JAMES STILL

CONTRIBUTIONS TO SOUTHERN APPALACHIAN STUDIES

# JAMES STILL

## Critical Essays on the Dean of Appalachian Literature

*Edited by* TED OLSON
*and* KATHY H. OLSON

CONTRIBUTIONS TO SOUTHERN APPALACHIAN STUDIES, 17

McFarland & Company, Inc., Publishers
*Jefferson, North Carolina, and London*

LIBRARY OF CONGRESS CATALOGUING-IN-PUBLICATION DATA

James Still: critical essays on the dean of Appalachian literature /
edited by Ted Olson and Kathy H. Olson.
p.   cm. — (Contributions to Southern Appalachian studies ; vol. 17)
Includes bibliographical references and index.

ISBN-13: 978-0-7864-3076-5
softcover : 50# alkaline paper  ∞

1.  Still, James, 1906–2001— Criticism and interpretation.    2.  American
literature — Appalachian Region — History and criticism.    3.  Appalachian
Region — Intellectual life.    I. Olson, Ted.   II. Olson, Kathy H.
PS3537.T5377Z73   2008          811'.52 — dc22          2007035259

British Library cataloguing data are available

James Still musing, typewriter at the ready,
at the log house, located beside Wolfpen Creek, Knott County,
Kentucky; (Inset) James Still sitting on stone stair (both courtesy
the Hindman Settlement School)

Manufactured in the United States of America

*McFarland & Company, Inc., Publishers
Box 611, Jefferson, North Carolina 28640
www.mcfarlandpub.com*

# Table of Contents

# Introduction

## TED OLSON

This volume is the first book-length collection of scholarly essays exploring the literary work of author James Still. Born July 16, 1906, he lived longer than most other authors of his generation, and he attracted considerable attention during his final years for his stylistically distinctive literary works, virtually all of which were set in eastern Kentucky yet which explored universal themes.

Integrally associated with eastern Kentucky and ultimately receiving the sobriquet "the Dean of Appalachian Literature," Still was in fact born and raised in east-central Alabama. Attending college at Lincoln Memorial University (in Harrogate, Tennessee), Vanderbilt University (in Nashville, Tennessee), and the University of Illinois (in Champaign-Urbana, Illinois), Still subsequently moved to Kentucky during the early years of the Great Depression. He would call the Cumberland Plateau home until his death on April 28, 2001, living primarily in Knott County, Kentucky (either at the Hindman Settlement School in Hindman, or 11 miles from that town in a log house on Wolfpen Creek). Despite the public's longstanding perception of him as a hermetic figure, Still was always a citizen of the world. He served three years in Africa and the Middle East for the U.S. military during World War II, and later, while based in Knott County, he gave frequent readings and talks across Kentucky and Appalachia and often traveled to other states and other nations both to conduct research and to experience other places and other cultures.

Best known as the author of the acclaimed novel *River of Earth*, published by Viking Press in February 1940, Still also wrote numerous short stories, many of which initially appeared in such prestigious periodicals as *The Atlantic*, *The Saturday Evening Post*, and *Virginia Quarterly Review*. Still's short stories were eventually incorporated into several book collections, including *On Troublesome Creek* (1941), *Pattern of a Man and Other Stories* (1976), and *The Run for the Elbertas* (1980). He received numerous honors for his fiction: *River of Earth* was co-recipient (along with Thomas Wolfe's *You Can't Go Home Again*) of the Southern Authors' Award in 1940, while several of Still's short stories were included in the anthologies *O. Henry Memorial Prize Stories* and *Best American Short Stories*. An equally vital component of his literary productivity during his early career was his poetry. During the 1930s, Still published poems in many of the most respected periodicals in America, including *The Atlantic*, *Esquire*, *The New Republic*, and *Poetry*, and his poetic output would be compiled in four books: *Hounds on the Mountain* (1937), *River of Earth: The Poem and Other Poems* (1982), *The Wolfpen Poems* (1986), and *From the Mountain, From the Valley: New and Collected Poems* (2001).

Upon their publication, Still's first three books—*Hounds on the Mountain*, *River of Earth*, and *On Troublesome Creek*—were reviewed in a wide range of periodicals, from *Time* magazine and the *Saturday Review of Literature* to the *Southern Literary Messenger*. His early work also garnered praise from other authors, including such contemporaries as Marjorie Kinnan Rawlings, Delmore Schwartz, Katherine Anne Porter, Carson McCullers, Stephen Vincent Benét, and Robert Frost. For his literary endeavors during those years, Still received two Guggenheim Fellowships and was invited to participate in the Bread Loaf Writers' Conference (located in Ripton, Vermont), the MacDowell Colony (Peterborough, New Hampshire), and Yaddo (Saratoga Springs, New York).

Still's initial burst of literary activity was curtailed by his involvement in World War II. After his return to eastern Kentucky in 1945, he wrote and published comparatively little for an extended period. Through the 1970s, he farmed at Wolfpen Creek, worked as a librarian at the Hindman Settlement School, and taught college at Morehead State University. While not writing as prolifically as he had in the 1930s, Still continued his lifelong practice of reading voraciously, devoting hours each day to perusing a range of books on various subjects.

Several events—including the appearance of Dean Cadle's influential article on Still in *The Yale Review* in December 1967, a 1968 paperback reprinting of the 1940 edition of *River of Earth*, and the emergence of the interdisciplinary academic field of Appalachian Studies during the late 1960s and early 1970s—led to the rediscovery of Still's work. During the mid-to-late 1970s, his short stories and *River of Earth* were republished in new editions by Gnomon Press (located in Frankfort, Kentucky) and the University Press of Kentucky (based in Lexington), and Still's literary standing improved dramatically, especially within Kentucky and across Appalachia. Accordingly, Still resumed writing. His most popular books from this period were primarily intended for young readers: *Sporty Creek: A Novel about an Appalachian Boyhood* (1977), which Still compiled from previously written short stories, and *Jack and the Wonder Beans* (1977). Other books from this phase of his career included three collections of folklore that Still gathered from the people he had met in eastern Kentucky—*Way Down Yonder on Troublesome Creek: Appalachian Riddles and Rusties* (1974), *The Wolfpen Rusties: Appalachian Riddles and Gee-Haw Whimmy-Diddles* (1975), and *The Wolfpen Notebooks: A Record of Appalachian Life* (1991)—as well as another book for children, *An Appalachian Mother Goose* (1998). During this latter phase of his career, Still received several literary awards, including the Marjorie Peabody Award of the American Academy & Institute of Arts and Letters, the Kentucky Arts Council's Milner Award, and the Southern Fiction Writer Award from South Atlantic Modern Language Association. Additionally, several writing scholarships were named after Still in recognition of his pioneering role in Appalachian literature. In 1995, he was named the State of Kentucky's first official Poet Laureate.

It is hardly surprising, given the unique trajectory of Still's literary career, that only two major scholarly interpretations of his writings—Dayton Kohler's 1942 comparative study of Still and Jesse Stuart, and the aforementioned *Yale Review* essay by Dean Cadle—were published before Still's "rediscovery" in the 1970s. Virtually all of the scholarship written in response to Still's literary legacy has come from writers, teachers, and students considerably younger than Still. Since the 1970s, people from both within and outside Appalachia have valued the author's work for its aesthetic integrity as well as for its representation of a world and a way of life that those younger readers have perceived as being endangered if not extinct.

It is hoped that the scholarly material in this volume will help James Still's readers better understand the many facets of his literary voice and vision. For the purpose of organization, this collection of critical essays is divided into separate sections offering scholarly responses to Still's works in various genres. This volume includes a section on his novel *River of Earth*, one on his short stories, one on his poetry, one on his writings for and about children as well as on his writings of folkloric interest. A final section features essays that reassess the achievement of James Still.

Not included in this volume are transcribed interviews with Still. Also not incorporated are materials on Still that are ephemeral or are expressions of marketing (such as book reviews and book jacket blurbs). Likewise excluded are writings of an emphatically personal nature, such as letters to or from Still, obituaries of Still, or memoirs in which people reflect upon their friendships with Still. Also not part of this volume are certain scholarly pieces that, though commendable for their interest in Still, are incomplete in their coverage of Still's life and work. (For instance, William S. Ward's scholarly overview of Still's career, which appeared in Ward's 1988 book *A Literary History of Kentucky*, is of limited utility today because it is both incomplete and too general, covering Still's activities only through 1980 and not analyzing in depth important aspects of Still's work.)

Most of the essays in this volume have been previously published in scholarly periodicals and books, though many of those publications are hard to find today. The inclusion of those essays here will enable wider dissemination of the existing canon of Still scholarship, allowing readers of this volume to encounter perceptive writing by such widely respected authors as Wendell Berry, Fred Chappell, Hal Crowther, Jeff Daniel Marion, Jane Mayhall, and Jim Wayne Miller, all of whom acknowledged Still as a significant influence on their own literary work. This volume also provides new visibility for previously published yet insightful essays by such scholars as H.R. Stoneback and Robert M. West. Additionally, in an attempt to fill in gaps lingering from the previous scholarship, five new scholarly essays prepared exclusively for this volume are included herein, written by Carol Boggess, Diane Fisher, Chris Green, Tina L. Hanlon, and Kathy H. Olson. Thanks are due those authors for these vital contributions to Still scholarship.

Any large project requires participation and interest from many individuals and organizations. This volume was rendered possible by widespread support, and I would like to acknowledge the following people for their help with this project: Michael Woodruff of the Office of Research and Sponsored Programs at East Tennessee State University in Johnson City, Tennessee; Mike Mullins and Rebecca Ware of the Hindman Settlement School in Hindman, Kentucky; George Brosi of *Appalachian Heritage* magazine in Berea, Kentucky; John Lang of Emory and Henry College in Emory, Virginia; Loyal Jones of Berea, Kentucky; Bob Jones, managing editor of *The Sewanee Review* in Sewanee, Tennessee; and Theresa Reynolds of Hindman, Kentucky. Crucial to the realization of this project were the many writers, editors, and publishers who authorized the reprinting of previously published scholarly essays within this volume, and deepest appreciation is extended to those people, all of whom shared the belief that this volume will help new generations of readers more fully understand and appreciate James Still's gift to the world — his literary legacy.

# I

# EARLY LITERARY AND PHILOSOPHICAL INFLUENCES

In one of his roles as Hindman Settlement School librarian, James Still carried boxes of books to students in rural schools across Knott County, Kentucky (courtesy of the Hindman Settlement School).

# Rivers of Earth
# and Troublesome Creeks:
# The Agrarianism of James Still

## H.R. STONEBACK

### Part I

*In those days everybody knew everybody else, and knew what he was doing,
and what his Father and grandfather had done before him, and you even
knew what everybody ate; and when you saw somebody passing, you knew
where he was going, and families didn't scatter all over the place, and people
didn't go away to die in the poor-house.— Giovanni Verga*[1]

In spite of a good deal of recognition in Appalachian circles, and in spite of ample acknowledgment of his achievement by fellow practitioners of the craft of fiction, we have not yet claimed James Still as an important Southern writer, a significant figure in the Southern Renascence. This essay addresses Still's place in the traditions both of Appalachian *and* Southern literature, to discover fresh perspectives, new avenues. Through examination of Still's association with Vanderbilt University, we may arrive at some useful sense of his version of agrarianism, his lyrical variation on one of the paradigms of Southern literature and experience. Through study of his masterpiece, *River of Earth*, we may find a way of according Still his place in literary history, a terrain which he shares not so much with other Appalachian writers, such as John Fox, Jr., and Jesse Stuart, as with such masters of the modern Southern novel as Elizabeth Madox Roberts, such acute chroniclers of various "postage stamps" of earth as Faulkner, and, in a wider sense, such delineators of place and the *genius loci* as William Wordsworth.

James Still was born in Lafayette, Alabama, in 1906. A rural area of ridges and low hills, a dying echo of Appalachia, Lafayette is an upland area similar in some ways to the Kentucky hills where Still has long been rooted. In 1929 he received his A.B. degree from Lincoln Memorial University in Harrogate, Tennessee. Much has been made of the fact that at Lincoln Memorial Still was a classmate of Jesse Stuart as well as a student of Harry Harrison Kroll, both important regional writers. In fact, however, Still never had a class with Stuart, and they

Stoneback, H.R. "*Rivers of Earth and Troublesome Creeks: The Agrarianism of James Still.*" The Kentucky Review 10.3
(1990): 3–26. *Reprinted with permission.*

did not, as Still observes, "run together." As for Kroll, though Still had a class with him, the contact was limited, and Kroll, as Still says, "never saw a manuscript of mine."[2] Another celebrant of the Appalachian myth, Don West, was at Lincoln Memorial University, though Still did not know him well until they were together at Vanderbilt. While it may be remarkable that four such writers identified with Appalachia were at an obscure college in the Tennessee hills at the same time, there is no evidence of influence or significant association. Indeed, the student of Appalachian literature will look in vain for the mark of Kroll or Stuart in the work of Still. If it is there, it is only as obverse reflection, as determination to avoid the sentimental deployment of the Appalachian myth, often tending toward caricature, which pervades the work of Kroll, Stuart, and West. From his earliest published efforts, the *Atlantic* and *Sewanee Review* and *Yale Review* stories and poems of the 1930s, Still's work is marked by a discipline, a precision, a restraint, and an economy which one seeks in vain in the work of his Lincoln Memorial University contemporaries.

James Still enrolled at Vanderbilt University in September 1929 after having considered attending either Duke University or the University of North Carolina. He was awarded his M.A. in English in June 1930. He had classes with Walter Clyde Curry, John Crowe Ransom, John Donald Wade, and Wilfred Walker. His advisor was Edwin Mims. His thesis, "The Function of Dreams and Visions in the Middle English Romances," directed by Curry, is signed also by Mims and Ransom. It was a "tough year," as Still recalls: "My two meals a day consisted of a ten-cent bowl of cereal in the morning and a thirty-five cent supper at a boarding-house: slim rations for a growing boy tackling Middle English." He worked very hard for Curry's Chaucer class, spending "seventeen hours in preparation for each of the two classes per week." Because of his intensive reading in American literature before he arrived at Vanderbilt, Still did not have to work as hard for Wade as he did for Curry. He recollects:

> During the first week in the American Literature class Dr. Wade tested us on our familiarity with the authors of note from the Civil War forward. He read passages from various works and we were to identify the authors. My score was perfect. Nobody else made a passing grade. Dr. Wade called me to his office and tested me further. The verdict was: "You don't have time to bother with my class. Just drop in once in a while and learn what we're up to." Or some such statement. I took him at his word and skipped every other class. My contribution to "The History of American Literature" the class composed was the chapter on Cotton and Increase Mather. Some twenty years later when Katherine Anne Porter told me she was writing a book on the Mathers I was prepared to discuss the subject at length.[3]

Such reminiscences yield a vivid sense of Vanderbilt in Still's student days. More important than such classroom recollections, for present purposes, is Still's recall of events beyond the classroom, events that define the tenor of the times in Nashville. He remembers attending several lectures by Mims at a Methodist Church, lectures "on the subject of Evolution, the monkey trials at Dayton being a sizzling issue of the day." He recalls the "considerable disregard," amply documented elsewhere, in which some faculty members held Mims's The *Advancing South*. Still's year at Vanderbilt was momentous:

> [T]he year of *I'll Take My Stand*, Ransom and Wade read their chapters to us.... Andrew Lytle was at Sewanee and came to read a play of his to us, but not from this book.... *I'll Take My Stand* was a pioneer undertaking, a seminal work.[4]

After Still left Vanderbilt in 1930, he took a degree in library science at the University of Illinois. In 1932, he became the librarian at the Hindman Settlement School in Knott County, in the hill-country of eastern Kentucky, where he has been rooted ever since. This aspect of Still's life and work — his immersion in place — has been remarked by every commentator on his work. In fact, over the past half century and with a quickening pace in the past decade, observers have more or less made Still out to be a kind of legendary autochthon of the mountains, the *deus loci* or at least the *genius loci* of the Kentucky mountains. All of this commentary, most of it in Appalachian regional reviews, has overlooked Still's connection with Vanderbilt agrarianism. More importantly, it has done Still the disservice of whittling his niche solely in the contexts of Appalachian literature. When an interviewer recently asked Still about "Appalachian literature" he allowed as how that would be "fairly restrictive"; "Southern literature," he said, "is good enough for me."[5]

It would be folly to construct an elaborate thesis regarding the influence of Vanderbilt agrarianism on Still. It must suffice here to say that Still's career as a poet and writer of fiction begins shortly after his 1929-1930 sojourn at Vanderbilt, a year and a place which mark one of the most fertile crossroads of twentieth-century literary and intellectual history. Few writers have been as free of the polemical temperament as has been Still. Readers will look in vain for agrarian exhortation in his work. Yet it might be argued that Still represents in all of the best senses the kind of stand—as man and artist—for which the Nashville agrarians called. While it may be true, as some observers have noted, that the agrarian manifestos overlooked the Appalachian South, that they were written from a point of view alien to the Appalachian sensibility, it must be asserted that the general conditions of deracination and dehumanization as a consequence of industrialism prevailed in the hills and minefields of eastern Kentucky. The qualities, moreover, which the Nashville agrarians valued as the pillars of resistance to the insidious spirit of progress and industrialism — tenacious family land tenure, sense of place, community, and tradition — were perhaps stronger in the Kentucky hills than elsewhere in the South.[6]

After Vanderbilt, then, Still settled in the hills. He describes his settling-in period:

> After six years of schoolkeeping at the forks of Troublesome Creek in Knott County, I moved nine miles farther back in the hills to a century-old log house between the waters of Dead Mare Branch and Wolfpen, on Little Carr Creek. These streams boxed me in. I raised my own food and stored vegetables and fruits for the cold months; I kept two stands of bees for their honey, and for the ancient custom of "telling the bees."... I joined the folk life of the scattered community, attending church meetings, funeralizing, corn pullings, hog butcherings, box-suppers at the one-room school, sapping parties, and gingerbread elections.[7]

Still's version of agrarianism, clearly, is not a call to political action, not a symbolic stance from which to go forth into the world of letters and a peripatetic academic career as it was for so many other Nashville agrarians. It is a design for living. It need not be insisted that this is a deliberate position, a conscious stand-taking for Still. Indeed in the same passage cited above, he goes on to say, "When I moved from Troublesome Creek to the backwoods of the county I had expected to stay only for a summer." Still remained there for many years. Yet it was, or soon became, a more deliberate matter than this last suggests. For example, in one of his early poems, "Heritage," which has the force of personal testament, Still asserts: "I shall not leave these prisoning hills.... I cannot leave." The speaker is one with the hills, "one with the fox / Stealing into the shadows, one with the new-born foal."[8]

The first time Still let his log-house "stand" for any period of time was in 1941, when he joined the army and went overseas:

> I was on another continent and longing for home when I penciled this verse of recollection: "How it was in that place, how light hung in a bright pool of air like water, in an eddy of cloud and sky, I will long remember.... Earth loved more than any earth, stand firm, hold last; Trees burdened with leaf and wing, root deep, grow tall."[9]

Still's postage stamp of adopted soil has been, then, a "stand," a terrain in which he has been able to hold tight, to "hold fast," and to gather the strength of a man rooted as a tree.

What are the consequences of this stand for his art? Looked at from the perspective of Nashville agrarianism, Still would appear to be the very artist called for in *I'll Take My Stand*. Donald Davidson, in "A Mirror for Artists," outlines how the arts have prospered, traditionally, in agrarian societies "where the goodness of life was measured by a scale of values having little to do with the material values of industrialism; where men were never too far removed from nature to forget that the chief subject of art, in the final sense, is nature." Under the insidious sway of industrialism, Davidson argues, this sense of life and art is lost; the artist becomes the adversary of the community, becomes alienated man, deracinated man. It is very rare to find in America an "artist slowly maturing his powers in full communion with a society of which he is an integral part." The more we consider the details of Davidson's formula for the artist in an agrarian society, the more we are likely to discern the face of Still in that mirror. For example, Davidson lists the artistic resources of the agrarian South:

> The South has been rich in the folk-arts, and is still rich in them — in ballads, country songs and dances, in hymns and spirituals, in folk tales, in the folk crafts.... Though these are best preserved in mountain fastnesses and remote rural localities, they were not originally so limited.[10]

These are the very resources that Still has employed skillfully in his work. Davidson concludes that the artist "will do best to flee the infection of our times" and take his stand within an agrarian tradition. It should not be interpreted that Davidson and the Nashville Agrarians were urging artists to "flee" to the hills and become subsistence farmers, subsistence poets — although some observers persist in reading them in that fashion. (One need not join with Jesse Stuart in laughing at the pathetic tomato plants he observed in the gardens of certain Nashville Agrarians — plants to which he often alluded.) Yet, one thrust of agrarianism is most certainly practical, and it makes as much sense to see *I'll Take My Stand* as a concrete pattern for life and work as it does to regard it as metaphor or as theoretical underpinning for an academic-literary career.

Indeed, there are "dropouts" of the 1960s and 1970s who cherish *I'll Take My Stand* as a kind of manifesto, still valid and vital — much of it — after all this time. They are not "dropouts" at all, in the usual journalistic sense of the term; rather, they have done precisely what Davidson and Lytle and others were talking about in 1930 — they have fled the infection of the times, fled the nightmare of urban America (or the daydream of suburban America), and they have "dropped in," into what remains of agrarian society, many of them to stay, to take root in place, in community, to cultivate the soil as well as the crafts and arts to which Davidson alludes, to sing the very songs and hymns and ballads which he so cherished. Many of them have followed Lytle's 1930 injunction: "Throw out the radio and take down the fiddle from the wall." If *I'll Take My Stand* yet possesses the power to inspire or affirm such action in subsequent times, what must have been its force in 1930 for a young man from the Alabama hills who, as a student at Vanderbilt, participated in the excited discussion of agrarian matters? An immense force, one may infer. "Pioneer," Still calls it, and "seminal" — both terms are charged and will serve to reinforce this thesis: of all the Vanderbilt writers, including those who have been students and teachers there in the past six decades and have gone on to careers as writers, James Still is the central exemplar of the agrarian tradition.

If agrarianism is the text here, then regionalism is the subtext, for more often than not the literary issue of agrarianism is one form or another of regionalism. It is the quality of this latter "-ism" which makes all the difference. If one deployed as paving stones all the books which have exploited ostensibly quaint and curious folks in isolated places, which have mishandled dialect and folk speech, which have awkwardly praised and patronized their "local color" subjects, we might have a broad new road from Nashville to the heart of the Kentucky hills. There is no space here to deal with this long-standing problem in American (and world) literature; perhaps a pedagogical anecdote will suffice. In the course of teaching seminars in regionalism, in Southern and Appalachian literature (or even Catskills and Adirondack lore and literature), one discovers how badly this novelist or that poet handles this or that problem of literary regionalism. These deficiencies should be examined against two touchstones. The first is Robert Penn Warren's essay, "Some Don'ts for Literary Regionalists":

> Regionalism is not quaintness and local color and folklore, for those things when separated from a functional idea are merely a titillation of the reader's sentimentality or snobbishness.... Regionalism based on the literary exploitation of a race or society that has no cultural continuity with our own tends to be false and precious.... Regionalism does not mean that literature is tied to its region for application..., does not imply in any way a relaxing of critical standards.[11]

The successful regional writer is never insistently self-conscious regarding his regionalism. He writes out of, not about, a profound sense of place. He sees in and through and because of intense localism, a way of seeing, a vision that is purged by a kind of ongoing sacramental relationship with the near and common things of his place and community. James Still's *River of Earth* represents one precise formal embodiment of these principles; it incarnates all of the best notions concerning how to write "regional" fiction. The second touchstone, and of similar significance, is Kentuckian Allen Tate's rumination, in a 1929 letter to Donald Davidson: "Our true Southern novelist at present is Elizabeth [Madox] Roberts, who does not write as a Southerner or as anything else." She is not a purveyor of sociological theses. Like Hemingway, she "sticks to concrete experience"; she has "that sense of a stable world, of a total sufficiency of character, which we miss in modern life."[12] The characterization of Roberts's fiction exactly fits the work of her friend, James Still; indeed, had Still's work been available a decade earlier, at the time of the agrarian deliberations concerning regional fiction, *River of Earth* would have served them well as a touchstone. Decades later, they had discovered this. (See, for example, Cleanth Brooks's praise of Still's mastery, in the foreword to *The Run for the Elbertas*.) In 1971, Tate wrote to Still:

> I have just read it [*River of Earth*] — one of the few novels I have read in a decade. I regret that I didn't see it years ago. It is a brilliant and moving novel. Moreover, in my opinion, it is a masterpiece of style. The subtle modulation between the mountain speech of the dialogue and the formal, yet simple, diction of the narrative is masterly.[13]

# Part II

> That was their way. Lonely folk, but a blessing to each other, for the beasts, and for the earth. — Knut Hamsun[14]

At the heart of Still's fiction and poetry is a master motif, a core image, based on the rivers and creeks which "glean the valleys."[15] Four of his books have titles which draw on this reservoir of river-creek imagery: *River of Earth, On Troublesome Creek, Way Down Yonder on Troublesome Creek,* and *Sporty Creek: A Novel About an Appalachian Boyhood.* Moreover, at least eighteen poems and seven short stories take their titles from creeks, and as many more draw key images from rivers or creeks. Consider some of the rivers and creeks, the prongs and forks and branches in Still's fiction: Big Ballard, Biggety, Big Greasy, Big Leatherwood, Big John Riggins Creek, Boone's Fork, Broad Creek, Buckeye Branch, Cain Creek, Crazy Creek, Cutshin, Dead Mare Branch, Defeated Creek, Dry Creek, Fern Branch, Fight Creek,

Goose Creek, Grassy Creek, He Creek (which joins She Creek), Keg Branch, Kentucky River, Lairds Creek, Lean Neck, Left Hand Fork, Left Troublesome, Letts Creek, Little Angus, Little Carr, Lower Flat Creek, Pigeon Roost, Quicksand Creek, Redbird River, Red Fox Creek, Roaring Fork, Rockhouse Creek, Salt Lick, Sand Lick, Shepherd's Creek, Shikepoke Creek, Shoal Creek, Short Fork, Slick Branch, Smacky Creek, Snag Fork, Snaggy Creek, Sporty Creek, Surrey Creek, Tight Hollow Branch, Troublesome Creek, Upper Logan Creek, Willow Branch, Wolfpen.

These are just some of the waters that flow through some of Still's fiction (*River of Earth, Pattern of a Man*, and *Run for the Elbertas*). Indeed, since more than fifty streams flow through one novel and less than two dozen short stories, one might state this premise: it's a mighty dry Still story that does not have a creek or two shaping it in some way.

What conclusions might be drawn from this riparian inventory? First, the student of place-names will observe that the Appalachian flair for naming is manifested amply here. Then, the scholar considering Still's career will note the author's enduring concern with the actual places of his chosen earth, a preoccupation going back to Still's earliest publications, such as his scholarly note, "Place Names in the Cumberland Mountains," published while he was a graduate student at Vanderbilt.[16] There, Still writes: "Names given to creeks, ridges, hollows, and villages in the Cumberland Mountains have a peculiarity all their own. They often represent some characteristic of the thing named which is overlooked by the outsider." Noting the difficulty of citing reasons for some of the designations, he concludes: "They seem to have sprung out of the fertile imagination of the mountaineer." It seems much to the point of Still's career as "Appalachian artist" to pay heed to his early mention of the possible incomprehension of the "outsider" as well as to the stress on the creativity of the hillfolk.

Other things might be said, too, about this rich plenty of streams, from the point of view of the geographer, the historian, and the social topographer of Still's corner of Appalachia. Streams in his fiction are — as, in fact, in some places they remain — the basic *roads* of that country. In addition, identity and sense of place are shaped, defined by creeks. When the narrator in "A Master Time," a story in *Pattern of a Man*, says he wasn't born on Logan Creek, but in a neighboring valley, a native of Logan exclaims: "Upon my word and honor! Are ye a heathen?" Political life, too, follows the design of the creeks: in "Pattern of a Man," which is concerned with the election of a county jailor, we find that "all the main creeks have one candidate." The fiction, then, accurately reflects the lay of the land, the flow of the creeks.

Far more important, however, is the way in which the creeks provide the deep form of Still's work. The litany of creeks recited above evokes—for the literary critic as for the topophile — a sense of the rhythm of life, a resonance of place and time, community and history. A pilgrim's progress through that creek-country reminds the wayfarer of history at Boone's Fork, of loss and danger at Dead Mare Branch, at Quicksand, Shoal and Snaggy Creeks, of suffering and triumph at Defeated and Fight Creeks, of complexity and paradox at Cain and Crazy and Troublesome Creeks, of nature's plenty as well as leanness and pollution at Pigeon Roost, Redbird, Red Fox, and Shikepoke, at Lean Neck and Tight Hollow, at Big Greasy. None of this is forced allegorical topography or heavy-handed *paysage moralisé;* it is natural, cumulative reverberation that issues finally in the sense that the core image of the work is in the creeks, the ritual lustration in the text and the sacred subtext of Still's Kentucky.

All of the foregoing concerns— and the very heart of Still's agrarian vision — are best exemplified in his masterpieces. When *River of Earth* appeared in 1940, one reviewer welcomed it as one of the best novels about hillfolk, declaring that "Mr. Still has distinguished himself principally in his restraint, avoiding Jesse Stuart's often faked heartiness and the cheap, easily written incidents which merely shock but which Erskine Caldwell thinks are good writing." In another review, Stephen Vincent Benét praised it: "It is rich with sights, sounds, and smells, with the feel and taste of things. And it is rich, as well, with salty and earthy speech, the soil of ballad and legend and tall story.... You can call it regional writing if you like — but to say so is merely to say that all America is not cut off the same piece." Another reviewer could find no one with whom to compare Still except Elizabeth Madox Roberts: "He is fully her equal in fusing the most realistic objectivity with the most intense inwardness of mood." Shortly after this spate of favorable reviews, an essay appeared in *College English* that considered the work of Still and Jesse Stuart to be a significant development in the hillfolk tradition, an important move away from the stories (such as those of Mary Murfree) which were "about a place rather than of it." The essay concluded that, especially in Still's work, "the Southern mountaineer has found his own voice for the first time. This regionalism is as genuine and untainted as any we have in America today.""[17] Such a judgment may be useful, but there is danger in it, too, danger of falling into an all-too-familiar "native son" parochial authenticity syndrome as the basis for evaluation. And surely it has been a disservice to Still to regard him solely under the rubric of Appalachian literature, and to yoke him with Stuart (a pattern established by this early essay). Rather, Still's primary credentials are those of the engaged artist. With the hand of a master stylist, he carves his regional materials into a vision of universal validity.

*River of Earth,* skillfully told from a boy's point of view, is a narrative achievement that deserves comparison with the finest work (especially that which employs a boy-narrator) of Sherwood Anderson, Faulkner, Hemingway, and Twain. The novel spans two years in the life of a Kentucky hill family, stretched over a cyclic framework which associates spring with the closing of the coal mines and a return to the farm from the grimy coal camps, and fall with the reopening of the mines and a return from the land to the slag piles, sooty mist, and oily flames of the coal camps. It is a pattern of agrarian-industrial contrasts which delineates Still's theme: in this world of motion, mechanization, and deracination, man needs "a place certain and enduring." The theme is a familiar one, but Still's engaged treatment gives fresh, vital force to this convention of the hillfolk tradition, of Southern and agrarian literature, of American experience.

Father, Brack Baldridge, is a coal miner who still owns his small subsistence farm but lives on it intermittently. He is forever moving to different coal camps as one mine closes and another opens. Mother, Alpha Middleton Baldridge, has no time for the coal camps; she wants to stay in one place where she can keep a garden and make a home. The children come alive in the voice of the narrator, who, by his seventh birthday, has seen enough of coal camps to know his own mind: "I would learn to plow, and have acres of my own. Never would I be a miner digging a darksome hole."[18] As the novel opens, the Baldridges are on their own farm on Blackjack Creek; food is so scarce that Mother burns down the house to get rid of some persistent kinfolk; then the Baldridges move into their smokehouse, where at last they feel "contented and together" (6).

Still's treatment of this situation may seem an ironic inversion of the usual agrarian or Southern sense of family; but, in fact, the extended family here has become not only a nuisance but a burden, as well. The visiting relations are outwitted in order, first, to protect limited resources from larger demands for food and, second, to meet the family's need for communion among themselves. While it is a slim existence they have in the smokehouse, it is not bleak; it is, in fact, a kind of triumph. And the people in the towns, in the coal camps, are not nearly as well off: "There was hunger in the camps. We believed that we fared well, and did not complain" (12).

But the primary business of the first part of the novel is to define the conflict between father and mother, a definition accomplished in discussions of the relative virtues of farm and town (or coal camp). Father spends his time anticipating the reopening of the mines:

> No use stirring the top of the ground if you're going to dig your bread underside.... I never tuck natural to growing things, planting seeds and sticking plows in the ground.... A sight of farming I've done, but it allus rubbed the grain. But give me a pick, and I'll dig as much coal as the next 'un. I figure them mines won't stay closed forever [35, 47].

On the other hand, when a move back to the coal-camp seems imminent, Mother asserts her reasons for wanting to stay on the home place: "I allus had a mind to live on a hill. Not sunk in a holler where the fog and dust is damping and blacking. I was raised to like a lonesome place" (51). Faced with her husband's stubbornness, she laments:

> Forever moving yon and back, setting down nowhere for good and all, searching for God knows what.... Where air we expecting to draw up to?... Forever I've wanted to set us down in a lone spot, a place certain and enduring, with room to swing arm and elbow, a garden-piece for fresh victuals, and a cow to furnish milk for the baby. So many places we've lived — the far side one mine camp and next the slag pile of another. Hardburly. Lizzyblue. Tribbey. I'm longing to set me down shorely and raise my chaps proper [51].

Although she always follows her husband she never ceases hoping for her "place." Again and again she speaks her mind: "Nigh we get our roots planted, we keep pulling them up and planting in furrin ground.... Moving is an abomination.... Since I married I've been driv from one coal camp to another.... I reckon I've lived everywhere on God's green earth. Now I want to set me down and rest.... We done right well this crop. We've got plenty" [179–82].

Alpha comes naturally by her agrarian vision, for her mother, Grandma Middleton, has never left the farm; she views the coal-camps as a strange intrusion in the hills. Bemoaning the fact that her daughter married "a coal digger, a mole-feller, grubbing his bread underground," she tells her grandson: "Allus I'd wanted her to choose one who lived on the land, growing his own victuals, raising sheep arid cattle, beholden to nobody" (130).

But the agrarian debate extends beyond family conversations, for appearing at significant moments in the tale is the legendary figure of Walking John Gay. The first mention occurs in juxtaposition with Mother's longing for her place; she describes and defines him:

> I saw Walking John Gay once when I was a child.... Walking John Gay traipsing and trafficking, looking the world over. Walked all the days of his life; seen more of creation than any living creature. A lifetime of going and he's got nowhere, found no peace [52].

Still focuses the reader's attention on Walking John Gay by skillful indirection; after Uncle Jolly mentions him in passing, the boy-narrator wonders, "Who is Walking John Gay? Somewhere I heered that name." Having received no answer to his last question, he persists, "Where does Walking John Gay live?" Finally, the boy is acknowledged and four pages of anecdotes follow. Uncle Jolly recalls how he saw Gay once long ago and asked: "Looky here, John Walkabout, where air ye forever going? What air ye expecting to see you've never saw yet? Hain't the head o' one holler pine-blank like the next 'un?" Grandma Middleton recalls how Walking John Gay had visited her and her husband, Boone Middleton, a long time ago on Lean Neck Creek, and how Boone had asked him questions till after dark:

> I got a bundle o' questions to ask you who've traveled these mountains.... What about them bee-gum rocks in the breaks of the Big Sandy? Tell where's that beech tree standing Dan'l Boone whittled his name on? I'm blood kin to ol' Dan'l. Have you seed a single pair o' wild pigeons the earth over?

And Grandma recollects what Walking John Gay said: "They's a world o' dirt flowed under my feet. I never crawled when I was a baby. Just riz up and walked at ten months. I'm a-mind to see every living hill against I die" (139–41).

There is a direct connection between the haunting figure of Walking John Gay and Brother Sim Mobberly's sermon, the important passage which gives the novel its title. The words used by Walking John Gay — "They's a world o' dirt flowed under my feet" — not only convey the sense of flow and motion which pervade the tale, but they also echo the preacher's words: "Oh, my children, where air we going on this mighty river of earth?" (76). A close look at this key passage is essential, since it centers the novel and exemplifies Still's mastery.

The boy-narrator watches the preacher come to the pulpit:

> A fleece of beard rose behind the pulpit, blue-white, blown to one side as though it hung in a wind. A man stood alone, bowed, not yet ready to lift his eyes. He embraced the pulpit block. He pressed his palms gently upon the great Bible, touching the covers as though they were living flesh. His eyes shot up, green as water under a mossy bank, leaping over the faces turned to him... [75–76].

The careful reader notices here that the creeks which shape the fiction flow *through* the preacher who is about to address his river of earth theme. He lifts a finger, plunges it into the Bible, selecting a text at random, and then looks down "to see what the Lord had chosen":

> He began to read. I knew then where his mouth was in the beard growth. "The sea saw it and fled: Jordan was driven back. The mountains skipped like rams, and the little hills like lambs. Tremble, thou earth...." He snapped the book to. He leaned over the pulpit. "I was borned in a ridge-pocket," he said. "I never seed the sun-ball withouten heisting my chin. My eyes were sot upon the hills from the beginning. Till I come on the word in this good Book, I used to think a mountain was the standingest object in the sight o' God. Hit says here they go skipping and hopping like sheep, a-rising and a-falling. These hills are jist dirt waves, washing through eternity. My brethren, they hain't a valley so low but what hit'll rise agin. They hain't a hill standing so proud but hit'll sink to the low ground o' sorrow. Oh, my children, where air we going on this mighty river of earth, a-borning, begetting, and a-dying — the living and the dead riding the waters? Where air it sweeping us? [76].

The boy is distracted, dozes off, does not hear the rest of the sermon. But when he walks home afterwards, he says "a great voice walked with me, roaring in my head."

The preacher's primary text is Psalm 114, a song in commemoration of Israel's deliverance from Egypt. Marvelous things take place in nature, the mountains skip, the earth trembles. After the preacher closes the Bible, he alludes to other scriptural passages: "My eyes were sot upon the hills" echoes the familiar Psalm 121. Then, echoing Isaiah 40:4, he considers the sinking hills: "Every valley shall be exalted, and every mountain and hill shall be made low." Finally, in his river of earth image, he returns, at some poetic remove, to the end of Psalm 114, where the rock is turned into water, "the flint into a fountain of waters."

What does this mosaic amount to as homiletic text? A hymn of wonder, a celebration of the deliverance of God's chosen people, and in the Isaiah passage, the promise of "comfort," of salvation in the Messiah, for not only will the valleys be exalted but the "crooked shall be made straight ... and the glory of the Lord shall be revealed." But we must ask, too, what the sermon accomplishes in the novel. Its immediate context is a "funeralizing." Thus it raises, in wonder and awe, the question of human destiny, man's place in time and eternity, and implies for those who know enough scripture to grasp the unstated connection, the hope of salvation. Yet, if this is the sacred text, we must also see that the sermon serves the novel as a subtext in which the skipping hills and trembling earth are directly associated with the ravaged garden of Kentucky, with eroded farmland, burning slag piles, coal-camps, and polluted creeks. Indeed, we have finally an anguished, ironic inversion of Psalm 114, desperately inquiring *are* we the Lord's people, *is* there deliverance, *is* there comfort for us?

The sermon echoes throughout the novel. For example, as the sermon ends, Father reads a letter that tells them that Uncle Jolly is in jail for dynamiting a mill dam. Mother says that no man has a right to hold back the waters, to let nothing up or down. Later we find out that Uncle Jolly has dynamited the dam so the fish can get upstream to spawn. Although his deed is done in the service of the plenitude of nature, he serves his time. When he is released, he opens the dam again. Jordan driven back, the earth must tremble.

The sermon resonates in other ways. The boy-narrator, for example, sees in terms of rivers. He watches his father build a roaring fire: "The top of the stove reddened, the cracks and seams of the cast iron becoming alive, traced like rivers on a map's face" (66). His general sense of wonder about rivers converges with the text of the sermon. In the chapter following the funeral, he is at school, where the talk turns to rivers, to "the biggest river ever was":

> "Biggest river I ever saw was the Kentucky, running off to the blue-grass, and somewhere beyond."
> "It's a river in South America, far off south, many thousands of miles."
> "There's a place called South Americkee, aver in Bell County. Now hit's the truth."
> "This river is the Amazon...."
> "I looked that word up in the dictionary and it said Amazon was a fighting woman. River or woman, I don't know which" [84–85].

Thus in a brief passage, without overt linkage, Still plays a subtle variation on the river of earth motif, evokes again the sense of wonder, particularizes, localizes the universal, and even, perhaps, suggests Mother's identity as a kind of Amazon, a fighting woman of the Kentucky creeks: river or woman, or "river-woman," *genius loci,* tutelary water spirit, enduring naiad of the hills.

In manifold ways, then, the sermon is both source and confluence of meaning, image, symbol. River of earth, or world of dirt, it flows as steadily as time and the creeks. When Uncle Jolly is teaching the narrator how to plow, how to "tend dirt proper," lest the hills "wear down to a nub" (the hills shall "be made low"), the boy has an agrarian epiphany:

> The earth parted; it fell back from the shovel plow; it boiled over the share, I walked the fresh furrow and balls of dirt welled between my toes. There was a smell of old mosses, of bruised sassafras roots, of ground new-turned.... The share rustled like drifted leaves. It spoke up through the handles. I felt the earth flowing, steady as time [134–35].

The narrator knows his dream at an early age — to avoid "digging in a darksome hole," to grow roots and tend the earth — but the novel is not a serene mountain pastoral, for the agrarian *locus arnoenus* is under terrific assault by the coal economy, and the hold of the Baldridges in the land is tenuous at best.

Toward the end of the novel, the connection between Walking John Gay and the Baldridges is made explicit. About to set off again to look for work in the mines, Brack says: "I was born to dig coal.... Somewhere they's a mine working. Fires still burning the world over, and they got to be fed. All the hearthstones in North Americkee hain't gone cold." To this Uncle Jolly replies: "Be-grabs if you folks hain't a pack o' Walking John Gays, allus a-going, don't warm one spot o' ground for long." Mother is in labor with imminent birth and thus she is not on the scene to reiterate her dream; so Uncle Jolly, who has at times seemed more akin to Walking John Gay — wandering the hills, spending time in jail for his pranks — becomes the spokesman for the opposition: "I aim to settle, I've got me a young mule, new ground cleared, and soon to have a doughbeater fair as ever drew breath. Bees to work my red apple trees, grapevines" (241–42). The novel ends, then, with Uncle Jolly staying on the land, and the Baldridges going off to find a working mine somewhere; but to the last, Mother holds to her vision of "a place certain and enduring."

Is this, then, an agrarian thesis novel? No, for there is nothing in it of the polemic, the exhortation. Still eschews the easy answers. Brack Baldridge is anything but a caricature of the deracinated man. Indeed, in his lust for the mines this earthy "mole-feller" is a haunting autochthon of another variety (akin to the miner in the song "Dark as a Dungeon," with his "lust" for the "lure of the mine"). Moreover, Still lifts the coal camp wandering of the Baldridges from the level of mere job-seeking by introducing the Walking John Gay motif and the "river of earth" imagery. The Daniel Boone allusions (and kinship) invite the reader to ponder the tale in larger terms. Boone, of course, was an ambiguous figure: was he one of the official makers of the American nation, preparing the way in the wilderness for homes and farms "certain and enduring," or was he the *ur-figure* of American rootlessness, ever fleeing the advance of settlements and civilization? As the novel speaks to concerns generally American, it poses the question: Is there room in a nation whose experience has been and continues to be primarily a matter of mobility and placelessness (in the deepest sense) for a "place certain and enduring"?

Much of the business of the novel suggests the motif of the intrusion of a "machine in the garden." In Still's world, there is yet something left of the garden — patches of soil "rich as sin," and the compellingly beautiful coming of spring to the hills, for example. But the "metal groan of the coal conveyor" has come to the once green mountain valleys and shattered and blackened a world. In the crowded coal camps, perfect miniatures of the industrial city, there is no room for a garden or stock, and when the mine slows, hunger comes; spirit and morals decay as the blanket of soot covers everything. Without a note of hortatory protest, Still enumerates the evils that have come with the machine into this particular garden. Children look for fish in a coal camp creek:

> The waters ran yellow, draining acid from the mines, cankering rocks in its bed. The rocks were snuffy brown, eaten and crumbly. There were no fishes swimming the eddies, nor striders looking at themselves in the waterglass [189].

The very rocks crumble; the river of earth flows darkly. Where the timber has been recklessly cut, the land is "a-wasting and a-washing," as Uncle Jolly says when he is teaching his nephew "how to tend dirt proper." And he asks that question which still reverberates: "What's folks going to live on when these hills wear down to a nub?" (134).

All of this amounts to the familiar motif of the ravaged American landscape. Indeed, according to long-established (since the mid–1800s) conventions of Appalachian literature, the hill-country landscape is seen as the most compelling and perhaps the most *American* landscape; yoked with this awareness in Still's work is the sense of the ruin, wrought in the hills by the machine, by the mines, which has been more complete and more devastating than anywhere else on the North American continent, taking the cycle of mountain gloom and mountain glory back to mountain gloom. Thus, in one sense, *River of Earth* provides the grim epitome of a pervasive image in Appalachian and American literature, with its version of the befouled "green breast" of the hills, something — to paraphrase F. Scott Fitzgerald's Nick Carraway — commensurate to man's capacity for horror. One can only wonder that there was never a Southern mountain *I'll Take My Stand,* since the issues were much the same, although intensified far beyond anything the lowland South could imagine.

It is in this context that Mother's longing for a "place," together with Uncle Jolly's agrarian vision, becomes the central thrust of the novel, played off against the design suggested by Father, the coal-digging wanderer, and Walking John Gay. *River of Earth,* then, belongs in the company of such hillfolk vignettes as Faulkner's MacCallum episode in *Flags in the Dust.* Still's novel stands as one of the finest novels of the hillfolk mythos and one of the more profound embodiments in fiction of agrarianism.

## Part III

*Et in Arcadia ego.*[19]

"Et in Appalachia ego": is this an apt rubric to inscribe on the rich canvas of James Still's life and work? And, if so, which reading of the old emblem are we to take as primary resonance? Is it the pastoral voice — in the classical convention, a shepherd, in the romantic tradition, more often than not, a hill-person — reminiscing on the idyllic life in an enchanted symbolic landscape? Often indeed, in Appalachian writing (and other hillfolk settings), hill people are depicted as simple, primitive people living charmed lives in a kind of mindless Arcadia. But this paraphrase of the old rubric is not intended to suggest such a "local color" reading of Still. Rather, it posits the rich complex of feeling implicit in the phrase, properly apprehended. Anyone who knows Erwin Panofsky's seminal study of the history of the motif in art, its ambivalence, its shifts in meaning, will catch the flavor of Still's Appalachian Arcadian world.[20] It is precisely in the tension between pastoral and tragedy, in the tension between the romantic mistranslation of the phrase — "I too have been in Arcadia" — and the older, darker, correct reading — "Even in Arcadia, there am I" (i.e., Death) — that one may locate the center of Still's work. In Still's Appalachian-agrarian world we find the plenitude of nature, a rich and living folk tradition, a sustaining sense of family and community, a vivifying sense of place, and an enduring sense of identity through place. We find also hunger, desperation, mechanization, deracination, violence, tragedy, and death.

To figure the matter another way, to move what may seem a great distance from Kentucky and Nashville agrarianism, let us briefly consider Still's work in the contexts of the oldest agrarianism of all, the ancient Chinese agrarian cults. In his classic study *The Religion of the Chinese People,* Marcel Granet writes about the "Holy Places," the "ritual landscapes" where the peasants experienced in trees and rocks, in creeks and rivers

> the presence of a tutelary power whose sanctity sprang from every corner of the landscape, blessed forces which they strove to capture in every way. Holy was the place, sacred the slopes of the valley they climbed zand descended, the stream they crossed .... the ferns, the bushes, the white elms, the great oaks and the wood they took from them .... the spring water .... the animals which teemed .... [all] shared in the holiness of the place.[21]

Granet writes of the communion and harmony of the peasants, with the land and each other, especially at festival times, of the sense of "rhythmic time," "creative joy," and "joyous power" expressed in the songs and games and rituals of the seasonal events of the community. At the Autumn Festivals, food was central, the bountiful table an omen of plenty and an act of generosity which was "a matter of some moment for the honor of the family." The Autumn Festivals ritually marked the end of cultivation: "earth was sacralized," not to be touched again until spring (45–46). What has all this to do with Still? Everything, for the *deus loci* which spoke to the ancient Chinese speaks eloquently in Still's work; the same "emblematism," as Granet has it, is at the heart of life in the Troublesome Creek country. The exact analogues for the ancient agrarian peasant festivals persist in the form of hog-killing gatherings and "stir-off" parties, the seasonal sorghum-making event marked by a feast, by games and songs, by a resacralization of the earth. In "The Stir-Off" depicted in *The Run for the Elbertas,* Still's proud host at that autumn festival welcomes his guests with words that fit precisely the ancient ritual formula:

> "We're old-timey people.... We may live rough, but we're lacking nothing. For them with muscle and backbone, Troublesome Creek country is the land o' plenty." He swept an arm toward

gourds of lard, strings of lazy wife beans, and shelves of preserves; he snapped his fingers at cushaws hanging by vine tails. "We raise our own living, and once the house and barns are full we make friends with the earth. We swear not to hit it another lick till spring" [61].

A great deal more could be said along these lines, and it is a good direction for future study of Still. The correctness of such an approach is confirmed by Still's preoccupation with Mayan civilization. He has made many study trips to Yucatan, to Guatemala, and Honduras. In a recent interview, he remarked: "I've always been interested in primitive peoples," and he stressed further: "the thing that holds me is the great mystery of the disappearance of the Mayan people."[22] Will future readers of Still's work ponder the mystery of the disappearance of the Appalachian people?

All of these matters—Nashville agrarianism, the Appalachian mythos, ancient agrarian peasant cults, and the mystery of Mayan civilization — are important touchstones for the study of Still. Yet we must not be led astray: He is not a polemicist; he is not, for all his interest in "primitive peoples," an anthropologist. And, while he is surely one of the finest "Appalachian writers" we are ever likely to have, he is much more — a regionalist in the finest Southern Renascence sense (and in that universal sense which we are reminded of by his carefully selected epigraphs for his work, from Verga, from Hamsun). A firm grasp of his "agrarianism" makes this clear. Yet the term agrarianism is a word that evokes a complex of values, a texture of experience, not likely to be much understood today.

Must we, then, find one last category, more contemporary and fashionable, for Still, for the man and his work as a symbol and a text for our times? It is ecological wholeness. For the man who established himself in an enduring place (not as autochthon, but as *anachthon*, to coin a term more universally apt for the optative agrarian of the twentieth century), for the man who deliberately "joined the folk life of the community," for the man who has always grown his own garden and experimented with plants, the "ecological wholeness" label is appropriate. For the writer, for the work, how useful is such a term? Karl Kroeber, in an essay concerned with Wordsworth's "Home at Grasmere," invokes Wordsworth as our contemporary, Wordsworth the ecologist who "speaks for the profound, biologically rooted need for territorial security common to all men and against the conquest of space, most vividly apparent in the urbanizing of technological civilization which daily consumes more of our planet.... Grasmere is no vacation spot, no mere place in respite from the fragmented restlessness of modern life. Nor is it a symbol of utopian existence. It is an authentic alternative. It is a genuine alternative because it is a real home?"[23]

Through this home, Kroeber suggests (in language that echoes Granet), Wordsworth appropriates a "truly 'primitive' response to nature," a sense of "primal unity," a sense of "innate ecological sensitivity," which issue in poetry that is, at its best, "simply, joyous worship" (138, 141). All of this constitutes what Kroeber calls "ecological holiness." Still and Wordsworth occupy the same terrain of the spirit. Wordsworth addresses the Grasmere hill-country: "Embrace me then, ye Hills, and close me in"; Still declares: "I shall not leave these prisoning hills." Prison or embrace, or both at once, Still and Wordsworth, each in his own Cumberland Mountains, takes a stand, a stand that is personal and vocational, ecological and hieratic, humanly and aesthetically life-determining. They do not romanticize the harshness, the hard truths of their mountains. They seek "the acknowledged voice of life," in Wordsworth's phrase, which speaks "of what is done among the fields, / Done truly there, or felt, of solid good / And real evil." They seek, and find, a song "more harmonious" than "pastoral fancies." Wordsworth asks: "Is there such a stream, / ... flowing from the heart / With motions of true dignity and grace?" There is indeed, and it takes its rise in James Still's Kentucky hill-country, flows through his lyrical chronicle, down all those troublesome creeks, and that vasty river of earth.

# *Notes*

1. This passage is the epigraph for James Still's *Pattern of a Man and Other Stories* (Frankfort: Gnomon Press, 1976) and is taken from Giovanni Verga's *The House by the Medlar Tree.*

2. All of the observations and quotations concerning Still's days at LMU and Vanderbilt are based on my conversations and correspondence with him. Also, see Still's published interviews, in *Appalachian Journal* 6 (Winter 1979): 120–41 and in *The Iron Mountain Review* 2 (Summer 1984): 3–10. The latter is a conversation with Jim Wayne Miller.

3. Author's communication with James Still.

4. Author's communication with James Still.

5. *Appalachian Journal* 6 (Winter 1979): 123.

6. The best study of the question is Jim Wayne Miller's "A Post-Agrarian Regionalism for Appalachia," *Appalachian Heritage* 8 (Spring 1980): 58–71.

7. "Afterword," *The Run* for *the Elbertas* (Lexington: University Press of Kentucky, 1980), p. 142.

8. Printed as "Mountain Heritage," *New Republic* 85 (1935); as "Heritage" in *Hounds on the Mountain* (New York: Viking Press, 1937); as a signed broadside, again entitled "Heritage," in 1968; set to music for the bicentennial celebration of Transylvania College in 1983.

9. *Run for the Elbertas*, p. 144.

10. Donald Davidson, "A Mirror for Artists," *I'll Take My Stand* (New York: Harper & Brothers, 1930), p. 55.

11. Robert Penn Warren, "Some Don'ts for Literary Regionalists," *The American Review* 8 (November 1936): 148–50.

12. John Tyree Fain and Thomas Daniel Young, eds., *The Literary Correspondence of Donald Davidson and Allen Tate* (Athens: University of Georgia Press, 1974), p. 245.

13. Tate's letter is in the correspondence held by Mr. Still.

14. This passage is the epigraph for James Still's *The Run for the Elbertas* and is taken from Hamsun's *Growth of the Soil.*

15. See Still's poem "Heritage."

16. *American Speech* 5 (December 1929): 113.

17. The first review is in *Commonweal*, 23 February 1940; the next is from *Books*, 4 February 1940; the last is from the *Boston Transcript*, 10 February 1940. The study of Still and Stuart is Dayton Kohler, "Jesse Stuart and James Still: Mountain Regionalists," *College English* 3 (March 1942). Other studies of Still include Cratis D. Williams, *The Southern Mountaineer in Fact and Fiction*, 1398–1432. (This is a Ph.D. dissertation, portions of which have been published in *Appalachian Journal*). Williams judges Still to be the most successful "mountain novelist" since Mary Murfree. Dean Cadle, in "Man on Troublesome," *Yale Review* 57 (1968), has high praise for Still and provides a good introduction to Still and his work. Recent essays by Fred Chappell, "The Seamless Vision of James Still," *Appalachian Journal* 8 (Spring 1981) and Jim Wayne Miller, "Appalachian Literature: A Home in this World," *The Iron Mountain Review* 2 (Summer 1984), offer perceptive readings of the work. The summer 1984 issue of *Iron Mountain Review* is entirely devoted to Still and includes a useful interview and bibliography. An M.A. thesis by Terry McCoy, "James Still: A Coal Field Agrarian," Tennessee Technological University, 1980, is concerned with the "desire to return to the land" which is "central to Still's work." As this survey of Still criticism suggests, the contexts of appreciation and analysis remain somewhat narrowly regional.

18. James Still, *River of Earth* (Lexington: University Press of Kentucky, 1978), p. 21; subsequent page references are to this edition and are included in the text.

19. Inscription on a tomb, depicted in eighteenth-century paintings by Guercino, Poussin, and Reynolds.

20. Erwin Panofsky, "Et in Arcadia Ego" in *Philosophy and History* (Oxford: Oxford University Press, 1936), pp. 223–54.

21. Marcel Granet, *The Religion of the Chinese People*, trans. Maurice Freedman (New York: Harper & Row, 1975), pp. 41–42.

22. James Still and Jim Wayne Miller, "'Daring to Look in the Well': A Conversation," *The Iron Mountain Review* 2 (Summer 1984): 6.

23. Karl Kroeber, "'Home at Grasmere'; Ecological Holiness," *PMLA* 89 (January 1974): 132, 134; subsequent page references cited in the text.

# Headwaters: The Early Poetics of James Still, Don West, and Jesse Stuart

## CHRIS GREEN

*"Are poems made by hands? … All that you can know and are and can be come together and [are] concentrated on a single point, like a glass drawing fire from the sun."— James Still, "I Sometimes Tell" 143*

The 1930s, the decade in which Appalachian writers themselves began to write about Appalachia, are commonly recognized as the headwaters of modern Appalachian literature. Five writers therein stand out: Harriette Simpson Arnow, Louise McNeill, Don West, Jesse Stuart, and James Still. This essay examines how James Still's early poetics were influenced by Don West and Jesse Stuart, the two poets with whom he came of age as a writer.[1] Still, West, and Stuart are important measures of one another because they shared a common set of experiences and cultural references, towards which each took remarkably different tacks. Specifically, they all attended Lincoln Memorial University — a school dedicated to educating mountain youth — and then proceeded to attended Vanderbilt University during the heyday of the Agrarians and the rise of proletarian literature.[2] From there, they became educators (of quite different sorts) in eastern Kentucky and established artistic personas as they published their poetry, found diverse readerships, and developed stances toward the literary world. Looking back from 1977, Still recounted,

> Don was a gifted man, he writes well, and if the day ever comes that he writes his autobiography, we'll have a volume to reckon with. I last saw him in 1937. The three of us— Jesse Stuart, Don West, and myself— have been referred to as "the barefoot boys." We have different careers. We chose the "path less traveled by." Don is the poet of the disinherited. And Jesse wrote the most books, some seventy-five of them, that came out of the Class of 1929 [Interview with Williamson 64].

But Still downplays their mutually definitive relationships. In their letters to each other, the authors discussed their literary and social experiences, and they came to define themselves by their relationship to each other's writing by pushing against one another's example — influence being more a matter of conversation and reaction than imitation. More than mere sibling rivalry, they represent three distinct approaches to the mountains, America, poetry, and the literary world.

Allow me to frame this investigation by asking how one might measure the influence of one author on another. How are we to gauge the effect of any particular influence from the myriad that an artist synthesizes into a piece that transcends them all? When three authors hold such widely different styles, how can we discern how one author influenced another's style? Given that these authors wrote each other about their work of becoming authors, perhaps we can begin to discern potential influences by considering the authors' poetics in poems that address select, definitive subjects about Appalachia: the impact of modernity on mountain youth, mountain culture and music, and — most importantly — the link between people and land. Hence, this essay compares examples of their poetry as a platform upon which we might hazard a few guesses about how these authors' influenced each other's poetics. Although my focus forbids full consideration of any one author's poetics, my hope is that the reader will feel invited to examine other aspects upon which I was unable to touch.

We might best begin with the poem that Still understood as his literary breakthrough: "Child in the Hills" (3–4).[3] The poem was first published in *The Atlantic*, whose editor Edward Weeks wrote to Still: "the stanzas are remarkable for their impulse, their authentic folk feeling, and for a diction which will appeal to readers far removed from your hills" (5 Sept 1936). The poem also begins *Hounds on the Mountain*, and Hindman Settlement School republished it in a four-page pamphlet of Still's poetry, seeking to harness both the ideas conveyed in the poem as well as the prestige of Still's publication with Viking (Still, "Poems"). In another pamphlet advertising the school, Hindman administrators gave a one-page list of books that would grant donors a "vivid understanding of the mountain country and a better appreciation of its people": the literary work of Lucy Furman, Ann Cobb, and James Still. Still's section announced the forthcoming publication of *Hounds on the Mountain* and carefully listed all the magazines in which his writing had appeared (Hindman). How could a poem appropriate for publication in *The Atlantic* also express an "authentic folk feeling," and why was such a feeling valuable to both Still and Hindman?

"Child in the Hills" presents the traces of an unnamed child from the mountains who has been swept away by the tides of civilization and has "Drifted into years of growth and strange enmeshment" (25). In the first stanza, the narrator asks where in the hills he can find the "tracks a small foot made" and "the echo of his voice" within "tall trees," "fallow earth," "sleeping years," and streams that flow before "his darkened door" (1–6). The narrator claims to hear the unseen child's "Shrill imperious" voice among "rain in the beechwood trees" and in the "dark hours" whence his voice creeps from "the mountain silence" (8–10). In the quiet, "deep night," the child's heart can be heard "ebbing and returning" (12). Against this ghostly presence encountered during moments of stillness and seclusion, the next two stanzas create the vigorous wonderment of the child who "once" (a word that begins five of the next ten lines) merged himself with the earth as he "thrust" his toes into the "gladness of soil" and "waded the clear stony waters of Carr" (14, 16). The fourth stanza is filled with concrete experience, and the child witnesses the world, listening "open-eyed" and "breathless" to unseen "geese flying over" in the night (18–19) — the same world where he listened to the echoes of horses upon his brother's death (20). Perception, in this poem, is no sure guarantee of encounter, for the thing perceived always surges just beyond the line of sight. And upon hearing the "swelling voice of the water's strength," the child too flees away and is "Swept with the waters down the winding mountain valleys" to the civilization beyond (22–24). The last stanza returns to the start of the poem, where the buried, "lost," and "drowned" child becomes a living presence only through his absence:

> He is waiting under the shadow of these hills,
> In the damp coolness of laurel and rhododendron;
> He is lost in the mossy coves, in the lynn's late sighing.
> His voice is drowned in the waters of Carr [27–30].

The form of the poem is haunted with its own lost fullness. Written in six stanzas whose line count slowly dwindles (6, 6, 5.5, 5, 4.5, and 4), ten-syllable lines evoke blank verse and frame the poem, with the 28 lines in between being fretted by an unfilled iambic hexameter (thirteen to fourteen syllables with five to six beats per line). Breaking midway through the poem, an amputated half-line draws attention to its lost words (line 14), as does the line before the stanza quoted above (line 26). Yet that search for completion of meter purposefully fails in the final four lines (quoted above), which are the shortest in the poem.

What did Hindman Settlement School appreciate about this poem: the call to *save* the lost child or the need to *preserve* him? For an answer, we might examine what feature of the poem led Weeks to praise its "authentic folk feeling." "Child in the Hills" appeals to the concept of a chthonic innocence that preceded the abandonment of the farm in the first stanza, whose door is "darkened" and whose fields lay "Unfurrowed" (6, 5). Even though the literal child, who is now "shod against the earth," has migrated with his family in search of work, the innocent child — the one not yet encumbered by the "strange enmeshment" of modern civilization — remains in "the shadow of these hills," the "coolness of laurel," and "the lynn's late sighing" (13, 15, 27–29). Paradoxically, this child whose presence now rises from the earth only does so because he has been buried, lost, and drowned — as if there had been an awful sacrifice. Hindman's ideal was to redeem those who had unencumbered phenomenal relations with nature, to honor those who had died, and to protect remaining children from such sacrifice. The "folk feeling" to which Weeks referred revises the classic American trope of the earth as woman: in the Appalachian mountains, America's children and their communal innocence have e/merged from/with the earth.

Although Still had been previously published in such prestigious literary journals as *Poetry* and *The Virginia Quarterly Review*, Still called the appearance of "Child of the Hills" in *The Atlantic Monthly* his first major publication ("I Sometimes Tell" 135). The story of how Still came to encounter and value *The Atlantic* is an essential part of understanding his poetics as well as his (and Appalachia's) place in the literary field. Still grew up on a small farm in east central Alabama near the Georgia border. When he was a senior in high school, Still came across a catalogue for Lincoln Memorial University, which had some 800 students mainly drawn from Kentucky, Tennessee, and Virginia. Because the school was predicated upon the fact that students paid their own way by working and Still's family had no extra funds, he decided to attend: "I had made a genealogical circle. Up the road in Virginia was the site of the Stills' pioneer home" ("James Still" 235). After working his first year in the limestone quarry, Still was too fatigued to study, so he became the janitor for the library, where he discovered a decade's worth of donated *Atlantic Monthly* back issues (Still, "A Man Singing" 12). Still relates,

> I kept scores of them and at the end of the term shipped them home. Those were the times of the Great Depression, and I had no employment, so I spent the summer reading. All of them. Every article, every poem, every word. I practically ate the paper. I learned from them more than I could state. Even the art of composition, if it can be said I ever obtained it. I decided to write for *The Atlantic*. First and foremost ["I Sometimes Tell" 135].

Still had been submitting poems to *The Atlantic* since late 1932, and it took three years for him to become published. In large part the editor's attention finally came because of the magazine's long investment in promoting the southern mountains to its readers.

In his correspondence with Still over the next year, Edward Weeks explained, "The

*Atlantic* has always had a soft spot in its heart for the Old Primitive, and your mountaineering sketches come to fill a place which has not been occupied since Lucy Furman last turned our way ... [And they] will have a bearing upon those many households which have grown crowded in these lean years" (23 April 1936). In a letter he sent along in acceptance of Still's story "Job's Tears," Weeks pointed out that "*The Atlantic* helped to lead the way to the literature of the mountains. Walter Page began the exploration and contributors such as Lucy Furman, Olive Tilford Dargan, and Maristan Chapman continued the good work" (25 August 1936). Weeks found Still to be the next step.[4]

The mountain youth — seen as lacking the means to become a functioning part of American society — had been a part of the national conversation since before the founding of the Hindman Settlement School in 1902. Don West wrote his religious studies thesis about Hindman and finished it with a poem about the mountain youth which struck quite a different note. Although West had been enamored of Hindman when he first wrote Still about it in 1930, West ended up forswearing how they educated students. He finished his thesis with a poem which also appeared in *Between the Plow Handles* (1932), published by and for his own Highlander Folk School. Rather than talking about the fate of the mountain youth to readers of national magazines, West was writing for and to the people in the mountains, seeking to inspire them to self-belief and action against the tides of modernity and capitalism.

In the poem, West directly addresses the "Mountain Boy" (26–27) as "you" (constructing a figurative reader) — a typical move for West who believed in direct communication, perhaps out of his training as a preacher. He implores the "boy" with clear, short lines that would be accessible to people from a wide range of literacies. Consider the first stanza:

> You are more than a dirty child
> In patched overalls,
> You mountain boy...!
> The hills are yours,
> Fragrant forests,
> Silver rivers
> And suffering people
> Are your heritage ... [ellipses in original] [1–8].

West counters their apparent poverty with the accessible wealth of nature — emphasized with trochaic bimeter lines whose staccato rhyme is parleyed with the softer accent of alliteration ('f') and assonance ('s'), which, combined, creates their "heritage." He calls on these "young hillmen" to be "Dreamers" as well as "Thinkers" (11, 9) and to build a new world from their experience of mountain culture and the "blue mysteries" of "jagged mountains" (18, 17). Seven of the nine lines in the third stanza start with an implicit command: "Rise up ... Sing ... Dream ... Climb ... Gaze ... Turn ... Nourish." At the heart of West's landscape is not the echo of children who once lived there but a call to the youth to unite intellect and soul as they fight for the hills that serve as their ground of being:

> Love the soil.
> Your father's blood
> Made it rich,
> His sweat has carved
> Your destiny.
> Shift the course dirt
> Between your fingers.
> Exult as you follow the plow.
> Yours in the poet's life.
> You rhyme the soil [23–32].

West calls on the young men to embrace life through song and work as a way of breaking the "bonds / of misery" (37–38). The poem's short lines emphasize the brief, clear sentences that spill down the page. While it is difficult to judge how the attitude that West expressed in such poems affected Still, people are more ephemeral in Still's poems, even though he explores their unity with the land.[5]

West's poetics differed from Still's because Still's work represented "a folk feeling" that outsiders could recognize through their associations (and value through his formal where-withal) while West's poetry was for the folk. Where they join is in recognition of mainstream America's encroachment into mountain life: Still appealed to outsiders to give aid to the mountain youth, while West called on them to save themselves. West would leave Hindman in 1932, and he lived in Kentucky again only from 1934–1937 as an organizer with the Communist Party. At Hindman, Still had found a place and people with which to make a home. Part of West's poetics involves his work to organize and educate people in the face of capitalist abuse. Still also served as an educator but in a less overt key: at first his poetry was not a direct tool to educate the folk, but later (from 1951 at Morehead through the establishment of the Hindman writers workshop until his death in 2001) he would become a leading mentor to writers from around Appalachia.

Between these extremes rests Jesse Stuart, whom Still knew as a writer and friend during their time at LMU. Throughout the 1930s, Stuart wrote Still about his career as a writer, and they challenged each other only to write letters upon publication of a poem (Richardson 100). Stuart was the first to publish widely, plowing the field for Still's later work and marking the national literary scene with the presence of his sonnets, which appeared in *The American Mercury* (Oct. 1933, 184–88), *Virginia Quarterly Review* (1933, 504–09), *Poetry* (May 1934, 61–65), and *Forum* (July 1934, 54–55). Indeed, Still's first poems in national journals were published just before *Man with a Bull-Tongue Plow*, which sold tens of thousands of copies, was released. When editors read Still's work over the next few years, they read it through the lens of Stuart. Although Still surely had read West's two small books, it is impossible to know which of Stuart's poems he read, as Stuart had written thousands and published 703 in *Man with a Bull-Tongue Plow* alone. What we can judge are the different stances and formal strategies the two took toward similar materials.

Continuing with the focus on modernity and the mountain youth, consider Stuart's sonnet 394, which shows how mountain adults were labeled as children according to their relationship with a mainstream culture that judged status and power largely upon literacy and education:

| | |
|---|---|
| Men say these are the children of the night, | A |
| These mountain men who cannot read and write. | A |
| They may not know the ways to shape a word. | B |
| They may not know the words when they are traced. | C |
| But they remember well the things they've heard | B |
| And soon forget the danger they have faced. | C |
| Some of these men are children of the sun — | D |
| Unnoticed things of earth one could show you, | E |
| And how to run your furrows straight and true. | E |
| They could teach many how to use a gun — | D |
| They are bronze men who have no fear of toil. | F |
| Their education is a book of soil — | F |
| They are men taught to work and pray and fight. | A |
| Let them be children of the darker night. | A |

Playing upon the phrase "children of the night," which refers to those outside the precincts of civilization, Stuart acts as a translator and a protector. Accenting his peers' illiteracy qualifies his own ability to "shape a word" as work as he writes his "book of soil" (4, 12). The poem addresses those who have the power to not "Let them be" but who, if they are open, might be shown "Unnoticed things of the earth" by mountain people (14, 8).[6] Stuart gains his authenticity as a mountaineer by his seemingly crude use of the sonnet (this one has 14 lines, though line count moves from 12 to 16 throughout the book). The structure of the poem, like the "furrows" that the men in the poem plow, "run[s] straight and true" (9): stops come at the end of the lines, and each line contains exactly ten syllables with five beats, flirting with iambic pentameter. Similarly, the rhyme scheme starts with a couplet followed by three quatrains— a reversed Shakespearean sonnet that gains its emphasis by starting with a couplet and ending with two of them. In the final line, Stuart revises the saying "children of the night," calling upon his readers to "Let them be children of the darker night." Like West's language, the poem's diction is simple, but provides just enough ambiguity to engage its educated audience. This combination showed people around America what they craved to hear: that poetry thrived in rural America outside of an elitist modernism. In his review for *The New York Herald Tribune*, Horace Gregory — himself the intellectual godfather of poets who combined proletarian issues with modernist writing — praised this poet from "provincial America," whom those tired of the "'intellectual'" poetry of the last ten years could read with "genuine relief" as well as being someone "the average man can understand." And people ate it up: Stuart found himself being read in New York as well as in Greenup, Kentucky.

Stuart sold himself as a mountaineer through whom the tradition of English sonnets lived in a form that was adapted to the roughness of the American mountains. Stuart was playing on the idea that outsiders had about survivals of English culture in the mountains, even through he learned most of what he knew about sonnets from the traditionalist agrarian Donald Davidson, his most influential mentor with whom he had repeatedly taken classes at Vanderbilt on Elizabethan poetry. But the savviest review — and the greatest appreciation — was Malcolm Cowley's in *The New Republic*. This recognition was critical, because Cowley's name was closely associated with Harlan County and Kentucky after he and other national leftist writers visited there to document abuse of the coal miners in 1931. Cowley recognized that Stuart's *The Man with the Bull-Tongue Plow* was the first book written about the mountains by "a poet who lives inside the cabin," so the book allowed outsiders to gauge mountaineers for the first time: "he is always speaking in his own words about his own people." Cowley begins by recounting how Stuart's life and poems demonstrate the living inheritance of the "pioneers themselves" who were "always driven on by their poverty," but like other reviewers he calls Stuart's poems "careless, trite, or perfunctory" and points out that the collection should be one-seventh its original length. Indeed, Stuart's poems are not about the craft of individual sonnets (many of which are relatively weak) but about the global process of representing a culture, at which this discussion can only hint.

If Stuart sold his connection with the past, so did Still — but Still's was valued by the people who had come into the mountains to try to preserve it. Given that the content of Still's work was shaped by his life in Knott County, the most critical influence on Still's writing was undoubtedly when Don West sent him a dulcimer from Hindman in 1930. The dulcimer was made by J.D. Thomas, whose brother had taught Jethro Amburgey, a crafts teacher at Hindman to whom Still would co-dedicate *Hounds on the Mountain* (the collection was also dedicated to Guy Loomis, a wealthy northerner who paid for Still's graduate education and provided critical literary contacts). While West was working on his Bachelor's of Divinity, he had gone to the Hindman Settlement School to work and collect data for his thesis on rural social infrastructure and its effect on values. During the time Still was in Illinois pursuing his degree in Library Science, West wrote that he had "at last captured one of those old instruments known as the 'Dulcimore'" [*sic*], and he sent it to Still along with testimony as to the "hopeless" case of the mountain youth (29 Nov. 1930). As a young man trained in the Social Gospel, West also related his despair at the school's "undersized" boys "without legal fathers," everyone of whom "smokes, swears, and drinks" (25 Oct. 1930). In an impassioned fourteen-page letter, West relates his "feeling of helplessness" and his desire to serve the suffering people who "will be a bunch of degenerates within a few more generations." West had first written to Still in October 1930 after hearing of his mother's death, and West appealed to Still to honor his recently deceased mother "like a real man" by coming to Hindman to uplift the people by helping them to be as clean and beautiful as the mountains they lived upon. Moreover, knowing his friend's interest in writing, West repeatedly promises that "I could give you material for stories and lots of them" (7 March 1931) and describes getting to know old men in the hollows and how he manages to reform some of the boys.

West would undergo a moral crisis, leading him to discount settlement-school methods, but the language he used portrays how many outsiders at Hindman Settlement School understood the mountaineers whom they sought to reform: victims degenerating morally and physically under the forces of modernity. Still's work gained notice by association with these understandings, but he never waged such judgments upon the people of Knott County. Still not only made a home at Hindman, but with an appreciative and sharp eye, he also witnessed the people among whom he lived and worked. Like other poets at the time such as William Carlos Williams, Still sought to represent the reality that modern culture had blinded Americans from seeing — in Still's case, the reality of life in the mountains. But the reality he first came to know was the one filtered, in part, through Hindman's project. In mutual validation, Still's association with Hindman familiarized him with the conventions of Appalachian authenticity that were recognized by the mainstream, and Hindman converted Still's cultural capital into fundraising pamphlets to help the folk survive in America.[7]

For the last century, one of the most well recognized cultural symbols for Appalachia has been the dulcimer, and Still's early poetry about dulcimers display the tensions and hopes underlying *Hounds on the Mountain*. "Mountain Dulcimer," *Hounds*'s second poem, concisely illustrates the contradictions and tensions of outsiders' beliefs about seeing Appalachia as a premodern space where contemporary Americans felt that people still lived in vital proximity to nature. In "Mountain Dulcimer" (5) no human voices are heard. Divorced from the human tongue, Still's "dulcimer sings," seemingly of its own accord, "Of the doe's swift poise, the fox's fleeting step / And the music of hounds" (1–2). The poem's ambiguous syntax strategically refuses to locate actors, blurring the distinction between the human and non-human world. The dulcimer's "fretted maple throat" allows the "creak of saddle-bags, of oxen yoke" to sound out next to the "Wild turkey's treble [and] dark sudden flight of crows," for the dulcimer has been crafted in the "quiet" by "the carver of maple" (1, 9, 10, 19, 20). This fine line between the human and natural is the "keen blade's edge" that carves the body of the dulcimer, an instrument whose "breast that sounds hunting horns / Strong as clenched hands upon the edge of death" (20, 7–8). And after the distant drumming of the "anvil's strength," the dulcimer vocalized the "silence" that "aches and cries unhushed into the day" (4, 5, 6). For in the mountain reaches where machines are silent, when one takes "Long drinks from piggins hard against the lips," one can hear the "breath of the lark" (15, 14). In this poem, a mountain dulcimer is the implement of an *unseen* people who, due to their minimal use of technology, live next to and can see through the valance between life and death, between the human world and the natural.

"Mountain Dulcimer" was Still's first major publication and appeared in *The Virginia*

*Quarterly Review* (July 1935), which served as the decade's premier journal about Southern politics and literature. In the age of modern artifice and industry from the turn of the century through 1929, Americans had poured into the cities to seek the promised shelter of higher standards of living under the fabric of civilization's umbrella. However, the Depression revealed to millions the failure of civilization, upon whose tools they had become dependent. Given the economic struggles most faced, newspaper readers in the Southern cities of Durham, Greensboro, and Norfolk (where Still's poem was also published on July 4, 1935) took solace from the soul-life portrayed in "Mountain Dulcimer."

Another of Still's poems called "Dulcimer" appeared in *Mountain Life and Work* in October 1934 (10).[8] In this poem, Still utilizes repetition, perhaps miming the relatively narrow range of the dulcimers; however, just as with the musicians whose hands made the dulcimer's croon, so Still strikes deep notes with limited chords:

> The dulcimer's three strings are the heart's cords.
> Tune them carefully, turn the pegs slowly,
> Plucking and listening to the sweetening voice
> Rising clear and articulate.
>
> Tune the first with the night, with shadows upon the mountain, approaching
>     thunder,
> The second with the morning, sheaves drowned in dew, sudden breaking of day,
> The third with the midday sun, ripe-hanging, swollen and lush mellow.
> Tune the strings carefully, turn the pegs slowly.
>
> Strum and play the merry heart, high hope and laughter,
> Play the child's thin voice, the wren in the maple tree,
> The rain upon a clapboard roof, the undissolving shadow,
> Play light, play dark, play unbound glee.
>
> Play swiftening wings in narrow predestined flight,
> Play heartbreak on the outward wandering way,
> Play time's slow evening, the quiet smile in sleep,
> Play love's first waking, play the yielding light,
> Play life, play death, play eyes that cannot weep.

The poem manifests the beliefs of the Council of Southern Mountain Workers, of which *Mountain Life and Work* was the official organ. Consisting primarily of home missionaries, charity workers, health reformers, educators, and social workers, that organization sought to honor the interconnection of handicrafts, culture, and environment, even as they aided the mountaineers in adapting to modernity. "Dulcimer" served as no less than a manifesto of preservation even as CSMW struggled to help the mountaineers adapt to modernization. The poem articulated the myth around the dulcimer that a people's unspeakable and unquantifiable intimacy with the environment was realized and deepened through their relationship with their handcrafted music.

Assuming an iconic status, "Dulcimer" would be republished in *Mountain Life and Work* some thirty-five years later during the magazine's 40th anniversary (1965) and the founding of the Appalachian Regional Commission as part of Lyndon Johnson's War on Poverty. In an accompanying article, senators from Kentucky and West Virginia explained that because these "hardy mountain people" are of "pioneer stock," they have "maintained their spirit and individualism in the midst of adverse economic conditions"; thus, with government aid to build social infrastructure and support business development, they could overcome their isolation and partake of "prosperity which might bring about the standard of living reached elsewhere in America" (Cooper and Randolph 31–32). These worn claims ignored the fact that Appalachian isolation had repeatedly been punctured by (and savaged for) raw-resource exploitation. Within this context, Still's poem takes on a desperate double meaning: the first harkening back to the struggles once indigenous to mountain culture, the second becoming a lament for the ongoing loss of that culture itself. The final phrase of the poem — "play eyes that cannot weep" — proposes the mountaineers' inability to grieve for the passing of their ways.

If Still's version of mountain music brought a certain spirit to life for readers of *The Virginia Quarterly Review* and *Mountain Life and Work*, Stuart and West wrote about the music of the mountains as the people there experienced it. Opposed to the mythology of the dulcimer, Stuart embraced the lived world of mountain jigs and narrated torn romances straight out of balladry. Sonnets 129–134 relate the musical prowess of the Fiddler named "Blind Frailey" (probably in reference to legendary fiddler Blind Ed Haley); sonnets 183–190 tell the doomed romance between Laura Day and Bill Glover, who narrates the sequence; but sonnets 379–382, to my ear, catch the participative movement of mountain reels the best. In particular, sonnet 380 enacts the motion of the dance as the caller's voice is juxtaposed via hemistich with the narrator's testimony. The poem runs 15 lines and laces together two layers of refrain, the enthusiasm of the narrator (who orders the listener's participation), and repetition of the end rhymes (*tell, Move, love, violin,* and *in*). The result is an animated villanelle that catches the order, mix, and resolve of a group dance. The first two lines draw attention to the basic rhythms of the call and why people seek it out: "Tomorrow may be bitter, who can tell / Oh, listen to that call: 'Move, children, move!'" The middle six lines quietly describe the "lonesome violin," "guitars," and "winter stars," but then lines nine and after paradoxically erupt into hemistich whose motion causes the reader to move:

> Now listen to that call: "Move Children, Move!"
> First couple out — waltz up and down the hall,
> "Move Children, Move!" Step lightly with your Love.
> . . . . . . . . . . . . . . . . . . . . . . . . . . . . . . . . . . . .
> You see the bird flies out — the crow hops in.
> "Move Children, Move!" Too slow that step you're in [9–11, 14–15].

The poem summons up and revises those picaresque images associated with mountain dance by yoking a plaintive quality — as demonstrated by Still — with this hotly-stepped, yet exactly measured, poetic reel.

Stuart wrote intensely about his mountain experience at the urging of Harry Harrison Kroll, his creative writing instructor at LMU who wrote about his experience growing up as a sharecropper in central Tennessee. Kroll would sell his first novel (*The Mountainy Singer* [1928]) while Stuart and West were studying with him, and his mark on them — and hence on all Appalachian literature since — was indelible.[9] Under Kroll's influence, exactly half of the poems in West's first collection, *Crab-Grass* (1931), were composed in dialect, another way of demonstrating intimacy with mountain culture that Still and Stuart minimized in their poetry as they sought publication in major journals. In "Sour-Wood Sprouts" (22–23), a poem narrating people setting out for a party, West interspaces the narrator's description (in dialect) with a character's song:

> Whoop em up thar, ye sour-wood sprouts,
> Scrooched in th' saddle like
> Sheep with th' gouts.
> Ole Newt Mealer's got a party on to-night
> An' good corn-licker fer to
> Make us all tight.
>
> "I got-a gurl in Sour-Wood Holler" [1–7].

The lines, which at first glimpse seem off-kilter, catch the focused mindset of folks setting out for a good time as rhymes and dwindling line length (nine [and eleven], six, and four syllables respectively) ebb and swell, stitching together their progress. But such a subject was abnormal for West, who looked down on drinking. Much more to his mature ken were poems in *Between the Plow Handles*, about the "Ballad Singer" (12)—who sang songs "Of corn in rocky soil" for those of "furrowed faces" and "calloused hand" (6, 13, 14)—or poems praising poets who "sang the songs / Of fresh plowd sod" ("For Jesse Stuart," p. 23, 11, 1–2). The poet and the life that West loved were those which refused "tractors / and reapers" and chose, instead, to sing for "hill people" even as they worked by the "hungry crow / In a dead chestnut tree" (3–4, 15, 12–13). West would cleave to such position as his life's work went on, and he would write reviews about Stuart and letters to Still that, essentially, accused them of betraying the mountains.[10]

During their years of contact and influence, all three authors developed a core belief about a *genus humi*, an Anglo-nativizing of the land, and all three—to different degrees and with varying means—sought to fight Appalachia's deterritorialization by the industrial and commodity forces of modernity. Nowhere is Still's move to distinguish himself from Stuart more vividly illustrated than in how Still shaped his sonnets to show the relationship between people and land. The second section of *Hounds on the Mountain*, "Creek County," renders the relationship of mountain farmers with nature. "On Redbird Creek" (18) considers the limits of what can be heard within purposeful cultivation.

Written in thirteen lines and two stanzas (7 and 6 lines long), the poem hints at the form of a Petrarchan sonnet but combines it with an Anglo ballad form (A-B-C-B) of the first quatrain with solidly-wrought, iambic pentameter lines. Forming the first sentence, these lines detail the "cloven soil," which "has penned the acres up / With greenness prim" (3–4). The second sentence makes up the next section, which, instead of providing the expected quatrain, includes only three lines that rhyme A-D-D. These lines point toward the "mist grown stark and tall" beyond the farm's edge to "the west / Of Redbird Creek where crows and blackbirds call" (7, 5–6). The missing fourth line of the quatrain perhaps represents that which rests beyond the bounds of what can be perceived from the folds of the farm. Until this point, the images and syntax are clearly rendered. However, the second stanza, through use of unspecified antecedents, points out the "foils of clouds" which "men and plows attend" (12):

> The vibrant canes crowding marshy ground
> Are tuneless pipes heard by bleeding ears
> Through blighted chestnut cankered to the heart
> And rousing all of memory's ancient fears
> These foils of clouds that men and plows attend
> Are tares and thistles strewn upon the wind [8–13].

Composed in one flowing, abundant sentence, the stanza is perhaps Still's finest formal showing. This sextet's rhyme hints at the shape of a Shakespearian sonnet, joining a ballad quatrain and an ending couplet (E-F-G-F-H-H). On the edge of the human ordered world, one must question just what causes the "ears," which hear the "tuneless pipes" of canes by the streambed, to be "bleeding" (9). The reference to blood suggests a corporal rupture on the edge of the visible.

The "ancient fears" (11) raised have less to do with the sound of "vibrant canes" than the fact that sound passes through "blighted chestnut" (8, 10), where the natural world is shorn by human manipulation. Thus, "these foils of clouds" (12) in the final couplet might be read as referring to both the "pipes" that have not been given human meaning (they are, after all, "tuneless") as well as to the consequence of not undertaking the rituals which are required to partake of substance from beyond the civilized world. To dispel such fears, "men and plows attend" to the tamable (and tunable) precincts of cultivated land (12). The "foils" become the "tares and thistles strewn upon the wind" and cannot be constrained via such purposeful cultivation (13). Yet the farm Still describes gains vigor from its proximity to the inhuman. Conversely, over-cultivation and exposure dehumanizes farmers and land. In "On Double Creek" (22), the final poem in this six-poem section, Still relates the consequences of such forced labor and misshapen poverty:

> Across the creek I saw the paupers plowing.
> I can remember their plodding in the furrows,
> Their palsied hands, the worn flesh of their faces,
> And their odd shapelessness, and their tired cries.
> I can remember the dark swift martins in their eyes [5–9].

Lush with grotesque alliterative "p" sounds and using first person (which was the first use of it in the collection), Still contrasts his own childhood on a cotton farm in the deep South against the experience of nature and farming in the mountains. This emendation is not shared with readers, which led many reviewers to take the poem as proof that Still was "mountain-born." Rather, Still was an empathetic immigrant who discerned much of his lowland experience in the mountains.

Still takes the position of a quiet witness, which perhaps led West and Stuart to share such intimate details with Still in their letters. But Stuart and West grew up as participants in the culture and portrayed how blood and land came together through process of toil, love, and death. Proclaiming that "These are the hills that's native to my blood" (sonnet 439,l. 1), Stuart's poems delve into the lives of those whose wild ways lead them to die young and those worthy farmers who have spent their lives bearing children and baring the ground. Regardless of their mortal dance, both types became "Forever brothers to weed, root, and stone" (sonnet 409,l. 13). Stuart's father speaks in sonnet 429, telling Stuart to "'Take you a mountain girl strong as a tree'" and "'get yourself about six right pert sons'" who will "'carry on their father's blood'" (2, 9, 10). In sonnet 561, Bunion Maddox speaks to his dead wife about their work on "the hill we wore out with the plow" and their "twenty children" who now all lie dead "beneath corn tassels now furled" (2, 5, 7). In sonnet 616, Tug Oliver rises to speak about how he and his wife "raised sixteen children," and

> In head-high oats and crabgrass in the corn
> We pushed the forest back — it grew again
> In second growth for our blood yet unborn [9–11].

But after years of wrestling with nature, their "cattle cutter plows" and their bodies become "rust" and "dust" (14, 15). Stuart documents how "the dust of generations" turns to loam and rises again in "blackberry blooms" (sonnet 695,ll. 2–3). Portraying the *genus humi* as a generational process of melding and renewal, Stuart shows the reader exactly how "Each life is dirt and time and rhyme and stone" (sonnet 678, l. 14).

The same smelting of spirit happens in *Between the Plow Handles*. Therein, West takes the reader into the quiet, long poems of daily life that are starkly juxtaposed against poems about the industrial depletion of the people and the land.[11] For instance, in "A'Callin' Home th' Hogs" (4–5), the narrator explains how the "echo" of "Pig-o, pig-o, pig-o-o-ee" calling across the "marshy bogs" belongs to the spirit of "ole Kim Mulkey," West's maternal grandfather (3, 13, 14):

> "Since last mast season
> When chestnut burs was spread,

> Ole Kim Mulkey's
> Been livin' with th' dead.
> Nearly bout a year now
> Ole Kim's been away —
> Sumpen calls th' hogs home,
> Eve of ever' day" [16–23].

As Stuart would do, West also called upon his ancestors as a direct connection to the past, particularly Kim Mulkey (see "Ole Kim Mulkey" [24] and "My Gran-Paw" [50] in *Crab-Grass* and "Scratching in Memory" [11] in *Between the Plow Handles*). If ancestors are integral to this densely textured landscape (which is reflected in the proportion of three stresses per 4–6 syllable line), the current generation is called to the cities and the mines. The next poem, "Dark Winds" (6), shows the consequences of this migration. This poem's diction is highlighted with dialect, which was in the process of becoming lost as the people were stripped of their connections to the land:

> Dark winds,
> Winds creepin' down frum th' mountins
> To stinky mills
> Callin' my longings
> Back to th' hills [1–4].

Even though West generally writes in short lines, the two beats per line in this poem are atrophied compared to line breadth in "A-Callin Home th' Hogs." The narrator becomes "dulled" by his or her "sufferin'" in factories, and even the suffering is no longer his or her own but is "blowed" with "sorrow … / Frum northern hills" (14, 16–17). All three poets wrote against industrialization, but West's stance and anger were the most pronounced. Yet after their undergraduate days, West and Stuart went in almost opposite directions. Stuart gained his inspiration and guidance from Donald Davidson, who was one of the three leading Agrarians at Vanderbilt and who sought to conserve the culture of the South. Meanwhile, West became a preacher and socialist under the guidance of Alva Taylor, one of the great leaders of the Social Gospel. All three authors joined in their love of mountain culture and anger at modernity, but they disagreed about how to fight the incursion of capitalism: Stuart appealed to an anti–Mammon morality and sought to become an American, appealing to the sanctity of mountain's connection with pioneer ancestry; West sought to catalyze his readers against capitalist domination in America by appealing to their cultural integrity; Still, however, took a quieter approach that focused on how people's daily perceptions were affected by the intrusion and appealed to an irreducible *genus humi*. [12]

Drawing on his studies at Vanderbilt, where he took classes with John Crowe Ransom and wrote his thesis on dreams in Middle English poetry, Still took the connection between people and land in a direction that appealed both to the left and to mainstream literary publishers. Soon after publication of his stories in *The Atlantic*, New York publishing houses began contacting Still, recognizing both the quality of his writing and the marketability of his subject. Still received an unexpected letter from an editor at Covici-Friede publishers, who had just published Harriette Simpson Arnow's novel *Mountain Path* in 1936. The editor wrote that someone had shown him Still's poem "Mountain Heritage," which "sharpened my editorial curiosity concerning your work" (Strauss, 10 Feb. 1936). Published in *The New Republic*, a magazine with which other Covici-Friede authors such as Horace Gregory had ties, the poem was retitled "Heritage" (55) as the final poem in *Hounds on the Mountain*. After Still's careful look into mountain life, the poem expresses an essence that could not be disintegrated by mining, deforestation, and the subsequent environmental consequences:

> I shall not leave these prisoning hills
> Though they topple their barren heads to level earth
> And the forests slide uprooted out of the sky.
> Though the waters of Troublesome, of Trace Fork,
> Of Sand Lick rise in a single body to glean the valleys,
> To drown lush penny-royal, to unravel rail fences;
> Though the sun-ball breaks the ridges into dust
> And burns its strength into the blistered rock
> I cannot leave. I cannot go away [1–9].

Given The *New Republic*'s and Covici-Friede's decided support of the American left, Malcolm Cowley (*The New Republic*'s literary editor) and Covici-Friede's editor no doubt admired Still's use of the pastoral to resist industrialism.

"Heritage" demonstrates the continuity of Western culture that has anthropomorphized America's topography (its hills shake their "barren heads," its forests "slide," its rivers "rise" in a "single body," and its "sun-ball breaks ... / and burns" [2, 3, 5, 7–8]). The poem is structured as a Petrarchan sonnet in two stanzas of nine and six lines, which "approximates a form," as one reviewer noted about the poem's rhythm (Holmes, "A Poet"). The first stanza, quoted above, contains three tercets (rather than two quatrains) that are structured by syntax rather than rhyme, an important nativization and modernization of the form. The poem begins with the narrator's declaration against abandoning the earth even though its flaying seems spontaneous with the resulting floods and droughts. Utilizing anaphora to emphasize the recurrence of environmental derogation, each tercet begins, "Though..." and sets the conditions of the narrator's determination. Against this momentum, the stanza ends with a halting, full-stop hemistich that gains intensification through that tercet's variance with the first two, which are unbroken: "I cannot leave. I cannot go away." This declaration of a naturalized Western heritage as a point of resistance generated the interest of editors and publishers who had to account for the proletarian surge in the 1930s without exiling mainstream readers.

One extended review for *The Boston Evening Transcript* begins by recounting Still's colonial heritage and his work with mountain literacy. The author explains that opposed to the work of Jesse Stuart and Thomas Wolfe, Still's "discrimination" and "craftsmanship" treats words "with scrupulous honor" (Holmes). Fully quoting the final two poems in the book, Holmes emphasizes the book's last section where he could "see the man most," and the presence of an authorial narrator steps forth only to meld with the mountains. The penultimate poem is "Horseback in the Rain" (54), where the narrator writes (and implicitly speaks) a series of unspoken second-person imperatives that unite reader and narrator as being mutually subject to the "you must" therein. This technique fills the poem with the feel of a scrambling continuity and the rush of a traveler searching for shelter in a storm that cannot be denied:

> To the stone, to the mud
> With hoofs busy clattering
> In a fog-wrinkled spreading
> Of waters? Halt not. Stay not.
> Ride the storm with no ending
> On a road unarriving [13–18].

Like the child in the first poem, the narrator has been turned out from human shelter in the mountains, but instead of leaving that which he knows his ghost would always haunt, he keeps going even though no end is promised. The surging pace of "Horseback in the Rain" contrasts with the "solemn pace" of the closing poem "Heritage," in whose quiet tone the reviewer proposes that Still is "most like his mountain people." Here is the second stanza of that naturalized Petrarchan sonnet:

> Being of these hills, being one with the fox
> Stealing into the shadows, one with the new-born foal,
> The lumbering ox drawing green beech logs to mill,
> One with the destined feet of man climbing and descending,
> And one with death rising to bloom again, I cannot go.
> Being of these hills I cannot pass beyond [10–15].

The review quotes the poem in full to demonstrate Still's organic quality: "[Still's rhythm] does not beat with any mechanical regularity, it approximates a form." Still's control of tone with syntax clarifies when we compare the careful pace of this final sextet, which contains only two end-stops, with the clatter of "Horseback in the Rain," whose stops within the narrow lines paradoxically accelerate its pace.

The last two lines of "Heritage," which Still might have seen as allowing one to transcend death by "rising to bloom" within a larger natural cycle, were frowned on by the reviewer who recognized a stock motif in regionalist literature and thought Still in danger of becoming like other "regional writers who insist that they are forever at home and happy in their chosen valley" (Holmes). The reviewer was on target: during the 1940s the regional issues of the 1930s, which seemed to counter the malignity of modernity, faded due to a ramped up economy and the Cold War. Moreover, attention to the plights and struggles of America's exploited and disinherited began to focus on racial segregation and civil rights.

Still had published with Viking Press, whose editors had undertaken a multicultural, progressive agenda, and they highlighted Still's work as their connection to the native soil of America. Nevertheless, Still's artistic persona was intensely introverted and committed to continuous, slow, private work. This position reinforced what he had been taught by the upcoming New Critics at Vanderbilt about the proper stance that one should take toward literature — it must speak for itself. But Still also enacted Donald Davidson's call from "A Mirror for Artists," his essay in *I'll Take My Stand*:

> The artist should not forget that in these times he is called on to play the part of both a person and an artist. Of the two, that of the person is more immediately important. As an artist he will do best to feel the infection of our times, to stand for decentralization in the arts, to resist with every atom of his strength the false gospel of art as a luxury which can be sold in commercial quantities or which can be hallowed in discreet shrines. But he cannot wage this fight by remaining on his perch as artist. He must be a person first of all, even though for the time being he may become less of an artist [60].

When Still undertook a life of service to literacy at Hindman, he was more than careful not to become lost in the seduction of the artistic field — he radically separated himself from it, even while writing poetry designed to function within it. By 1968, few people in the region of Hindman had actually read anything by Still, who had a policy of "flagrant disregard" for self-promotion and, instead, "worked diligently to protect his privacy and to insure separation between his personal life and any critical acclaim that might adhere to the name James Still" (Cadle, "Man on Troublesome" 236). Still felt he was entrusted to witness the people among whom he had come to live. When asked by Dean Cadle if there was a contradiction between his life as a writer ("whose duty is to preserve mountain people as they are, with their folk-customs and often primitive attitudes") and his dedication as an educator and librarian at Hindman (who sought "to teach them to read, to improve their living conditions, and to bring them closer to culture and so-called modern thinking and living"), Still replied: "No. None at all. I would still write about them as they would be under changed conditions. For it's the people rather than the conditions I'm writing about" (Cadle, "Pattern" 114). Yet the very terms of Cadle's question and Still's response divulge underlying assumptions. Words such as "preserve," "primitive," and "about" demonstrate a contradiction at the heart of Still's stance: instead of becoming directly involved *in* the artistic practices of the local population, Still wrote *about* a people whose habitus was valued by Hindman, and he wrote *for* an exterior audience of highly literate readers. Still created literary work that sought to catch the spirit of a passing moment, but with the imposing forces of labor exploitation and the raping of raw resources, his stance was questioned by those who assumed confrontational tactics. Nowhere is this conflict more clearly demonstrated than in Stuart's and West's responses to his work. Before his first acceptance to *Poetry*, Stuart had been writing to Still since they went their ways after graduating LMU in 1929. In January 1935, Stuart wrote how "fine" it was to see Still "climbing in poetry," and in November 1935 wrote how "honestly glad" he was to see Still's poetry appearing in *The Atlantic, Household*, and *Esquire* all within the same week. While both poets were writing about similar culture and geography, not a tinge of jealousy was registered. In June 1936 upon reading "All Their Ways Are Dark," the first story Still published in *The Atlantic*, Stuart wrote him about how he had seemingly "got over what Don [West] has been trying to put over all of his life" (18 June 1936). Stuart refers to how Still had managed, in just three pages, to portray the crisis of a mountain family who participated in the economy of a coal mine during the Depression. This move brought the family into strife over the use of resources, forcing the narrator's mother to solve the problem by burning down their home. Indeed, Don West did not appreciate Still's description of internalized class conflict.

West had returned to Kentucky in 1934 with the Communist Party to help unionize coal miners, whose lives and struggles served as a central subject for his writing. Accordingly, in each letter that Stuart wrote Still, he ranted against West's answer of political action, which Stuart saw as creating an "old sad-faced world" and denying the joy and "grand time" the world offered. Instead of frowning on moral decay, Stuart chortled to Still, "Boy, life's just a can of applesauce. Woodrow Wilson's vice [president] said the best thing that has ever come from the whitehouse. Said what this country needed was a good fivecent cigar. Say, if you come up here don't fail to stick a San Felice in your pocket" (18 June 1936). Stuart's take was that West, who was then the State Organizer for the Kentucky Workers' Alliance (and regional organizer for the Communist Party, though that was not public knowledge), was a charismatic but failed leader and poet. Stuart put it directly: "[Don] Wants his name before the public on the sweat and blood of other men's labor and others' writings" (30 Jan. 1936), and he predicted that "Don will pass in a blowing wind unless he does a book of his own" and settles down (8 Sept. 1937). Yet Stuart continued, "There's something in Don West that makes him go on. There is a thirst unbearable in him." Against West's political energy and Still's literary bearing, Stuart noted his own complicit use of images that he knew would sell: "I'm afraid about all my virginity is gone. I've been more or less a prostitute among the magazines" (18 June 1936). Like smoking, drinking, and other moral delinquencies, West also spurned such prostitution to the literary field.

That November (1936), West had written Still on precisely this point. He had been speaking at Sue Bennett College in London, Kentucky, about Kentucky writers and his hope for a new way. He dismissed the representations of Kentucky by John Fox, Jr., and Elizabeth Madox Roberts—the latter of whom Still would become quite close to before her death—and even spoke against Still and Stuart (6 Nov. 1936). West condemned Stuart for being "hungry for a career [and] exploiting the old romantic, sentimentalism which outsiders hook up to the mountains." Then he launched into "Still," whom he writes about in the third person, a telling defamiliarization: "As for Still, he is still a very confused young guy, honest in his work, sincere in his desire to picture the mountains—but tends to idolize and idealize. Fails as yet to get into the vital stream of present day life. Still holds on to the old romantic approach." He then says that Still's recent story in *Mountain Life and Work* had "nothing new, not even a new approach"; besides, he went on, "you still make the mistake of fumbling mountain language." He continues, "This story ["One Leg Gone to Judgment"] is as trite as all the poems I've seen of yours in the same magazine and in the *Sewanee Review*." West no longer confided his dilemmas to Still. By this time West had been blacklisted from *Mountain Life and Work*, which he called "that reactionary sheet" catering to "the old maids of Hindman," so he published stories about mining conflict there under the pseudonym Mack Adams. In the fury of his righteousness—and perhaps from his anger at his own lack of literary success—West was preaching to Still.

In May 1937, West revealed to Still that "I find myself constantly on a nervous edge with all kinds of commotion, fights [and] unpleasantness." He shares his appreciation of Still's ability to get him to listen quietly to stories and says he appreciates that Still is "pushing ahead" and sticking to his writing: "Of course, a man goes as far in any way as his vision allows. I do not expect you to go the same way I do socially in thought or action. We have two different outlooks, different set of values, as much as I love peace...." But West's calm was only momentary; after reading *Hounds on the Mountain*, West realized their distance and voiced his disapproval: "seemingly our interests are a million miles apart, [but] we once did have quite a close friendship which I have always appreciated in spite of the feeling that I have that you and your writing are barely scratching the surface of things" (9 Aug. 1937). West concludes by admitting that Still might find West's contempt hard to bear but that "we can still get a hell of a kick out of talking together." Such words were poignant since West had acted as a big brother to both Still and Stuart when they were at Vanderbilt and had inspired Still to come to Hindman when he sent him the dulcimer seven years earlier. This letter was essentially their last contact.

Perhaps the writer who most situates Still's place in the literary landscape of the late 1930s is Elizabeth Madox Roberts, whose literary prestige both came of age and faded with regionalism. Editors at Viking had passed *Hounds on the Mountain* along to Roberts, who wrote Still that she found the "verses beautiful, contemplative, a personal record that mirrors the hills themselves—the reflection being in the impression more than in the physical descriptive picture" (Best, 23 June 1937). Roberts felt strongly about Still's work and offered to write a blurb for *River of Earth*, although she had never done so for any other writer. In appreciation of this offer, and of her 1940 novel *Song in the Meadow*, Still sent her a dulcimer, perhaps one made by Jethro Amburgey. Roberts gave her thanks but shared, "I do not know how to tune it" (6 May 1940). Still sent her directions, a copy of one of his stories in *The Post*, and praised reviews of her book. Roberts replied in sadness, "I am glad you have seen some reviews of my book. I have seen only three, and it almost seems as if it fell upon an indifferent world" (May 1940). She would die ten months later.

In the decades since, Still has become one of the foundations for Appalachian literature. In the 1960s and 70s during the cross-country ethnic and racial renewal, cultural activists in Appalachia harvested Still's work as source of ethnic awareness. In those same years, national appreciation for Stuart's work waned and is now almost entirely absent (and few ever grappled with his voluminous poetry, let alone theorized about its role in American culture during the 1930s). As for West, though he lives almost as a myth among Appalachian activists, national attention to his work has only begun with the University Press of Illinois releasing his selected works *No Lonesome Road* (2004) and a biography (by James J. Lorence, 2007). Under the necessary and beautiful burdens of identity and the reign of new criticism, the poetics (and hence the aesthetics) of these authors have become all but lost. Even though Still became an unquestioned insider, his poetics—which mated the nuances of modernist free-verse with his close understanding of pre–Restoration English poetry—were designed to operate within a national literary system, which came to define how poetry was understood in America. This combination explains why contemporary poetry readers might find his work of interest, but—more importantly—Still's graceful and exact empathy has also translated the dignity of his encounter with a people's spirit.

## *Appendix A*

| James Still | Hounds on the Mountain (1937) | The Wolfpen Poems (1986) | From the Mountain, From the Valley: New and Collected Poems (2001) |
|---|---|---|---|
| "Child in the Hills" | 1–2 | 27 | 50 |
| "Dulcimer" | NA | NA | NA |
| "Horseback in the Rain" | 54 | 74 | 74 |
| "Mountain Dulcimer" | 3 | 20 ("Dulcimer") | 37 ("Dulcimer") |
| "Heritage" | 55 | 82 | 43 |
| "On Double Creek" | 22 | 48 | 79 |
| "On Redbird Creek" | 18 | 13 | 68 |

| Jesse Stuart | Man with a Bull-Tongue Plow (1934) | The World of Jesse Stuart: Selected Poems (1975) | A Jesse Stuart Reader (2003) |
|---|---|---|---|
| 380 "Tomorrow may be bitter, who can tell" | 194 | NA | 301 ("Go, Dance Tonight") |
| 394 "Men say these are the children of the night" | 201 | 147 ("Night Children") | NA |
| 409 "The sky's washed-in with ribbon clouds and stars" | 410 | NA | NA |
| 429 "'Son,' said my father, 'take you a strong wife" | 219 | NA | NA |
| 439 "These are the hills that's native to my blood." | 224 | NA | NA |
| 561: Bunion Maddox "'At last, my Laura, we are taking rest" | 288 | NA | NA |
| 616: Tug Oliver "I plowed these fields—I pushed the forest back" | 315 | NA | NA |
| 677 "Don Davidson, if I have stolen words" | 348 | NA | NA |
| 695 "This pasture land is filled with blackberry blossoms" | 357 | NA | NA |

| Don West | Between the Plow Handles (1932) | In a Land of Plenty: A Don West Reader (1982) | No Lonesome Road: Selected Poems and Prose (2004) |
|---|---|---|---|
| "A-Callin Home Th' Hogs" | 4–5 | 43–44 | 112 |
| "Ballad Singer" | 12 | NA | NA |
| "Dark Winds" | 6 | 38 ("Factory Winds") | 113 |
| "Mountain Boy" | 26–27 | NA | 108 |
| "For Jesse Stuart" | 23 | NA | NA |
| "Sour-Wood Sprouts" | In *Crab-Grass* (1931) 22–3 | NA | NA |

# *Notes*

1. By "poetics" I mean the way that a poet's aesthetics cohere with their content, context, and intended audience. Hence, poetics investigates how poems were designed to function in specific contexts, each of which has a differing understanding of and purpose for poetry.

2. All three graduated from Lincoln Memorial University in 1929, where Stuart and Still had developed a close rapport. West became close friends with both of them when all three attended Vanderbilt University — Still and Stuart working on Masters in English (Still 1929–1930, Stuart 1930–1931) and West completing his Bachelor's of Divinity in the School of Religion (1929–1932).

3. Versions of the poems herein come from the following publications, which represent an early gestalt of the authors' poetic vision: Still, *Hounds on the Mountain* (Viking, 1937); Stuart, *Man with a Bull-Tongue Plow* (E. P. Dutton, 1934); West, *Between the Plow Handles* (Highlander Folk School, 1932). Citations to poems are made in reference to these texts, but "Appendix A" lists other, more accessible republications, in which the poems (or versions thereof) may also be found. When poems are first introduced, I cite the page number from the book in which it appears; when poetry is quoted the numbers that follow signify the particular lines being drawn from.

4. Weeks underestimated the role *The Atlantic* had played. This trend continued the work begun by William Dean Howell's publication of Mary Murfree in 1878, but its roots go deeper even than that with Elizabeth Harding Davis's publication of "Life in the Iron Mills" (1861). Louis Menand's *The Metaphysical Club* (2001) conducts a brilliant intellectual history of American pragmatism and its influence on pluralism starting with a discussion of The Saturday Club, which included such figures as Ralph Waldo Emerson, James Russell Lowell, Oliver Wendell Holmes, and Henry Wadsworth Longfellow. He might have expanded consideration to The Atlantic Club, a gathering of the magazine's original editors, publishers, and contributors, which included many of the same members. Contributors to *The Atlantic* went far beyond the purely literary authors Weeks mentioned, and the following essays about "the Southern Mountain Whites" were published from 1929 through 1933, an influential time of growth for Still: Charles Morrow Wilson's "Elizabethan America," August 1929: 238–44; E. T. H. Shaffer's "Heredity," Sept. 1929: 349–54; Eleanor Risley's "Wildcat Settlement" (story), January 1930: 67–77; Alfreda Worthington's "The Mountain Doctor" (the most well written and informative of any article published), Sept 1932: 257–67, Oct 1932: 469–72, Dec 1932: 768–774; Wendell Brooks Phillip's "Students in a Hick College," April 1933: 412–18.

5. Poems in *Hounds on the Mountain* that focus primarily on people rather than landscape include "Infare" (10–11), "On Troublesome Creek" (17), "Court Day" (21), "Nixie Middleton" (36), "The hill-born" (43), and "Uncle Ambrose" (47). Conversely, few of West's poems focus on landscape, and while most of Stuart's poems in *Man with a Bull-Tongue Plow* narrate human existence, he is well known for his poems therein that focus purely on nature as well.

6. Interested readers might consult other poems in which Stuart announces his anger at higher education: 234, 396, 681, 689, and 693. Another Stuart poem, "Mountain Boy," which appeared in *Forum* (July 1934), takes an approach much more similar to West's: in it, Stuart calls on mountain boys to use the strength gained from "summer toil" to "stand and hand [a world of men] blow for blow" (p. 54,11. 5, 14).

7. See David Whisnant's "'Hit Sounds Reasonable': Culture and Change at Hindman Settlement School," in *All That Is Native and Fine: The Politics of Culture in an American Region*. Chapel Hill: University of North Carolina Press, 1983. 17–101.

8. The poem is reprinted in its entirety, because — perhaps due to its titular similarity — it is not included in any of Still's books.

9. See West's "Harry Harrison Kroll: An Essay" (1986) in *No Lonesome Road* (18–21) and Stuart's "The Crazy Professor" in *Esquire* (April 1939): 72–73, 179–80; "Lesson in a Liberal College Education" in *The Saturday Review* 16 Feb. 1946: 26–27, 55–57; "Harry Kroll as I Knew Him," *Peabody Reflector* July-August 1967: 177–180; and "Three Teachers and a Book" in *Pages: The World of Books, Writers, and Writing*, Ed. Matthew Bruccoli, Detroit: Gale Research, 1976. 90–103.

10. Even though in his first two books West had poems praising Stuart as a mountain poet and Stuart wrote the introduction to *Crab-Grass*, West would not republish those poems and later wrote poems decrying Stuart.

11. The reader might also consider the first poem I discussed by West, "Mountain Boy," in terms of how blood and land are joined.

12. West first brought Still to witness a mine strike in Wilder, Tennessee. Of Wilder, Still wrote, "It was my first inkling that folk could starve to death in the United States of America in plain view of a largely indifferent populace" ("A Man Singing" 14). No doubt this experience furthered his own appreciation of "the traditional kind of community" that existed around Hindman (20). Although I've not taken room to do so here, we might also compare the starkly human version of West's gruff poems about Harlan (see "Harlan Portraits" [14–15] and "The Thief" [19] in *Between the Plow Handles*) versus Still's oddly disembodied but dramatically physical and quiet poems about mining (see the "Earth-Bread" section of *Hounds on the Mountain* [23–27]). Included in this comparison might be the plentiful poems that Stuart wrote about modernity's intrusion in terms of Mammon.

# Works Cited

All of the letters in this essay came from James Still's papers at Morehead State University: James Still Manuscripts and Correspondence, 61st02, Department JS Morehead of Special Collections and Archives, Camden-Carroll Library.

Cadle, Dean. "Man on Troublesome." *Yale Review* 57 (1968): 236–55.

_____. "Pattern of a Writer: Attitudes of James Still." *Appalachian Journal* 15.2 (1988): 104–43.

Cowley, Malcolm. "Man with a Hoe." Review of *Man with a Bull-Tongue Plow. The New Republic* 31 Oct. 1934: 342–43.

Davidson, Donald. "A Mirror for Artists." *I'll Take My Stand.* 1930. New York: Harper Torch Books, 1962. 28–60.

Gregory, Horace. "A Farmer Singing Behind His Plow." Review of *Man with a Bull-Tongue Plow. New York Herald Tribune Books* 14 Oct. 1934: 8.

Hindman Settlement School. Promotional Pamphlet. Hindman, KY: Hindman Settlement School, [1937]. James Still Manuscripts and Correspondence, 61st02, Department JS Morehead of Special Collections and Archives, Camden-Carroll Library, Morehead State University. Box 7, Folder 11.

Holmes, John. "A Poet from the Rugged Hills of the South." Review of *Hounds on the Mountain. Boston Evening Transcript* 17 July 1937: 2.

Richardson, H. Edward. *Jesse: The Biography of an American Writer — Jesse Hilton Stuart.* New York: McGraw-Hill, 1984.

Still, James. "Dulcimer." *Mountain Life and Work* Oct. 1935: 10. Reprinted in *Mountain Life and Work* Summer 1965: 15.

_____. *Hounds on the Mountain.* New York: Viking Press, 1937.

_____. "I Sometimes Tell People I Was Born in a Cotton Patch." *Foxfire* Fall 1988: 132–49.

_____. "James Still." *Contemporary Authors Autobiographical Series.* Vol. 17. Ed. Joyce Nakamna. Detroit: Gale Research 1993. 231–48.

_____. Interview with J. W. Williamson. *Interviewing Appalachia: The Appalachian Journal Interviews, 1978.* Eds. J. W. Williamson and Edwin T. Arnold. Knoxville: University of Tennessee Press, 1994. 49–65.

_____. "A Man Singing to Himself: An Autobiographical Essay." *From the Mountain, From the Valley: New and Collected Poems.* Ed. by Ted Olson. Lexington: University Press of Kentucky, 2001. 5–24.

_____. "Poems." Knott County, KY: Hindman Settlement School, [1937]. Dean Cadle Papers, 1919–1986, 1M87M46, Special Collections and Archives, University of Kentucky. Box 5, Folder 10.

Stuart, Jesse. *Man with a Bull-Tongue Plow.* New York: E. P. Dutton, 1934.

West, Don. *Between the Plow Handles.* Monteagle, TN: Highlander Folk School, 1932.

_____. *Crab-Grass.* Nashville, TN: The Art Print Shop, 1931.

# Jesse Stuart and James Still: Mountain Regionalists

## DAYTON KOHLER

A curious parallel links the careers of Jesse Stuart and James Still. Products of the same general environment, graduates of the same small college on the Tennessee side of Cumberland Gap, they live less than one hundred miles from each other as the crow flies in the mountain section of eastern Kentucky. This is the region of ridge farms and lonesome hollows about which each has written, first in poetry and later in prose. In a way this similarity is misleading, for the effect of their writing is completely unlike. James Still is realistic where Stuart is melodramatic, Still is poetic where Stuart is often sentimental. Between them, however, they have given shape and life to their green Appalachian hills.

The background of their work is familiar enough. At the end of the century Mary Noailles Murfree and John Fox, Jr., reclaimed the Tennessee and Kentucky hill country as a segment of older America. But one can describe a region without participating in its life. Today this sense of participation is the very center of all regional matters. A generation of local-color writers from Miss Murfree to Maristan Chapman exploited only the picturesque and sentimental in the lives of mountain characters; their stories failed to reveal the essential humanity of the people themselves.

Jesse Stuart and James Still have an advantage over these earlier writers in having been born into the life they write about. They use the materials of the local colorists, but it is clear that much of their freshness and gusto derives from a sense of identity with a place and its people. We can mark a stage in the development of southern fiction if we put one of their books beside one by Miss Murfree, for example. The older writer demonstrates a landscape literature: bright scenes of local color enlivened by quaint dialect. Her stories are about a place rather than of it. No writer's notebook, filled with tourist observations of dress, weather, sayings, manners, crops, could give the casual yet familiar picture of a way of life which we find in Stuart's and Still's best work. Even their language has emotional roots in the common experience, for it takes its color and rhythm from the speech of people who have lived a long time in one place. This writing has value quite apart from its importance as regional documentation.

Like the best apple butter, good regional writing is always made at home. Jesse Stuart

*Kohler, Dayton. "Jesse Stuart and James Still." College English 3.6 (March 1942): 523–33. Reprinted with permission.*

Page from *The Railsplitter*, Lincoln Memorial University yearbook, featuring photographs of James Still (on left) and Jesse Stuart (on right), 1929 (courtesy of the Hindman Settlement School).

has written five books without going far beyond the borders of W-Hollow in his native Greenup County. Ten or twelve families live in the hollow, and he has written poems and stories about all of them. These real people behind his stories would make an interesting article in themselves. There is the old railroadman in "Huey, the Engineer." He operated the small train on the thirty-six-mile branch of the Eastern Kentucky Railway, and Stuart used to wait to see his engine come puffing out of Barney Tunnel. Uncle Fonse of "Uncle Fonse Laughed" was a country schoolteacher whose children Stuart himself taught later on. Having known these people, he says, he tries to tell their stories as vividly and truthfully as he can.

Stuart came into literature in 1934 with an amazing collection of 703 sonnets, *Man with a Bull-Tongue Plow.* Many of these poems were pure description, a re-creation in lyric language and mood of the Kentucky landscape in all weathers and seasons. Others told with innocent frankness of the adventures, loves, and dreams of Jesse Stuart, poet and plowman of the hills. Then in the third section, the book came roaringly to life when the writer resurrected more than two hundred dead in Plum Grove churchyard to tell the stories of their humble lives. The method suggested *Spoon River Anthology,* but these stories— grim, humorous, profane — had nothing in common with Edgar Lee Masters' studies in pessimism and defeat. The poetry was often trite and prosy and crude. It was also as native as a whippoorwill and as full of provincial flavor as a persimmon. Critics, viewing Stuart's book with mixed feelings, tried to account for his earthy vigor by calling him a Kentucky Robert Burns. The true explanation of his talent, I believe, lies closer home. These poems and the prose which followed show us something of the pioneer experience as it has survived on a ruined frontier. In everything he has written we can find evidence of a tradition which goes back beyond the Sut Lovingood papers and Augustus Longstreet's *Georgia Scenes* to the anonymous storytellers of the frontier.

The early American was by nature a storyteller. The realities of pioneer living and his own hard comic sense created a literature of oral anecdote which flourished in the trading post, the groggery, the trappers' rendezvous—wherever men met on the edge of the wilderness. Folklore and fantasy appeared at every halt on the westward march, and the best hunters and rail-splitters passed into legend: Davy Crockett, Dan Boone, Honest Abe. More fabulous heroes—Paul Bunyan, John Henry, Pecos Bill—came out of the common experience and imagination. These stories had a geography, a mythology, and a lingo of their own. Some were streaked with ballad sentiment. Others crackled with bawdy humor. But mostly these tales were comic elaborations of character or drawling reminiscence in which the frontiersman dramatized himself with shrewd appraisal and salty enjoyment.

This literature was of the country and the times. Through the frontier yarns goes a procession of hunters, traders, prophets, settlers, land speculators—the raggle-taggle of a nation on the move. The musterings, auctions, infares, feuds, and frolics are here, the holdup, the war whoop, eagle oratory, revival shouts, hard work and hard times, and every aspect of pioneer morality from the bashful lover at the bean pot to the camp-meeting baby. Behind all this is an awareness of the beauty of river and forest which gives our literature its most authentic theme. It is the brief, westering American dream in the language of the people who lived it.

In his short stories Jesse Stuart has caught the echoes of this frontier world. *Head o' W-Hollow* and *Men of the Mountains* are filled with pioneer tags of realism and rough humor. Sometimes he reports on local custom, such as the rowdy charivari described in "Bellin of the Bride." His mountain politicians are as shrewd as in the days of Davy Crockett. Uncle Casper is a homespun state senator who wins a vote by telling tall stories. Another backwoods candidate tricks two feuding families with some political skullduggery that might have come out of Crockett's dealings with the electorate. Religious fervors shake his people. In "300 Acres of Elbow Room" a Forty-Gallon Baptist gets the word that he will die that night. He invites all of his Free-Will neighbors to be present so that they can see the error of their belief. The leader of an uncouth shouting sect digs up the body of his dead wife but is bitten by a copperhead in her coffin. A constable arrests him on a charge of public indecency for violating the grave. Red Jacket, the shade of a murdered Indian, upsets a spiritualist meeting by telling sly crossroads gossip. Patterns of violence are always present. Grandsons of the men who shot it out with squirrel rifles break up a dance with guns and brass knuckles. Thickety laurel hides a smoking still. The farm wife of "Woman in the House" spends a night of terror in a cabin with her brutal husband and drunken brother. The hero of "Whip-Poor-Willie" can never get a wife because he had an eye shot out at a church meeting. "Dark Winter" records a season of poverty and hunger in the lives of the humble Powderjays.

He has a frontiersman's delight in tall talk and tall deeds. "The Blue Tick Pig" has weird overtones of the Paul Bunyan legends in its account of a runt that learned to milk cows. There is genuine folk fantasy in the story of a quiet tramp, a champion worker in the cornfields, who is finally arrested for stealing all the brass in the neighborhood. Grandpa Grayhouse asked his family to keep his body salted down in the house for six months while they held a party every week in his memory. These doings become the scandal of the countryside. "Huey, the Engineer" and "Uncle Jeff" belong to the John Henry tradition, stories of strong mountain men beaten in the end by the machine. These tales have the tall-story blend of sharp, dry realism and fantastic invention.

Jesse Stuart tells his stories without apology or comment. Whether grimly realistic or wildly humorous, they bear the manner of tales that have been common for a long time. Part of this effect comes, I think, from his use of the present tense and a first-person narrator through whom the experience is presented. These stylistic devices make it plain that he thinks of the short story as a narrative told, for on the printed page they approximate the tones of voice, the pauses, the decisive accents of speech. His colloquial language adds also to the oral manner that we find in frontier yarns. Sometimes this style makes for vivid reporting: "Mom comes to the door with me. She takes a piece of pine kindlin and sticks it between the fore-stick and firebrands and gets a tiny blaze with a tiny black smoke swirlin up. She lifts the lantern globe and wipes off a speck of mud with her checked apron. I can see the tears roll down her cheek without the curve of her lips for cryin." Less expertly handled, it falls into the flat, declarative rhythm of meager prose. "Tarvin sees the redbird on the bank above him. It sings in the leafless brush. It is a pretty redbird. It is the rooster redbird. Its feathers are red as beef blood. It sings to its mate. The mate answers the rooster redbird. She is up on the hill picking up straws."

In *Beyond Dark Hills* he tells of his own life on the arrested frontier. A provincial innocence and cocksureness touches the chapters on his hardy ancestors and his boyhood, and the account of his struggles to get an education reveals a provincial distrust of cities; but his pictures of mountain life are written with great feeling and sincerity. There had been no book quite like this in our literature since Hamlin Garland described another late frontier in *A Son of the Middle Border*. Stuart's autobiography is pure regional writing, simple in finish and tone, and more effective than his novel in showing us the piety and violence of his people. *Trees of Heaven* presents another phase of the frontier experience, the old grudge fight between the settler and the squatter. Anse Bushman is a patriarch of the hills, proud of his cleared acres, his cattle, his crops. Boliver Tussie is a squatter living in idleness and squalor. When Anse buys the tract of land on which the Tussies live, he tries to hold his shiftless tenant in line with a bill of particulars to which the Tussies must conform. But the quarrel of the man of property and the landless man takes a new turn when young Tarvin Bushman falls in love with Tussie's daughter, Subrinea. The romance of this backwoods Romeo and his Juliet ends, as all such stories must, with the feud settled forever. At times the novel reads like a parody of all the hillbilly fiction ever written. Its faults are obvious. The plot is sentimental and trivial, its dialogue extravagant, its social problem unresolved. Stuart's imagination is free and vivid, but sustained passage work between the scenes of his novel is impossible for him. *Trees of Heaven* lives only in single episodes like the frolic at a sorghum boiling or the night watch in a blizzard when Tarvin and Subrinea nurse the newborn lambs.

After five books his writing remains a frontier talent for anecdote and character drawing, and the chief impression from his work is one of much power poorly controlled. He is by turns a reporter, an atmosphere man, a poet, and a racy fabulist. He has the mixed strains of pioneer fatalism and broad humor which produced the lonesome ditties and tall stories. He also has the pioneer's morbid concern for death, a subject which he treats either with sentimentality or with the cruelty of casual humor. At his best he seems to know instinctively the meaning of life in terms of a people and a place, and he can describe the look and feel and smell of things with joyous certainty. But as an artist he is without discipline — perhaps incapable of it. The truth may be that he is not temperamentally a writer at all but a conversationalist with a quick eye and ear and a lively gift of expression. As such, he stands at the end of a tradition in American story-telling rather than at the beginning of a new one.

If Jesse Stuart has escaped from strict localism by a renewal of frontier types and themes, James Still has gone beyond local emotions through the working of a poetic imagination which finds in regional experience the feelings common to very simple people everywhere. This was also the method of Elizabeth Madox Roberts, the one novelist to whom Still can best, although imperfectly, be compared. He is like her in his ability to join outward realism with intense inwardness of mood.

In Still we confront a serious writer. He has specifically those qualities that Stuart lacks: the precision and restraint which reflect a literary discipline of humility as well as sincerity in the handling of his material. Both men exhibit the same regional theme, the relationship between man and his natural world. In Stuart's fiction this kinship of man and nature leads him at times into vague landscape mysticism. Still has wisely given his sensibility a frame of reference and a point of view. His novel and short stories have been told by a boy whose recognition of objects in nature becomes a measure of his awareness of the world about him. This sensibility is effective because it sets a contrast between a boy's knowledge of the familiar natural world and the bewildering, mysterious world of human relationships.

The territory of Still's fiction is the region of hill farms and coal camps scattered along the branch waters of Little Carr and Troublesome creeks. For him this is adopted country. Born on Double Creek in the Alabama hills, he came into Kentucky by way of Tennessee. His boyhood ambition was to be a horse doctor like his father, and among his earliest recollections are nights he spent with his father while they nursed a sick animal on some neighbor's farm. At Lincoln Memorial University, where he worked in a rock quarry and in the school library to pay his way, he became interested in writing. After some postgraduate study at Vanderbilt he went to Hindman as librarian at the Hindman Settlement School. There, one of his duties was to carry boxes of books over mountain trails to supply one-room schools that had no libraries of their own. He has tramped over every ridge and hollow mentioned in his books. At Hindman he wrote his first poems, published in 1937 as *Hounds on the Mountain*.

These poems are minor but authentic. Their subjects are those of much regional verse — people, a horse-swapping, a court day, the sights and sounds of nature — but the quiet tones of his lines surprise us with a sudden sharp image that reveals the true poet. His descriptions of the hill country are always warm and homely and clear. There are overtones of music and emotion in "Mountain Dulcimer":

> The dulcimer sings from fretted maple throat
> Of the doe's swift poise, the fox's fleeing step
> And music of hounds upon the outward slope
> Stirring the night.

"Earth-Bread" tells of the miner's life: "This is the eight-hour death, the daily burial." "Year of the Pigeons" stirs ancestral memories. "Heritage" is his regional affirmation:

> Being of these hills, being one with the fox
> Stealing into the shadows, one with the new-born foal,
> The lumbering ox drawing green beech logs to mill,
> One with the destined feet of man climbing and descending,
> And one with death rising to bloom again, I cannot go.
> Being of these hills I cannot pass beyond.

One way of becoming an artist is to accept those limitations of material imposed upon the individual by the nature of his social experience. This acceptance implies an act of discipline, the necessity of the writer to distinguish what is his own from what he admires in other men's books. It was this discipline which Thomas Wolfe, for example, could never learn, but which turned Willa Cather from the Jamesian manner of *Alexander's Bridge* to a use of native materials in *O Pioneers!* James Still has known this discipline from the first. All of his writing is of one piece, for it comes straight out of the region which has shaped his own life. Per-

haps that is why he reverts to a boy's world in *River of Earth,* where the experiences of a growing boy make the regional pattern clear.

*River of Earth* covers two years in the life of a mountain family. The novel begins shortly
before the boy who tells the story has his seventh birthday, and it ends two winters later, after
he has learned something of a man's responsibilities. The boy is one of Brack Baldridge's
young ones. Brack is a miner, moving his family about from one coal camp to another as he
follows the precarious wages the big companies pay. Although he will take to farming when
work in the mines grows slack, he has no desire for the homeplace his wife talks about. She
wants a house with windows and a real puncheon floor, a garden patch, and some trees without smoke-grimed leaves. She is one of the mild Middletons, but she speaks her mind when
Brack's worthless cousins and lazy old Uncle Samp come to live with them at the end of a
hard winter. But Brack says, "As long as we've got a crust, it'll never be said I turned my folks
from my door." Mother has another plan. She moves the furniture into the smokehouse and
burns the cabin. It is a life of hardship and violence. School closes when the teacher is shot
for whipping one of the pupils. After Uncle Jolly has been taken off to jail, the boy goes to
Lean Neck Creek to look after Grandma Middleton through a starvation winter. At seventy-
eight Grandma is still spryly carrying on her secret feud with the man who killed her husband years ago. Next spring the baby dies. In September the Baldridges hold a funeralizing,
with Preacher Sim Mobberly from Troublesome Creek to preach the text. "Oh, my brethren,"
he begins, stroking his white beard, "we was borned in sin and saved by grace." Lifting his
hands toward the sky, he thunders, "We have come together to ask the blessed Saviour one
thing pine-blank. Can a leetle child enter the Kingdom of Heaven?" In Blackjack they face
another hungry winter after the mines close. Then Grandma Middleton dies. "Send nary
word to my chaps," she says. "They wouldn't come when I was low in health. No need they
haste to see me dead."

From incidents like these James Still has made a simple but moving regional novel. There
is no dramatic structure to his book, for it is a boy's story that falls into a clear pattern of
memory as he tells what he saw and did during those two full years. He has learned the feel
of tools in his hands and back-breaking labor in the fields. Birth and death, men's anger and
hate, women's tolerance for clumsy masculine ways, summer's plenty and winter's hungry
pinch have become as much a part of his life as the sights and sounds of mining camp and
farm, the smells of plowed ground, an empty house, cooking food.

*River of Earth* is regional, but it is first of all a novel about people, not more literary business about folkways in the manner of so much regional literature. People are never folk to
any but outsiders, and Still happens to be writing about friends and neighbors into whose
lives he has entered with the instinctive knowledge and feeling of true imagination. They
belong to the life he himself shares. The signs are hopeful for his future. The writer who can
reveal the life of his own region with perception and meaning usually ends up by writing about
the world.

Beneath the regional feeling of the novel there is another meaning which is never put
into words because it lies just outside the boy's understanding of his world. Brack's son can
describe his mother's fears and his own hunger, but he can only listen to talk of puzzled
resentment and bitterness when men are out of work. He knows Uncle Jolly's anger over good
farmland ruined when the timber was cut off, leaving the plowed fields to wash away in gul-
lies during the summer storms. But if he is too young to realize what is happening, the reader
can understand the terrible importance of work and food to America's dispossessed. The
Baldridges are not Joads or Lesters; nevertheless, they speak to the social conscience of our
time.

*On Troublesome Creek* is a collection of short stories in the same clear, luminous pattern of measured emotion and unstudied drama. At first glance it may seem that Still is trying to write a lesser *River of Earth* in these stories, for some use the same background and the same theme and all are loosely linked by the bright-eyed boy who tells them. Although the book as a whole is likely to give an impression of sameness because the point of view does not vary, most of the stories, taken singly, will stand on their own merits. In any collection like this each reader must find his own favorites. One of the best is "I Love My Rooster," in which the boy's longing for a gamecock and a striped shirt becomes an expression of the desires of an inarticulate class in which the sense of possession is strong but seldom satisfied. "Snail Pie" is a pathetic picture of old age. "Brother to Methusalem" shows that Still can write fantasy and humor in the tall-story tradition. A boy's revenge on a miserly cattle-driver gives another kind of humor to "On Quicksand Creek." "The Moving" tells what happens to these people when the mines close, and several of the stories deal with the hardships of finding a new home in a new place.

James Still has been praised for his simplicity. Much of the effectiveness of his writing comes from a clear and often lovely style with the occasional incorrectness of folk speech in its idiom. This is the best kind of style that a regional writer can have, for it shows the habits of thought and language found in the sayings, stories, and proverbs that indicate the history and simple wisdom of a region. "Even come spring," says Grandma Middleton, "we've a passel of chills to endure: dogwood winter, redbud, service, foxgrape, blackberry.... There must be seven winters, by count. A chilly snap for every time of bloom." Still's style is flexible enough for more than one effect. It can bear a considerable burden of emotion that is within a boy's range of response, and it can record sensory impression with poetic finality. Here is a picture of the back country in autumn:

> Fall came in the almanac, and the sourwood bushes were like fire on the mountains. Leaves hung bright and jaundiced on the maples. Red foxes came down the hills, prowling outside our chicken house, and hens squalled in the night. Quin Adams's hounds hunted the ridges, their bellies thin as saw blades. Their voices came bellowing in the dark hours. Once, waking suddenly, I heard a fox bark defeat somewhere in the cove beyond Flaxpatch.

In Preacher Sim Mobberly's sermons this style broadens with homely metaphor into rude folk poetry. It can also weight a situation with a deeper meaning that adds to our understanding of life. In *River of Earth* there is a scene in which Brack, newly hired at the mines, brings home several sacks of food from the company commissary. The mother sits quietly touching the meat and flour and then suddenly throws her apron over her head as she bursts into tears. The words of that passage are not the language of realism, but something as flat and final as the realist can offer has been said about a way of life.

Perhaps one should not grow too critically solemn over the books Stuart and Still have written. Stuart has probably shown us the whole range of his talent. Still has the manner of a young writer feeling his way, and as yet he has not attempted a direct portrayal of the larger adult world. But as regionalists they have added another panel to the long record of American life, for in their books the southern mountaineer has found his own voice for the first time. This regionalism is as genuine and untainted as any we have in America today.

# II

# River of Earth

James Still as an older man (courtesy of the Hindman Settlement School).

# The Still Life in
# *River of Earth*: Exploring the
# Novel's Biographical Context

## CAROL BOGGESS

At the conclusion of most novels, readers know both how the story turned out and who the narrator is. But *River of Earth,* James Still's classic tale of a Kentucky mountain family, leaves us with questions—does the family move and does it survive? What becomes of the boy? Though we have shared a critical part of the narrator's young life, we never know his first name. In a congratulatory letter written to Still on February 6, 1940, the day after the book's release, his editor at Viking Press, Marshall Best, closed with the comment that a number of the people who read the work in advance of publication were curious about the boy: "I wonder if you had any name for him in your mind when you were writing the book and if you would care to mention it so that we can pass it on to them" (Morehead Collection. Viking Letters). Because *River of Earth* was Still's first novel, readers also wondered about James Still.

Mary Caperton [Bingham] begins her 1940 review, "Some books have the power to reveal the quality of mind and character of their authors to such an extent that to review the book seems somehow embarrassingly like reviewing the writer," then goes on to observe in both the novel and the man a quality of simple goodness. The spirit of this early response indicates the tone and direction of much subsequent attention given Still, yet, unlike Caperton, most critics have not been embarrassed or hesitant to "review the writer." The mind, character, and habits of James Still have intrigued people for over 60 years, sometimes eliciting more comment than his writings.

While several of the early reviews openly label the book autobiographical, others only imply a connection, perhaps taking a hint from Viking's promotional description: "Mr. Still calls his book fiction, but the youngster ... must be close kin to the author's own boyhood" (Morehead Collection, Box 11). Scholars who have sought to connect the work to Still's life have avoided specific claims because they lack clear biographical evidence and because Still resisted such connection. In the 1991 *Wolfpen Notebooks* interview, Still insists that, although most novels are autobiographical, his is not. He does acknowledge, however, that his childhood informs the book (35). In a 1994 interview, Still admits that almost any book has elements of the author's childhood, but he also says *River of Earth* is not a story of his life but, he hopes, a work of art that came true as he wrote it. In a conversation with Elisabeth Beattie, Still erases himself further from the story when he says *River of Earth* is a novel that "exists in nature. James Still is not there and never has been" (365). In spite of these assertions, critics and readers have continued to wonder about the life of the man who created this book.

Still's public image of honest simplicity was not seriously questioned until 1983 when Joe Glaser in the essay "Slick as a Dogwood Hoe Handle" described Still as a person who presents himself as a "plainspoken country man" but whose life and work seem to abhor simplicity (4). The most accurate description of James Still exists somewhere between simple mountain writer and devious trickster. He grew up in a large family in Alabama and went to college in Tennessee and Illinois. Looking for work during the Depression, he took what he could get, a job as a librarian in Hindman, Kentucky. He liked the place, so he stayed.

Beneath the surface, Still had an interesting complexity that led Jim Wayne Miller to describe him as "endlessly surprising" in Miller's 1986 essay "Jim Dandy." Still lived in Knott County from 1932 to 2001, but he also made numerous journeys out and back, including a stint in the Army during World War II, 14 different visits to Central America to study Mayan civilization, and a decade of teaching at Morehead State University. Although he usually gave the impression of being unconcerned with publication, his correspondence indicates that he was very conscious of both how often and where his works were published. He developed lasting friendships with his mountain neighbors, but also knew personally many of the nation's prominent writers. He took part in bean stringings, corn shuckings, and hog killings; he rambled in the hills and told tales with his cronies, but he also attended prestigious writing workshops, recited poetry on college campuses, spoke regularly on National Public Radio, and read three or more hours a day. A local acquaintance captured the paradox of James Still in his comment: "You talk smart but you've got hillbilly wrote all over you" (*Wolfpen* 21).

James Still's complex image, while intriguing, is a topic too large for this article. The focus here is only the relationship between the first 34 years of Still's life and *River of Earth*. Parallels between the facts of his life and the fictional world of *River of Earth* are numerous: he fashioned characters after real people in his family, and he drew on childhood experiences for incidents of plot and situation. Since his narrator is a child between the ages of seven and ten, Still's early years provide the most direct influence. Yet his experiences of young adulthood also helped mold the story. When he wrote the novel, he was a 30-year-old man who had left home at age 18 and had earned three college degrees by age 26. His search for a job eventually landed him in Knott County, the place that became his permanent home and the geographical context for all his writing. With the publication of *River of Earth*, James Still had changed his focus from movement to permanence, from hunting a job to establishing himself as a writer.

The first 30 years of Still's life separate into three phases: childhood in Alabama (1906–1924), education in Tennessee and Illinois (1924–1932), and early work career in Kentucky (1932–1940). This biographical study explores general concerns that emerge from these periods and ties them to the novel's theme of searching for identity, place, and meaning. His childhood provided both security and mobility for the boy: his pursuit of education allowed the young man to wander and learn; and finally the adult selected a place and found a purpose.

# Growing Up

People in Still's early life parallel certain fictional characters in *River of Earth*. For example, Brack Baldridge is a "horse doctor" as was Still's father, James Alexander Still, Sr. Concerning their education, both men claim to have gotten only as far as "baker" in "the blue-back speller" (*River of Earth* 80; *Contemporary Authors* [hereafter abbreviated *CA*] 232), though we can assume that the older Still had more formal training since he held a veterinary license and at one time ran a drugstore. Still's father appreciated a joke just as Brack enjoys Uncle Jolly, the fun-loving "born fool" of the book. Although never acknowledging a connection between the two fathers, Still does claim that Jolly is modeled on distant relatives. "Uncle Jolly was my great-grandpa, with some of the attributes of a cousin, as near as I've come to using actual persons in my fiction."[1] Despite using real life models for characters, Still does not mask reality with a fictional veneer as did his contemporary, Thomas Wolfe; nor is Still's protagonist narrator the author in disguise.

Yet parallels between the young James and his boy narrator are noteworthy. Although his real family had five more children than his fictional one, the position of the narrator among the siblings is similar to that of Still himself—each is the first male. Euly, the older sister of the narrator, reminds Still of Inez, the sister three years his elder. He remembers them both as tomboyish (personal interview, 10 July 1997). Still's memories of walking to school with his sisters, eating lunch from his pail, and needing a box to reach the blackboard (*CA* 233) mirror experiences of the narrator and Euly, who walk together and eat their lunches out of a shoebox. Like young James, the narrator is so short that the teacher comments, "Little man, I'm going to hammer together a box for you to rest your feet on" (94). Although younger than his sister and smaller than the other children at school, the boy narrator receives privileges as the family's oldest male child: when he celebrates his seventh birthday by making a trip with his father, he notes that his younger brother's "face was shriveled with jealousy" (23). A friendly competition between the close siblings surfaces throughout the story.

The narrator feels himself grown up as he starts to school because his brother Fletch was "only five, and too young to go" (81). The two-year age difference between the brothers affects them — taking from the older some of the dependence of infancy while inspiring in the younger an earlier maturity — and presents an interesting contrast. Several times during the story the narrator, who wants to be a horse doctor,[2] compares himself to Fletch, who proves with unflinching determination that he is better suited to the profession (62, 65). Fletch is fearless but also careless as he demonstrates in his dramatic dynamite experiment. The narrator, who is thoughtful and sensitive, begins that same scene hidden behind the meat box to study the Indian Doctor Almanac because any "feller going to be a doctor ought to know the insides of beings" (217). But later in the chapter he cannot watch as Father amputates Fletch's two mangled fingers.

No hard evidence proves that James' brother William Comer served as a model for Fletch, but we do know that the boys were two years apart in age and, just as in the book, a third baby boy followed. Still acknowledges that a brother had kicked him out of the cradle almost before he could walk and that had been "a deciding factor" in his development ("Man Singing" 6). In a personal interview, Still described Comer and himself as different personalities with different interests, Comer appearing tough and preferring the life of an outdoor sportsman, like Fletch. Still spoke of himself as a quiet child, observant and independent-minded. His position as eldest son in a large family was one factor contributing to his independence (10 July 1997). The narrator of *River of Earth* is also a mature, observant, self-reliant, but quiet young boy.

More significant than these specific parallels is the general pattern of Still's childhood and the way in which he shaped it into fiction. In the many interviews that Still granted over the last 20 years of his life, he made anecdotal reference to his childhood, but the best written source is the autobiographical sketch he prepared for the *Contemporary Authors Autobiography Series* and adapted to be the introductory piece, "A Man Singing to Himself," in the collected poems, *From the Mountain, From the Valley*. In addition, Wade Hall taped Still when they traveled together in 1993 and published a short biography of Still's early years in *Portrait of the Artist as a Boy in Alabama*. The general impression created in these oral and written accounts is that he was a normal, happy child surrounded by immediate and extended family — he worked in the fields, went to school and experienced the typical adventures, joys, and hardships of a boy growing up on an Alabama cotton farm in the early part of the 20th century.

He enters his own story by positioning himself in time, place, and family: "I appeared in this world July 16, 1906, on Double Branch Farm near LaFayette in Chambers County, Alabama. I was the first boy after five girls" ("Man Singing" 6). A few sentences further, he describes himself as running to the house of his black wet nurse as soon as his legs were long enough. In the next paragraph, he relives one of his earliest memories of running about in a cotton patch as a boy of four. He pictures himself as a farm boy who is confident of his place in a limited world. In some ways this portrayal parallels the opening of the novel. When the seven-year-old narrator begins his story on a farm near the coal mines on Little Carr, three children are running barefoot in a small house where eight people live (3). The rural family setting, which suggests security and stability, contrasts to the movement of the children who run about, the adults who walk or wander, and the family that continually relocates out of economic necessity.

No evidence suggests that the Still family was as poor as the Baldridges or that most of their moves were forced, but move they did. They left Double Branch to live with his grandfather Still when James was five. A year later they moved to the Carlisle Place, two miles out of LaFayette. After a couple of years, they shifted to a house in town, where they stayed temporarily until they went back to the Carlisle Place. Later they moved to Shawmut and finally into Jarrett Station. None of the moves involved a distance of more than 20 miles, and the actual locations were not as important as the fact that the family relocated at least six times during the 18 years James lived at home. In conversations about this semi-transient life, Still expressed no regret for the changes, nor did he explain them except for the vague reference to problems with the mortgage on the Carlisle Place (personal interviews, 1994, 1997). As might be presumed, the children did not know the details of the family's finances, but clearly cash was not abundant, and the children were expected to work hard. The act of changing places that spread through his childhood becomes a major theme in *River of Earth*.

Lack of a dependable source of work and thus money is a driving force for the Baldridge family. The motif of family relocation pervades the story, as they move five times in less than three years and face a more distant move to Grundy at the end of the book. The first chapter finds them established in their own place above Blackjack and presents their prevailing problem — too little food for too many mouths. Here, Alpha makes her most dramatic gesture of the novel when she burns down the house to rid them of the kinfolk that the big place had drawn "like a horse draws nitflies" (7). She tells Brack in the first of many disagreements, "We've got to start over again, hand to mouth, the way we began.... We've got to tie ourselves up in such a knot nobody else can get in" (8–9). Ironically, Brack echoes those words in the last chapter, though he seems to have ignored them in the first. He tells Jolly that they are leaving Blackjack to make a three-day move to Grundy: "Can't haul all our belongings. We'll sell and give away. We've got to begin over again. We've got to start from scratch" (241).

Beginning over is the key to their endurance, but sadly each beginning represents less security and stability for the family. They own their first house and their second — the smokehouse — where they live for the first year of the story. Their third residence we only hear about because the narrator is staying with Grandma at Lean Neck when the family moves to Blackjack coal camp for a few months and then moves away to their fourth residence, a rented farm called Little Angus. When the boy returns to his family, he joins them at this rented farm, but already the father is planning a move back to Blackjack, which the mother is resisting. By the second chapter of Part III, they have returned to the coal camp and Brack has found steady work. With prosperity, however limited, come kinfolk — Tibb, Harl, and Uncle Samp — but nothing seems permanent in the life of the camp; the young men nearly die pulling a prank, and Uncle Samp runs away to marry the local fortune-teller. By the end of the tale, the Baldridge family is without property, money, or job. They can only contemplate the next, more distant move.

Motion, whether by choice or force, is a central trope for Still's life and art and is basic to both his metaphor of the river and to the recurring question it embodies: where are we going? The figurative form of the question reverberates throughout the text, beginning with Sim Mobberly's first sermon, "Where air we going on this mighty river of earth … ?" (76). The final and most profound rendering of the question occurs when the narrator speaks to the corpse and memory of his grandmother: "I looked at Grandma in the dark of my head where I could see her living face. 'Grandma,' I spoke, 'where have you gone?'" (245). The mother understands the notion of movement not figuratively but literally as does her brother. Jolly asks Brack, "Where on God's square earth did they go?" when he notices 27 empty houses in the coal camp (240). Jolly's approach to life may be light-hearted, but land and permanence are essential to him and to his chosen work as a farmer. In the manner of her brother, Alpha always responds to Brack's proposals to move with words like these: "I'm a-longing to stay on here … I'm sot again moving … Moving is an abomination" (182). The mother has, throughout their marriage, wanted to settle in "a place certain and enduring," to raise her children properly (51, 52).

We do not know the attitudes of James Still's family toward going and moving.[3] Indeed, the issue may have lost some of its force in the last decades of the 20th century when mobility became the norm, but in the first half of the century, when Still and his narrator were young, both the real and the fictional families embodied an unusual tension because of their frequent moves. This tension continues into the second phase of Still's life, a time when his movement is motivated by a yearning to wander and learn. The juxtaposition between traveling and settling is not fully evident until the third phase of Still's life when he finds his permanence in place and profession, but before he reaches that stability, he must live through his middle period of wandering and searching.

## Walking Jim Still

Complementing the motif of the family's movement in *River of Earth* is the mysterious character, Walking John Gay. The mother first mentions the wanderer in one of her many conversations with her husband on the virtues of staying put: "Walking John Gay traipsing and trafficking, looking the world over…. A lifetime of going and he's got nowhere, found no peace" (52). Though Father initiates all the family moves and is a foil to his settled wife, he is quick to disassociate himself from the walker who has neither family nor job. Brack has both. He chooses the work he knows, mining, so he must follow the mines. John Gay is a loner, a searcher, a symbol of restlessness. In Part II, Jolly likens Grandma's setting out before daylight to the traipsing of Gay, a man who is "forever going" and lives anywhere he "pegs his hat" (140, 139). Grandma joins in the storytelling by recounting a cold February years earlier when John Gay had thawed out by walking "back and forth before the fire" as he answered her husband's questions. A wanderer, like Gay, who has been "the earth over," is assumed to know all, and Boone wants him to share that knowledge (140). Although he plays a minor role in the plot, John Gay is important to the novel because through him walking and moving are connected to knowledge and experience. The only words he speaks show that he has embodied a purposeful restlessness his whole life; he wants to see and experience every place. "They's a world o' dirt flowed under my feet. I never crawled when I was a baby. Just riz up and walked at ten months. I'm a-mind to see every living hill against I die" (140.41).

Gay's short statement pulls together two important metaphors of movement — the river of earth, which for him is the "world o' dirt flowed," and the baby's walking. The youngest Baldridge, Green, illustrates how walking is significant to the development of an infant. In Part II when the narrator is homesick for his family, he asks Grandma if she thinks his baby brother can walk yet. She answers, "He's bound to walk in time, bounden to rise up and find his own way" (128). But Green dies before he learns to walk. Later in the story when Alpha plans the funeralizing for the baby, Brack argues that the celebration is an unnecessary extravagance because "Green hadn't even larnt to walk" (174). Learning to walk marks the first stage in becoming a person in both the story and in Still's family life. In his self-portrait, Still tells of his own experience of a childhood accident which required him to learn to walk again, concluding, "With so many children coming along, in our family, once you learned to stand alone, you were treated as an adult" (Hall 4).

Standing alone and moving about are critical to the journey motif and the maturation story of the novel. Walking and exploring are associated with learning and growing. In the last chapter of Part I, Euly and the narrator walk to school; Part II also ends with the narrator walking, this time alone from the jailhouse back to Grandma's; near the end of Part III, the narrator tells of his solitary barefoot walks through the coal camp to see "what there was to see" (224). He matures as a result of these walks: learning about the camp, the ways of men, and his own ambitions for the future. Through small journeys out from home and back, the young boy gradually learns what it means to be swept along on this mighty river of earth. He also knows something of the strength required to resist the flow, the fortitude he will need to be anything other than a coal miner. The boy wants to control his own destiny, but the words of the unemployed men "throbbed in his heart" when he ran from the camp store: "Whate'er you're aiming to be, you'll end snagging jackrock" (228). As readers, we know that the boy becomes something other than a coal miner, for already he is a storyteller and a poet who reveals truth by relating his experiences through his own remarkable voice.

In the journey-equals-growth theme, movement provides knowledge and experience to children who are developing and to adults, like Walking John Gay, who are endlessly searching. Between the ages of 18 and 26 (from 1924 to 1932), James Still was in motion, and his life combined the characteristics of a learning child and a searching adult. In our society, young adulthood is a transition time to prepare for a career or to marry and establish a family. To Still it was both more and less than that; he did not marry, and his college degrees — all earned during this period — had not "qualified" him for his chosen profession as writer. Instead, these eight years gave him life experiences, broader knowledge, higher education, and personal growth. Also, just as it did for the boy in the story, wandering contributed to the development of his voice as a storyteller and poet. By 1932 his walking phase inspired a need to find permanence in a place where he could write.

The Still family owned few books. Young Jim's favorite was the *Cyclopedia of Universal Knowledge,* an eclectic volume that introduced him to a wider world and invited him to travel in his imagination before ever leaving Alabama. The only fiction he claims to have read as a boy were public library volumes like *Treasure Island* which motivated him to attempt to write his first novel, one of boats, sailors, and whales. Although he wrote a few stories, he had no specific ambition to be a writer and apparently received no encouragement, except for learning the magic of oral storytelling from his sister Inez. Neither did his family encourage him to go to college, but he went, earning his own way and finding a generous benefactor (personal interview, 29 Mar. 1994). His college years, indeed this whole period, seem an interesting mixture of directed purposeful pursuit and submission to luck or chance. He appears to have been wandering toward a goal, without being sure what the goal was and where or how it might be reached.

While a senior in Fairfax High School, Still came across a catalogue from Lincoln Memorial University, at Harrogate, in the Cumberland Gap area of Tennessee. He set out with a little money in his pocket which he had earned as an office boy and paperboy. His plan from the beginning was to work his way through, and reports indicate that he worked hard both inside and outside the classroom. According to a January 27, 1940, *Lincoln Herald* article, "He came with forty dollars in the pocket and made a trembling, hesitant appeal to the business manager, C. P. Williams, for a chance to work out his expenses.... With an inflexible will and unfailing determination he set to work on the business of getting an education" (qtd. in England 14). His memory of those college years generally focuses on fatigue and hunger. Yet it seems an act of fate that his work assignment for his last two years was as janitor of the library. Each evening he would sweep floors and empty wastebaskets, then have a world of books to himself. There he discovered writers that became important to him: Hardy, Conrad, Hawthorne, and Whitman (*Wolfpen* 14). But he also discovered journals and magazines to which he could submit early writings. The two most important were *American Speech,* for which he wrote two articles (published in 1929 and 1930), and *The Atlantic Monthly,* which was to become his favorite short story publisher.

Even better fortune than his library job was the relationship that Still began to develop at Lincoln Memorial with his scholarship donor, Guy Loomis, a wealthy, elderly gentleman who helped students in the Southern mountains. The story goes that Still was the first to find out the benefactor's address and invite him to a college graduation; Mr. Loomis responded by arriving in Tennessee from New York in his chauffeured limosine.[4] He attended the commencement which must have been memorable, at least in retrospect. Still impressed his visitor by winning prizes in several essay contests. Loomis responded with an offer to support Still for a year of graduate study anywhere in the South. Still chose Vanderbilt and an M.A. in English (personal interview, 10 Aug. 1998).

Loomis had wanted to make the experience possible, not easy. The year was difficult for the young graduate student. He took classes with Walter Clyde Curry, John Crowe Ransom, John Donald Wade, and was advised by Edwin Mims (UK Collection, Vanderbilt). In his article exploring Still's agrarianism, H.R. Stoneback describes the Vanderbilt experience in Still's own words as a "tough year" (4). His tight budget was less of a problem than his demanding classes. Still describes the writing of his thesis—"The Function of Dreams and Visions in the Middle English Romances"—as a journey to a foreign land where he had to study a different language before he could begin work, but when he arrived, he met Chaucer, who became one of his favorite writers (personal interview, 29 Mar. 1994). Why did Still choose such a difficult thesis topic? Why did he choose to go to graduate school at all except for the adventure?

His specific choice of Vanderbilt did not depend on the illustrious collection of poets and agrarian spokesmen assembled there in the 1920s and '30s. Yet he must have known the poetry of his professor, John Crowe Ransom, who had been a founding member of The Fugitives, the group of writers who met regularly on campus to read poetry and discuss ideas. Still was aware that the important collection of agrarian essays, *I'll Take My Stand,* was published the year he was at Vanderbilt, and even recalls that Ransom and John Donald Wade read their essays to their classes (Still's letter to Stoneback). But the young man from Alabama was primarily concerned with passing his courses and feeding himself. Any influence the agrarian philosophy had on Still was indirect and would not manifest itself during this period of wandering. In 1930 he hoped his searching would eventually result in his finding a job.

When Still had finished his studies at Vanderbilt but had no better opportunity for employment, Loomis again offered support, but this time he chose a more practical program and sent the young man to the University of Illinois to earn a B.S. in library science. Few details are known about Still's experiences in Illinois, but he did complete the program within the year and began once again searching for work — or perhaps, since the prospect of a job was dim, he was merely drifting. One classmate and friend at Illinois was Anna Roberts. In a letter dated March 7, 1932, she shows Jim her view of his luck and life:

> Your wandering career — maybe that isn't the correct expression — sounds rather attractive to a confirmed stay-at-home.... I read with interest of your jaunts. Somehow I hate to think of your having to settle down to a job and have always thought it quite fortunate that you had your seventy year old guardian angel to stand by while you tried out your wings [UK Collection, Correspondence, 1920–40].

"Wandering career" is the correct expression because beneath the appearance of personal drive and self-direction, Still was a wanderer and searcher, set on getting his own education outside as well as inside the classroom.

On several occasions during his six years in college, he spent time traveling, sometimes by choice, usually through necessity. In *The Wolfpen Notebooks,* he tells of a jaunt during the summer before his junior year at Lincoln Memorial University. Not having the train fare to go back to school for the fall semester, he decided to look for work.[5] He walked, hitchhiked, and rode the rails through the South, picking cotton in Texas, applying for jobs in Georgia. He found himself "one of hundreds on the move believing there was a job somewhere." What looked like hard luck was really a positive experience for him in the end because it changed his perspective in a way he could not have imagined (16). Finally, a professor at Lincoln Memorial heard of his situation and sent him the train fare back to school. Still experienced another memorable travel adventure, this one when he was at Vanderbilt (1929–30). Don West had been a student at LMU with Still, but they did not become well acquainted until they were both at Vanderbilt, where West was studying religion. Their friendship consisted mostly of wandering about Nashville on Sundays and listening to street-corner preachers. But they took a longer jaunt together when West persuaded Still to accompany him to a coal mine at Wilder, Tennessee, on a mission to distribute food and clothing to the striking miners. The predicament of the people impressed Still, the adversity they faced and the resolve with which they faced it: "They were held together by their common misery.... It was my first inkling that folk could starve to death in the United States of America in plain view of a largely indifferent populace" ("Man Singing" 14). Although Still never wrote of striking coal miners, the social difficulties and the human will to endure which he witnessed on that trip became part of his general life experience and transferred to his writing.

After six years, he had, as he often told audiences, graduated three times in the same pair of shoes. Yet he had no prospect for employment. In the summer of 1931, he was ashamed to go home and also felt that home was different since his mother had died in 1930, so he set out to find something to do. What led him to Knott County, Kentucky, can again be attributed to a combination of chance and personal connections. Don West was conducting a Bible school there during July and August, and his brother-in-law, Jack Adams, was running a recreational program involving Boy Scouts and baseball teams. Jim Still joined their efforts as a volunteer.

One of the sites of the summer activities was the Hindman Settlement School. A draft of a letter Still wrote (probably in July 1933) to Miss May Stone at the school gives several clues to the critical career decisions he was in the process of making. He tells Miss Stone that for some years he had been interested in writing and that recent encouraging letters from editors of *The Atlantic Monthly* and the *Virginia Quarterly Review* led him to believe now he should give it more attention. Also, a friend who had taken an interest in his education (presumably Guy Loomis) was willing to pay him a salary of $25 a month if he would return to Hindman, where he could resume working with the children and pursue his writing. In this way, Still volunteered his services to the Hindman Settlement School library and to the recreational program in exchange for room and board (UK Collection, Correspondence 1930s). The exact details of the arrangement are unknown, but Still frequently described his first work experience as six years with the Settlement School library (from 1933 to 1939), the first three for no pay and the last three for a modest salary beginning at $15 a month. He figured that the money the school paid him over the six-year period would average out to six cents a day.

Clearly Still did not anticipate accumulating riches or fame as his period of wandering drew to a close, but he had taken the first step toward setting down roots in Knott County, and he admitted to himself and others that he wanted to write. He had come to the end of the road, an image that his own description of the Settlement School's location evokes: "The hardtop road stopped dead in town, and a rutted wagon road took over. The bridge had washed out. You walked a plank, waded, or used a jumping pole.... I had come to the jumping-off place" *(Wolfpen* 18). Since leaving his parents' home in Alabama, Still had been to Harrogate and Nashville, Tennessee, as well as to Champaign, Illinois, to study; and he had wandered throughout the South looking for work and adventure. Now, by choice and chance, he had come to the end of his journey; at least the nature of the journeying would change.

## *Finding a Place and a Purpose*

If his college years were a time of figurative roaming for Still in the manner of Walking John Gay, the period from 1932 until 1942 — which began with his work in Hindman and continued until he was drafted into the army — suggests a commitment to stability, community, and an agrarian way of life which would allow him time to write. This third phase in Still's life strongly suggests attitudes of the Middleton family in *River of Earth*. Like Jolly who at the end of the novel says of Brack's plans to move to Grundy, "Be-grabs if you folks hain't a pack o'Walking John Gays, allus a-going.... I aim to settle. I've got me a young mule, new ground cleared, and soon to have a doughbeater fair as ever drew breath" (242), Still at this point intended to settle. He did not have his own house until 1939 and never had a wife, but by

1933 he was beginning to feel a commitment to his new-found place in Knott County and to acknowledge a calling to write. In answer to the question why he stayed at the Settlement library for six years for so little pay, he says, "No amount of money could have substituted for the joy I felt from 1932 to 1939. The literary juices were flowing" (Williamson 126).

In a sense, Still found a stable place to live in order to pursue his life's work. However, his initial move to Knott County had not been carefully planned to further his career and must have raised some doubts. For example, how might Still's wealthy benefactor have taken the news that his protégé was working in a library and writing poetry in the hills of Kentucky? When "Mountain Dulcimer" was published in 1935 by *Virginia Quarterly Review*, Still sent a copy to Loomis. Curious about the young man's talent or perhaps about the future of his "investment," Loomis sent the poem on to the columnist and poet Edgar Guest for his reaction. The reply was prompt and terse: "Leave this young man alone. He may draw up at a place you know nothing of" (Miller, "Madly" 231). After years of literal and figurative roaming, much of it financed by Loomis, Still did draw up at this little-known place.

His move to Hindman did not mark the end of his walking, but now it became part of his job as opposed to a restless searching. Working at the library, he quickly saw a need for books in the surrounding area and began traveling on foot to take reading material to different schools. Reports vary on the number of schools he visited and the quantity of books he carried. One interesting account comes from the pen of an observer and supervisor. Elizabeth Watts, an executive director of Hindman School, praises the project in a letter of appreciation which she wrote to Still's father:

> If you ever come to Kentucky, we should very much like to have you visit the Settlement and see for yourself the work your son is doing with the library and in other ways. You would be particularly interested in the work he has done with "travelling libraries" carrying twenty books on his shoulders, and often walking as many as sixteen miles in a day in order to take books into communities where there are very few if any [9 July 1936 letter, Morehead Collection. Correspondence: Hindman].

Walking through the county familiarized this outsider with the local geography, customs, and people. No doubt it also helped the mountain communities accept him, but that acceptance did not come easily and sometimes not at all. For example, one official prevented Still from bringing "them old books" into his school on the grounds that they were taking the children's minds off their studies.[6] The students and the administration of the Hindman Settlement School were receptive to the librarian. His status was special because he was the first unmarried male to reside at the Settlement (Stoddart 131). While there, Still got to know some of the children. He claimed at times that one young boy in particular, William Lee Parks, served as a model or inspiration for the narrator of *River of Earth*. On one of William's visits to Still's room, Still typed a story as the boy spoke and later immortalized his lively voice and will to survive in a 1942 *Courier-Journal* article, "Hit Like to 'a' Killed Me."

During the summer of 1935 Still's walking took him into people's homes when he served as a substitute social worker for the Federal Emergency Relief Administration (FERA). His territory was lower Knott County, and his task was to visit homes by invitation in order to inventory their belongings; observe their gardens, crops, and livestock; and estimate the health of the family members. The data he collected would be used to evaluate need for government assistance. He penciled notes in school copybooks, which he claims furnished some of the background for *River of Earth*.[7] These contacts with the people of the local communities provided him with the raw material that would be the basis of all of his stories, poems, and notebooks. His walking and learning experiences during this third phase were intricately tied to the life and place that fed his writing.

As Still acknowledges, he "scribbled a little" during his college days (note in *Hounds*), and in his childhood he had played with literary forms, but it was only in 1935 that he began publishing poems seriously. That year ten poems appeared in magazines such as *Virginia Quarterly Review, Saturday Review of Literature, Poetry, The Sewanee Review,* and *The New Republic.* A year later, he increased his output to 22 poems and initiated his career as a prose writer with his first five stories. In January, Edwin Grover from Rollins College in Florida encouraged Still by complimenting his storyteller's gift: "While I would continue to write short stories, I would *at once* begin planning for a novel — not a long one, about 50,000 words" (letter of 25 Jan. 1936, UK Collection, Correspondence). Whether Still needed this advice we cannot know, but he has said that he began writing *River of Earth* in 1935 or '36 (Williamson 127). In this same letter, Grover suggested that Still would get a higher price for his stories through a literary agent and recommended Hill and Peters. Apparently Still did follow up on this suggestion because Carol Hill wrote a letter to Still on May 27, 1936, concerning his story "On Defeated Creek" (UK Collection, Correspondence). His publication record and his correspondence indicate that by 1936, while working at Hindman, Still was becoming serious about both the production and publication of his writing.

Although he had committed himself to living in a relatively remote community, he traveled in the summers to prestigious writing workshops where he made important professional connections. In the summer of 1936 Still was in Blowing Rock, North Carolina, where he met Marjorie Kinnan Rawlings. In 1937, with the publication of Still's first book, his editor at Viking, Marshall Best, recommended him for a fellowship to Bread Loaf's Writers' Conference in Middlebury, Vermont. There he met Carson McCullers and Paul Green and began a long friendship with Robert Francis. The following summer, Still attended the MacDowell Colony conference where he met John Gould Fletcher, who won the Pulitzer Prize for his *Selected Poems* (1938). He also made friends with Joy Davidman, the American writer who later married C. S. Lewis. A letter she wrote him in 1939 indicates that she envied his strong, precisely detailed prose and that she yearned for his peaceful "log house deep in the hills" (Morehead Collection, Correspondence). In 1939 Still again attended a writers' conference, this time at Yaddo in Saratoga Springs, New York, where he met Katherine Anne Porter and Delmore Schwartz. This partial list of summer travels between 1935 and 1940 shows that although he had chosen to live and write in a remote situation, Still was by no means isolated from a vital community of writers.

During the five years leading up to the publication of *River of Earth,* publishers, agents, friends, and fellow writers were all taking an interest in James Still. Marjorie Kinnan Rawlings began corresponding with Still in 1936. In a letter dated July 13 of that year, Rawlings wrote to Still concerning a recommendation from Miss Kenyon at Rollins College that Still take a class in versification. Rawlings disagreed and in her letter calls him a "natural artist" who needs no formal lessons. His place, she points out, is his best teacher:

> Your lessons, James, are in your Kentucky hills. They are in the waters of Troublesome Creek. They are in the strange minds and destinies of your mountain people. They are most of all in your own innate good taste in writing — and in your own heart, sensitive and raw ... all you have to do is find time and opportunity to do as much writing as possible [Cadle Collection, Box 14, Folder 4].

Throughout the middle of the decade he must have been searching for more time and opportunity to write. He remembers the Saturday morning when he went to the storeroom of the high school and began writing the novel: "I always retreated for my one-hour break during the school day, and on Saturdays when my duties allowed. The principal was to remark, 'He goes in, bolts the door, and only God knows what he does in there'" ("Man Singing" 18).

Still never said that his library duties were too time-consuming, but after six years at the school and with the help of Viking Press and his friend, Jethro Amburgey, he made a move. According to Still, Viking asked him to take a year off to finish the novel and offered a salary in return. But his pride would not allow him to accept money for something that was unfinished (Miller, "Daring" 5). Yet encouragement from Viking must have been a factor in his decision to quit his job and go to "the backside of Nowhere" to finish *River of Earth* ("Man Singing" 20).

More critical than this offer from his publisher was finding the place and time to concentrate on his writing. Jethro Amburgey, the noted dulcimer maker and woodworking teacher at the Settlement School, had known Still since he first came to Hindman; by 1939 they were good friends.[8] Still accompanied Amburgey on several visits to his mother at the family homeplace. Located 11 miles from Hindman, over a wagon road and creek bed, the two-story log house was built by German immigrants in 1836. Having been in the family for a century and having served as his birthplace, the house held great value for Amburgey; Still quotes him as saying, "I'll never sell it; I might give it away" (*Wolfpen Notebooks* 59). After his mother's death, Amburgey wanted the house occupied, and he offered it to his friend in the summer of 1939. At first Still planned to stay only a few weeks, but the place quickly became his home. Amburgey gave Still a lifetime deed to the house and the parcel of land on Dead Mare Branch.

Still's move away from Hindman represented a retreat from the working world to a personal world of writing, a change from living in a student dormitory to an independent existence in an isolated setting. In a 1960 interview with Joe Creason, Still denies a philosophical basis for his relocation. Rather, he says, it suited his needs: "I wasn't satisfied with the place where I was living. Then one day I saw this place and knew it was what I had been looking for all my life — remote, picturesque and quiet." The move was also practical; he had no money (9). By living in Amburgey's house rent-free and growing much of his own food, Still could be frugal. His financial records from the 1930s indicate that he had and needed very little cash (UK Collection. Financial). Like the Baldridge family, he was making life-changing decisions based on economic necessity.

His relocation signified a commitment to a new lifestyle. As he put down roots, wandering became a diversion rather than a way of life. He had settled in a place "certain and enduring" to use Alpha's words, and he was no longer a Walking John Gay. He was destined to become more Middleton than Baldridge, more settled than mobile. His life in 1939 and '40 was Walden-like.[9] In addition to writing, farming, and gardening, he experimented with wild strawberries and violets, studied insects, and spent his evenings reading by lamplight (*CA* 241). He was happy and productive, but not the hermit that some local people called him. His quiet life was neither isolated nor friendless. He began to attend community events and associate with three men who became his cronies: Sam and John Stamper and "Shorty" Smith. They rambled the hills, visited graveyards, and told tales (*Wolfpen* 19). Still soon became acquainted with all of Jethro Amburgey's five brothers, who were his neighbors, and he frequently ate supper with the Melvin Amburgey family.

Still was becoming accepted as a neighbor and a member of the local community. Yet the people of the area did not know him as a writer. His first book, *Hounds on the Mountain,* had appeared in 1937 with good reviews. Herschel Brickell concluded his column about the volume of poetry with the declaration that Still "is at the outset of a distinguished career ... You'll be hearing of this young man or I shall give up prophecy." But as Rena Niles observed in 1939, Still was not well known in Kentucky — and in Hindman he was completely unknown as a writer. "To the people of his community he is a hard-working school teacher ... and James Still would be the last one to want things changed." Fame and riches were not his goal. He shunned publicity. Between 1939 and 1942 Still wanted, most of all, the time and peace to write. When he moved to his log home, he did so with the intent of completing the novel. His account reads:

> I finished the manuscript in 1939 in the log house on Dead Mare Branch where I still live. Not having a suitable table, I perched the typewriter on two steamer trunks, one atop the other. I had expected to write an additional chapter, had it clearly in mind, so clearly that I could produce it today, but when I wrote the last sentence of the book as it now stands I realized I had ended the journey. In my relief I jumped to my feet and ran around the stacked trunks a couple of times [Williamson 126].

His use of steamer trunks for a typing table may have been a practical matter, but in the telling, the trunks add an image of travel to his journey metaphor. His tendency to roam in his young adulthood took a different turn when he became a settled writer. Firmly planted in his area and house, he engaged in travel of a different kind, a creative and literary journey, accomplished through reading and writing.

Although most local people were not aware of his writing, he was critically aware of them and built his fictional world around them. One story that he actually lived took place on February 5, 1940 — the day *River of Earth* was published. Still was awaiting a late train in a railway station at Jackson, Kentucky, when a deputy sheriff was shot down in front of him. He boarded the train and wrote a letter to *Time* thanking them for kind words on the forthcoming novel but also describing the shooting incident he had just witnessed in Breathitt County. He concluded, "Long have I looked to this day [because of the publication of his novel], but I've got no pleasure out of it. I have seen a man die" ("Bloody" 2). When *Time* published the letter as "Bloody Breathitt," the citizens of Jackson were furious at Still because, in his own words, he had given "a local matter national attention" ("Man Singing" 21).

Giving national attention to the region is exactly what *River of Earth* did, but the people of the area were undisturbed by this publicity, perhaps because few were aware of the book until its reissue in 1978, or perhaps because those who did read it recognized its picture of mountain life as both realistic and sympathetic. That Still could achieve such a balance is the result of the life he had led: he was both outsider and insider, writer and librarian, stranger and neighbor. He had come to know and appreciate his own adopted place by traveling in other places. His ability to blend himself with the folk setting while keeping an objective, artistic distance was important to his success.

In the novel, he achieved a similar mix of memory and make-believe. Mingling the experiences of his youth with the life he was observing as an adult yielded a poignant picture of his world. The process of growing and learning that the Baldridge boy undergoes during the story reflects the maturation and discovery that Still himself had experienced up to 1940. Both man and boy seek control over their destinies, a control that each gains, in part, through telling a timeless story. Readers are never on a first-name basis with the child, but we know him to have the sensitivity of an artist. We know more about James Still. He had control over his destiny in the sense that he chose his place and vocation. The tension between fixity and flux that he had experienced during his first 30 years was a central issue in the novel, but an important difference is that the Baldridges are moving on at the end of their story, while Still had found a home and occupation, a place and purpose.

Still's writing explores change and permanence as they relate to individual characters and to the culture of the region. In *River of Earth,* Still depicts a traditional society on the brink of change and creates a fluid picture where the geography itself can be altered, a phenomenon described by Preacher Mobberly's words, "These hills are jist dirt waves, washing through eternity" (76). Within this setting of potential motion, Still and his characters, according to

Martha Billips Turner, "cling tenaciously to a sense of place, to a sense of permanence in a world of subtle but constant flux" (13). The search for permanence is at the core of the Baldridge family's life and of James Still's life, his writings, and the history of the region.

The permanent mark that Still's canon makes in American literature will result chiefly from the enduring quality of this one novel, *River of Earth,* due in part to the profound complexity beneath its surface simplicity. As Robert J. Higgs notes, the novel succeeds because it can "move in various directions yet remain secure at the center." When we try to isolate elements of the work, we find them attached to everything else in that fictional world. James Still noted this same kind of unity when, as a result of his naturalist experiments on a tiny insect called the leaf miner, he came to concur with John Muir's statement: "When we try to pick out anything by itself, we find it hitched to everything else in the universe" (*Run* 143). Just so, the world of the story is connected to the life of the man. The two cannot be separated. Still's experiences inform the story, and, in turn, the story reveals to us something essential about its creator.

Since the publication of *River of Earth,* readers have wondered about this intriguing person who lived and worked in eastern Kentucky where he says he "exercised as much freedom and peace as the world allows" (*Wolfpen Notebooks*). John Stephenson compared Still's life to a voyage down a river:

> small in its geographic measurements but infinite in the depth and variety of human experience encountered there.... His is the journey of the artist-naturalist who enjoys his feeling of wonder about it all. He stops to watch closely the small things which others pass by. He sees the relation of the part to the whole and does not sacrifice detail for generality.

Still is the artist-naturalist who appreciates with the wonder of an innocent child and understands with the perception of an experienced philosopher. For almost 70 years he made notes on the life around him —collecting folklore, creating stories, and writing poems that convey the particularity of his place in the universal language of art. His voice was not loud or shrill or garrulous. He chose his language carefully and spoke through his writings with characteristic humor, restraint, and wisdom. Like his boy narrator in *River of Earth,* James Still's life and art have given us "a word to endure."

## Notes

1. Still is quoted here from his *Contemporary Authors* autobiographical entry (234). Family records show that he did have a relative, whom he could not have met, by the name of Jolley James Still (1786?–1849) who was his great-great grandfather.

2. In his autobiographical note to the 1937 edition of *Hounds on the Mountain,* Still acknowledges that as a boy he, like the narrator, wanted to follow his father and become a horse doctor: "My father is a 'horse doctor.' As a boy I expected to follow him in this profession and went about with him a good deal, often sitting up all night in a barn lot waiting on a sick horse" (note on flyleaf).

3. One anecdote from Still's life sheds light on his mother's attitude toward moving and is rewritten into the story. Before he was born, his parents were settled in Texas, but on a trip back home to Alabama, his sister Nixie died of scarlet fever. The mother had promised the sick child that she would not leave her and kept the promise even after the burial. As a consequence, the family did not return to Texas as planned but remained

in Alabama. In Part III of the novel, Alpha wants to remain on the rented farm because the baby is buried there, but unlike Still's mother, she does not get her wish.

4. Guy Loomis began his correspondence with James Still with a short letter addressed to "Jimmy" on May 18, 1929, in which he indicated his intention of attending the commencement. The James Still Collection at Morehead State University contains 141 letters or notes sent from Loomis to Still between 1929 and 1951.

5. Although the details are essentially the same, Still varies the context of this job hunting experience. In the Wolfpen interview he describes it as coming before or after his junior year at LMU (1926 or 1927); in the *Contemporary Authors* sketch, he tells of the same attempts to find work but dates the experience after he graduated from University of Illinois in 1931 (237). When asked about the inconsistency in a private interview, Still could not date the periods of job hunting, but he remembered there were at least two different times when he traveled extensively hunting for work. He also admitted that he

always liked to travel even under conditions such as these, always "had a yearning to go places."

6. See Miller's "Jim Dandy: James Still at Eighty" (17) for a discussion of the difficulties Still faced in his early years at Hindman.

7. The composition notebooks associated with the 1935 FERA work are located in the James Still Collection at Morehead State University.

8. The James Still Collection at Morehead State University contains 165 items from Jethro Amburgey to James Still between the years 1929 to 1946. Many are undated casual notes and fulfill the function of today's telephone messages; others are longer business or personal

letters. (See Correspondence, Box 1A, Files 5–8 Amburgey, Jethro.)

9. Still did not make much of possible parallels between his choice of lifestyle in 1939 and Thoreau's experiment of a hundred years earlier. However, it may not be coincidence that the only book Still took with him when he left Knott County for the army in 1942 was a paperback copy of *Walden*. Underlined passages would indicate that he read the book, but the long and obvious comments are not about the text. Still used the early pages as a diary to record his first army experiences on his way overseas. The volume is available in the Morehead Collection.

## Works Cited

Brickell, Herschel. "The Debut of a Highly Gifted New Poet." [c. spring 1937] news clipping. Book Reviews, UK Collection.

Caperton, Mary. "James Still's Beautiful First Novel." Review of *River of Earth*. *Courier-Journal* [Louisville, KY] 11 Feb. 1940: n.p.

Creason, Joe. "Some things a man does just for himself." *Courier-Journal Magazine* [Louisville, KY] 14 Feb. 1960: 7–9.

England, Rhonda George. "A Literary Biography of James Still: A Beginning." MA. Thesis. Morehead State University, 1984.

Glaser, Joe. "Slick as a Dogwood Hoe Handle: Craft in the Stories of James Still." *Appalachian Heritage* 11.3 (Summer 1983): 4–9.

Hall, Wade. *James Still: Portrait of the Artist as a Boy in Alabama*. Lexington: The King Library Press, 1998.

Higgs, Robert J. Review of *River of Earth*. *Tennessee Folklore Society Bulletin* (December 1978): n.p. Book Reviews, UK Collection.

Miller, Jim Wayne. "'Daring to Look in the Well': A Conversation." *The Iron Mountain Review. James Still Issue*. 2.1 (1984): 3–10.

___. "Jim Dandy: James Still at Eighty." *Appalachian Heritage* 14.4 (Fall 1986): 8–20.

___. "Madly to Learn." *From the Fort to the Future: Educating the Children of Kentucky*. Eds. Edwina Doyle, Ruby Layson, and Anne Thompson. Lexington: Kentucky Images, 1987. 230–43.

Niles, Rena. "Obscurity Begins Back Home For Kentucky's James Still." *Courier-Journal Magazine* [Louisville, KY] 30 Apr. 1939. n.p. Book Reviews, UK Collection.

Stephenson, John B. Tribute in *River of Earth: The Poem and Other Poems*. By Still. Lexington: The King Library Press, 1982–83. n.p.

Still, James. Autobiographical Notes. *Hounds on the Mountain*. By Still. New York: Viking Press, 1937. Flyleaf.

___. "Bloody Breathitt." *Time*. 26 Feb. 1940: 2.

___. "Hit Like to 'a' Killed Me." *Courier-Journal Roto-Magazine* [Louisville, KY] 19 Apr. 1942: 22.

___. Interview. *Conversations with Kentucky Writers*.

By L. Elisabeth Beattie. Lexington: University Press of Kentucky, 1996. 357–72.

___. "James Still 1906–" [autobiographical sketch] *Contemporary Authors Autobiography Series*, Vol. 17. Detroit, MI: Gale Research, 1993. 231–47.

___. Letter to H. R. Stoneback. 20 Jan. 1985. James Still papers in storage. Hindman, Kentucky.

___. "A Man Singing to Himself: An Autobiographical Essay." *From the Mountain, From the Valley: New and Collected Poems*. Ed. by Ted Olson. Lexington: University Press of Kentucky, 2001. 5–24.

___. Manuscripts, correspondence, photographs, and memorabilia of James Still are held in two libraries in Kentucky: The Special Collections of Margaret King Library at the University of Kentucky in Lexington has the James Still and the Dean Cadle Collections. The Camden-Carroll Library of Morehead State University in Morehead has the James Still Room and Collection. In addition some materials are stored in Hindman, Kentucky.

___. Personal interviews with Carol Boggess. 29 March 1994, 6 July 1994, 10 July 1997, 10 August 1998.

___. *River of Earth*. 1940. Rpt. Lexington: University Press of Kentucky, 1978.

___. *The Run for the Elbertas*. Lexington: University Press of Kentucky, 1980.

___. *Wolfpen Notebooks: A Record of Appalachian Life*. Lexington: University Press of Kentucky, 1991.

Stoddard, Jess. *Challenge and Change in Appalachia: The Story of the Hindman Settlement School*. Lexington: University Press of Kentucky, 2002.

Stoneback, H. R. "Rivers of Earth and Troublesome Creeks: The Agrarianism of James Still." *Kentucky Review* 10.3 (1990): 3–26.

Turner, Martha Billips. "A Vision of Change: Appalachia in James Still's *River of Earth*." *Southern Literary Journal*. 24 (Spring 1992): 11–25.

Williamson, J. W. "An Interview with James Still." *Appalachian Journal* 6.2 (Winter 1979): 121–41. Edited form is available in *Interviewing Appalachia: The Appalachian Journal Interviews, 1978–1992*. Eds. J. W. Williamson and Edwin T. Arnold. Knoxville: University of Tennessee Press, 1994. 49–94.

# Sense of Place in
## *River of Earth*

### RUEL E. FOSTER

"Place is one of the lesser angels that watch over the racing hand of fiction" wrote Eudora Welty at the beginning of her essay "Place of Fiction" (*Three Papers on Fiction*, Eudora Welty, Smith College, Northampton, Massachusetts [1962], pg. 1). She goes on to remark that Place must be second to "feeling," which in her mind wears the crown in fiction. But if Place is one of the *lesser* angels, it is nonetheless an angel and we should pay proper attention to its angelic habitude. I will argue in this paper that Place is indeed an important fundament in Mr. Still's *River of Earth* and that his skill in evoking his unique mountain place gives an enviable cachet to his novel. I hope to show that it does more than this, that it is, in fact, the catalytic agent for the best effects in his novel.

Mr. Still joins a number of great American writers in emphasizing place in his fiction. American writers throughout the 19th century and into the 20th have lavished much of their talent on a loving evocation of Place in their work. Walden Pond's bean fields and pickerel linger in our minds as long as Thoreau's pithy aphorisms. William Faulkner lost his touch whenever he moved his fiction out of that tiny postage stamp of soil that cradled his Yoknapatawpha County. Mark Twain's picture of the Mississippi River, as seen through the eyes of young Huck Finn, has an immortality equal to any achieved by other American novelists. Thomas Wolfe's Altamont has a vigor and veracity that makes it come alive for each new generation of young readers. Sherwood Anderson continues to fade a bit for the present generation, but his *Winesburg, Ohio* as place influenced Hemingway, Wolfe, and Sinclair Lewis in their fiction.

Since the concept of "Place" is so important to this paper, I would like to linger for a moment on what I imply by it in the following discussion. May I continue here with Eudora Welty's remarks on Place? I condense and paraphrase them as follows.

"Place," she says, provides the base of reference for the experience out of which the author writes. All the arts celebrate the mystery of "Place." Its mystery lies in its having a more lasting identity than we have. The magic lies partly in the name of the place since that's what we gave it. The moment the place in which the novel happens is accepted as true, it will begin to glow in a kind of recognizable glory with the feeling and thought that inhabited the novel in the author's head and animated the whole of his work.

*Foster, Ruel E. "Sense of Place in James Still's* River of Earth." *In* Sense of Place in Appalachia. *Ed. by S. Mont Whitson. Morehead, Ky.: Morehead State University, 1988. Pp. 68–80. Reprinted with permission.*

Feelings are bound up in Place, and in art, from time to time, Place undoubtedly works upon genius. How else can we explain a *Wuthering Heights* out of Yorkshire, or a *Sound and the Fury* out of Mississippi, or a *River of Earth* out of Kentucky.

Place in fiction is the name, identified, concrete, exact and exacting, and therefore credible, gathering spot of all that has been felt, is about to be experienced in the novel's progress. Location pertains to feeling; feeling profoundly pertains to Place. Every story would be another story, and unrecognizable as art, if it took up its characters and plot and happened somewhere else. Imagine *Swann's Way* laid in London or *The Magic Mountain* in Spain or *Green Mansions* in Appalachia. All feelings — recognition, memory, history, valor, love — all the instincts of worship and endeavor are bound up in poetry and praise.

In regard to the writer, the question of Place resolves itself into point of view. Place, to a writer at work, is seen in a frame. The writer sees two pictures at once in his frame, his and the world's. His task is to make the reader see the author's picture under the pleasing illusion that it is the world's picture. For the *spirit* of things is what is sought.

What can Place not give? It cannot give Theme. Place can only suggest, but *must* suggest, what that theme is. Human life is fiction's only theme, and it is made fiction in order that it be communicated between writer and reader.

Miss Welty concludes by saying that art that speaks most clearly and passionately from its *place* of origin will remain the longest understood. And James Still does this. Through Place we put down our roots, wherever and whenever birth, chance, or our traveling selves may set us down; but where these roots reach toward is the deep and running vein of human understanding.

Whatever our theme in writing, it is old and tried. Whatever our place, it has been visited by the stranger; it will never be new again. It is only the *vision* that can be new, but this vision is enough.

Miss Welty's comments on Place carry considerable authority because she herself has been most adept at its use in such stories as "A Worn Path," "The Petrified Man," and her novel *The Ponder Heart*. With your permission, I would like to add a brief comment by Jacques Maritain, who was not a formal creative artist but was skilled in metaphysics and aesthetics. I wish to present his statement because later in this paper I will argue that Still's *River of Earth* is in many ways a *poetic* production and that Place itself is presented therein under the rubric of poetry. In his well-known work *Creative Intuition in Art and Poetry*, Maritain makes certain statements I would like to draw on briefly. They follow:

• Art and Poetry cannot do without one another. Yet they are not synonymous.

• By Art I mean the creative, or producing, work-making activity of the human mind.

• By Poetry I mean, not writing verses, but a process more general and more primary: [namely] that *intercommunication* between the *inner being* of *things* and the *inner being* of the *human self* which is a kind of divination (as was realized in ancient times; the Latin *Vates* was both a poet and a diviner). Poetry in this sense is the secret life of each and all of the arts [pg. 3, *Creative Intuition in Art and Poetry*, Bollingen Series XXXV. I, Pantheon Books (1953)]. [I believe the intercommunication referred to here is found very strikingly in Mr. Still's *River of Earth*.]

Later in his work Maritain deals with "Things and the Creative Self" in such a way as to throw light on Mr. Still's achievement. Again I quote:

> The mutual entanglement of Nature and Man — the coming together of the world and the self in relation to artistic creation —[in this] we have to do with Poetry.
> I need to designate the secretive depths and the implacable advance of that infinite host of

beings with which man the artist is faced. And I have no word but the poorest and tritest of the human language — the things of the world — the *things*. But I invest this word with the feelings of primitive man looking at all the pervading force of nature or of the old Ionian philosophers saying that — "All things are full of gods" [Idem, pp. 9 & 10].

And now to speak more explicitly of *Place* in *River of Earth*. The story opens in March on Little Carr, a creek in the eastern Kentucky mountains early in the 20th century. We see a small house, holding to a scrap of land, and a black birch, the only tree on all the barren slope above Blackjack. We meet Brack Baldridge, coal miner, and his wife Alpha. Inside their house move three children: Euly the oldest at twelve; our first person narrator, a young boy who is seven and our center of consciousness but is never named; and Fletch, five years old. Alpha, the mother, carries a fourth on her hip as she works over the rusty stove in the shed room. Outside it is March and there are robins by the house because they never left for the winter, and sapsuckers have come early to drill the black birch beside the house. The yeast of nature dropped so early into our text will work its way all the way through the book. In a sense, nature both frames and interpenetrates most scenes in the book.

The last chapter opens on a windy March evening several years later. The Baldridges are in another mining camp and another company house, this one with two real glass windows in every room. Since the opening scene of the novel, the baby has died in the winter and been buried with a funeralizing in the summer. Grandmother has died and now rests in a coffin supported by two chairs in the front room of her daughter's house. Alpha, Brack's wife, is again with child and about to give birth. Our young narrator, now eleven, sits up with his dead grandmother. Late in the night as sleep drops upon him, he speaks — "Grandma, where have you gone?" Morning comes and he wakes, trembling with cold. The coffin box has been taken away. He runs outside and there are only wagon tracks to mark where death had come into his house and gone again. He turns suddenly toward the house and listens. "A baby was crying in the far room." And with that sentence the story ends.

Such is one way of describing Place in *River of Earth*. In the intervals between these two scenes we follow the Baldridge family in a seemingly endless Odyssey of moves from one mining camp to another, with an occasional pause on a small patch of rural life. And this Odyssey throws into relief for the reader a fundamental conflict in temperaments between husband and wife, between Brack and Alpha. Alpha is passionately an agrarian; she loves the earth and its vegetables and flowers. She is a very private person and cherishes the solitude of the farm where she is enclosed with the people she loves, her husband and her children. Brack is a pragmatist. He likes coal mining, which brings him "the big money," doubly welcome in a cash poor economy. He has no sentimental attachment to home or farm and seems to take easily to the nomadic life of the coal miner. He thinks Alpha is a sentimentalist, although he loves her and would like to humor her as much as he can. In effect this conflict, a major one in the novel, grows naturally out of the Place inhabited by the Baldridge family. We can now focus on Still's depiction of that place in greater detail.

Still, adhering to one of the most ancient axioms in the writing trade, has written about what he knows. Although he grew up in the Appalachian foothills of Alabama, he moved to an eastern Kentucky farm between Wolfpen Creek and Dead Mare Branch in Knott County, where, to the best of my knowledge, he continues to live and write in an ancient log cabin today.

It is a matter of interest to me that Still was at Vanderbilt around 1930 taking a Master's degree and that he was thus cognizant of the work and ideas of the Fugitives and the Agrarians. One of the more famous of these was Allen Tate, poet, critic, and novelist. Tate, in one of the better-known utterances of the movement, wrote that "only a return to the provinces, to the small self-contained centers of life will put the all destroying abstraction of America to rest." Still, like William Faulkner, has studiously avoided involvement with any organized group. In spite of this, I feel that the sense of Still's work is to return to the small, self-contained centers of life and to put the abstraction of America to rest — as indeed he does in *River of Earth*.

It is a marvelous thing Still does when he transposes the mountainous world of eastern Kentucky into the crisp, pellucid fictional world of *River of Earth*. He describes the physical contours of this world with a sharp reality — it is a kind of realism, but as we read the following passage we feel something else moving in the consciousness of our young boy narrator: "January was a bell in Lean Neck Valley. The ring of an ax was a mile wide, and all passage over the spewed up earth was lifted on frosty air and sounded against fields of ice" (pg. 110). And in the following passage as the boy plows for the first time: "Then Uncle Jolly stood aside and let me hold the handles. The mules looked back, but he kept going. The share rustled like drifted leaves. It spoke up through the handles. I felt the earth flowing, steady as time" (pg. 135).

That last line, "I felt the earth flowing, steady as time," is a marvelous line and has a deep poetic lilt which is carried throughout the novel as a great river of poetry. In fact, one is deeply reminded of the poetic realism of Elizabeth Madox Roberts in her great novel *The Time of Man*. The matrix of the poetic realism in both Still and Roberts seems to be their mysterious attraction to nature, their deep compulsion to celebrate over and over the powers and rituals of nature. Each writer gives us time signals, seasonal signals on almost every page as the great wheel of the year rolls forward. The cumulative effect of reading *River of Earth* is to be convinced that James Still is indeed a poet in the Maritain sense; namely, in "that intercommunication between the inner being of things and the inner being of the human self which is a kind of divination." Consider the grace of the following description as winter is dying into spring in the mountains and the boy longs to leave Granny's cabin and go home.

> Before a tip of green showed in any brushy place you could feel spring growing through the sky. The robins came early, cocking heads in the cold. The gray bodies of goldfinches yellowed, for all the world like pussy buds blooming. And where no other sign held on wood or field, finger twigs of elder and willow and service smelled beneath their hull of bark [pg. 126].

So much of the richness and evocativeness of Place in *River of Earth* depends on Still's poetic sense. One thinks of Dylan Thomas's "Fern Hill" or of Gerard Manley Hopkins' "The Windhover." One thinks, too, of how much the poetic auras of *The Great Gatsby* and *The Time of Man* contribute to their projection of place; *River of Earth* benefits by an equal use of poetic place. Still's novel at times has a kind of *pageant* quality; reality and action seem to slow down in a stylized contemplative manner as the boy, our center of consciousness, broods, in the manner of Walt Whitman, by the great ongoing stream of mountain life. Thus, Still creates a world, a place whose resources resound and echo beyond the last word to the fullness of the reader's capacity to understand. This is all made possible by the tonally perfect style of our child narrator — clear, dry, unsentimental, and seemingly non-judgmental.

I'll foreshorten the rest of my argument. Let me put it this way: Henri Bergson, the French philosopher, defined reality as "a flux of mutually interpenetrated parts unseizable by the intellect." My idea of Place is that it is a unity of mutually interpenetrated fictional modes whose unity can only be intuitively grasped. This is especially true of the unity of *River of Earth*. What we call conflict, symbol, tone, style, etc., are all intimately related to Place and mutually interpenetrated.

Since it would take too much time to comment on these factors in any detail, let me at least name them before I draw a conclusion. Consider each of these modes as being in an intuitive way related to Place.

A) Life is hard for the Baldridges. At times hunger becomes their familiar; poverty is accepted and endured. They know to live out their life in hunger and cold.

B) What we might call the Family-rumble — husband and wife differ on the farm and the mines. Pa believes kinfolks conquer all. Ma believes that your children come before your relatives.

C) The Ulyssean Motif — the family ever on the move.

D) "River of Earth." This theme is stated in Brother Sim Mobberly's sermon:

> My eyes were sot upon the hills from the beginning. I used to think a mountain was the standingest object in the sight of God. Hit says here they go skipping and hopping like sheep, a-rising and a-falling. These hills are jist dirt waves, washing through eternity.... Oh, my children where air we going on this mighty river of earth, a-borning, begetting and a-dying — the living and the dead riding the waters? Where air it sweeping us?... [pg. 76].

In Brother Mobberly's vision, the earth takes on the character of the Heraclitean flux — all things flow, you never step in the same river twice because it is a different river. There is a hidden irony in Brother Sim's vision because in the lifetime of our narrator, he was to see mountain earth, pulverized by surface mining and deluged by cloudbursts, literally become a river of earth and flow away (the Cheat River flood in West Virginia in November 1985 literally washed topsoil down to rock in farm after farm).

E) The mystique of nature. In his own way Still is as sensitive to the nuances of nature as Thoreau, John Muir, or Walt Whitman. Nature is the most central piece in Still's mosaic of place — and the most beautiful.

F) There is humor, a light, dry humor, nothing heavy-handed. An example: When the novel opens, times are hard for the Baldridges. Pa has been laid off at the mines and the only food in the house is corn meal and shucky beans. It is December; and this mite of food won't last till spring and garden time. They have no money. To make matters worse, three freeloaders have lodged themselves on the family: big-eaters Han and Tibb, cousins of Pa, and Uncle Sapp, who eats regularly but never dirties his hands with work. Mother is carrying a baby and can't get enough food to sustain it. Her anger boils over. She speaks to father.

> "We have enough bran for three more pans of bread.... It won't last us all more than three meals. Your kin will have to go today."
> Father put his spoon down with a clatter. "My folks eat when we eat," he said, "and as long as we eat" [pg. 8].

The next day was clear and the menfolks traipsed off to Blackjack. Ma marshals the children, moves the furniture and stove into the large dry smokehouse, then puts a torch to her house. When the neighbors in the valley below arrive the walls have fallen in, and Mother stands among the scattered furnishings, her face calm and triumphant. When the freeloaders return, there is no place to roost. "The Revolt of Mother" is complete.

Another example: Jimmy's Uncle Jolly is a free spirit who has landed in the state penitentiary. Granny learns that Jolly is coming home early with a pardon and is delighted. She cooks up a fine meal and receives him with great hooraws and gratulations. Jolly eats gigantically and tells about the fire in the penitentiary, which he fought and put out when everyone else ran off like a chicken with its head wrung off. "Then the Governor heard how I fit the fire and never run, and he gave me a pardon." Granny spoke up.

> "Whoever sat that fire ought to be whipped with oxhide.... Who lit that fire, son?"
> [Uncle Jolly] dropped his eyes and swallowed. "I sot it, Mommy."

The humor is much in the tradition of the old Southwest humor of Sut Lovingood and Huck Finn.

What can we say then in conclusion about Still's extraordinary novel? In the child narrator and in his parents and siblings and in the mountain folk who cluster about them, inured to hunger, hardship, and poverty, Still celebrates convincingly the courage which enables the human race to push outward against the great overlying barrier, the enveloping dark. It is a novel both indigenous and universal; the insights into life and character are original and profound. His control of his laconic, undercut style is masterful, a rare example of the successful welding of realism and poetry. The individual scenes have the ageless quality of folk song and the sharp impact of life truly and unflinchingly observed. The lyric runs of language are virtually faultless and remind you of the best of such lyrics as "Another Grace for a Child," and "Corinna's Going A-Maying' by Robert Herrick, whom poet Algernon Charles Swinburne called "the greatest song-writer ever born of English race" (c.f. Herrick entry, pg. 458, *The Oxford Companion to English Literature,* Margaret Drabble, 5th ed.).

What Elizabeth Madox Roberts in her great novel *The Time of Man* did for the wandering tenant farmer and tobacco sharecropper of the Kentucky Bluegrass region, Still has done for the coal miner family, equally nomadic, of the eastern Kentucky mountains. Although each novel is unique, there are distinct parallels between the two. It is fitting that they should keep each other company — they are among the graceful best of Kentucky's fiction and of American fiction.

# A Vision of Change:
# Appalachia in *River of Earth*

## MARTHA BILLIPS TURNER

James Still's earliest short stories and his first volume of poetry, *Hounds on the Mountain* (1937), established his reputation as a serious, talented writer of the Appalachian region of Kentucky, a reputation confirmed by the publication in 1940 of his best-known work, the novel *River of Earth*. Like his early fiction and poetry, Still's subsequent literary endeavors have continued to deal almost exclusively with life in the mountain area of eastern Kentucky — a fact suggested by many of their titles. Since 1940 Still has published three collections of short stories, *On Troublesome Creek* (1941), *Pattern of a Man* (1976), and *The Run for the Elbertas* (1980); a novel for adolescent readers, *Sporty Creek: A Novel about an Appalachian Boyhood* (1977); two collections of Appalachian riddles and rusties (playful tricks involving the formulaic use of language), *Way Down Yonder on Troublesome Creek* (1974) and *The Wolfpen Rusties* (1975); a book for children, *Jack and the Wonder Beans* (1977); and a volume of collected poetry, *The Wolfpen Poems* (1986).[1] In addition, the University Press of Kentucky published *The Wolfpen Notebooks* in the spring of 1991. This collection, records of remarks Still overheard or incidents he observed in the mountains roughly between 1932 and 1965, offers, in his words, "a picture of the region not otherwise provided" ("Interview," Foxfire 140).[2]

Still's interest in eastern Kentucky comes as no surprise to those familiar with his biography. A native of Alabama, Still earned an A.B. degree from Lincoln Memorial University, a B.S. from the University of Illinois, and an M.A. from Vanderbilt before moving to Hindman, Kentucky, in the early 1930s. In Kentucky, Still began his life-long relationship with the Hindman Settlement School, serving as the institute's librarian from 1932 until 1939. During those Depression years, Still estimates that the school paid him about six cents a day but adds that the "publication of a few poems and short stories ... kept me in razorblades and socks" ("Interview," Foxfire 137). In June 1939, Still moved to an isolated, century-old log house between Dead Mare Branch and Wolfpen Creek in rural Knott County, where he completed *River of Earth*. He still owns the house and frequently goes there to write, but for the last several years he has lived in the town of Hindman. Despite his career

Turner, Martha Billips. "A Vision of Change: Appalachia in James Still's River of Earth." The Southern Literary Journal 24.2 (Spring 1992): 11–25. Copyright 1991 by The Southern Literary Journal and the University of North Carolina at Chapel Hill Department of English. Reprinted with permission.

as a writer, his journeys outside the area, and his teaching at Morehead State University, James Still remains very much a part of the mountain community; or, as he puts it in his poem "Heritage," "[b]eing of these hills I cannot pass beyond" (*Wolfpen Poems* 82).

At this time of increased interest in Appalachia and Appalachian literature, it seems particularly important to have a full understanding of Still's vision of the area to which he has dedicated his life and his life's work, yet his literary treatment of the mountain region he so clearly loves has received relatively little sustained critical attention — probably for two major reasons.[3] First, Still is a master stylist, and the craft of his art has tended to occupy the few critics writing about him; secondly, Still's portrait of pre–World War II Kentucky seems, on the surface, fairly straightforward: poverty and the escalation of coal mining have scarred the region, but it remains rich in folklore, humor, and basic human dignity. As critics such as Randolph Paul Runyon, Joe Glaser, Dean Cadle, and Jim Wayne Miller have pointed out, however, Still's apparent straightforwardness often proves deceptive; in fact, the most notable characteristics of his writing — the lack of allusiveness, the employment of child narrators with their restricted point of view, and the severely economical use of language — an editor once accused Still of trying to eliminate "all the words" (Miller, "Jim Dandy" 18) — may initially mask rather than reveal his deeper meaning.[4] Such proves the case, undoubtedly, with Still's treatment of Appalachia, especially as it occurs in *River of Earth*. In this deceptively simple text, Still not only presents a traditional folk society poised on the brink of change — the accomplishment with which critics most frequently credit him — but also creates a complex, strangely fluid portrait of the region, one in which the geographic area itself becomes subject to alteration and to literal physical destruction. Within this world of actual and potential motion, Still's characters — and perhaps the author himself — cling tenaciously to a sense of place, to a sense of permanence in a world of subtle but constant flux.

Still's central image, the river of earth, powerfully conveys this sense of change, of motion underlying the seemingly fixed. Drawn from Psalms 114, the concept of a river of earth receives its fullest expression in the novel during Brother Sim Mobberly's sermon.[5] In this key passage, Mobberly tells his congregation:

> I was borned in a ridge-pocket.... I never seed the sun-ball withouten heisting my chin. My eyes were sot upon the hills from the beginning. Till I come on the Word in this good Book, I used to think a mountain was the standingest object in the sight o' God. Hit says here they go skipping and hopping like sheep, a-rising and a-falling. These hills are jist dirt waves, washing through eternity. My brethren, they hain't a valley so low but what hit'll rise again. They hain't a hill standing so proud but hit'll sink to the low ground o' sorrow. Oh, my children, where air we going on this mighty river of earth, a-borning, begetting, and a-dying — the living and the dead riding the waters? Where air it sweeping us? ... [76; final ellipsis is Still's].

At first glance, Mobberly's vision may seem peculiarly his own; the other characters do not see the hills as fluid or mutable, and the mountains dominate the physical landscape. A careful examination of the novel's tripartite structure and its major themes — the relationship of birth and death, the search for continuity, the desire for permanence — suggests, however, that the work as a whole affirms a position consistent with the one implicit in Mobberly's sermon. Permanence in *River of Earth* does not lie in the physical haven seemingly offered by the Appalachian mountains; instead, it lies in human endurance, in the unchanging cycles of human life, and in the annual passage and renewal of the seasons.

Still explores these issues in *River of Earth* through the story of the Baldridges, a Kentucky hill family of six. During the novel's three-year span, the family moves from farm to coal-camp; the youngest child, one-year-old Green, dies; brother Fletch loses part of his hand in an accident with a dynamite cap; the maternal grandmother passes away; and the mother, Alpha, gives birth. Still presents these and other events in the narrative entirely from the viewpoint of the oldest Baldridge son, an unnamed boy whose seventh birthday occurs in the novel's opening pages. We learn, therefore, of the novel's central conflict from the boy; when he recounts his parents' conversations, he reveals, almost without comment, the tension between Brack Baldridge's desire to give up farming and "follow the mines" and his wife's longing "to set ... down in a lone spot, a place certain and enduring ... and raise my chaps proper" (51–52).

Still devotes much of the novel's first and longest section to the exploration of the conflict between farming and coal mining, between establishing an "enduring" home and accepting constant migration; the section as a whole, however, does not clearly resolve the issue. Instead, it juxtaposes Alpha Baldridge's poignant and convincing longing and her brother Jolly's refusal to be "buried" in a coal mine (35) to the fact that the family is nearly starving on their farm; at one point, the narrator comments that "[w]e had come through to spring, but Mother was the leanest of all and the baby cried in the night when there was no milk" (13). With the advent of summer, the family's garden promises to help alleviate their hunger, but necessity often forces them to harvest its produce too soon; thus, Alpha peels "knotty and small" potatoes, "lifting paper-thin [skins], wasting none of the flesh" (55–56). Even when fully grown, the garden cannot satisfy the family's craving for meat (58); the money Brack earns in the mines provides this "luxury." Alpha herself recognizes, somewhat reluctantly, the advantages of steady wages. "When your pap sets to work," she tells the narrator, "I can buy a tonic. The baby will fatten then. I've been drinking 'sang [ginseng] tea, but it does no good" (68–69).

Still's early handling of the opposition between Alpha and Brack Baldridge has important ramifications for his treatment of Appalachian Kentucky; or, to put it more specifically, his refusal to clearly resolve the conflict in Alpha's favor proves subtly consistent with the conception of the mountains as part of "a mighty river of earth" (76). Because he stops short of unqualifiedly affirming Alpha's dream of an isolated, inviolate haven "on a hill" (51), Still seems to admit — albeit unwillingly — the possibility that such a dream of permanence may remain unattainable in an area characterized by motion. And although the first section of *River of Earth* depicts a seemingly static environment, it repeatedly suggests — through both Mobberly's sermon and Still's handling of the conflict between Brack and Alpha — that the underlying characteristics of the area are change and movement. Moreover, this sense of motion can be quite logically expressed through both a literal migration to the coal camps and a cosmic vision of the mountains as dirt waves, for in Still's multi-layered, masterfully crafted novel, the literal nearly always reinforces the visionary.

Still's treatment of the tension between permanence and change within the context of a marital conflict links him to another important Southern novelist, his friend Harriette Simpson Arnow. In her masterpiece *The Dollmaker* (1954), Arnow also chronicles the destruction of a family's agrarian existence; despite the mother's protests, the Nevels family leaves Kentucky so that the father can pursue the "big money" in the factories of wartime Detroit. Even more clearly than does the tension between Brack and Alpha Baldridge, the conflict between Gertie and Clovis Nevels comes to represent the conflict between a traditional, almost Jeffersonian, farm life and the growing preference for a rootless, wage-oriented existence. And while Arnow clearly sympathizes with Gertie, she too acknowledges that the dream of a self-sustaining life on the land may be unattainable for many people.[6] After fifteen years of harsh economizing, Gertie has barely half the amount she needs to buy her own farm; only her brother's death and unexpected bequest provide her with the funds she needs to complete the purchase. Even with cash in hand, however, Arnow's heroine cannot resist the forces—social, religious, economic—pressuring her to join Clovis in Detroit, and, like Alpha Baldridge, she succumbs to her husband's need for change and movement, and allows her family to be uprooted in an illusive search for economic security and a "better" life.

Both *River of Earth* and *The Dollmaker* contain, then, many of the tensions Leo Marx has described as characteristic of American literary pastoral. According to Marx, the pastoral or garden world in American literature is constantly threatened by a "real world" counterforce; thus, its permanence remains illusory.[7] Texts such as Thoreau's *Walden*, Twain's *The Adventures of Huckleberry Finn*, or Norris's *The Octopus* depict this counterforce as the machine which intrudes into, and destroys, the pastoral landscape. Still and Arnow go a step further. In their novels the conflict between the pastoral or agrarian existence is threatened not only by the intrusion of the machine but also by acquiescence to a spouse.[8]

In the second section of *River of Earth*, Still continues to explore the tension between motion and stability, although he does so in a much less overt manner than in the novel's earlier chapters. In this section Brack and Alpha Baldridge virtually disappear from the novel, for Still's narrator goes on to live with his seventy-eight-year-old Grandmother Middleton while his Uncle Jolly serves time in the state prison at Frankfort. Jolly returns earlier than expected (he receives a parole for putting out a fire in the prison workshop, a fire that prison officials do not realize he also started), but the narrator nonetheless remains with his relatives for a full year. As readers of Still's fiction know, this long interlude with the grandmother occupies a rather unique position in his canon, for although he often tells the story of a family similar to the Baldridges and frequently includes events from *River of Earth* in his other work, only in this instance does he develop a sustained relationship between a child and a member of the grandmother's generation.[9] By depicting this relationship, Still manages to convey—to both the narrator and the reader—a sense of the boy's familial past; or, as the seven year old puts it, Grandma's "hair trunk was peopled with keepsakes and recollections. She held up things for me to see, naming, giving them meaning" (122). The grandmother also endows the past with meaning through her stories, and from her conversation we learn of Alpha's childhood and early womanhood; of the grandfather's operation on his infant son's deformed hand (an incident which strongly anticipates Fletch's accident); of the death of another son in childhood; and of the grandfather's murder by an angry neighbor, Aus Coggins. To Still, as this section makes clear, the oral tradition (the "naming") functions as a vital means of passing knowledge from one generation to another; it is, in essence, the only means available to Grandma, as she can neither read nor write (109).

In addition to conveying this sense of family history and continuity, however, the second section of *River of Earth* also allows Still to depict the lives of people who share Alpha Baldridge's commitment to tradition and stability. In fact, Still goes to some lengths to attribute a philosophy of life quite similar to Alpha's to both the grandmother and Jolly. Grandma admits, for instance, not only that she wanted her daughter to choose a husband "who lived on the land, growing his own victuals, raising sheep and cattle, beholden to nobody," but also that she wishes Brack would "settle some place and grow roots" (130). For his part, Jolly Middleton emerges as almost the direct opposite of his brother-in-law; he remains, despite his mischief making, a serious, deeply-rooted "natural" man, one closely attuned to the needs of the land and vitally aware of the processes of nature—witness the fact that he goes to prison for blowing up a dam which keeps the fish from spawning (109). But perhaps most important for Still's purposes, this section demonstrates that Grandma and Jolly—unlike Alpha—manage to live in a manner consistent with their vision of a good life. Mother and son work hard for meager rewards, yet they maintain their self-sufficiency, their independence, and, above all, their allegiance to a particular place.

In many senses, then, the second section of *River of Earth* presents an alternative to the Baldridge's migratory way of life. This alternative seems, moreover, a relatively secure one; despite the Middleton's poverty, no overt tensions between characters exist to mar their traditional, agriculturally based existence and no external pressures (like the need for cash) force them to move. Even during the interlude on the farm, however, cracks appear in the facade of permanence, for Still introduces an element of doubt about the stability of both the place he depicts and the way of life it sustains. He repeatedly points out, for instance, that although the grandmother imbues one grandchild with a sense of family history and continuity, she cannot do the same for other family members; lamenting her lack of contact with her descendants, Grandma tells the narrator, "I'd give a year o' my life to see all my children and all their chaps.... A year's breathing I'd give. Never they come to see their mommy. Old, and thrown away now" (131). And although Grandma may overstate the case against her absent children, they do visit infrequently or not at all. Their absence, coupled with the fact that only Jolly lives much as his parents did (his brothers, like Alpha and Brack, adopt a relatively rootless existence of day labor and sporadic farming), strongly suggests the breakdown of family continuity and of a way of life.[10]

Somewhat ironically, however, the most powerful suggestion of change in this section comes from the character most firmly committed to maintaining his roots in a particular place — Uncle Jolly. When the narrator asks Jolly to teach him to plow, his uncle replies in language highly reminiscent of Mobberly's: "Hain't many folks know how to tend dirt proper," he tells the boy. "Land a-wasting and a-washing. Up and down Troublesome Creek, it's the same. Timber cut off and hills eating down.... What's folks going to live on when these hills wear down to a nub?" (134).[11] Jolly's ecological concerns remain, of course, far removed from Mobberly's spiritual ones, yet the words of both men create strikingly similar images of the potential alteration or destruction of the apparently immovable mountains.[12]

In much the same way that Jolly's dramatic statements echo Mobberly, certain apparently minor details from *River of Earth*'s second section also recall the sense of motion inherent in the minister's sermon. In keeping with the idea of a river of earth, Still often uses verbs and employs expressions which indicate fluidity: thus, Grandpa Middleton's "life's blood flowed a river" (121); the narrator feels "the earth flowing, steady as time" beneath the plow handles (135); and Walking John Gay — a compulsive journeyer whose migratory life stands as the antithesis of Alpha's dream of permanence — comments that "[t]hey's a world o' dirt flowed under my feet" (140). Granted, Still might have chosen these means of expression under any circumstances, but given his frequent comments on the importance of precise word choice — and the overwhelming evidence that he adheres to his own personal dictum — they more likely reflect the conscious effort of the careful artist to recall, once again, the sense of movement vital to his novel's central passage.[13]

If the first two sections of *River of Earth* subtly underscore the conception of the Kentucky mountains — and a way of life traditionally associated with them — as part of a fluctuating, ever-flowing river of earth, the novel's final portion stands as Still's clearest acknowledgment of change and movement. This section actually breaks down into two diametrically opposed parts, one taking place on a farm, the other in a coal camp. The much shorter agrarian portion opens with the narrator's return to his family and his dispassionate assessment of their situation: the mines have closed, the family has moved to a rented farm, and the baby has died of croup (169). In spite of the losses and hardships the Baldridges experience on the farm, however, Still presents their existence there as a largely satisfying one:

relatives and friends gather for Green's funeral; Alpha and the children feel at home (Alpha, in fact, describes the farm as "the nighest heaven I've been on this earth" [176]; and a bountiful harvest ensures sufficient food for the winter. Against this benign backdrop, the coal camp emerges as a harsh, almost hostile environment, and the narrator's description of the arrival at Blackjack indicates both the desolation of the place and Still's ability to convey the child's sense of wonder at anything new:

> We reached Blackjack in middle afternoon. The slag pile towering over the camp burned with an acre of oily flames. A sooty mist hung over the creek bottom. Our house sat close against a bare hill. It was cold and gloomy, smelling sourly of paint, but there were glass windows, and Euly, Fletch, and I ran into every room to look out [184].

Subsequent events do little to alter the initial impression of Blackjack, and in the novel's final pages, we learn without surprise, that the mines have shut down once again and that Brack plans yet another move — this time to Grundy, a coal town "three days' travel" from his present location, but one where work may be available (241). By projecting this trip, Still leaves little doubt that the Baldridges will continue to "follow the mines" even after the narrative's close (52).

Still has commented that when he re-reads parts of *River of Earth* he finds them "sad," primarily because of "the bleakness, the hopelessness" of the characters' futures ("Interview," *Appalachian Journal* 140). Although Still does not identify the portions of the book to which these remarks refer, they most aptly apply to its final section; not insignificantly, much of the section's bleakness results from the characters' inability — both in the novel and in the projected future — to establish a permanent haven in the mountains. The outward events of the narrative indicate this failure, of course, but Still underscores it in the novel's closing section with a complex — and highly appropriate — symbol of dislocation and transience. In the weeks following Green's death, Alpha and Euly decorate a small willow tree with eggshells, hoping to cover all the branches before the funeral. (In order not to violate Alpha's character, Still points out that decorating the egg tree does not involve the waste of family resources; as Alpha explains, "[e]ggshells hain't a grain o' good except to prettify with" [173].) When Brack begins to talk of moving to the coal camps, the egg tree becomes the composite symbol of all the things Alpha hates to leave — the baby's grave, the land, the security of remaining in one place. "Nigh we get our roots planted, we keep pulling them up and planting in furrin ground," she tells Brack. "Moving is an abomination. Thar's a sight of things I hate to leave here. I hate to leave my egg tree I set so much time and patience on. Reckon it's my egg tree holding me" (182).

Brack replies that, unfortunately, "thar hain't a seed so it can be planted again" (182), but Still makes clear that the exchange between husband and wife involves more than the impossibility of planting an egg tree. Within the context of the section, Alpha's tree represents, quite literally, her efforts to put down roots, to make a rented farm her own, to create a lasting reminder of her child's funeral, and to establish the "certain and enduring" home she desires for her family (51). These efforts, according to Still, cannot be successfully transplanted; when Brack attempts to move the egg tree to Blackjack, it arrives with cracked shells, exposed willow branches, and shallowly buried roots. Alpha's comment on the undertaking — "It takes a man-person to be a puore fool" (185)—could be Still's. Both character and author recognize that establishing roots and traditions necessitates staying in one place; reader and author recognize, however, the difficulty of doing so in a world characterized as part of a "mighty river of earth" (76).

As the novel draws to a conclusion, the narrator himself gains an insight into the difficulty of controlling one's own existence, of putting down roots where and when one chooses. Throughout the narrative, the boy insists that, as an adult, he will be a horse doctor, not a miner, yet when a Blackjack resident tells him "[y]ou can't get above your raising.... [W]hate'er you're aiming to be, you'll end up snagging jackrock" (227), the words reverberate in his mind "like truth" (228). His own future, the boy gradually realizes, may well be as bleak — and as migratory — as his parents' past.

This reading of *River of Earth*'s final section should not suggest that the novel ends on a note of despair or that Still views the attempts of Kentucky hill residents to establish firm roots as hopeless; after all, the evidence indicates that Uncle Jolly will continue to live on his farm, in Still's words, until "the day of his death, without apparent change" ("Interview," *Appalachian Journal* 140). The entire analysis of the novel thus far should suggest, however, that Still goes to some lengths in *River of Earth* to associate the eastern Kentucky mountains — and the way of life they have traditionally sustained — with the fluid and the mutable. On one level, this pervasive sense of change and motion acknowledges shifts in local socioeconomic factors, such as the decline of agriculture and the rise of coal mining.[14] But on another, more universal level, the apparent instability of the Appalachian mountains reflects the difficulty, in a modern world, of finding any place that remains certain, enduring, and unchanging; or, as Jim Wayne Miller puts it, "Still's people, swept along on the 'mighty river of earth,' constitute a metaphor of the essential human experience" ("Jim Dandy" 20).

Still does, however, view certain aspects of this experience as changeless, and although he hesitates to affirm the permanence of a place, he does affirm in *River of Earth* the timelessness of the seasons and of the on-going cycles of human life. Still implies this first affirmation through the structure of the three parts of his novel. Each section begins in either a time of planting (one and three) or of harvest (two); sections one and two also end in harvest times, and three concludes with the coming of spring (the final chapter opens "on a windy March evening" [235]). By tying the sections of his narrative to the periods of the earth's production and by enclosing his characters' actions within these seasonal boundaries, Still seems to suggest that wherever human beings travel on the "river of earth" certain fundamental natural cycles will remain unaltered. And by ending his novel in spring — the traditional time of rebirth and renewal — Still suggests an element of hope in the Baldridge's apparently bleak future.

*River of Earth* also ends with a literal birth; or, more accurately, with the juxtaposition of birth and death, as the most recent Baldridge child arrives on the same night Uncle Jolly brings Grandma's corpse to Blackjack. In a characteristic display of Still's artistry, nearly every major narrative incident up to this point prepares reader and narrator for just this combination of events. Throughout the novel, Still consistently exposes the narrator to what Harriette Simpson Arnow called the realities of a life experienced without the barriers of "institutional walls." As both Still and Arnow recognize, children in the Kentucky hills witnessed births, deaths, amputations, and other operations, all carried out, as Arnow put it, "with no help from that man so seldom found in impoverished communities — the physician." Still's novel also depicts, however, the horror involved — especially for the sensitive individual — in confronting first-hand the more painful realities of existence. Without fail, therefore, his boy narrator reacts strongly to or turns away from experiences which reveal these realities, whether they assume the form of the birth of a colt ("I knew then the pain of flesh coming into life, and I turned and ran with this sight burning before my eyes" [27]); a primitive operation to remove a cob from a calf's throat ("[t]he horror of it ran through my limbs. It shook me as a wind shakes a tree" [64]); or the severing of his brother's fingers ("I felt bound to see this thing happen. Fletch would want me to see. But I chilled and backed away" [221]).

As a hill child, living free of "institutional walls," the narrator also encounters death quite frequently, yet early in the narrative he understandably resists exposure to this reality as well: where an angry parent murders the local schoolmaster at the end of part one, the narrator turns and runs "down the creek road, sick with loss" (97); when Uncle Jolly's mare, Poppet, dies, the boy locks the stall door and does "not go back to the barn ... that winter" (110). But by the novel's final section, the narrator's reaction to death has subtly altered. At Green's funeral he can acknowledge that "there had been death in our house" without turning from the fact (181); when Grandma's body arrives at Blackjack, he can view the corpse and comment that "[h]er face was like a mold of tallow, quiet, and unbreathing" (237). During the night watch over her body, however, the boy's reaction to death undergoes its most powerful transformation, and he recognizes the mystery involved in the end of life: "My eyes dwelt on Grandma. Now that we were alone I longed to speak a word to her, a word to endure, a word to go with her to the burying-ground. What word? I could not think" (238); ultimately, he asks, "Grandma ... where have you gone?" (245). At the moment he articulates this question, the boy hears— almost in answer — the cry of his newborn sister or brother.

Highly effective in itself, this ending also reveals the fine structural and thematic unity of *River of Earth*. Structurally, the ending recalls many earlier incidents in the narrative, particularly the previous juxtaposition of birth and death involving the colt, an incident which leaves the narrator with little real knowledge, but only the "cruel wisdom that the colt had been spared Oates's [a neighbor boy's] rusty hand" (32). In the final scene, however, Still suggests that the cycles of human birth and death, like the cycles of the earth, continue even when actual places alter. His boy narrator reacts to this unchanging reality of human existence; his adult reader recognizes its affirmation as one of the most important thematic conclusions of a masterfully-crafted novel.

In the final analysis, then, Still's treatment of Appalachian Kentucky in *River of Earth* proves much more complex than is usually recognized. On the one hand, Still clearly loves the place he depicts and wants— with characters like Alpha and Jolly — to affirm its permanence; on the other hand, however, he undercuts any sense of real permanence with poetic visions of change — like Mobberly's "river of earth" — which the novel consistently reinforces in very conscious and artistically sophisticated ways. As someone coming to the mountains from outside, Still can, it seems, recognize and express the gradual but inevitable alteration of the region's way of life. As a modern American artist, he can also recognize the forces working against the permanence of any tradition or any place — no matter how firmly rooted and secure they appear. In *River of Earth*, Still's masterful treatment of the eastern Kentucky mountains— the seemingly permanent mountains— reflects this multi-leveled recognition of change.

In much of his work since *River of Earth*, Still chose to continue writing about a folk culture which has largely disappeared; in fact, many of his more recent endeavors— particularly the collections of riddles and rusties and *The Wolfpen Notebooks*— are in large part attempts to preserve something of that culture.[15] Although Still acknowledges certain alterations in his world, then, he neither embraces them nor ceases to value the manner of living they destroy; instead, like Alpha Baldridge, he treasures the old ways.[16] Still's preferences should not surprise us; after all, even *River of Earth*— with its subtle and poetic suggestion of change — remains, to its author, a "sad" book.

# Notes

1. In 1989, the University Press of Kentucky also released a one-volume combined edition of *Way Down Yonder on Troublesome Creek* and *The Wolfpen Rusties* (both of which had been out of print for several years). The new volume, entitled *Rusties and Riddles & Gee-Haw Whimmy-Diddles*, includes the full texts of the original books, including Still's explanatory notes, and Janet McCaffery's original illustrations.

2. For a discussion of *The Wolfpen Notebooks*, see *Foxfire* 22 (Fall 1988). The entire issue is devoted to Still and the publication of his notebooks.

3. Dean Cadle comments briefly but perceptively on Still's treatment of Appalachia and its residents: "More than twenty years before the region was labeled a 'poverty pocket' and prior to the surprised reactions of experts and government officials to the problems of destitution, as though they had encountered some recent wonder, James Still had presented the heartbreaking account of what it means for a human being to live out his life hungry and cold. His is not a socioeconomist's collection of figures, causes, and possible cures, but the dramatized plight of human beings accepting poverty without accusations or judgments or rantings against outside institutions" (Foreword viii–ix). In an insightful article on Still's connection to the Nashville agrarian and his relationship to regional literature, H. R. Stoneback notes the author's unsentimentalized depiction of eastern Kentucky: "In Still's Appalachian-agrarian world we find the plenitude of nature, a rich and living folk tradition, a sustaining sense and community, a vivifying sense of place, and an enduring sense of identity through place. We find also hunger, desperation, mechanization, deracination, violence, tragedy, and death" (22). The fullest discussion of Still's treatment of change in the area is Fred Chappell's. According to Chappell, most of Still's "stories depict his Appalachia as sealed away in time and space, resistant to and mostly unknowing about the forces of larger history. The changes his fiction depicts are the most ancient ones, the changes of seasons, the changes of human life, from youth to maturity to old age to death" (200). While I agree that Still's fiction depicts "ancient" changes, my reading also argues that the author subtly admits the possibility of other kinds of change in Appalachia. Moreover, Still's characters may be more aware of a larger world beyond their immediate environment than Chappell's comment suggests. Brack Baldridge, for instance, refers to conditions on the Great Lakes as affecting the market for eastern Kentucky coal (66–67).

4. See, for example, Runyon 56–64, Glazer 4–9; Miller 14–16; and Cadle, "A Man on Troublesome" 246–51.

5. Stoneback offers a full analysis of the sermon and the ways in which it reverberates throughout the rest of the novel (16–19). As Stoneback correctly notes, "The sermon is both source and confluence of meaning, image, symbol" (19). In his introduction to Still's *The Wolfpen Poems*, Jim Wayne Miller also recognizes the centrality of Mobberly's sermon, not only to *River of Earth*, but also to much of Still's other work, both poetry and fiction. As Miller accurately observes, "[D]etails, imagery and syntax of this important passage are anticipated in early poems, and later poems and stories are variations and further elaborations of it" (xi). Perhaps the most striking example of a "further elabo-

ration" is the poem "River of Earth" (first collected in *The Wolfpen Poems*). The poem alludes to the same biblical text as Mobberly's sermon, and its closing stanzas again evoke the sense of motion underlying the apparently permanent mountains:

He can but stand
A stranger on familiar slopes and drink the restless air,
Knowing that beneath his feet, beneath his probing eyes
A river of earth flows down the strident centuries.
Hills are but waves cast up to fall again, to rise
Still further down the years.
Men are held here
Within a mighty tide swept onward to a final sea [21].

6. For a fuller analysis of Arnow's attitude toward the increasing difficulty of maintaining the kind of life Gertie prefers, see my article, "The Demise of Mountain Life: Harriette Arnow's Analysis," *Border States: Journal of the Kentucky-Tennessee American Studies Association* 8 (1991): 37–42.

7. Marx points out, for instance, that most early American writers tended to employ "a variation upon the contrast between two worlds, one identified with rural peace and simplicity, the other with urban power and sophistication, which had been used by writers working in the pastoral mode since the time of Virgil" (19). By 1854 (Thoreau's *Walden*), however, "a new, distinctly American, post-romantic industrial version of the pastoral design" had emerged (32). The intrusion of the sound of the train into the Concord woods, Marx argues, "implies a radical change in the conventional pattern [of pastoral]. Now the great world is invading the land, transforming the sensory texture of rural life — the way it looks and sounds — and threatening, in fact, to impose a new and more complete dominion over it" (32–33). Stoneback also discusses *River of Earth* in terms of The Machine in the Garden but focuses his discussion primarily on Still's depiction of the coal camps (20–21).

Both *River of Earth* and *The Dollmaker* might also be considered in terms of Wendell Berry's argument that the history of America has been largely the history of two opposed attitudes toward life and the land, the dominant being the relatively rootless pursuit of "our ideas of affluence, comfort, mobility, and leisure," and the other the "until now subordinate tendency of settlement, of domestic permanence" (13).

8. Arnow had treated this theme in a similar manner in her earlier fiction as well. Her unpublished novel, *Between the Flowers* (1936–1939), deals with the marriage of Marsh and Delphine Costello Gregory, a young farm couple whose conflicting desires create a growing estrangement between them. *Between the Flowers*, however, reverses the situation found in *The Dollmaker*, for in this novel the husband wishes to stay on the land, while the wife longs for a life away from the farm and the small community.

9. The most noticeable repeated event is that of Fletch losing his fingers. This event recurs in *On Troublesome Creek* with the younger brother Lark and in *Sporty Creek* with brother Dan, although this time the boy loses his fingers in an accident at a sawmill, not by playing with a dynamite cap.

10. Perhaps Still also underscores this break in continuity through an apparent error in the text. At one point, Jolly tells Grandma that one of her other sons,

Luce, has named his infant daughter Cordia after Grandma (113). Later, we find out that the baby's name is actually Foan (178).

11. Although Still often uses a-prefixed verbs (a common feature of Appalachian speech) in *River of Earth*, he seldom uses them in sequence as he does in Mobberly's sermon ("a-rising and a-falling" and "a-borning, begetting, and a-dying") and in Jolly's comments about the hills ("a-wasting and a-washing"). By using these forms, I think, Still intends to strengthen the connection between the two passages.

12. Dean Cadle quite accurately notes, however, in the Foreword to *River of Earth* that "[r]ead today with the strip-mined region as a map — the scalped hills and gashed mountainsides, the ruined farmlands, the dead streams, the flash water the earth can't contain — even the title of the novel assumes a prophecy of doom undreamed of by Brother Mobberly" (x).

13. See, for instance, Still's comments throughout Cadle's "Pattern of a Writer: Attitudes of James Still."

14. For a thorough analysis of this change, see Ronald D. Eller's *Miners, Millhands, and Mountaineers: Industrialization of the Appalachian South, 1880–1930*. Chapters 4–7 in particular deal with the rise of coal mining in eastern Kentucky and the surrounding area, as well as the effect of this industrialization on the mountaineer. According to Eller, by the 1930s (the time of *River of Earth*) mountaineers "[s]uspended halfway between the old society and the new ... had lost the independence and self-determination of their ancestors, without becoming full participants in the benefits of the modern world" (242).

15. Several of Still's more recent stories do, however, deal with post–World War II Kentucky. Important examples include "A Ride on the Short Dog" and "Pattern of a Man" in the 1976 volume *Pattern of a Man and Other Stories*, and the title story of the 1980 collection *The Run for the Elbertas*. Like *River of Earth*, each of these narratives also involves a journey: "A Ride on the Short Dog," the bus trip to the mountain town of Roscoe (and perhaps the death of Godey Spurlock); "Pattern of a Man," the return to the Appalachian Kentucky community of a World War II veteran, whose stories about the Middle East upset the erroneous notions of a local preacher; "The Run for the Elbertas," the journey from Kentucky to North Carolina to pick up peaches, and the drive back with the quickly rotting load. Although Still clearly values the traditions, folklore, and way of life of Appalachian Kentucky, and although he actively seeks to preserve them in much of his work, these stories — like *River of Earth* — demonstrate his steady awareness of alterations within the region; likewise, they indicate the frequent evocation of a "vision of change" in his fiction.

16. Still addresses the issue of the "new" Kentucky directly in the *Foxfire* interview: "Roads, telephones, shopping malls. This would appear to be all good. It's opened up the world and broken down barriers.... There are losses. A sense of community is lost" (141).

## Works Cited

Arnow, Harriette Simpson. Introduction. *Mountain Path*. Berea, KY: Council of the Southern Mountains Publishers, 1963.

Berry, Wendell. *The Unsettling of America: Culture and Agriculture*. San Francisco: Sierra Club Books, 1977.

Cadle, Dean. Foreword. *River of Earth*. James Still. Lexington: University Press of Kentucky, 1978.

_____. "A Man on Troublesome." *The Yale Review* 57 (1968): 236–55.

_____. "Pattern of a Writer: Attitudes of James Still." *Appalachian Journal* 8 (Winter 1988): 104–43.

Eller, Ronald D. Miners. *Millhands, and Mountaineers: Industrialization of the Appalachian South, 1880–1930*. Knoxville: University Tennessee Press, 1982.

Glazer, Joe. "Slick as a Dogwood Hoe Handle." *Appalachian Heritage* 11 (Summer 1983): 4–9.

"An Interview with James Still." *Appalachian Journal* 6 (Winter 1979): 120–41.

"An Interview with James Still." *Foxfire* 22 (Fall 1988): 123–49.

Marx, Leo. *The Machine in the Garden: Technology and the Pastoral Ideal in America*. Oxford: Oxford University Press, 1964.

Miller, Jim Wayne. Introduction. *The Wolfpen Poems*. James Still. Berea, KY: Berea College Press, 1986. xi–xxiii.

_____. "Jim Dandy: James Still at Eighty." *Appalachian Heritage* 14 (Fall 1986): 8–20.

Runyon, Randolph Paul. "Looking the Story in the Eye: James Still's 'Rooster.'" *Southern Literary Journal* 23 (Spring 1991): 55–64.

Still, James. *River of Earth*. 1940. Lexington: University Press of Kentucky, 1978.

_____. *The Wolfpen Poems*. Berea, KY: Berea College Press, 1986.

Stoneback, H. R. "Rivers of Earth and Troublesome Creeks: The Agrarianism of James Still." *Kentucky Review* 10 (Autumn 1990): 3–26.

# "This Mighty *River of Earth*": Reclaiming an Appalachian Masterpiece

## TED OLSON

### *I.*

In 1978, nearly four decades after its original publication and many years since it was last available in print, author James Still's novel *River of Earth* was reissued by the University Press of Kentucky. In his foreword to this new edition, scholar Dean Cadle reassessed the novel:

> *River of Earth* and *The Grapes of Wrath* are the only books chronicling the demoralizing Depression years that have continued to gain readers in more affluent ones. The major difference between them is that Steinbeck's story deals with a calamity that has struck America only once in its lifetime, while Still is writing of the struggles that have plagued the mountain people since the country was settled [Still vii–viii].

Cadle was right to compare *River of Earth* to *The Grapes of Wrath*. Still's novel not only appeared less than a year after Steinbeck's, but both novels were published by the same publishing house — The Viking Press. More significantly, *River of Earth* and *The Grapes of Wrath* are Depression Era social novels with remarkably similar plots: both portray working class families struggling to endure the crippling effects of an unsupportive, often belligerent social/economic/political system.[1]

In asserting that *River of Earth* is as enduring a novel as *The Grapes of Wrath*, Cadle challenged the longstanding assumption that Steinbeck's was the greatest social novel written by an American author during the Depression Era. Before Cadle, literary critics and scholars usually awarded *The Grapes of Wrath* the highest position in the hierarchy of works reflecting the social struggles of Americans during the Great Depression. Critics and scholars generally agreed that this hierarchy included, among other works, an earlier novel by Steinbeck (*In Dubious Battle*), a novel by Erskine Caldwell (*God's Little Acre*), a play by Clifford Odets (*Waiting for Lefty*), and a work of non-fiction by James Agee (*Let Us Now Praise Famous Men*). Despite

Olson, Ted. "'*This Mighty* River of Earth': *Reclaiming James Still's Appalachian Masterpiece.*" Journal of Appalachian Studies. *1.1 (Fall 1995): 87–98. Copyright 1995 by the Appalachian Studies Association. Reprinted with permission.*

Cadle's efforts to foster wider appreciation of Still's work, and despite strong interest in Still among students of Appalachian culture, *River of Earth* has seldom been included in this hierarchy. However accurate it is in depicting one phase of the Southern Appalachian mountain people's historical experience, and however successful it is aesthetically, Still's novel has never achieved more than marginal status in national literary circles.

In suggesting that Still's and Steinbeck's novels are equally significant literary responses to the Great Depression, Cadle begged an important question: why isn't *River of Earth* better known outside of Appalachian Studies' circles? In this essay, I will attempt to answer that question. In this essay's second section, I will recount the critical reception for both *The Grapes of Wrath* and *River of Earth*, in the hope of exposing the primary reason for the latter novel's ongoing marginal status, which I believe to be the timing of its publication. *River of Earth* has been overshadowed by *The Grapes of Wrath* not because Steinbeck's novel was aesthetically superior to Still's, but because *River of Earth* had the misfortune of being published in the wake of Steinbeck's literary blockbuster. In this essay's third section, I will defend Still's novel from attacks (both actual and hypothetical) from unsympathetic critics and scholars who might distrust Cadle's restructuring of the American literary canon to include a little-known Appalachian novel. In a short fourth section, I will summarize the reasons *River of Earth* deserves to be more widely read and taught. The fifth section will offer a few closing comments about Still and his overlooked masterpiece, *River of Earth*.

## II.

Since its publication on March 14, 1939, *The Grapes of Wrath* has never been out of print. When it first appeared, though, no one would have guessed that Steinbeck's novel would become Viking's best-selling title to date and one of its most widely acclaimed. The publishing company served little advance notice of the book's release. Also, *The Grapes of Wrath* was greeted by mixed critical reception. While certain literary critics and writers immediately recognized the novel's importance (Alexander Woollcott, for instance, upon reading a pre-publication copy of the novel, called *The Grapes of Wrath* "the great American book" [Woollcott 218]), book reviewers for such influential mainstream magazines as *Time* and *Newsweek* found fault with the novel. Some critics were troubled by the fact that the novel's author interspersed narrative chapters with chapters offering detailed journalistic commentary; others felt that the latter half of *The Grapes of Wrath* was weaker than the first half, with an ending that some found offensive (French 107–8). Even critics for left-leaning periodicals like *The Nation* and *The New Republic*—critics, one might surmise, who should have been especially sympathetic towards the novel for its socialistic overtones—echoed the general displeasure for the novel's ending; they also took Steinbeck to task for fudging the distinction between fact and fiction (108).

Nevertheless, even without the benefit of book club sales, advance promotion, or whole-hearted critical support, *The Grapes of Wrath* soon generated a level of excitement seldom bestowed upon serious literary works: the novel became a mass culture phenomenon. It was the best-selling book of 1939—over 430,000 copies were sold in that year alone. From May 6, 1939 (less than two months after its publication date), through the end of that year, the novel remained at the top of the *Publishers Weekly* list of national best-selling books. In 1940, *The Grapes of Wrath* continued to sell extremely well and was one of the top ten best-sellers for that year (French 106).

What prompted such massive support for a novel published to little initial fanfare? For one thing, when *The Grapes of Wrath* appeared in 1939, Steinbeck had a broad-based literary reputation, having already published novels highly regarded in literary circles for their skillful storytelling (particularly *Of Mice and Men*), their quirky sense of humor (especially *Tortilla Flat*), and their daring treatment of social and political movements in Depression Era America (*In Dubious Battle*).

Also, *The Grapes of Wrath*—which continued the investigation of Depression Era sociopolitical issues that Steinbeck had begun with *In Dubious Battle*—received considerable promotion from unlikely sources. For instance, First Lady Eleanor Roosevelt, in the June 28, 1939, edition of her nationally syndicated column "My Day," confessed that she had found *The Grapes of Wrath* to be "an unforgettable experience in reading" (French 131). In defense of the novel's frank realism, the First Lady wrote: "The book is coarse in spots, but life is coarse in spots, and the story is very beautiful in spots just as life is" (131). Given the respect granted her by the American public, Mrs. Roosevelt's endorsement of *The Grapes of Wrath* surely convinced countless American readers from all walks of life to participate in that "unforgettable experience in reading." With the novel's controversial treatment of timely subject matter triggering widespread discussion, *The Grapes of Wrath* became favored reading in unlikely places, among persons who did not usually read "serious" literature. As one Oklahoma City bookseller recalled, "People who looked as though they had never read a book in their lives came in to buy it" (118). Accordingly, for several years *The Grapes of Wrath* was the book most commonly checked out from community libraries nationwide—it was more popular than the other blockbuster novel of that era, *Gone with the Wind* (118). After its release in early 1940, John Ford's hit movie version of *The Grapes of Wrath* further thrust Steinbeck's novel before the American public.

Witnessing the novel's phenomenal popularity and recognizing its epic strengths, critics, scholars, writers, and mainstream readers began to consider *The Grapes of Wrath* the quintessential American social novel. Steinbeck's novel drew attention internationally as well as nationally: *The Grapes of Wrath*, for example, was a key reason why Steinbeck received the 1962 Nobel Prize for Literature.

The widespread enthusiasm of readers for *The Grapes of Wrath* was not transferred to Still's own Depression Era social novel after its publication in early 1940. Ironically, however, *River of Earth* received more unqualified critical acclaim in 1940 than had *The Grapes of Wrath* the year before. In the February 3, 1940, edition of *The Saturday Review of Literature*, W.J. Gold remarked that *River of Earth* is "told with ... clarity and strength born of restraint.... The economy of its style and the directness of its aim give evidence of a mature and intelligently used talent" (May and Lesniak 407). An anonymous reviewer, in the February 10, 1940, edition of the *Boston Evening Transcript*, considered Still to be as fine a writer as Elizabeth Madox Roberts: "He is fully her equal in fusing the most realistic objectivity with the most intense inwardness of mood" (Stoneback 13). In the February 23, 1940, edition of *Commonweal*, another anonymous reviewer suggested that *River of Earth* proved Still a more capable writer than some of his better-known contemporaries: "Mr. Still has distinguished himself principally in his restraint, avoiding Jesse Stuart's often faked heartiness and the cheap, easily written incidents which merely shock but which Erskine Caldwell thinks are good writing" (12).

Literary critics were not the only ones to laud *River of Earth* after its publication: several established writers publicly acknowledged their interest in the novel. Marjorie Kinnan Rawlings described the novel as "vital, beautiful, heart-breaking and heart-warmingly funny," while Delmore Schwartz called it "a symphony" (Still vi). Katherine Anne Porter and Carson McCullers also praised *River of Earth*. Robert Frost reported that he stayed up all night reading the novel; impressed by what he read that night, Frost later invited Still to attend the dedication of Amherst College's Robert Frost Room ("Man on Troublesome" 238–9).

Revealingly, in their efforts to position the little known author of *River of Earth* in the public's consciousness, none of these critics or writers mentioned Steinbeck or *The Grapes of Wrath* as possible touchstones; instead, they compared Still and his novel exclusively with Southern and Appalachian writers and their works. From the start Still was seen as a writer of strictly regional significance — an attitude that no doubt has contributed to the lingering exclusion of *River of Earth* from the American literary canon.

Yet, when *River of Earth* was first published, not everyone pigeon-holed it as a novel of strictly regional significance. Three reviewers clearly understood that Still's aesthetic intention was to render universal the essential localness of his chosen subject matter. In the February 5, 1940, edition of *Time* magazine, an anonymous critic wrote: "James Still tells of [the Kentucky mountain people's] japes and sorrows and near starvation, the rich archaic poetry of their talk and customs, in a clear, dry style as unsentimental as his seven-year-old [protagonist's] eyes.... The problem it [*River of Earth*] fairly solves is that faced by many Southern novelists: how to be sectional without being affected.... [Still] has produced a work of art" (*Time* 64). Writer and critic Stephen Vincent Benét, in the February 4, 1940, edition of *Books*, commented that *River of Earth* is "rich with sights, sounds and smells, with the feel and taste of things"; Benét then defended Still against those who would marginalize his work because of its regional identity: *River of Earth* is "rich, as well, with salty and earthy speech, the soil of ballad and legend and tall story.... You can call it regional writing if you like — but to say so is merely to say that all America is not cut off the same piece" (Stoneback 12–13).

In the March 1942 edition of *College English,* scholar Dayton Kohler asserted that Still's regionalism — Still's knowing depiction of one Southern Appalachian locale and its people in his fiction and in his poetry — dramatically improved on the efforts of "local color" authors (like Mary Murfree) whose writings about Appalachia were, because they were "about a place rather than of it," inaccurate and dangerously romanticized. Kohler then determined the importance of Still's work to the national literary scene — as a model of accomplished regional writing: "[In the writings of James Still] the Southern mountaineer has found his own voice for the first time. This regionalism is as genuine and untainted as any we have in America today" (Stoneback 13).

Although *River of Earth* received more unqualified critical support when published in 1940 than had *The Grapes of Wrath* in its publication year of 1939, Still's novel attracted only a fraction of the public support garnered by Steinbeck's novel. Both novels may have traced the plight of a group of dispossessed Southerners coping with the devastating effects of the Great Depression, but *The Grapes of Wrath* better reflected the everyday social realities of Depression Era Americans. In the early years of the 1940s, the American reading public, exhausted by the Depression and seeking solutions for socioeconomic woes, could more easily identify with Steinbeck's plot and characters (Oklahomans who desert their environmentally and economically devastated native region for the "promised land" of California, on the way coming into contact and conflict with a wide range of Americans) than with Still's (Kentuckians who refuse to leave their similarly desecrated homeland, choosing instead to remain in their native region, geographically, economically, and socially isolated). And though both novels featured markedly original prose styles, readers could more easily identify with the more accessible journalistic style of *The Grapes of Wrath* than with the literary approximation of an Appalachian dialect employed in *River of Earth.*

When published in 1940, Still's novel not only had to compete with *The Grapes of Wrath,* it had to contend with the fact that American readers, exhausted by the cumulative effects of the Great Depression, were tired of the disturbing realism of social novels and were losing interest in the works of "regionalists" (Faulkner's novels, for instance, were little read at this time). By 1940 the separate experiences of regional groups in the United States—particularly of rural dwellers like the mountain people of eastern Kentucky—were beginning to seem remote indeed to many Americans. *River of Earth* seemed out of step with the era, because one of its dominant themes—that the forces of Industrialization were endangering the traditional life of Appalachian people—contradicted a view on the subject that was quickly gaining popularity. While Industrialization is depicted negatively in *River of Earth* (as in many other social and regional novels written in the 1930s), the preponderance of Americans by 1940 were beginning to believe that Industrialization, however destructive it had proven to be in the past, might now be the best way to surmount the socioeconomic problems lingering from the worst years of the Depression.

In its quest to find a reading audience, *River of Earth* also had to contend with the fact that by 1940 Americans were increasingly preoccupied with international events. A German dictator was attempting to conquer Europe. Widespread fear concerning the United States' imminent involvement in a global war further wrenched the attention of Americans away from the circumstances of American regional groups. When the United States entered World War II in late 1941, Depression-era social novels concerned with domestic social issues suddenly seemed obsolete.

Considering the fact that American minds were understandably preoccupied with recuperating from their own socioeconomic struggles and with confronting international events, it hardly seems surprising that *River of Earth*—a novel about the economic and cultural survival of Appalachian people (a group that, because of media-created stereotyping, mainstream America already thought of as abnormal)—was soon out of print.

## *III.*

*River of Earth* has never been widely read, and many literary critics and scholars—not to mention mainstream readers—have never heard of James Still. A major factor leading to the marginal status of the novel and the novelist in the American literary canon has been Still's disinclination to promote his own career. According to Cadle, "Three patterns of living, perhaps more the result of inclination than of design, have contributed to [Still's] obscurity. He has chosen to live and write in isolation, he has refrained from inviting attention to himself and has run from it when he could, and he has published relatively little" ("Man on Troublesome" 237). By living and writing in geographical and emotional isolation from the New York literary establishment, Still did not receive the same level of attention and support that fueled the careers of more accessible authors (such as Steinbeck).

Thus, many literary critics and scholars, having never read Still's work, would react skeptically today to Cadle's declaration that *River of Earth* is as deserving of placement in the American literary canon as *The Grapes of Wrath*. Some of these people, perhaps distrustful of multi-culturalist railings against the literary establishment, might question Cadle's literary tastes. The deeply skeptical might wager that *River of Earth* was simply one author's attempt to cash in on the success of *The Grapes of Wrath* (or, if in a particularly benign mood, they might hypothesize that *River of Earth* was one author's effort to imitate Late Modernist "regional" fiction writers like Steinbeck and Faulkner). Cynics, especially those vulnerable to conspiracy theories, might conjecture that The Viking Press itself had commissioned *River of Earth* as an exercise in literary opportunism; as such thinking would have it, the publishing company, recognizing in the spring of 1939 that *The Grapes of Wrath* was going to be a best-seller, might have hired Still to pen a similar type of novel.

It is interesting to note that a cursory knowledge of Still's biography could be used, albeit unfairly and inaccurately, to reinforce skepticism toward *River of Earth*. Resistant critics and scholars might question how Still could possibly have understood the mountain people, since the author was not a native of the place of which he wrote — he moved to eastern Kentucky as an adult. These critics and scholars might also wonder why *River of Earth* should be considered as anything more than a formulaic "local color" novel — after all, many other novels about specific American locales by non-native authors fall into the pseudo-literary "local color" tradition.

Hostile reaction to the proposition that *River of Earth* is a forgotten masterpiece deserving of a wider audience — though here presented hypothetically, it does exist within the academy — stems from one source. Clearly, such people have not read *River of Earth* closely. If they were to do so, literary critics and scholars would soon realize that, because its author intimately understands his subject and possesses an artistic mind capable of shaping fact into highly original fiction, *River of Earth* is anything but a "local color" novel. Cadle is far from the only critic/scholar who considers the novel a literary masterpiece.

In fact, deeper investigation easily defends Still, *River of Earth*, and the Viking Press from all the aforementioned accusations. Regarding both artistic vision and subject matter, *River of Earth* owed no debts to *The Grapes of Wrath*. When Steinbeck started to conduct research toward the writing of *The Grapes of Wrath* in 1937, Still had already established himself as a significant new voice on the American literary scene — his short stories and poems had appeared in major periodicals like *The Atlantic, Esquire, Poetry*, and *The Saturday Evening Post*. By the time Steinbeck's novel was published in 1939, Still had already been under contract to The Viking Press for two years (in 1937 that publishing company had issued *Hounds on the Mountain*, a book-length collection of Still's poetry). And Still's empathy for the dispossessed eastern Kentucky mountain people predates *The Grapes of Wrath* by a decade, a fact quite evident in Still's earliest published work and in autobiographical statements from interviews. In the 1920s, Still, an Alabaman attending Vanderbilt, accompanied Don West, a fellow student, on a relief trip to aid striking coal miners at a coal camp near the Tennessee-Kentucky border; it was there that Still first identified with the plight of mountain people:

> When I entered graduate school at Vanderbilt [in late 1929], Don West was there in the School of Religion. I hadn't known him well at LMU [Lincoln Memorial University] but in Nashville we became better acquainted.... A strike which lasted three years was going on at a coal mine at Wilder, up near the Kentucky border, and Don recruited me to go with him to distribute food and clothes that medicine students had got together. This was the strike where Barney Green was machine gunned to death. It was my first sight of people starving in America. In America! [Lee 136].

Still empathized so strongly with the plight of the mountain people that in 1932, after completing graduate work in library science, he moved to eastern Kentucky to work as a librarian for the Hindman Settlement School in Knott County. His identification with this place and its people was already firmly established when, in the middle years of the Depression Era, a flurry of newly published social and "regional" novels (by Steinbeck and other writers) directed the public's attention to the complex local realities of various American regions. Still's own work, though, developed not from any premeditated attempt to latch onto a national trend, but from his own personal experience.

Because the American literary canon has to date excluded Still's work, readers (specifically, literary critics and scholars, historians, and students) not directly involved with Appalachian studies are not exposed to *River of Earth* and thus are unaware that the novel is arguably the most objective and enlightening fictional depiction of the effects of Great Depression on a particular American region and its people. Although *River of Earth* documents the impact of Industrialization on one group of Appalachian people at a particular historical moment, the novel's underlying theme — Cadle describes it as "acceptance of life as it is and refusal to admit defeat" ("Man on Troublesome" 247) — is anything but parochial. According to Cadle, *River of Earth* exhibits Still's uncanny understanding of the universal nature of poverty:

> More than twenty years before the Appalachian region was labeled a poverty pocket and before the somewhat artificial reactions of experts and government officials to the problems of poverty, as though they had encountered some recent wonder, Still had presented in *River of Earth* the heartbreaking account of what it means for a human being to live out his life hungry and cold. His is not a socioeconomist's collection of figures, causes, and possible cures, but the dramatized plight of human beings accepting poverty without accusations or judgments and without rantings against ephemeral institutions [247].

Still renders his fictionalized exploration of the universal nature of poverty much more believable and compelling by grounding it in a regionally specific cultural context. The end result of Still's efforts, writes scholar H. R. Stoneback, is that *River of Earth* "incarnates all of the best notions concerning how to write 'regional' fiction" (10):

> The successful regional writer is never insistently self-conscious regarding his regionalism. He writes out of, not about, a profound sense of place. He sees in and through and because of intense localism, a way of seeing, a vision that is purged by a kind of ongoing sacramental relationship with the near and common things of his place and community. James Still's *River of Earth* represents one precise formal embodiment of these principles [9–10].

Since a primary goal of "regional" writing is the reconciliation of the local and the universal, many of the novels in the aforementioned hierarchy of Depression Era literature — including *The Grapes of Wrath* — could be considered "regional" fiction, as could some of the most acclaimed novels in twentieth century American literature (such as Faulkner's Yoknapatawpha novels). Obviously, the fact that a given novel is set in a particular time and place has never in and of itself determined whether or not that novel should be accepted into the national literary canon. Therefore, it is unjust that the academy (when it has shown any interest at all in Still's novel) has primarily read *River of Earth* as an historic document (i.e., in terms of the accuracy with which Still depicts one phase of the Appalachian experience).

The importance of *River of Earth* is certainly as much aesthetic as historic. In a 1971 statement that both lauds the novel's stylistic excellence and laments its obscurity, Allen Tate, among the most rigorous critics of twentieth century American literature, wrote:

> I have just read it [*River of Earth*] — one of the few novels I have read in a decade. I regret that I didn't see it years ago. It is a brilliant and moving novel. Moreover, in my opinion, it is a masterpiece of style. The subtle modulation between the mountain speech of the dialogue and the formal, yet simple, diction of the narrative is masterly [Stoneback 10].

Clearly, *River of Earth* should be read as much for its artistic accomplishments as for its documentary value.

## *IV.*

In addition to being an aesthetic masterpiece and an important historical document, *River of Earth* is an excellent tool with which to correct the widespread national stereotyping of Appalachian people. The teaching of *River of Earth* to a national audience would not only promote an underappreciated novel that is, to quote from Tate, "a masterpiece of style," it would also expose diverse Americans to a poignant yet unsentimental depiction of the Appalachian region and its people, which would help to correct the American public's century-old stereotyped image of Appalachia and the Appalachian people (an image largely manufactured by the media via "local color" novels, print and broadcast journalism, "hillbilly" recordings, Hollywood movies, and syndicated television programs).

## V.

Although the University Press of Kentucky's reissue of *River of Earth* has not yet regained for the novel a substantial national readership, it has ensured the novel a prominent place in the canon of literature about the Appalachian region. Nonetheless, Still's work deserves a wider audience. According to H. R. Stoneback, "[I]t has been a disservice to Still to regard him solely under the rubric of Appalachian literature, and to yoke him with [Jesse] Stuart.... Rather, Still's primary credentials are those of the engaged artist. With the hand of a master stylist, he carves his regional materials into a vision of universal validity" (Stoneback 13). Cadle likewise believes that Still should be considered not an Appalachian writer, but an American writer: Still's "skillful use of the English language and his clean, spare style elevate the regional to the universal" ("James Still" 429).

## Notes

1. The two novels employ remarkably different strategies in exploring this predicament. According to Leon V. Driskell, "Both books treat forced movements in search of work and food, but the Baldridge family in *River of Earth* moves only a few miles and, unlike Steinbeck, Still does not introduce political or sociological comment into his narrative" (Driskell 69–71). In this latter statement Driskell is referring to Steinbeck's frequent insertions of journalistic commentary into the narrative of *The Grapes of Wrath*.

## Works Cited

Cadle, Dean. "James Still," *Southern Writers: A Biographical Dictionary*. Ed. by Robert Bain, Joseph M. Flora, and Louis D. Rubin, Jr. Baton Rouge: Louisiana State University Press, 1979. 429.

———. "Man on Troublesome," *The Yale Review* 57 (December 1967): 236–55.

Driskell, Leon V. "James Still," *Dictionary of Literary Biography, Volume 9, American Novelists, 1910–1945, Part 3*. Ed. by James J. Martine. Detroit: Gale Research, 1981. 68–72.

French, Warren, ed. *A Companion to The Grapes of Wrath*. New York: The Viking Press, 1963.

Lee, Laura et. al., eds. "August 17, 1988: 'I sometimes tell people I was born in a cotton patch,'" *Foxfire* (Fall 1988): 132–49.

May, Hal, and James G. Lesniak, eds. *Contemporary Authors* (New Revision Series, Vol. 26). Detroit: Gale Research, 1989. 406–08.

Still, James. *River of Earth*. Intro. by Dean Cadle. Lexington: University Press of Kentucky, 1978.

Stoneback, H.R. "Rivers of Earth and Troublesome Creeks: The Agrarianism of James Still," *The Kentucky Review* 10 (Autumn 1990): 3–26.

Woollcott, Alexander. *The Letters of Alexander Woollcott*. Ed. by Beatrice Kaufman and Joseph Hennessey. New York: The Viking Press, 1944.

# III

# THE SHORT STORIES

James Still reflected in mirror at his log house, located beside Wolfpen Creek, Knott County, Kentucky (courtesy of the Hindman Settlement School).

# Slick as a Dogwood Hoe Handle: Craft in the Short Stories

## JOE GLASER

I came somewhat late to Appalachian literature, but I came with one thing in my favor. I have always had a weakness for scofflaws and scamps—fellows whose profession and amusement it is to confound the unwary. It seems to me that a disproportionate number of Appalachian writers and characters fall into this category, and no one fits there more perfectly than James Still. Still is a supremely artful man who mixes misdirection into everything he does. In his public statements about his work, there is a large element of recreational flimflam. In his fiction, the same duplicity is put to more complicated uses. It shapes his plots, controls the unfolding of events in his stories, enriches his characterizations with unexpected turns, and even determines the basic tone of his fiction. With Still, guile is a prime ingredient of art. His trickery is essential to his work's fundamental nature and appeal.

In interviews, of course, Still presents himself as a plainspoken country man, but it would be a mistake to trust this appearance far. In fact, his life as well as his work is marked by an abhorrence of genuine simplicity. Like a number of writers he admires (Twain and Frost, to name two), he is instinctively devious. Not only is it hard to tell what he wrote and when he wrote it, but even the form into which his fiction fits is debatable. He is generally credited with two novels and three collections of stories, but these figures are misleading. The total number of episodes and stories in his hardcover work is just fifty-four, enough material for only two books the size of his classic novel *River of Earth*. The other volumes are full of repetition (much of it obscured in entertaining ways by his copyright pages), with several pieces appearing in as many as three places. As episodes migrate from one book to another, titles and names of characters change, and there are often extensive revisions as well. Throughout his career, Still has doubled and redoubled his tracks like a fox, creating a literary trail of bewildering complexity.

The precise nature of Still's writing is another problem. One book, *On Troublesome Creek*, is half novel and half short story collection; and much of Still's work seems to deliberately blur the line between novel and story as forms. Some readers feel that none of his books is

*Glaser, Joe. "Slick as a Dogwood Hoe Handle: Craft in the Stories of James Still."* Appalachian Heritage *11 (Summer 1983): 4–9. Reprinted with permission.*

really a novel at all. Even *River of Earth* is a collection of episodes so distinct that it is hard to think of the book as a continuous narrative.[1] It is another example of Still cheating the usual expectations to create something uniquely his own. It is part of his nature, even in such commonplace areas as the printing history and genre of his work, to keep his readers at arm's length and off balance.

In an ordinary writer this taste for mystification might be merely interesting, but in Still it is an essential facet of a first-rate artistic intelligence. His work's simplicity is only another of its deceptive features. A typical Still episode starts almost randomly and seems almost to meander to its conclusion. But this artlessness is pure illusion. His stories grip a reader early and sweep him along with a power that can be difficult to account for. One feels that nothing remarkable is happening, and yet the reader cannot wait to see it through. And the endings of Still's stories strike like revelations. One comes away feeling that some vital link has been established, something important affirmed. Still's best stories are as resonant as imagist poetry or good haiku — and just as difficult to analyze.

No one achieves such effects unconsciously, but Still is predictably evasive about technique. He hints that the writing process is unknowable, citing such organic maxims as "All the seeds of all the flowers of tomorrow are in the flowers of today" and "An apple is a modified leaf."[2] But he is a consummate craftsman. His writing may have points in common with flowers and apples, but it is also as sophisticated as the latest thing in programmable welders. The author's shaping touch is everywhere, and nowhere does it operate to better effect than in the seamless efficiency of his plotting, the dexterity with which he orchestrates action and detail.

I hope I can show this orchestration at work in a representative Still story, "I Love My Rooster." The version I am using is the one that appears in *On Troublesome Creek* (1941) and *The Run for the Elbertas* (1980). The story is also included in *Sporty Creek* (1977), but there it is called "Low Glory" and is substantially different.

"I Love My Rooster" is a first-person account of an eight-year-old boy's campaign to get a store-bought shirt and/or a fighting cock, but it touches on many other things as well. As the boy speaks, the life of the coal camps of Eastern Kentucky — in boom times for once — rises about us. Also evoked is a mining family (the same one Still wrote about many times under different names) of strong, conflicting personalities yoked together by even stronger loyalties and common purposes. At a deeper level, the story is also a parable of hidden beneficence, unfolding as a series of small ironic reversals moving like eddies on a broad current of providence. Narrator, characters, and readers are all subjected to a succession of disappointments, but disappointments that work ultimately for the best.

The principal conflict is between a mother and her family. She wants to save her husband's salary during good times at the mine; the others burn to spend the money as it comes in. Her determination results in a whole stack of unopened pay envelopes for the family to fall back on when the boom breaks and the father is laid off. But while the mother is winning her basic struggle, the story's foreground is crowded with other incidents. The narrator gains part ownership in a rooster and finally obtains a genuine, machine-made shirt. His friend accumulates enough money to buy a glass eye. His baby brother learns to talk. The seasons roll round to another spring.

The story is marvelously successful at infusing meaning and pattern into these commonplace events. The narrative is simple and spare, but it is alive with unspoken significance: "We lived in Houndshell mine camp the year of the coal boom, and I remember the mines worked three shifts a day. The conveyors barely ceased their rusty groaning for five months. I recollect the plenty there was, and the silver dollars rattling wherever men walked; and I recollect the goldfinches stayed that winter through, their yellow breasts turning mole-gray."[3]

Each detail in this first paragraph is echoed and elaborated as the story develops.[4] Money rattles all the way through the tale. The satisfied groaning of the conveyors underlies the whole narrative, until their sudden stopping at its conclusion signals the end of the boom. Even the finches come up again and again as hallmarks of this marvelous year. There is something wonderful about a winter mild enough to keep the finches from migrating, just as there is about the coal boom. But blessings in Still's fiction are rarely unmixed. The wonder of the finches dulls with their yellow breasts. As the year wears on, they blow "like leaves, piping their dry winter song above the conveyor's ceaseless rattle."[5]

The story makes notable use of such rueful sidelights, most of them connected some-how to the sealed envelopes hoarded in the mother's draw sack. Each hope that starts up runs straight into a snare. Announcing the boom, the father exults, "Yon blue sky might be the limit," but when the family instinctively look out the window they see "only the night sky, dark as gob smoke."[6] The main characters are outside the general prosperity. The father goes without the flashy boots he wants. Fern does not get her factory dress. Fedder Mott cannot save the money for his glass eye. The narrator lusts impotently after striped and spotted shirts and fiery roosters. And underlying these troubles are further worries. Sooner or later the boom will burst. And then there is the baby. Old enough to talk, all he does is gurgle and make bird sounds. Even the cat that moves in with the family is denied her dearest wish — a few minutes alone with their crate of salt fish.

Aside from reflecting disappointments, none of these plot elements seems connected to the others. The narrative gives the appearance of resolute naturalism. But we learn early that there is more to it than that. In an opening section that works as an overture to the story, Still gives a foretaste of his method. Like a juggler, he moves around his stage picking up details of various kinds, adding each one to the whirling mass, keeping everything in the air. The details he juggles may be unspectacular, but his treatment of them is not. I mentioned the way money, conveyor sounds, and finches flit in and out of the story as a whole; this open-ing section is brimming with the same sort of fugue-like repetition.

When the family first hears of the boom, they are in the kitchen, and it is warm. The baby is playing in a plate of shucky beans, and the mother is shaking a coffee pot to clear the grounds from its spout. All through the conversation that follows, she is distracted. She puts the pot on the burner and from time to time feeds the stove another stick of wood. The father proclaims an end to "hardscrabble skimping" and the dance of cross-purposes is on. He wants a pair of high-top boots. The baby clucks. The other children appeal for presents. The nar-rator's wish for a gamecock makes his father angry. The father's comments on gambling cause the narrator to think of one-eyed Fedder Mott, who haunts the cockpit. Not for the first time, he wishes he could look into the socket behind Fedder's eyepatch.

It gets hotter. The father envisions a supply of dried mackerel to replace the beans. The baby makes a bird sound, and the mother finally speaks. She wants to save the money the others are so intent on spending. Sweat pops out on the father's forehead, and he strips off his coat. He scorns the idea of "living barebones in the midst o' plenty."[7] The narrator renews his clamor for a store-bought shirt. But the mother is determined. "Where there's a boom one place, there's bound to be a famine in another," she says. "Coal gone high, and folks not able to pay. Fires gone out. Chaps chill and sick."[8] At this point she remembers the coffee pot may have boiled dry. Checking, she absently pokes up the fire, and the heat in the room, which has intensified along with the family's emotions, becomes unbearable. Imperceptibly, the stove has grown into a symbol. It has come to represent the mother's will to protect her family from the cold times ahead. Dimly aware of this, the narrator notices a last detail: "Drops of water began to fry on the stove. She was crying." "Be-grabbies!" exclaims the father in distress. "Stop poking that fire! This room's already hot as a ginger mill."[9]

Throughout the story, Still continues and extends this intricate weaving of details. The children get a nickel-a-week allowance and beans give way to dried fish and mush, but most of the father's pay goes unopened into the mother's cache. The father still wants his boots—he has his eye on an eighteen-dollar pair with "toes so sharp you could kick a blacksnake's eyes out."[10] But he would give all his money to hear the baby talk. The baby, meanwhile, is chiefly interested in a nanny cat that haunts the house, drawn by the mackerel.

The narrator spins off along another line of development. He agrees to accompany Fedder Mott to the cockpit if, when the time comes, he can look into the other boy's eye socket. Fedder tries selling seeds to save up for a glass eye and the narrator plans to save up for a shirt, but neither project seems promising. The gloom deepens when the narrator proves unable to slip away to the cockfights.

Then, slowly at first, the plot starts to turn, and its scattered strands begin to draw back together. The goldfinches show the way. Gray all winter, in March they return to their former selves. Their breasts are as yellow as rubbed gold. Soon after, the boys obtain their rooster. The owner of the famous Red Pyle gives his bird up for dead when it is defeated in the pit. Fedder carries it off, only to have it revive on the road home. Fedder sells a half share in the cock to the narrator for the nickels he had been saving for his shirt.

Things are not all rosy, however. The rooster has to be hidden, a proposition made difficult by its activity and crowing. Besides, the warm weather may mean the end of the coal boom. It is also clear that the baby's condition is not improving. The father reluctantly puts a word to it, acknowledging the child may be a mute. And Fedder is still short of the five dollars needed for his artificial eye. His hopes are almost extinguished. All he has left to sell are dill and rutabaga seeds.

It is with all this as background that the story launches into its conclusion, and the barriers between the separate plot elements collapse in dazzling succession. Fedder sells his half of Red Pyle to the original owner, a man in a beautiful candy-striped shirt, finally completing his glass-eye fund. As the narrator is deciding whether he too should sell, he notices the faint *per-chic-o-ree* of the finches. He realizes the conveyors have stopped at last and miners are trooping home, their lamps burning in broad daylight. He chooses to sell, but only for the striped shirt *plus* a peep into Fedder's empty socket. The sight frightens him so that he runs home, the precious shirt balled up in his hand. Going through the kitchen door with his father, he feels the sow cat stealing in between his legs. There is his mother surrounded by crumpled pay envelopes. The hoarded greenbacks are piled before her on the table, enough to build a house on the family acres in the country:

> "Hell's bangers!" Father gasped, dropping heavily upon a chair and lifting the baby to his knee; and when he could speak above his wonder, "The boom's busted. I've got no job." But he laughed, and Mother smiled.
> "I've heard already," Mother said. She laid a hand upon the money bills, flicking them under a thumb like a deck of gamble cards. "There's enough here to build a house, a house with windows looking out o' every room. And a grain left for a pair o' costy boots, a boughten shirt, a fact'ry dress, a few pretties."
> The baby opened his mouth, curling his lips, pointing a stub finger. He pointed at the old nanny smelling the fish kit.
> "Cat!" he said, big as life.—[11]

For all its homespun details and diction, "I Love My Rooster" is as elegantly plotted as a scene from Restoration drama, and almost any other Still story or episode would show the same narrative deftness. The story's clockwork construction has roots in early Southern fiction and the picaresque, but in Still's hands it has a special authority. Many of the traits for which his writing is noted—for example, his complete lack of sentimentality, his ability to mix sophisticated observation and unsophisticated observers with no sense of strain, and the convincing, *achieved* positiveness of his outlook—owe everything to his handling of complication and denouement. Terrible things can happen to his characters, and the world they live in can be grim, but at the same time Still's polished plots and the way they repeatedly bring events into unpredictable alignment work against materialism and hopelessness. The design that shapes his world is not always clear in its operation, but it is present in great things and in small, and it has sustaining power.

## Notes

1. Still supports this impression in a recent interview by maintaining that he himself has never read *River of Earth* straight through. He has only read isolated episodes as they have come up for anthologizing or reprinting. "Interview with James Still," *Appalachian Journal* 6 (Winter 1979), 130.

2. "Interview with James Still," p. 127.

3. "I Love My Rooster," in *The Run for* the *Elbertas* (Lexington: University of Kentucky, 1980), p. 1.

4. Dean Cadle sees this technique as a special feature of Still's work (Cadle calls it "foreshortening"). "Man on Troublesome," *Yale Review* 57 (1968), 249.

5. "I Love My Rooster," p. 8.

6. *Ibid.*, p. 2.

7. *Ibid.*, p. 4.

8. *Ibid.*, p. 4.

9. *Ibid.*, p. 4.

10. *Ibid.*, p. 6.

11. *Ibid.*, p. 15.

# "Menfolks Are Heathens": Cruelty in the Short Stories

## FRED CHAPPELL

My subject in these scattered and ramshackle remarks is the presence of cruelty in James Still's short stories. It is not an easy subject to define, and not always easy to recognize.

I expect that a sociologist would tell us that in a poverty-stricken society, among a people largely without education and with fiercely insular interests, a people whose daily anxieties are concerned with the effort toward bare survival, cruelty is a form of release and a necessary though regrettable mode of communal discourse. That is one indication why sociology is mostly pretentious humbug while good fiction is enduring and engaging truth.

Of course, I have set up a straw man to knock down and trample upon. So far as I know, sociologists have left Still's stories mercifully alone. That is a good thing because the author would, I believe, disagree with almost every one of a sociologist's premises about his Kentucky subject matter. If I read correctly the tone and temperament of these stories, then Still would not describe the condition on Troublesome Creek as poverty. The people have no money, it is true; but it is also true that one is poor only in comparison to someone who is wealthy, or at least better off than oneself. As no one is wealthy on Troublesome Creek, then no one is poor either. The lack of money is such an ordinary fact that, like the weather, it is simply taken for granted, usually not even noticed. If survival is sometimes a narrow squeak, it is this danger that gives relish to it and helps to define the character of the place and of the people. Poverty — insofar as it is isolated as a fact unto itself — is seen in Still's work as a positive value rather than a negative one.

The same with education. Very few of the characters in these stories have much book-learning. So what? The older characters — and even some of the younger ones — voice a deep and abiding skepticism about the value of education. They do so not because they are envious and barbarian by nature, but because they recognize institutional education as an intrusion upon their native cultural values and think of it as fanciful and irrelevant to the world in which they live. There are some important exceptions to my description, but I think it is largely correct. And it is notable as marking Still apart from his colleagues in Appalachian fiction. If there is one single large theme that dominates the bulk of

*Chappell, Fred. "'Menfolks Are Heathens': Cruelty in James Still's Short Stories." The Iron Mountain Review 2.1 (Summer 1984): 11–15. Reprinted with permission.*

Appalachian fiction, it is the coming of education to the backward knobs and hollers. From Thomas Wolfe to Jesse Stuart to Lee Smith, this story has much exercised our writers.

But education is a paradoxical theme. If the characters in these books are proud to have pulled themselves up by their multiplication tables, then they are forced to recognize that in doing so they have put some distance between themselves and the culture that nurtured them. They have become — to greater or lesser extent — outsiders, and have made themselves objects of wonder and scorn. And this queasy bit of alienation makes them, I would submit, not entirely trustworthy as reporters.

If I read Still's attitude correctly — and, to be honest about it, I'm never certain that I do — he has no illusions about education as panacea. He believes that Appalachia might have done as well without education as with it. He sides as much with the most thoroughly unlettered of his characters as with the proud readers. Education is associated with the inhumane coal mines and the scurvy attempts at industrialization as well as with the pleasures of Daniel Defoe and Jonathan Swift.

*He takes one side as much as the other:* this ability, or propensity, is one that perhaps distinguishes Still's writing from all the rest of Appalachian writing; the rest of us are apt, consciously or unconsciously, to editorialize. And to editorialize, I must say, in an ambiguous and illogical fashion. "The old way," we say, "was often harsh, unfeeling, cruel, unhealthy, and disastrous. Isn't it a shame that it is passing away?" We seemed proud of our birthright, sure enough, but are also willing to sell it for a mess of algebra.

Poverty and lack of formal education are two parts of Appalachian life that have drawn much liberal concern. Enormous and complex government programs have been set in place to combat these two evils which I believe Still does not regard absolutely as evils but simply as historic cultural conditions with their own cultural validity. I do not know how he feels about health care, another target of liberal governmental programming; perhaps he feels the same distrust.

And maybe he is correct in these views that I have imputed to him. It is difficult to understand and accept the inner values of a culture when they collide with the notions of the larger American culture about what is right and wrong. We are all too quick to leap to judgments without closely observing what it is that we judge.

Cruelty is a case in point. I certainly am not going to aver that James Still sees human cruelty as a necessary part of Appalachian culture and approves of it. I think, in fact, that he condemns it as much as a literary artist is at liberty to condone or to condemn; but I also think that he is clear-eyed about cruelty; he takes it in stride in his fiction and is at some pains never to sensationalize it.

But first we must distinguish what cruelty may be defined as in Still's work. He sees, in the first place, one mode of Appalachian social intercourse as a complicated series of dares and challenges among the males. The story called "The Stir-Off" is a good — and good-natured — example of his delineation of the sort of behavior I am talking about. In this story the young boy goes to a molasses stir-off, a traditional social event, sponsored by the family patriarch, Gid Buckheart. This rambunctious father has five sons, "tough as whang leather," and four daughters. Plumey, one of the daughters, is to be married — seemingly against her father's wishes — to a fellow named Rant Branders. This impending surprise marriage requires the presence at the shindig of Squire Letcher, a "law-square" who is to legalize the wedding. Not only does old Gid Buckheart oppose the young Rant Branders, he also seems to feel that he has an ancient score to settle with Squire Letcher. The stage is set for many different conflicts.

Which begin soon enough. Jimp Buckheart is the narrator's friend and has invited him to attend. They are about the same age—both quite young. Jimp is in favor of the marriage because the prospective bridegroom has promised to hammer out for Jimp a pair of brass knuckles. The narrator protests: "Hit's not honest to fight with knucks unless a feller's bigger'n you." But his sense of honor is assuaged when he finds out that Jimp only wants to fight his brother Bailus. Jimp, it seems, owns a pet weasel, which Bailus wishes to borrow for rabbit hunting. "Ere I'd let Bailus borrow, I'd crack its neck," Jimp says.

The two boys then make a tour of the grounds, as Jimp explains the complexities of the situation and characterizes several members of his family for his guest. Then they stop to rest in a weed patch "where noggin sticks grew tall and brittle." Here Jimp comes up with a civilized suggestion for a pastime. "Let's crack each other's skulls and see who hollers first," he says. The narrator admits that he "winced, dreading the pain," but he does not back down. "We broke five sticks apiece, and felt for goose eggs on our head."

As the story continues, the narrator takes a ride on Jimp's "fly-jenny," a kind of crude Kentucky mechanical bull like those the urban cowboys test their manhood on nowadays. Two unnamed fellows provide the party with entertainment by "rooster-fighting," that is, by boxing without the use of fists. The tough father, Gid Buckheart, challenges Squire Letcher to a fight and menaces him into falling into the "sorghum-hole." The squire comes out "green as a mossed turkle."

This event is the signal for a pitched battle. "And then it was Old Gid's boys began punching, and fellows shoved and fought to keep clear of the hole. Jimp and I were in the midst of the battle. Gid's boys soused a plenty; they soused folk invited or not, and they ducked one another too."

Then the father, Old Gid, challenges his prospective son-in-law, grasping his hand, and Rant Branders satisfies him that he is indeed a proper man. "He stood prime up to Old Gid, and wouldn't be conquered." The wedding is allowed to take place.

Then jimp must challenge his guest. "Me and you hain't never fit," he says. "Fighting makes good buddies." Of course, it is not in the other boy to withdraw. They fight, observed by Jimp's younger sister, Peep Eye, who has taken a liking to the narrator. "We fought with our fists, and it was tuggetypull, and neither of us could out-do." When they stand apart, reconciled, Peep Eye runs up, strikes the narrator in the mouth, and runs away again. "Jist a love lick," Jimp explains. "The blow hurt," the narrator says, "but I was proud." Rough and ready stuff. When Amy Vanderbilt throws a party, this is not how the guests go at it. But maybe they don't have as much fun, either.

There is, however, no cruelty in "The Stir-Off," apart from Jimp's threat to crack his pet ferret's neck. I might even go so far as to say that there is not much aggression, if by aggression we mean serious intent to do another person bodily harm. Bodily pain is not regarded as harm but almost as the memorable part of friendly communication. The pain is real enough, and the narrator admits that he dreads it—but there is no anger in it. In order to stage the final fight that makes them "good buddies," the two boys have to trade ritual insults, working up enough artificial cause to make the blows convincing.

But we can admit that it takes a special cultural context to enjoy this kind of party. The cheerful willingness to give and take painful blows—especially to take them—is not a talent all of us are born with; and I imagine that an observer with a different cultural background, someone from Rome, say, or from Newport, Rhode Island, might see this molasses stir-off as a convocation of murderous lunatics. Still intends it as an account of a genial and quite well-behaved social event. "The Stir-Off" is a happy story.

It is in unhappy stories that we find cruelty, and it is interesting to compare the cheerful violence of "The Stir-Off" with the sullen nonviolent cruelty we find in another story, "The Moving."

The central narrative of "The Moving" is quite simple, as with most of Still's work. Hardstay mine has closed down and family is moving out, probably for good. Other members of the community come out to see them off. These include Lo Tramble, a jeering man with a misshapen sense of humor, Cece Goodloe, a mischievous fellow, Rig Sommers, a retarded person who gets events reversed in his head, and Sula Basham, "tall as a butterweed, and with a yellow locket swinging her neck like a clockweight." There are some other characters who mostly just stand about.

The people of the settlement bid the family goodbye, exchange a few remarks among themselves, and then the family departs. That's all there is, in probably not more than 3000 words. Yet in these few words a great deal is shown and intimated; there are many impressive shifts of tone and feeling and judgment.

I surmise that in order to interpret a possible reading of "The Moving" we must understand that the mining community is sad to see the family leave. We are not told that the citizens are sad; sentimentality is not James Still's stock in trade. The one indication the reader gets is in the widowed Sula Basham's exchange with the mother. "You were a comfort when my man lay in his box," she tells her. "I hain't forgetting. Wish I had a keepsake to give you, showing I'll allus remember." The mother replies that she will always remember Sula, and Sula says, "I'll be proud to know it."

From these brief remarks we learn that the departing family is of a kindly nature and has fulfilled its community responsibilities. It is a family well thought of. But the sorrow felt at their departure is couched in language that is mostly scornful and querulous. Sill Lovelock says, "Hit's mortal sin to make gypsies of a family. I say as long's a body has got a rooftree, let him roost under it." Lovelock is not accustomed to voicing sadness; words of frustrated anger are as close as he can come, and his last farewell is: "You're making your bed in Hell!" It is likely that the mother and father can interpret the sad feelings behind Lovelock's harsh sentences, but the story is told by a young boy who cannot. For him it is a comfortless leavetaking.

During the process of departure, Cece Goodloe pulls two practical jokes, "rusties," as they are called in Appalachian dialect. He snatches off the hat of the retarded man, Hig Sommers, and he unhooks the harnessing of the mare to the departing wagon. "Father smiled while adjusting the harness. Oh, he didn't mind a clever trick." In fact, this sort of rusty really is regarded as a clever trick, but it may seem to the reader a particularly inopportune time for one to take place. It is not in itself a cruelty, though the occasion may make it seem so to the narrator.

What is most cruel in this story is the ill treatment of Sula Basham, the tall widow-woman, by a character named Loss Tramble. As soon as he lays eyes upon her he begins to torment. "If I had a woman that tall," he says, "I'd string her with gourds and use her for a martin pole." And the young narrator records the fact that a "dry chuckle rattled it, the crowd."

Again, when the father wants someone to return his house-key to the mining commissary, Tramble volunteers. "I'll deliver that key willing if you'll take this beanpole widow-woman along some'eres and git her a man." Sula remarks with some heat that it's a certain fact there's no man in Hardstay worth her time. Tramble will not let go his single ugly joke. "I allus did pity a widow-woman," he says a few moments later. "In this gethering there ought to be one single man willing to marry the Way Up Yonder woman." By now Sula has had enough of this guying and takes a threatening step towards Tramble — and Sula is a formidable physical specimen. "I want none o' your pity pie," she says.

I hope that you-all are as happy as I am to discover that Sula's patience finally runs out.

In the last paragraph of the story, the narrator hears the smashing of glass; someone has heaved a rock through a window of the family's deserted house, and the boy looks "back upon the camp as upon the face of the dead." More happily, he sees "the crowd fall back from Sula Basham, tripping over each other. She had struck Loss Tramble with her fist, and he knelt before her, fearing to rise." My heart leaps for joy when I read that sentence. Earlier in this episode, the mother has felt constrained to calm Sula, to soothe her in her vexation at Loss Tramble, in her anger at the heartless crowd gathered round. "The Devil take 'em," she says. "Menfolks are heathens. Let them crawl in their own dirt."

*Menfolks are heathens:* that seems to be about the size of it. The mother, in her remark here, shows the depth of her weary resignation to what she regards as an inescapable fact. Men are heartless violent creatures who lack not only gallantry and any respect for the dead, but also have not the least conception that other people have feelings and may be hurt. Men have, in her view, no true sense of humor; humor is for these heathens merely an excuse for cruelty, merely a pretext for excoriating the feelings of another person in a socially acceptable way. The worst is, there is not even that much purpose in it. Tramble intends to vex Sula; the point of the joke is to get her riled and cause her to lose her temper. But he cannot see how far he has transgressed the bounds of charity, of ordinary human decency. It is not as much his petty malevolence, but his ignorant blindness that makes him a "heathen"; he has not the imagination to place himself in another person's shoes. That kind of sympathy is as alien to him as the concept of the neutrino would be.

This blindness, this total incomprehension, on the part of men is summed up in "The Moving" in the figure of Hig Sommers, the witty. Hig is not a cruel person, but well-meaning; but he is retarded and reacts to situations in a backward, upside-down manner. When the departing father wants someone to take his key to the commissary, Hig volunteers. "I'll fotch it," he says. "I'm not a-wanting it fotched," the father says. "You've got it back'ards, Hig. I'm wanting it tuck."

And the final image we get of the mining settlement as we leave it behind forever is that of the witty. "And only Hig Sommers was watching us move away. He stood holding up his breeches, for someone had cut his galluses with a knife. He thrust one arm into the air, crying, 'Hello, hello!'"

These are the last sentences of the story and they follow immediately those sentences which had made me so happy, the ones in which Sula Basham knocks down Loss Tramble with a blow so powerful that he is afraid to get up again. Such a compact juxtaposition of contradictory emotions is rare in fiction and, I would think, extremely difficult to bring off. There are many stories that leave the reader not knowing whether to laugh or cry, but there are very few stories that leave him actually disposed to do both.

We know who has cut the galluses of Hig Sommers' overalls. It was Cece Goodloe, who also unhooked the trace chains of the family wagon. To cut the galluses of someone's overalls is regarded as an acceptable and even a clever rusty; it is recorded as such other times in Still's fiction. But surely it is not acceptable, surely it is despicable, to pull rusties on a retarded person. If, up to this point in the story, we had regarded Cece Goodloe as a mischievous but probably harmless joker, our perceptions of him must now change. He goes into the crowd with the rest of the "dead," the "heathens." And perhaps we were wrong all along. Maybe these men of the mining community feel no inarticulate sadness at the family's departure; maybe they are only little, sneaking, hard, unfeeling men who lack the courage to move from this one place they know and are envious of the father's courage. It is Sula who tells them that "This mine ham' opening ag'in. Hit's too nigh dug out." And their answer to that is: "They's Scripture ag'in a feller hauling off the innocent."

I admitted early on that I am often uncertain how to read some of Still's finely laconic stories. And here I don't know how to read the character of this group of men. Are they saddened at the family's leaving but with no way to voice their sadness? Or are they only contemptibly ugly little creatures to be left to stew in their own pettiness?

I think that I finally incline to the latter reading for two reasons. The first reason is that the family is leaving Hardstay, which is a mining settlement. Mining communities are generally seen in Still's fiction as bitter ugly places that one ought to escape as soon as possible. That powerful novel, *River of Earth,* is careful to oppose the hell of a mining community with the paradise of a mountain farm. Nowhere in Still's work is the mining settlement life seen as a happy experience; an individual family may be happy at times—as in "I Love My Rooster"—but as a social and communal life it is usually portrayed as being quite dreadful.

That is an extraneous reason for my seeing the group of men in "The Moving" in such an ugly light. It is not an entirely convincing reason because of the fact that no writer is obliged to be consistent in his attitudes from story to story, from one literary work to another. Each single story or poem has its own needs and laws, and both writer and reader must be content to abide by them.

My other reason for preferring a gloomy reading of the characters of "The Moving" is attached to a detail in the story. When we first meet the tall woman, Sula Basham, we see that she has "a yellow locket swinging her neck like a clockweight." It is a characteristic of Still's writing to portray scenes with dark or gray backgrounds and then to set just one single bright primary color against this background. In "The Moving" the yellow locket is this single bright color. I have already quoted the passage in which the mother and Sula exchange endearments and in which Sula wishes she had a keepsake to give the mother to remember her by. The mother has already, a few minutes earlier, looked at the locket, "not convetously, but in wonder." The little boy thinks of his mother's "unpierced ear lobes where never a bob had hung, the warm stems of her fingers never circled by gold, her plain bosom no pin-pretty had ever hooked." Then, when the father at last clucks up the mare and the family drives away with that cheerful admonition, "You're making your bed in Hell!" ringing behind them, the little boy makes a discovery. "Then it was," he tells us, "I saw the gold locket about Mother's neck, beating her bosom like a heart." Sula has given the mother as keepsake what was her own one thing of value.

The importance of the locket is not only to show the love and friendship that obtains between the two women, feelings of a sort the miners can never know or participate in. It is important that the mother is carrying it away, taking out of Hardstay the last bit of bright color. There is to be not one speck of joy left in Hardstay, not for the callous men and—more terribly—not for Sula either. The tall woman is condemned to stay behind to endure the insults and the mockery of these men, perhaps—most terrible of all—to marry one of them. Small wonder then that the boy looks back upon the camp "as upon the face of the dead."

All this is dramatized, as I noted, in a story probably not more than 3000 words long. "The Moving" ought to be for writers an object lesson to show what effects can be got out of cruelty in fiction when that cruelty is not gratuitous or sensationalized or used as an excuse for the author to indulge in a sermon. When it is observed dispassionately, drawn in a work as a cultural condition, it can arouse in readers feelings not of anger or indignation but of tenderness and compassion and regret. To get a sharp idea of what Still has accomplished, we have only to imagine how Erskine Caldwell might have handled the same material.

Would James Still agree with the mother's weary generalization? I doubt it. I don't think he sees all menfolks as heathens; that was just the attitude that "The Moving" called for. In another equally masterful story, "Snail Pie," it is the woman's coy sentimentality that amounts to cruelty, in a more complex situation.

Cruelty in Still's fiction is a large topic, and that is why I chose two comparatively simple stories to talk about in my limited space of time. I think that it is a subject worth pursuing for some scholar more intrepid and more adventurous than I. But it must be a scholar who understand the ways of Appalachia and who can discern what cruelty actually amounts to in this context.

Here I am content simply to let the topic show how beautifully Still can handle a single one of the elements of his fiction. I might have chosen any other subject matter — animals, memory, girlhood, money — and examined it in his work and have come to the same conclusion: that James Still is one of the best writers we ever had.

# "The Nest": Images of
# Lost Intimacy

## RON WILLOUGHBY

In *The Poetics of Space,* Gaston Bachelard refers to "primal images, images that bring out the primitiveness in us" (Bachelard 91). Primal images conjure similar feelings, visions, and emotions in all human beings, though the intensity of these images is certain to vary greatly. The concept of a "nest" is one such primal image, producing predictable feelings in all who hear the word. Bachelard uses the term to refer almost exclusively to the homes of birds, but acknowledges its poetic use in the broader context of a cozy habitation of any sort, and most readers will respond to the word in that broader context. We all know, to one degree or another, how it feels to withdraw to one's own small corner of the universe, how it feels to be physically and spiritually close to other human beings or to be alone in comforting surroundings. These feelings, evoked by the concept of "nest," are generally described by words like "contentment," "security," "comfort," and "happiness."

Another primal image to which Bachelard refers almost in passing is that of "lostness." Everyone has been lost at one time or another, if not physically, then surely spiritually. We are all familiar with the blend of fear, confusion, and frustration engendered by being lost, and that familiarity produces an instant rapport with another who is lost.

Bachelard makes an interesting connection between the primal images of lostness and nests. There is, he says, sadness underlying the association of a nest with the home: "If we return to the old home as to a nest, it is because memories are dreams, because the home of other days has become a great image of lost intimacy" (100). A nest is a place ignorant of the world's hostility, a place of well-being and security (103). When we are beset by the world, we long for the comfort and security of the nest, and our attempt to return to the nest (our old home) is evidence of the pain we feel.

In his short story "The Nest," James Still makes use of these two intertwined primal images. Several different nest images are used to intensify the impact of this story of a lost child. The lostness of a child and her yearning to return to the nest evoke immediate empathetic feelings in the reader, feelings the writer can build upon as the story moves toward its conclusion. Having called upon such images to evoke these responses, however, the writer must be careful to avoid losing the story to sentimentality. Still does this by telling the story

*Willoughby, Ron. "The Nest: Images of Lost Intimacy." In* The Poetics of Appalachian Space. *Ed. by Parks Lanier, Jr. Knoxville: The University of Tennessee Press, 1991. Pp. 95–101. Reprinted with permission.*

103

in a spare, dispassionate narrative that lets the situation speak for itself, relying on the power of the images to carry the story. For this reason, Still wastes no time in introducing the two principal images. The nest image appears in the title, and lostness in the first paragraph.

"The Nest" is the story of Nezzie Hargis, who is, as the story opens, resting on a clump of broomsage while the wind flows "with the sound of water" through leafless trees on the ridge (Still 43). She is cold, tired, and lost. Nezzie's struggle to find her way is the focus of the story, and we learn about her in flashbacks as the story progresses. Each of these flashbacks contains at least one nest image; and, with one exception, all the nest images serve a dual purpose. First, they tell us more about Nezzie; and second, they intensify our appreciation of Nezzie's dilemma by contrasting her cold, lonely lostness with the warmth and companionship for which anyone in her situation would yearn.

As Nezzie rests on the clump of broomsage, we encounter the first of the nest images in the story. She is thinking of her home, of her father, the baby, and Mam, "the woman her father brought home to live with them after [Nezzie's] mother went away" (43). We learn that Nezzie is a young girl who is, as her father reminds her, "half past six by the calendar clock" (43). She is old enough to walk by herself to Aunt Clissa's, where she will spend the night while her father and Mam visit Nezzie's sick grandfather. Nezzie wanted to go visit her grandfather, and most of all she did not want to leave the baby. But Mam tells Nezzie that "young'uns get underfoot around the sick" (43). Mam apparently considers Nezzie to be "underfoot" most of the time, constantly crying at her to "go tend the chickens" (44). Even Nezzie's devotion to the baby, with whom she enjoys playing, often prompts Mam to send her out. Nezzie's father, siding with Mam, offers to bring Nezzie "a pretty" if she will go willingly, and he instructs her simply to follow the cattle path that they usually take. But the cow paths become a "puzzle of trails going nowhere" (43), and after hours of searching for the right path, her hands are numbed by the winter wind, her feet have become "a burden," and she is resting, wondering what to do (43).

Perhaps, she proposes, she could find her way back home. The house would be locked, but she could stay in the brooder house with the chicks. Here we encounter the second of the nest images in the story. She remembers the warmth and closeness of the brooder as she played with the chicks, feeling "snug and contented, almost as happy as before her mother went away" (45). It is an inviting memory, but then she thinks of smoke rising from the chimney of her aunt and uncle's house, of the dogs dashing out to meet her, and of the warmth of the hearth, and it is a more compelling vision. Deciding to try again to find her way across the ridge, Nezzie rises and starts upward.

She still cannot find her way, but now darkness is moving up the side of the ridge, and Nezzie feels she cannot go back. She is very cold, her hands so numb she cannot tie her shoelaces. She longs for the sound of a cow or cowbell to guide her, but there is only the sound of the wind and a spring that she cannot find. She sees a rabbit's bed, steaming pellets beside it. This nest image, unlike all the others, is not comforting to her. It is cold and empty, like her home with her parents gone. She takes little note of it, but it foreshadows the image that ends the story.

As she continues the climb, Nezzie begins hallucinating, hearing the baby's voice. Pushing on through the vines and briars, she reaches the crest of the ridge at dusk. She can see no light, hear no sound. She calls out, but there is no answer. She hurries on, her teeth chattering, and at about dark, she comes to a rock wall. She sinks to the ground in disappointment. Hungry and thirsty, she imagines her aunt's table — "biscuits smoking, ham fussing in grease, apple cake rising" (48). But now the stronger image is the saucer of water left for the chicks in the brooder. She thinks of her father and his pride in the baby, a boy he is certain will one day amount to something, an opinion which Mam does not share. When Nezzie thinks of the baby, she jerks back to reality. She decides to go back home and spend the night in the brooder. But her gait is stiff-legged now, and it so dark that she can scarcely see the trees. Stumbling and falling in the cold silence, she eventually curls up in a ball, exhausted. She thinks of her father again, seeing him at her grandfather's house, by the hearth. She thinks of the baby, of holding him on her lap. And she thinks of her mother, of being in the "warm, safe nest of her arms" (51); and Nezzie falls asleep. This is the last of the nest images before the ending, perhaps the most powerful of all to Nezzie, and it sets the stage for the final image soon to come.

Nezzie awakes the next morning in the snow, to the sound of an ax in the distance. She does not hurt now, as she starts back down the ridge in the direction from which she had come. She is unaware of the cows that pass her, unaware of the briars stealing her bonnet, unaware of losing her shoe in the snow. She does not hear the fox horn blow, the horn her father said he would blow to call her home. She is so sleepy, too sleepy to bear it. She crawls into a clump of broomsage, curls into a ball, and "rounded the grass with her body. It was like a rabbit's bed. It was a nest" (52).

The story ends suddenly, just when there seems to be hope that Nezzie may yet find her way home. She has survived her night on the cold ridge; there are sights and sounds to guide her now. Surely she will manage to get home. But it is not to be. She is simply too drowsy from the cold, and she just wants to curl up in her mother's lap. The contrast between Nezzie's mother's lap and the nest she finally settles into is stunning in its poignancy. We want Nezzie to find a nest, a haven, to return to the comfort and security of her home. Our natural tendency to hope for such a result is reinforced in a remarkable, subtle way by the title the author has chosen for his story. Because of the images the title calls to mind, the story — though generally bleak — always seems to hold some promise, or at least some suggestion, of a happy resolution. Nothing in the narrative itself leads us to believe that anything other than disaster is imminent, but nevertheless a hopeful tone underlies the narrative. This is partly the result of the alternation in the narrative between the despair of being lost and the inviting, longing images of safe havens. But the hopeful tone is set primarily by the title, which, due to the power of the image, leads us to expect, consciously or subconsciously, that Nezzie will somehow find her way. The title is therefore an integral part of the story, for the choice was not made to trick the reader, but to lend ironic power to the story's conclusion by allowing us to maintain hope for Nezzie to the very end. And just as the title suggests, Nezzie does indeed find a nest. But it is not the nest of our images. The nest Nezzie finds is not the warmth of her aunt and uncle's home, with its friendly dogs and laden table. It is not the comfort and security of her mother's lap. It is, instead, the cold emptiness of the abandoned rabbit's nest, and it is this ironic inversion of the image of nests that intensifies the impact of the story's conclusion.

The theme of lostness and its interrelationship with nests is a universal one, one that speaks to us across time and space. Individuals and groups of people throughout history have wandered in search of haven — sometimes succeeding, as often failing. These wanderings have been chronicled — sometimes factually, sometimes in fiction — by skillful writers ranging from the unknown author(s) of the book of Exodus to Homer and on into modern times. It is an inexhaustible theme because lostness itself is universal and apparently inexhaustible as well. So it is not surprising that writers find themselves using this theme; nor is it surprising that good writing on such a theme continues to have appeal. All good writing, while set in a particular time and place, has the ability to rise above its parochial setting and speak to us across time and space of important human emotions. "The Nest" is such a story. Many parallels can be drawn between the story of Nezzie Hargis and the plight of other individuals or groups. But it seems especially appropriate that a story with an Appalachian setting should speak so strongly about the Appalachians from the coal fields of eastern Kentucky, southwestern Virginia, and southern West Virginia.

During the 1940s and early 1950s, the Second World War and then the mechanization of coal mining lured or drove thousands of Appalachian families out of the mountains. Usually out of work, they felt, as Nezzie did, underfoot—stepchildren of an indifferent stepmother. And, like Nezzie, they set out for a place where they hoped to find security—the industrial cities of the North. They found themselves in a strange land, where networks of roads must have looked to them like Nezzie's cow paths—puzzles going nowhere. Unlike Nezzie, however, most of the migrant Appalachians managed to find their way.

Another Appalachian author, Harriette Simpson Arnow, has written the definitive novel about this out-migration. The characters in the Nevels family epitomize the various reactions individual Appalachians had to their new surroundings. Some, like Clovis, the father, put the old life and ways behind them and blended readily into their new surroundings. Others, like Reuben, the oldest son, never adjusted and went back where they came from, back home. Some found refuge in empty nests, and like Nezzie, met with tragedy. The daughter, Cassie, for example, found comfort in her imaginary friend, Callie Lou; and when that friend was banished from the house, Cassie began to secretly meet her outdoors. A spot under the train car must have seemed to Cassie a close, cozy place—a nest—in which to meet Callie Lou, and the rail a convenient place to sit. But when the train began to move, Cassie's nest, like Nezzie's, became a place not of haven but of tragedy.

Many Appalachian emigrants—the most visible group if not the most numerous—were like Gertie, the mother. They managed to come to terms with their new existence, but they never shook the feeling that home is somewhere else, where they came from rather than where they currently were. And like Gertie they longed to return to their old homes "as to a nest because the home of other days has become a great image of lost intimacy" (Bachelard 100). They yearned for the nest-like intimacy of their homes in the hills and hollows, but realized that they could not return, at least not permanently. So they left work on Friday, drove into the night to get home, and returned north late Sunday evening. In the fifties, on any weekend and all summer, Appalachian streets and roads were full of cars with Illinois, Ohio, and Michigan license plates.

The group that left the coal fields in the 1940s and 1950s is aging now, and aging seems to strengthen the impulse to nostalgic yearning. There is always that fondness for the earlier time and place where everything was—or at least seemed—happier, more secure; but that fondness seems particularly strong in the Appalachian heart. Displaced Appalachians, forced from their homes at the point of an economic bayonet, adjusted as best they could. Most adjusted well, a few not so well. But, to one degree or another, all hold images of lost intimacy, of home, which they would like to regain—if only for a moment—in whatever way they can. So they spend a week's vacation visiting old friends and old places. Or they hold reunions for towns that no longer exist. Or they subscribe to weekly newspapers from hometowns that in some cases they haven't visited in years or even decades. Like Nezzie, they long to return, somehow, someway, to the nest.

## Works Cited

Bachelard, Gaston. *The Poetics of Space*. Trans. Maria Jolas. Boston: Beacon, 1969.

Still, James. *Pattern of a Man and Other Stories*. Frankfort, KY: Gnomon Press, 1976.

# Creative Energy in "Mrs. Razor"

## JOYCE A. HANCOCK

*"The only image of Appalachia and Appalachian people that can sustain us is the image that Appalachians themselves create."— Jim Wayne Miller (quoted on the back cover of* Dialogue with a Dead Man, *1978).*

The narrator of James Still's story "Mrs. Razor" tells about a problem at home. Things just aren't right when the story begins. The family is eating supper too early, while "the day still held and the chickens had not yet gone to roost in the gilly trees." And everyone is all upset: sister Elvy is "crying behind the stove, her throat was raw with sobbing." The narrator and his brother are at table, but they are not eating their bread, Mother and Father are at odds. Only the fire in the stove behaves normally at this uneasy mealtime: "The firebox of the Cincinnati stove winked, the iron flowers of the oven throbbed with heat."

Things are all out of kilter in this household because Elvy, one of the children, has imaginatively constructed a parallel domestic existence for herself, and a tragic one at that: "She was married, to hear her tell it, and had three children and a lazy shuck of a husband who cared not a mite for his own and left his family to live on her kin. The thought had grown to truth in her mind."

As we give attention to the first paragraph of Mr. Still's story, we see a pattern beginning to emerge. It is an ancient pattern, which has shaped civilizations as surely as it has shaped short stories, and is a pattern given many names. Here, the pair of energies shaping the story is expressed as a conflict between Mother and Father, and the nature of which is contained in these words "Mother tipped a finger to her lips, motioning Father to hush. Father's voice lifted: —"

From the information given us in the first paragraph of "Mrs. Razor," we do not know what event has caused the domestic crisis to emerge, but Father's first words, "We'll have to do something about that child," give two hints about the fundamental forces involved. First, we know that the disorder of events in the household stems from the behavior of one of the children in the family. Second, it is clear that Father's solution is one of corrective action, and, as is confirmed by the father's next words, concerned aggression. There is a problem,

*Hancock, Joyce. "Creative Energy in James Still's 'Mrs. Razor.'" Appalachian Heritage 8 (1980): 38–46. Reprinted with permission.*

and Father wants to "do something," to take control, but Mother counsels patience and passivity: "Mother tipped a finger to her lips, motioning Father to hush."

So we, as readers, are vicariously and immediately involved in a crisis of world views, a difference of opinion about how to deal with a disruptive situation. We recognize right away that ancient and basic division of outlooks, a primordial pull between letting things be (Mother's way) and trying to do something to make them right (Father's way). Father, his voice lifting, is heard first, while, significantly, Mother's only words concern nourishing the family. Father's next words, carrying over into the second paragraph, emphasize his response to the problem and give us a clue as to its nature: "I figure a small thrashing would make her leave off this foolish notion."

"Foolish notion." Aha! So the conflict is generated over the question of how to manage a mind. In particular, Elvy's mind, her imagination. And it is Elvy's "foolish notion," we learn at this point in the story, which has led to suppers being served earlier than usual, and to the display of Mother's and Father's difference of opinion.

Structurally, Elvy's imagination, a nonmaterial phenomenon, has had an effect on the material, lived order of the family: The effect is expressed in terms of a temporal disruption, the early supper, and what disrupts time disrupts life. Although the displacement of one meal, objectively speaking, may not seem worthy of note, here, in terms of the story's structure, that early supper is emblematic of the natural order of things being out of joint. The resolution of the story depends upon their being set right again.

And the thing to be set right, from Father's viewpoint, is Elvy. More specifically, he wishes to re-establish the previous harmony of the household by somehow dispelling the alternative order of experience provided by Elvy's imagination. Elvy's unsuitable and usurping order has come to bear on all members of the family. Her fiction is powerful enough to create a world in which little brother Morg, who is not a fiction-maker, eventually participates. It is precisely when Morg becomes caught up in Elvy's fiction, and cries at the supper table, that Father does take action that reconciles Elvy's fictional world with the family's life. But that action, as we discover, succeeds only because Father employs an extraordinary and creative measure to solve this problem — a measure that resides in the realm of the creative imagination and in Morg's ensuing belief in that alternative structure. Father finally takes the family on a real journey to a made-up place, a journey which reconciles the male and the female ways, a journey which brings sleep, and, finally, a return home for them all.

With that resolution in sight, let us take a look at the story as it is told to us by the narrator. "Mrs. Razor" has at its core an impressive lesson about the practical application of the creative powers of the mind. In short, "Mrs. Razor" demonstrates that fiction-makers hold a powerful influence upon people in the world who do not create fiction, and that the invented worlds or creative people combine and move upon each other to shape the worlds and beliefs of the more literal-minded. Elvy's fiction-making has got Morg's family into a domestic dilemma, and Father's real action, which finally embraces the fictional models involved, resolves the dilemma.

Of the five members of the family, three are fiction-makers and two are not. Mother and Morg are not fiction-makers. Mother has few words in the story; she exists, on a level other than the predominantly verbal, as a passive, but sure and receptive, force, willing to trust nature to take its course, advising peaceful silence and providing food for the family. Little Morg is not a fiction-maker, and, appropriately, has no speech at all in the story. Even the narrative flashbacks portray Morg as being wordless. Morg is a believer, not a make-believer. And Morg, speechless little brother that he is in the story, provides a valuable example about the consequences of irresponsible fiction-making, as we shall soon see.

The three fiction-makers in the story are Elvy, her father, and the unnamed brother who tells the story. And their fictions are as unlike each other as can be. Each represents a different order of creative activity, differences that become apparent when we look at the ways in which the creative impulse is expressed, the effect it has on others, and the range and quality of imagination involved.

The narrator is the truest artist in the story. His imagination, he tells us, enables him to exist in the world any way he chooses. The only qualification the narrator places upon his creative powers is that he retain his masculine identity: "I could be any man body," he says. Within that limitation, the narrator is totally free to act out any way of being he wants. The words he chooses to define the extreme variants of his imaginative existence, aptly enough for the theme of this story, reflect the opposition in the world-view externalized by his father and mother, an opposition as basic and integral to the human consciousness as the two hemispheres of the brain.

Listen to the narrator's imaginative alternatives, which provide absolute freedom for the creative person: "I could play at being Brother Hemp Leckett, climb onto a chopblock and preach to the fowls; or I could be Round George Parks, riding the creeks, killing all who crossed my path; I could be any man body." His choices here embody passivity and aggression; nature's mystic gentleness and nature's destructive violence, Saint Francis of Assisi on the one hand and Saint George the dragon-killer on the other. The narrator, having internalized the extreme variants of action in the world (variants sometimes called feminine and masculine, or anima and animus) and having accepted the co-existence of these extremes, represents a creative vision which is whole and healthy, and one which does not impinge upon the external order of events in the story. The brute element in the human psyche is experienced by the narrator creatively, safely, and responsibly, because he understands the integrative value of make-believe. Brutishness—a clear and forceful element in Appalachian fiction (Wilma Dykeman and Harriette Simpson Arnow portray the Brute excellently, as does Still in other fictions)—is portrayed in three ways in "Mrs. Razor." It is implicit, but overcome, in the Mother/Father conflict; it is handled as an internalized balancing force by the narrator; and finally, Elvy invents a mean-man persona (associated in her mind with "Old Scratch," evil) to balance out the incompleteness of "little girlism." But Elvy is devastated by her own projection of the brutish, and in the process, involves her family in that projection in an unhealthy manner. This narrator-brother, however, is a wise observer: he sees the workings of Elvy's imagination, of Morg's mind, of his father's tales of Biggety Creek, and comments without passing judgment. He acts out the saint and the sinner, he tells his story, and, like Mother, lets things be.

Father's fictionalizing is of another sort. His fictions are designed to have an effect upon his children's minds, although he himself does not participate in his own fiction. Father's fiction is utilitarian: his stories of Biggety Creek are designed to instruct the children against the follies of high-brow folks.

When, in Elvy's imaginative existence, her husband, Razor, dies, she wants to go to Biggety Creek to get her children before the gypsies come. "'Is he doornail dead?' Father had asked. And he smiled to hear Biggety Creek named, the Nowhere Place he had told us once at table. Biggety Creek where heads are the size of water buckets, where noses are turned up like old shoes, women wear skillets for hats, and men screw their breeches on, and where people are so proper that they eat with little fingers pointing, and one pea at a time." Satiric, didactic, and riddled with the kind of nonsense that is supposed to delight children, Father's stories of Biggety Creek make an impression upon six-year-old Elvy and come to play an important part in her "foolish notion." The narrator points out the purposefulness of Father's fictions by commenting that "Father rarely missed a chance to preach us a sermon." But Father's sermonizing has an effect he didn't anticipate. Whether or not the sermon on manners was lost on Elvy, she was impressed with "the Nowhere Place" and came to include Biggety Creek in her imaginative vision. She insists, to Father's consternation, that she be taken there forthwith to save her children. And it is, ironically enough, a family trip to Nowhere Place of Biggety Creek that brings about a resolution to the conflicts embodied in the story.

While Father's fiction is sermonizing and purposeful, the narrator's reconciling and liberating, Elvy's fiction is realistic and imitative. And confining. Elvy has imagined for herself a sorry existence, and one she may have witnessed in the lives played out around her. The narrator is well aware of the difference between the creative life and life in the ordinary world of events, but Elvy becomes caught up in her own imagination and is made miserable by it: "Elvy imagined herself old and thrown away by a husband, and she kept believing."

Elvy's persistence in her imaginative existence, and her growing desperation with the events that make up her fiction world, precipitate the family crisis that is the focus of "Mrs. Razor." As Elvy's misery continues, more and more of the normal family life is disrupted.

When the narration takes place, at suppertime, the force of Elvy's fiction has reached an intolerable level as far as Father is concerned. He has tried to humor her throughout the summer, and tease her out of her notion. Once, the narrator recounts, while shaving Father was attempting to humor Elvy, as he had done "the summer long … trying to shake her belief." He asked her, "What ever made you marry a lump of a husband who won't come home, never furnishes a cent?"

At this point the story achieves one of its most delightful matrices between fiction and fact. Morg and the narrator are standing by Father while he shaves, waiting "to spread leftover lather on our faces and scrape it off with a kitchen knife." The boys naturally imitate adult life here, as Elvy has in her creation of the hard life of an abandoned woman, but Elvy prolongs her imitation to a point of disorder. As the boys wait to pretend to be men and shave with the kitchen knife, Father, for the moment participating in Elvy's fiction, "glanced slyly at Elvy. 'What's his name? Upon my honor, I haven't been told.'" In a criss-cross of fact and fiction, Elvy pulls her answer out of the air of the real world:

> Elvy looked up. Her eyes glazed in thought. "He's called Razor."
> "Given name or family?" Father asks.
> "Just Razor."

What an innocent, childish, honest maneuver Elvy makes here. Her father's question left a vacuum in her imaginative structure, so she fills it quickly and surely, with six-year-old ingenuity, by pulling the answer out of the real world, like a magician materializing a dove.

But Elvy's imaginary marriage to Razor begins to wear thin with Father. She becomes a widow, "the news having come in an unknown way" and after telling her mother, "waited dry-eyed and shocked until Father rode in from the fields in middle afternoon, and she met him at the barn gate to choke out her loss."

Fiction meets fiction when Elvy tells Father that they must go to Biggety Creek right away "and fetch my young'uns ere the gypsies come…. They're left alone." Father asks her, "Do you know the road to Biggety Creek?" "Elvy nodded. Father keened his eyes to see what manner of child was his own, his face lengthening and his patience wearing thin. He grabbed his hat off and clapped it angrily against his leg; he strode into the barn, fed the mules, and came to the house with Elvy tagging after and weeping."

Father's already short temper is detonated when, at the early supper he has ordered, Morg converts to Elvy's invented life. Morg's progression from disbelief, to half-belief, to total belief in Elvy's fiction convincingly illustrates how the forces of the creative (or destructive) imagination influence the lives of those who *do not* create imaginary worlds.

Morg is the only character who undergoes a change of belief during the events of the story. The narrator tells us at the beginning of the story that "Morg couldn't make-believe. Morg was just Morg." But Morg has the capacity for believing, and as Elvy continues to spend her days in her imagined unhappiness, Morg begins to be caught up in it too. "Once we spied on her in the grape arbor making to put a jacket on a baby that wouldn't hold still. She slapped the air, saying, 'Hold up, young'un!' Morg stared, half believing."

Morg's participation in Elvy's fiction grows, until he becomes completely engrossed by the strength of his sister's fiction: "As we sat at supper that late afternoon, listening to Elvy sob behind the stove, Morg began to stare into his plate and would eat no more. He believed Elvy. Tears hung on his chin." Morg's nature remains constant, a nature that is trusting, but he undergoes a conversion in belief.

But Morg provides "Mrs. Razor" with its most profound political point, one that deserves attention by all word people, whether politicians or poets. Morg's mind is the sort that, once it subscribes to a belief system, performs actions based on that belief and gives shape to the social and physical world. The Morg-like mind is given shape and direction by the liveliest, most forceful view of the world presented to it. Once made up, minds the likes of Morg's will act in utter conviction and trust on the basis of the world-view by which it has been captivated. None of these observations should be taken as negative criticism of the Morg mentality. Most of us are Morgs: we believe in the world as presented to us—by our parents, our professors, our politicians, our writers. And then we act on that belief to shape the world.

Take, for example, this simplified view of the far-reaching consequences of projected world-view (the accuracy of views is not a question here, but rather the persistence and strength of them). Once, say, many years ago, an articulate and progressive-minded person with convincing word-power came to Appalachia and saw that people didn't have much money or many things. Say his world-view made him see the world in such a way that not having many things signified poverty, which, in its turn, signified misery. So this man, acting in good faith, began to tell Appalachians how poor and miserable they were. And, like Morg, most Appalachians believed because this man presented his view persistently and forcefully. People began to think poor and get help and more money, to be happier. They acted in innocence and good faith, with unmalicious efforts to improve their lot and the lots of their children.

But what if, for the sake of this discussion, someone looked upon Appalachia with a very different set of attitudes. A person, say, who was less materialistic than the previous man, and who looked upon the people of Appalachia and said: "Here is a land of beauty, where the people know the value of music and kinfolk and spiritual energy. America would do well to learn of these ways." These are exaggeratedly simplified extremes, to be sure, and only two of any number of viewpoints possible, but they illustrate the way in which projected fictions, which the sociologists often call models, work to shape the minds of non-imaginative people, people who, in their turn, work to shape our world. Morg represents the masses; his view of things is profoundly crucial to what happens in the world.

Morg's capacity for believing whatever model or world-view is offered him is balanced by his inability to imaginatively create worlds of his own, and herein lies a grave danger. Morg is, in his honesty and literal-mindedness, a model of most men's minds: he is capable of building a life based on whichever description of the world has the greatest persuasive power, and he accepts, without question, the accuracy of any view of life presented to him most effectively. There is no reason given in the story to think that Morg is any less than a good honest, normal child. Like most of us, he believes what he is told, and acts upon that belief.

It is not curious, then, once Elvy's fiction has gained sway in Morg's mind, that he is less able to dispel it than he is to project it. The narrator, knowledgeable of the creative and destructive powers of the imagination, counsels Morg, in the presence of Father's angry explosion, to use his mind to understand that Elvy's imaginary life is imaginary: "Father's face tightened, half in anger, half in dismay. He lifted his hands in defeat. 'Hell's bangers!' he blurted. Morg's tears fell thicker. I spoke small into his ear, 'Act it's not so,' but Morg could never make-like." Morg lacks any antidote for dangerous fictions.

This last quoted sentence completes one cycle of the story, that of Morg's progression from disbelief to belief. It is an echo of the narrator's first description of Morg at the beginning of the story: "Morg couldn't make-believe; he was just Morg." But now, the events in Elvy's imaginary life have brought about an ironic reversal in Morg's situation. He cannot "make-believe," so when his mind becomes convinced of the truth of another's fiction, that fiction in turn becomes truth in Morg's mind, and he is unable to "act it's not so." Thus the mind of the literal-minded man is more surely shaped by fictional processes than the mind generating those processes, because the creative minds — healthy ones, anyway — understand the difference between their created world and the ordinary world. But it is as impossible for non-imaginative minds to see through a false world-view as it is for them to create one. It is the Morgs who, in their total belief in the predominant imaginary, perceptual, or social construct available to them, take action in the day-to-day world: build houses, raise children, engage in religious activity, go to the polls to vote. And the configurations of those activities are determined by the world-view that is the most forceful and convincing at any given time.

Elvy has maintained her fictional life of pain and abandonment long enough for Morg to begin to share her emotional anguish. And Morg, unlike his brother, has no freedom in this adopted fiction; since he has no creative power, he also lacks the power to subordinate other fictions to his own perception of the world around him.

But Elvy has created a model of life which has bewitched Morg. The relationship between Morg and Elvy constitutes nothing less than a spell: Morg has come under his sister's power, and she creates for Morg a blighted and unhappy life. The suggestion that this is so occurs within the names of the characters themselves, within the language, however intentionally or accidentally on Mr. Still's part. "Morg and Elvy": "Morgan le Fay," we recall, was the sorceress sister and enemy of King Arthur. (Moreover, "Elvy" resonates the sounds of "elve" and "elfin," an order of creatures notorious for playing havoc with the realities of honest folk.)

Other elements of "Mrs. Razor" support the kind of scrutiny usually reserved for writers like James Joyce — for instance, the use of fire as a sustaining symbol throughout the story. Mr. Still is a deliberate and literate artist, and I suggest that his fiction deserves the sort of critical attention that presupposes that every word of his prose exists in its place for a purpose. Mr. Still's fiction is of such a caliber that the truths built into language emerge of their own energy and accuracy. The best literary artists are allowed to participate in a mystery which sets conscious awareness aside to do its work. Mr. Still's "Mrs. Razor" is a story in which his awareness joins sheer creative energy to open the way for that mystery to enjoy one of its finer moments.

The conclusion of the story must be read with an eye capable of viewing the structure of the story and also the story's meaning as embedded within language itself. Taken simply as plot, as another step in the sequence of events, Father gets mad and loads the whole kit and caboodle in the wagon, and drives around until Elvy wears out and goes to sleep. There is, in truth, a fascinating ambiguity surrounding the ending of "Mrs. Razor," and the following interpretation is, of course, my own reading of it.

Does Elvy drop her miserable fabrication or not? I believe that the structure of the story and the language of its conclusion suggest that she does, and that she wakes up the next day being Elvy again, that Morg, disenchanted, is again "just Morg," and supper tomorrow will be served when the chickens go to the gilly trees to roost.

Father's decision to take "the whole push" of them to Biggety Creek solves a problem existing on the level of imagination by uniting the imaginative and the real. He had previously tried to solve the problem on the level of the problem itself — that is, by humoring Elvy, offering Razor a job, and even inviting him to Sunday dinner, for which Elvy "had Mother fry a chicken, the dish he liked the best, claiming the gizzard was his chosen morsel." But this solution didn't work. Elvy — put on the spot by her family's waiting "noon through, until one o'clock" — tells them to "Go ahead and eat. Razor allus was slow as Jim Christmas." Between dinnertime and supper, Elvy declares her man dead. Razor's death, Elvy's consuming grief, and Morg's acceptance of the situation push Father to his limit: "Father's face tightened, half in anger, half in dismay. He lifted his hands in defeat."

The contest has been over world views: first, Mother and Father are engaged in a deep, nearly unspeakable crisis of opinion about how to handle this child's mind, and then the contest becomes one of the durability of Elvy's fiction versus Father's tolerance of it. Father is defeated, finally, but it is only in his defeat, his letting go of his insistence on the primary nature of the real world (i.e., not Razor's world), that he discovers the solution to the problem. He does this by capitulating to Elvy's imaginary woes and taking her to Biggety Creek, a creation of his own imagination. And the trip to Biggety Creek is, moreover, a real trip in the real world, a solution which combines action with acceptance. Thus, Father's authority is re-established, and Mother's wise passivity is incorporated in the one gesture of taking the whole family to Biggety Creek.

At the point of Father's defeat, genius informs his actions, and the nature of the domestic situation is suddenly changed. The change is heard in the rhythm of the next two sentences: "Elvy's sobbing hushed. Morg blinked." Finally, Father has made contact with Elvy through her fictitious web. Nothing he has done to this point has affected Elvy's insistent fiction. Morg's blink suggests that his senses are returning, that Elvy's spell is broken, and the enchantment he has fallen under is dissolving. Normal order is being restored to the household.

In terms of formal structure, the ending of the story conforms to the beginning, giving unity of action and image. It begins and ends in a silence broken by Father's voice. The fire, which has served throughout the story as a symbol of the creative imagination, informs both beginning and ending. The fire in the Cincinnati stove burns throughout the day of the story, and is the only source of light besides the light of the dwindling day. No other source of light appears in the story: "The day was still so bright the wall bore a shadow of the unkindled lamp. Elvy had hidden behind the stove, lying on the cat's pallet, crying." In the first paragraph, "Elvy was crying behind the stove," and toward the ending of the story, she is still there: "As we sat at supper that late afternoon, listening to Elvy sob behind the stove, Morg began to stare into his plate and would eat no more." The present action of the story places Elvy behind the stove; she remains removed from her family by the fire until Father's reconciling action at the end. After Father's declaration that he is taking the whole family to "Biggety Creek," the narrator relates, "The room became so quiet I could hear flames eating wood in the firebox."

*Flames eating wood* — this phrase triggered something in my mind, and giving in to a hunch I looked up the hexagram in the *I Ching* that was associated with wood and flame, placing flame under wood. I realized that I was stretching the usual framework of literary criticism, and had no real intention of allowing the *I Ching* to enter into my reading of "Mrs. Razor" until I turned to the appropriate hexagram to discover, to my surprise and delight, that flame under wood comprised the hexagram called *Chia Jen* (The Family or The Clan). There I read words that conformed with my reading of the story up to the point I had yielded to my intuition and opened the *I Ching*. "The Family shows the laws operative within the household that, transferred to outside life, keep the state and the world in order.... When the family is in order, all the social relationships of mankind will be in order." And more, a lot more.

I decided that to eliminate this discovery from my article on "Mrs. Razor" would be an injustice to readers and to the natural energy of the story itself. The fact that the arrangement "flames eating wood" appears in James Still's story about natural order within a family and also comprises the hexagram The Family/The Clan in an ancient treatise on social conduct affirmed the force of the creative imagination for me. I am not suggesting that James Still consciously drew either ideas or images from the *I Ching* to make his story, but that, more significantly, the creative intellect works through artists of Still's caliber to continuously reflect and recreate an indestructible natural order in our human world. This relationship between ancient and modern wisdom, between primary order and storytellers, comprises the mystery and the reliability of creativity. It is very tempting here to enter into a discussion of the details of the *I Ching*'s comments on The Family/The Clan, but I shall invite the reader to participate in this discovery by consulting the *I Ching* directly.

Natural order is restored to Elvy's family when Father acts, and the story comes to a conclusion which suggests reconciliation of Father's views and Mother's views. The image that, at the story's beginning, had suggested the disturbance of natural order, reappears at the ending: "Chickens walked toward the gilly trees, flew to their roosts, sleepy and quarrelsome." Things are returning to normal.

For Elvy, sleep and nighttime restore the normal world. As the family drives toward "Biggety Creek," directed by Elvy, they are drawn together by Father's authority and calmed by the coming of nighttime. The trip to Biggety Creek brings the story to its full circular close. "The shapes of trees and fences were lost and there were only the wise eyes of the mules to pick the road when the ground had melted and the sky was gone." There is nothing to separate the family; Elvy is no longer behind the stove, removed by her feverish imagination from the rest of the family. Father takes the family on their symbolic journey to Nowhere Place, and then, after traveling six miles, they go home again.

# Looking the Story in the Eye: "I Love My Rooster"

## RANDOLPH PAUL RUNYON

In sheer quality, if not in abundance of production, James Still should surely be considered a major Appalachian writer. By coincidence, both Still and the much better known Jesse Stuart graduated from Lincoln Memorial University in the 1920s—and spent a year at Vanderbilt University when some of the Fugitives still taught there. If Stuart overproduced, Still by contrast has with lapidary precision written a mere handful of short stories (and one remarkable novel—*River of Earth*) of astonishing beauty. Some two dozen stories originally published between 1936 and 1959 were made available again in two collections, *The Run for the Elbertas* and *Pattern of a Man* (Still is a poet, too, of considerable gifts—as recent collections abundantly show).

In an interview, Still spoke about his work and the effort he requires of his reader in these demanding terms: "The static rating of my fiction is rather low, and I press for absolute clarity. I demand of a reader his whole attention, his eyes and ears and his understanding. He must meet me halfway, not expect me to do the whole job" (139). In proposing a close reading of his short story "I Love My Rooster" (from the collection *The Run for the Elbertas*), I am trying to go that halfway distance, though it is altogether possible that, once one begins to read such a text as Still's, one will be led by that text a little farther, or even in another direction, than its author had in mind for one to go. But such a direction, and distance, is what his stories themselves require.

In his Foreword to the re-issue of *River of Earth*, Dean Cadle makes a remarkable claim for the simplicity of Still's fiction: "An emotional response is the one quality above all for which Still works. There are no games, no literary or historical allusions, no puns, no symbolism.... He simply sets down the experiences of a few human beings ... in a manner that is simple and unposed" (x). Elsewhere, in his valuable study "Man on Troublesome," Cadle states his argument in similar, though more accurate, terms: "there is little conscious use of symbols, no allusions to classical or other literatures, and no reference to anything outside the immediate situation in which the characters are involved" (240). This absence of outside symbolic reference is evidently what is meant in the other passage by the claim of "no symbolism"

*Runyon, Randolph Paul. "Looking the Story in the Eye: James Still's 'Rooster.'" The Southern Literary Journal 23.2 (Spring 1991): 55–64. Copyright 1991 by* The Southern Literary Journal *and the University of North Carolina at Chapel Hill Department of English. Reprinted with permission.*

(though attenuated here to "little conscious use"—leaving open the possibility that there is some, and that it is unconscious). The assertion, however, that there are no allusions to classical or other literatures is in fact contradicted by Still's clever integration of *Gulliver's Travels* into his story "School Butter" (in *The Run for the Elbertas*). And that there are neither games nor puns in the fiction of a writer who has compiled two volumes of Appalachian riddles and wordplay (*Way Down Yonder on Troublesome Creek* and *The Wolfpen Rusties*) would seem an especially dangerous claim to make. Puns in particular are precisely what one is quite likely to find in Still, as I intend to show here. His manner may be simple, but it is deceptively so.

"I Love My Rooster" is the story of a boy—the narrator—whose father has found employment in a coal mine but whose mother knows the boom won't last; she persuades her husband to bring home the pay envelopes unopened and let her manage the household expenses. The boy has a friend, Fedder Mott, who wears a black patch over a missing eye and who wants the boy to come with him to the watch the local cock fights.

> I studied the eye patch. It was the size of a silver dollar, hanging by a string looped around his head. What lay behind it? Was there a hole square into his skull? I was almost ashamed to ask, almost afraid. I drew a circle on the ground with my shoe toe, measuring the words: "I'll go to the rooster fight sometime, if one thing—"
> "If'n what?"
> "If you'll let me see your eye pocket" [7].

Winter comes and the rooster contests are called off until spring, and the narrator does not get to see what is behind the "great dark eye" of the patch until the end of the story. Meanwhile, the narrator's family scrapes by on his mother's extraordinary domestic economy, while she saves against the day when the boom will bust and they can leave the coal camp and build a house on land they have inherited, to live in rural self-sufficiency. But there is one nagging problem: the baby has yet to speak his first word, and the father is afraid he will turn out to be a mute. On the day he came home with his first two-week "pay pocket," he gave him the unopened envelope to play with:

> ...The baby opened his mouth, clucking, churring. He made a sound like a wren sitting on a nest of eggs.
> "Money, money," Fern said, trying to teach him.
> He twisted his lips, his tongue straining. But he could not speak a word.
> "I'd give every red cent to hear him say one thing," Father said [4–5].

As Joe Glaser has pointed out in a commentary on this story ("For all its homespun details and diction, 'I Love My Rooster' is as elegantly plotted as a scene from Restoration drama" [9]), one of the most consistent qualities of Still's fiction is the profusion of subplots, and the way these several stories are so interwoven that each responds to the rest in intricate ways. The title is not necessarily a guarantee that the narrative strand to which it refers is the principal plot, if indeed there is one. But if we take the story to be in the main about the narrator's love of his rooster—the one in which he bought half-ownership from Fedder Mott for eleven nickels when Fedder brought him back from the cock fights, vanquished and to all appearances dead, but who came back to life—then that story finds some intriguing echoes in the subplot of the baby's apparent muteness. For one thing, the baby is specifically identified with a rooster, the one the narrator had told his father he wanted before Fedder's salvaging of Steph Harben's Red Pyle brought that wish to unexpected fruition.

> Father poked a finger at the baby. "By gollyard, if he'd just speak one word!"
> The baby lifted his arms, mouth wide, neck stretched. He crowed.
> "Thar's your rooster," Father chuckled, setting his eyes on me.

"I aim to own a real gamer," I bragged, irked by Father's teasing. "I aim to." I spoke without hope, not knowing that by spring it would come true [10].

Given that equation of infant and bird, it is perhaps not illegitimate to ponder for a moment the possible analogy between the baby's apparent muteness and the rooster's apparent death, especially in light of the fact that not only does the rooster in the end come back to life but also that the baby, in the last lines of the story, finally speaks. If in fact a short story's conclusion could speak as loudly as its title in suggesting which of its several plots is the principal one, "I Love My Rooster" may not be about the narrator's beloved pet, but about his infant (in the true sense of the word, in this instance: *infans*, "not yet speaking") brother. In this regard the short story would itself resemble its protagonist, not yet speaking until the very last moment, not revealing until that very last moment its true nature.

In either event, in the perspective of the father's suggestion of a resemblance between the baby and the rooster, some other details of the story begin to reveal their significance. Take the nature of the wound itself that made the rooster Fedder rescued look as if he were dead. "They was a cut on his throat and you'd a-thought him knob dead. Steph give him to me, and ere I reached the camp, he come alive. That thar cut was jist a scratch" (12). The baby, too, in Father's estimation, may have something terribly wrong with his throat — if that's what it is that prevents him from speaking. It is worth noting that Fedder didn't say, though he just as easily could have, that "They was a cut on his neck...." The throat of the voiceless child is indeed menaced in a more particular way at the very moment Father points out his resemblance to a rooster, for he has just bitten off the eraser of the pencil Father had been using to try to figure out, without looking inside the unopened pay envelopes, how much he had earned at the mine. The sequence of events is perhaps significant:

> The baby sat up, threshing the air, puckering his lips. We looked, and he had bitten the rubber tip off the pencil.
> "Hain't he old enough to be saying words?" Father asked [10].

The narrator's brother Lark reports that the baby once spoke to a cat. The mother said that wasn't speaking,

> ... "Just a sound he made. Cats follow stealing in since we bought salt fish. Can't keep the cat hole plugged."
> "He said 'kigid.'"
> "That hain't a word," Fern said.

Then follows the passage cited earlier, where father exasperatedly wishes for just one word from the child, who then crows like a rooster. One could almost conclude that the eraser in his throat had something to do with that bird imitation, something to do with his momentary metamorphosis into what would appear to be, according to the title, the central image of the story; the two events at least coincide. Then, "Mother searched the baby's mouth for the pencil tip.... She didn't find the rubber tip, for the baby had swallowed it down." Why is it that it's an eraser the baby swallows, instead of any other item lying around the house? Because Still's fiction is tightly woven, because everything is connected to everything else — because it was the eraser from the pencil with which the father had been trying to calculate the sum hidden in the unopened pay pockets. But surely also because of the remarkable appropriateness of a throat that doesn't speak ingesting the very thing that makes words disappear.

The eraser disappears, too, into the inaccessible interior of that throat — into a place that cannot but remind us of another inner void, the most haunting image in the story, the hole behind Fedder Mott's eye patch, the "eye pocket" the narrator both desires and dreads to behold:

> ... I was suddenly afraid, suddenly having no wish to see.
>     The patch was lifted. I looked, stepping back.... I turned, running, running with this sight
> burnt upon my mind [15].

Fedder and the baby share, too—almost—the quality of being deformed children—that is, the baby would if the father's fear turned out to be true.

It is not, perhaps, by accident that the near-miracle of the baby's finally speaking should have something to do with yet another kind of hole. We have seen a hint of this already, when Lark points out that he said "kigid" to a cat and Mother then complains that they can't keep the cat hole plugged. "I Love My Rooster" abounds in holes: (1) the one behind the eye patch ("Was there a hole square into his skull?"); (2) the one into which the eraser vanishes; (3) the hole in the back door through which Mother predicts, correctly, the neighborhood cats will come in if Father buys the saltwater fish his paycheck now makes affordable ("'Right today I'll buy that kit o' fish.' 'They're liable to draw every cat in Houndshell holler. Better you plug the cat hole in the back door first'" [6]); (4) the other hole for which fish are the attraction, and of which the narrator speaks immediately after the definitive disappearance of the eraser is established:

> ... She didn't find the rubber tip, for the baby had swallowed it down.
>     I told Fedder of Mother's prophecy [that the boom would bust] as we sat by a fire on the
> creek bank. We had fish-hooks in an ice hole [10].

And, (5) the hole, unspoken but present, into which Father disappears every day to earn those biweekly pay pockets that Mother amasses unopened (all but the first, which was large enough for them to live on those entire five months). In any case, it is one of those creatures that can so freely go in and out of holes that draws, finally, speech out of that infant's mouth: The narrator has run home, the image of what lay behind Fedder's eye patch burnt upon his mind; Father has come home, too, to announce that the boom is busted and he's out of a job; Mother has finally opened all the pay pockets—

> I ran all the way home, going into the kitchen door as Father went, not staying the sow cat
> that stole in between my legs. Mother sat at the table, a pile of greenbacks before her, the
> empty pay pockets crumpled [15].

—and is smiling, knowing now that they have enough to build a house. And, so that everything can finally fall into place:

> The baby opened his mouth, curling his lips, pointing a stub finger. He pointed at the old
> nanny smelling the fish kit.
>     "Cat!" he said, big as life [15].

We know the child is really speaking this time, is really using language (and not just making a sound as arbitrary as "kigid"), because he actually links signified with signifier through his accompanying gesture, "pointing a stub finger" at the cat at the moment he says its name. But at the very moment he does this, the story does some naming of its own, for the adjective that describes the finger that makes this linking gesture (linking sound and sense, word and referent) participates in another kind of linkage, recalling (because it calls both by the same name and because the word appears nowhere else in the story) that other linguistic tool, the pencil whose eraser the baby had swallowed—the "stub pencil" with which Father tried to calculate the content of the sealed pay pockets.

If the precision of Still's text extends to the appearance and reappearance of such a word as this—and I believe it does—then perhaps we can also hold the text of his story accountable for the multiple yet meaningful appearances of pockets: (1) the "pay pockets" whose opening coincides with the baby's acquisition of language; (2) clothes pockets that, like the pay pockets, carry money ("Boys' pockets clinked money" [9]; "He [Fedder Mott] moved toward the gate, the nickels ringing in his pocket" [12]); and (3) most intriguingly, the "eye pocket" (7, 14) behind Fedder's eye patch that the narrator wants to see and, to his horror, does. There is a certain appropriateness in the fact that the envelopes in which Father is given his wages and that part of Fedder's and other boys' clothing in which coins are kept should be called by the same word, given their similarity of function—but isn't it remarkable that the narrator should call the place of Mott's empty eye a pocket too? And isn't it all the more remarkable that the association between pockets and money that the other uses of the word maintain should persist here as well? For it does, in two ways: First, as we have seen in a passage already cited, the narrator tells us that he "studied the patch. It was the size of a silver dollar" (early on, we hear the noise silver dollars make in pockets: "silver dollars rattling wherever men walked" [1]). Second, it was to cost him money to see that eye patch lifted, for he had to give up his half interest in the rooster that the title tells us he loved and that he had conceded his life savings of fifty-five cents to acquire. The original owner of the rooster, who had given it to Fedder when he thought it was dead, wanted it back after its resurrection, and Fedder grabbed the chance to make enough money on the deal to buy a glass eye, selling his interest for some undisclosed sum and persuading the narrator to sell his for the chance to see into the eye pocket beyond that patch the size of a dollar (he acquires, too, Steph Harben's store-bought shirt): "'If'n you sell,' Fedder promised, 'I'll let you spy at my eye pocket. Now, while it's thar, you kin look. Afore long I'll have a glass 'un.'"

By now the narrator is not so sure he wants to know what's in that pocket—"I was suddenly afraid, suddenly having no wish to see"—but by this point he really has no choice; what he is about to see will leave a lasting impression: "The patch was lifted. I looked, stepping back, squeezing the shirt into a ball. I turned, running, running with this sight burnt upon my mind." Surely something more than just the horror of an empty eye socket is present here—what else is it that the boy is afraid to see but, at this moment, must?

It would be easy, almost frighteningly so, to speculate, to leap to a psychoanalytic interpretation—to see this hole, this bodily pocket, as a screen for another, to read the story as an allegory of the acquisition of sexual knowledge, to wonder what it might mean for the narrator to give up his cock for a chance to look into the nothingness of that hole. Surely that's not what we are meant to read in this tale of Appalachian innocence. Yet, "I Love My Rooster" has its ways of letting us into its secrets, into the text within the text; and one of them is through the words and gestures it repeats. Consider a passage already cited—"I was almost ashamed to ask, almost afraid. I drew a circle on the ground with my shoe toe, measuring the words: 'I'll go to the rooster fight sometime, if ... you'll let me see your eye pocket'"—and how this attention to the narrator's shoe toe may make us want to rethink a similar attention paid to the toe of his father's boots on the page just before: "The pair my head was set on cost eighteen dollars. Got toes so sharp you could kick a blacksnake's eye out. Reckon I'll just make these clodbusters I got on do" (6). This wished-for footwear is the equivalent of the store-bought shirt for which the narrator expressed a similar desire—

> "I need me a shirt," I said. "A store-bought shirt." More than a game rooster, more than anything, I wanted a shirt made like a man's. Being eight years old, I was ashamed to wear the ones Mother sewed without tails to stuff inside my breeches [3–4].

—and that he will acquire on his own, without the assistance of his father's pay pockets, in the trade that will also net him the chance to look into Fedder's empty eye. But it's what Father does with it, or could do with it, that is most intriguing. He could do to a blacksnake what something, or someone, did to Fedder. It is a rather disturbing thought given the power of the Oedipus myth in our culture and the inescapable association, both within that myth (in *The Interpretation of Dreams* Freud notes that the "blinding in the legend of Oedipus, as well as elsewhere, stands for castration" [433n–434n]) and in our culture, between castration and blinding — that Father could have such a power. The son, in this instance, acts out what he hears his father say he could do in his own way, not by putting out an eye but by drawing an empty circle in the dirt with the toe of his shoe at the same moment as, "measuring the words," he expresses his ambivalent desire, at the same moment he alludes to the empty circle that lies behind Fedder's black patch. As well befits a boy who will become a teller of tales (the narrator of the story, if not its author), he is careful with his words, measuring them as he traces his desire in the dirt.

The gesture will return, though in different guise, at the moment of exchange, when the narrator contemplates what he must do to acquire both the shirt (store-bought, and not mother-made, like those eye-poking boots his father also wanted) and to unveil the mystery of the eye:

> I dug my toe into the ground, scuffing dirt. "I love my rooster," I said. But I looked at Steph's shirt. It was very beautiful.
>   "If'n you'll sell," Fedder promised, "I'll let you spy at my eye pocket...."
>   I kicked a clod into the road. "I'll swap my part o' the rooster for that striped shirt..." [14–15].

I don't think it too much to point out that even the clod he kicked bears a significant relation to the "clodbusters" his father said would have to do.

There are two more things about Fedder that ought to be said. One is his name, which appropriately evokes what it is that makes roosters, and other birds, flock together (as well as, somewhat more distantly, "Father"). The other is that he carries around something like the paternal pay pockets the narrator's mother soon acquires and hoards, for the family nest egg, his "seed papers" (14), the envelopes he has bought and plans to sell at a profit to those who can see beyond winter to spring. The seeds represent, potentially, money, and these "[p]ackages of seeds rattled in his pockets" (11), like the money that clinked in other boys' pockets and the nickels that would ring in his own after the rooster transaction. But as seeds they can bear another meaning, one of a piece with the sexual imagery that seems to run just beneath the surface in Still's story (as it does for another seedsman in Melville's "Tartarus of Maids" — where a tour through a paper mill becomes a journey into the human reproductive system).

In the same way that "I Love My Rooster" is the site of competing plots and subplots (is it the story of a boy's love for his rooster, or of the baby's conquest of speech, or of the family's survival, or all of these and more?), so also is the subtext that its repeated and parallel words and gestures define a site of rival meanings. For though there is more than a hint of sexuality in "I Love My Rooster," that sexuality must compete for our attention with another category of meaning, that of commercial exchange, whether that be the exchange of labor for money, or of nickels for a rooster, or of that rooster for the opportunity to gaze upon the mystery of the missing eye. Subtext aside, what the story is most apparently about is the conflict, apparent in *River of Earth* and other Still stories, between the older Appalachian culture of rural self-sufficiency from which money was absent and the newer one of an especially pernicious form of wage slavery. The fact, however, that Still casts this conflict in terms of a mother who prefers the former and a father who would rather work in the mines results in its being inextricably intertwined with the issues of fathers and sons and sexuality. The mother effectively forbids the father from opening the pay pockets and thereby keeps the family from entering into the capitalist economy that company towns foster (the better to enslave their workers: some coal companies actually brought in "social workers" to encourage mining families to "want" in order to increase their loyalty to the wage system and their indebtedness to the company store). The other families ate better, the other children "wore store clothes. They bought spin-tops and pretties at the commissary. Boys' pockets clinked money. Only Fedder Mott and I had to wind our own balls and whittle our tops" (9). The narrator's longstanding desire to gaze into the hole behind the patch has, given the context outlined above, undeniable sexual overtones. But because of the vocabulary of the text, the parallel between his wanting to look into this eye pocket and his father's desire (evident when he tries to calculate how much they contain and in his teasing: "What say we count the greenbacks? My curiosity is being et raw" [10]) to know what the pay pockets contain is just as undeniable.

Yet in the end it is by no means certain that considerations of cultural change and monetary exchange entirely govern the weave of Still's text, for even this is couched in what are surely sexual terms: the pay pockets become the mother's purse, an enclosed feminine space to which she alone can grant access. And surely Appalachian fiction is not always best served by a purely sociological reading. For the words—especially with a writer with the craft of a James Still—count too.

# *Works Cited*

Cadle, Dean. "Man on Troublesome." *Yale Review* 57 (1968): 236–55.

Freud, Sigmund. *The Interpretation of Dreams*. Tr. James Strachey. New York: Avon, 1965.

Glaser, Joe. "Slick as a Dogwood Hoe Handle: Craft in the Stories of James Still." *Appalachian Heritage* 11.3 (Summer 1983): 4–9.

Still, James. "An Interview with James Still." *Appalachian Journal* 6 (Winter, 1979): 121–41.

_____. *Pattern of a Man and Other Stories*. Frankfort, KY.: Gnomon Press, 1976.

_____. *River of Earth*. 1940; repr. Lexington: University Press of Kentucky, 1978.

_____. *The Run for the Elbertas*. Lexington: University Press of Kentucky, 1980.

_____. *Way Down Yonder on Troublesome Creek: Appalachian Riddles and Rusties*. New York: Putnam, 1974.

_____. *The Wolfpen Poems*. Berea, KY.: Berea College Press, 1986.

_____. *The Wolfpen Rusties: Appalachian Riddles and Gee-Haw Whimmy-Diddles*. New York: Putnam, 1975.

# IV
## THE POETRY

James Still standing in the doorway of the log house, located beside Wolfpen Creek, Knott County, Kentucky (courtesy of the Hindman Settlement School).

# Introduction to
## *The Wolfpen Poems*

### JIM WAYNE MILLER

More critical attention has been given to James Still's novels and short stories than to his poems, but Still is rightly admired for his prose because he is first of all a poet. After reading the novel *River of Earth* (1940; rpt. 1968, 1978) and the poems in the 1937 collection, *Hounds on the Mountain,* Katherine Anne Porter said in a letter that the two books should be read together. The novel was "an extension of the poems," while the poems were "further comment on the experience that made the novel." Still's poems are thus doubly deserving of critical attention. Rewarding in themselves, they also belong to any assessment of his overall achievement.

The poems establish themes, birth imagery and motifs beautifully and subtly elaborated in the fiction. Thematic and imagistic continuities exist also between the poems of the 1937 volume and the later poems collected here [in *The Wolfpen Poems*]. A passage central to Still's work is Brother Sim Mobberly's sermon in *River of Earth.* The mountain preacher declares:

> I was borned in a ridge-pocket ... I never seed the sun-ball withouten heisting my chin. My eyes were sot upon the hills from the beginning. Till I come on the Word in this good Book, I used to think a mountain was the standingest object in the sight o' God. [But] These hills are jist dirt waves, washing through eternity. My brethren, they hain't a valley so low but what hit'll rise again. They hain't a hill a standing so proud but hit'll sink to the low ground o' sorrow. Oh, my children, where air we going on this mighty river of earth, a-borning, begetting, and a-dying — the living and the dead riding the waters? Where air it sweeping us? ...

Details, imagery, and syntax of this important passage are anticipated in early poems, and later poems and stories are variations and further elaborations of it. In the manner of Brother Mobberly, the speaker of the poem "I Was Born Humble" begins: "I was born humble. At the foot of mountains / My face was set upon the immensity of earth / And stone." Mobberly's vision of the mighty river of earth is implicit in the poem "Heritage," in which the speaker vows never to leave the hills

> Though they topple their barren heads to level earth
> And forests slide uprooted out of the sky.
> Though the waters of Troublesome, of Trace Fork,
> Of Sand Lick rise in a single body to glean the valleys,
> To drown lush pennyroyal, to unravel rail fences.

*Miller, Jim Wayne. "Introduction."* The Wolfpen Poems. *By James Still. Berea, Kentucky: Berea College Press, 1986. Pp. xi–xxiii. Reprinted with permission.*

A previously uncollected poem bearing the same title as the novel *River of Earth* and drawing upon the same biblical text (Psalm 114) presents the mountain preacher's vision of hills as "dirt waves": "Hills are but waves cast up to fall again, to rise / Still further down the years." A later poem, "The Trees in the Road," works a variation on the image: a cliff has given way, allowing a slope on which oak trees grow to slide down into a road. The oaks have ridden down upright and "possessed the road." The bringing low or raising up of the "standingest" objects is repeated humorously in the short story "The Stir-Off," whose child narrator describes riding a flying-jinny at a sorghum making: "The earth whirled, trees went walking, and tiptops of the mountains swayed and rail fences climbed straight into the sky."

Still's early poems are a headwaters where the river of earth rises. The "Child in the Hills" is "Swept with the waters down the winding mountain valleys" as are the stallions in "Journey Beyond the Hills." In "Mountain Fox Hunt," hounds "flow down the slope in a narrowing sweep / And up again in brown tidal strokes." In "Farm," crows "flow from their perch in heavy pointless flight," and a lizard "runs up the sky with liquid feet." "Passenger Pigeons" are "an aerial river of birds." In "Year of the Pigeons," the birds arrive "in a darkening flood." The river imagery is present in "Horseback in the Rain," where the speaker asks: "Where turn from the flow / Of day slanted greyly / Toward earth...?" Caught up in "a fog-wrinkled spreading / Of waters," he rides "the storm with no ending / On a road unarriving." Again in "Rain on the Cumberlands," the speaker is a wanderer "Caught up with broken horns within the nettled grass, / With hoofs relinquished on the breathing stones / Eaten with rain-strokes." The speaker knows that "Rain has buried her seed and her dead. / They spring together in this fertile air / Loud with thunder." The situation prefigures Brother Mobberly's vision of humanity being swept along "a-borning, begetting, and a-dying — the living and the dead riding the waters." The juxtaposition of "seed" and "dead" has its parallel in the image of a locust post in *River of Earth* used to mark Grandfather Middleton's grave (a post which has taken root); and in the novel's conclusion where, after the grandmother's body has been carried from the house for burial, a child is born in another room. A similar juxtaposition occurs in the story "The Nest," where Nezzie Hargis, imagining her grandfather "stretched gaunt and pale on a feather bed," then thinks of her little brother growing old, "time perishing his cheeks, hands withering and palsying."

Since creeks and rivers are natural highways, implicit in the river image is the motif of the journey. The creek in "Drought" is "a highway wandering." The journey forms an important part of the narrative structure of *River of Earth, Sporty Creek,* and of many short stories. Echoing Brother Mobberly's "Where air it sweeping us?," the mother in *River of Earth* complains of the family's life: "Forever moving yon and back, setting down nowhere for good and all, searching for God knows what ... Where air we expecting to draw up to?" The family in *Sporty Creek* also shuttles back and forth from subsistence farm to mining camp. Finally, the narrator and his brother journey to a settlement school. Variations on the journey motif occur in such short stories as "The Moving"; "On Quicksand Creek"; "The Burning of the Waters"; in "Mrs. Razor," where the father loads up the family and sets out for the mythical Biggety Creek; in "A Ride on the Short Dog"; "The Run for the Elbertas"; and in *Jack and the Wonder Beans,* Still's reworking of the familiar Jack and the Beanstalk.

Whether in the poems, novels, or short stories, Still's characters typically journey out into the world like Jack, "get their barrel full" and return gladly home. The young narrator of *River of Earth* models himself after the legendary Walking John Gay, described as "traipsing and trafficking, looking the world over." The boy dreams of "going to the scrag end of creation." Settled in a coal camp, he says: "I tramped the camp over. I saw what there was to see."

Many spatial metaphors associate the journey motif with acquisition of knowledge. In *River of Earth* the narrator wonders "how it would be to know square to the end of everything." The boys in "Journey to the Forks" speak of and experience knowledge in spatial terms. The narrator remarks to his brother: "They never was a pure scholar amongst all our folks ... Never a one went all the way through the books and come out yon side." The boys descend a ridge to a settlement school at nightfall, picking their way "through stony dark." The situation suggests the effort, which lies before them, of going through the books and coming out "yon side."

Firmly established in the early poems and prose, and associated with knowledge, the journey motif is further elaborated in Still's later work. In "White Highways," from the 1937 collection of poems, the speaker has "gone out to the roads that go up and down / In smooth white lines...." But like the mother in *River of Earth,* who yearns to "set down in a lone spot, a place certain and enduring," the speaker in "White Highways" has come home, with a sense of the wider world, but happy to live quietly in peace "curved with space / Brought back again to this warm homing place." A later poem, the autobiographical "On Being Drafted into the U.S. Army...," focuses on the circumstances of another journey beyond the hills. Weather and time have made a crack in the cabin wall "for inside to look out / And outside to peer wonderingly in." The planet "Mars hung bright in the Wolfpen sky / And glared and met me eye to eye. / Mars looked in and routed me out." In the humorous short story "The Sharp Tack," a young man who has gone off and seen the world during World War II outrages Preacher Powell by claiming to have seen the Holy Land. Powell's conception of the hereafter is challenged by the report of the returning soldier. Powell is forced to travel, vicariously, through the reports of the returned soldier, and must admit, "I learnt a speck." But ultimately, at least to his own satisfaction, he accommodates irrefutable geographical facts to his narrow theological preconceptions. "Apple Trip," a post-war poem, relishes the details of another journey, which, though it does not take the speaker far from home, is still "a worldly wonder."

The earliest poems suggest that knowledge resulting from a journey is a kind of self-knowledge. Knowledge gained from journeying brings, paradoxically, an understanding that there is a spot of "earth loved more than any earth" ("Wolfpen Creek"); a realization of how deeply one is attached to one's home place. As Still puts it in the poem "Heritage," "Being of these hills, I cannot pass beyond." The narrator in *Sporty Creek,* leaving home for a settlement school, says: "I experienced a yearning I could not name. I knew then that Sporty Creek would forever beckon me." In the early poem "Eyes in the Grass," the speaker is completely identified with the earth; he is "lost to any wandering view" and describes himself as a "hill uncharted ... / ... horizon ... earth's far end." Such imagery suggests that the journey can be a journey into the self and that the resulting self-knowledge is not unlike that expressed by Eliot in "Little Gidding," where the goal of our journey is said to be to arrive at the place we started from and to understand that place for the first time.

But the journey in Still's poems and narratives is not always successfully completed. And the knowledge gained is sometimes bitter indeed. The mountains, a home and haven, can also be a prison. The journey can end in defeat or death. The fox pursued by hounds in the poem "Hounds on the Mountain" is walled in by the "arched leanings / Of hill on hill." Trapped at the head of a cove, the fox turns to the hounds and is killed. The poem "Pattern for Death," a meditation on a spider's cleverly and intricately woven web, suggests that there is often no escape. The speaker asks: "Who can escape through the grass? ... / Who reads the language of direction? Where may we pass / Through the immense pattern sheer as glass?" The question echoes Brother Mobberly's "Where air we going?" as well as the mother's "Where air we expecting to draw up to?" and Uncle Jolly's "What's folks going to live on when these hills wear down to a nub?"

An attempt to pass through the "immense pattern" and arrive at a "warm homing place" is the subject of one of Still's finest stories, "The Nest." A little girl, Nezzie Hargis, becomes lost attempting to cross a ridge to stay with her aunt and uncle. She cannot read the language of direction. "Cow paths wound the slope, a puzzle of trails going nowhere." She grows cold, tired, confused. Night is coming. Like the fox at the head of the cove, Nezzie finds her route of escape cut off. "Dusk thickened. Not a star showed. And presently the flat [where she is walking] ended against a wall of rock." She wants to weep but chokes back tears and perseveres, because her father has asked her to "Be a little woman." The actual terrain Nezzie covers is limited, and she is never far from her home or from that of her aunt and uncle. Yet the story encapsulates a mythical journey, like the journey to Biggety Creek in the story "Mrs. Razor," like Jack's journey to the giant's house. Nezzie's small world symbolizes the great world, her journey over the ridge the transition from childhood to adulthood — her journey into the world. The bench of rock on which she takes refuge has, for her, "the width of the world." Her journey produces knowledge, a "hateful wisdom" that "caught at her heart and choked her throat."

Dead from exposure on the ridge, where wind "flowed with the sound of water" through trees, Nezzie is one with the dead riding the waters of the river of earth. The failed journey of "The Nest" is prefigured in the early poems and prose. References to the death of a brother in the poem "Child in the Hills" and to a child's grave in "Death on the Mountain" anticipate the death of the young in the stories and in *River of Earth*. When the mother complains about the difficulty of raising guineas, the father observes: "Bounden to lose some. It's the same with folks. Hain't everybody lives to rattle their bones. Hain't everybody breathes till their veins get blue as dogtick stalks." The father's observation is borne out in the death of a colt at birth and by the death of the Middleton baby from croup.

James Still's achievement as literary artist largely rests on the success with which he blends sophisticated and self-conscious storytelling with a folk mode found in the oral traditions of Appalachia. Writing in 1905 in *The Spirit of the Mountains*, Emma Bell Miles stressed the potential of the folk language and oral traditions of the southern highlands and thought them the basis of a contribution to the national literature. Still exploits that potential, illustrating Eliot's observation that literature takes its life from common speech and Frost's belief that literary form is the amplifying and elaborating of folk speech.

The color and concreteness of Still's language often stems from his use of the folk simile. The mother in the short story "The Proud Walkers" complains of a windowless house: "Nary a window cut ... A house blind as a mole varmit." The father in "Locust Summer," observing his unkempt children, remarks that their hands are "rusty as hinges." The hyperbole characteristic of folk speech occurs frequently. A character in "On Quicksand Creek" quips: "A mouse wouldn't raise young'uns in that trampy quilt." A cattleman has a pair of boots with toes so sharp "You could nigh pick a splinter out o' yore finger with them."

Still's narrators are as much at home with the local language as are other characters. Therefore, folk similes and local expressions occur not just in dialogue but naturally and unobtrusively in the narrative. The child narrator of "The Proud Walkers" observes: "So sleepy baby was, his head rolled like a dropped gourd." The young narrator of "School Butter" describes the day Uncle Jolly rode past the school as "an August afternoon when heat-boogers danced the dry creekbed and willows hung limp with thirst." Still is so thoroughly at home with the terse vividness of folk speech he can simulate it, as he has done in "School Butter" when he describes children listening "still as moss eating rocks."

Still blends elements of folk speech with more refined elements as effectively in the poems as in prose. In the poem "On Double Creek," the county poor farm has "furrows as crooked as an adder's track." In "Apple Trip," apples are "tooth-ticklers" and "grin-busters." Still is never far from folk speech. In the poem "Memorial Day: Little Carr Creek," artificial flowers are as "lifeless as doorknobs," a variation of the folk simile, "dead as a doorknob." Still's subtlest metaphors accommodate, or arise from, local terms or expressions.

Still effectively blends the folk and the fine not only in expressions and turns of phrase; he also appropriates folk forms in the oral tradition — the anecdote, the tale, the folk sermon, and themes and situations associated with folk experience generally — and amplifies and elaborates these for sophisticated literary purposes. Stories such as "A Ride on the Short Dog" and "The Run for the Elbertas" consist of elaborated series of rusties, or mischievous pranks. Other stories resemble folk tales or ballads in their narrative structure. Whether tramping about a coal camp, taking part in a cattle drive or leaving home for a settlement school, Still's young protagonists forever set out into the world, open to experience, at once innocent and shrewd, like Jack of Jack and the Beanstalk. Nezzie Hargis sets out for her aunt and uncle's, as a critic has suggested, much as Little Red Riding Hood sets out for her grandmother's or as does Nelly in the ballad "Footprints in the Snow." When Still's narrator is someone more nearly like himself, as in the poems, the speaker is still a kind of Jack, going out to white highways, going to Hurricane Gap to buy apples, being drafted into the army. Still's protagonists do not even have to be human. The colt in "Foal" is turned in wonder toward the wide world, about to begin its "timid quest" no less than Nezzie Hargis or Still's nameless child narrators.

Still's achievement as literary artist can also be appreciated by comparing his depictions of mountain life with the way the Appalachian region of America has been typically depicted. The French critic Roland Barthes (*Mythologies,* 1972) maintains that there is an inherent difficulty in writing about mountains and mountain people, the result of a bourgeois Alpine myth that causes writers and readers to take leave of their senses "anytime the ground is uneven." Whatever the cause or causes, Appalachia appears in American writing as a funhouse of distorted and contradictory images which, since the mid-nineteenth century, have suited the needs, motives, and perspectives of abolitionists, social workers, Protestant missionaries, industrialists, and entrepreneurs. Appalachia has been known through an either/or literature — either as a place of problems, poverty, and peculiar people or as a preserve of fundamentally American values, sterling Anglo-Saxon and Anglo-Celtic qualities. The region entered the popular American mind during the 1880s by way of local colorists (chief among them Mary N. Murfree, pseud. Charles Egbert Craddock), who noted the quaint and sensational aspects of a way of life suddenly perceived to be old-fashioned. By the 1920s, a careful student of Appalachia remarked that more was known about the region that was not true than about any other part of the country.

At a time when it was fashionable, indeed almost obligatory for poetry about Appalachia to be either a witless romanticizing of mountains and mountain people, or proletarian verse, Still took a different approach. He presents no diagnosis of economic ills, preaches no social gospel, offers no program. He declines to participate in the either/or literature, ambitious to do no more — and no less— than to show people in their place and tell how it was with these people at a particular time.

As a consequence, Still's poems discover not just a landscape of beauty and wild freedom and not just visual blight, exploitation, and hard, unremitting conditions. All these things are caught up in a vision both local and universal. Still's poems embody certain universal themes implicit in the experience of people in a particular time and place — the themes of endurance, perseverance and self-preservation under harsh and perilous circumstances.

Details and images create an impression of a difficult life at subsistence level. Danger and death are ever-present. Life under such conditions is characterized by stark contrasts—between the bitterness and sweetness of experience, between toughness and tenderness. Beauty and blight, untrammeled freedom and imprisonment co-exist. From birth to death, the circumscribed life of man and beast is difficult, uncertain, constantly endangered. The response to these conditions is to endure.

The characteristic qualities of his style blend with Still's ever-present themes in the representative poem "Spring." The restraint and understatement of the opening line is gently insisted upon by repetition that suggests conversation, or a ballad: "Not all of us were warm, not all of us." Subsequent lines illustrate Still's simple diction and objective reporting of concrete details: "We are winter-lean, our faces are sharp with cold / And there is a smell of wood-smoke in our clothes; / Not all of us were warm, though we hugged the fire / Through the long chilled nights." The poem concentrates Still's themes of endurance, perseverance, and self-preservation: "We have come out / Into the sun again, we have untied our knot / Of flesh." (In its imagery and concrete detail, the poem anticipates the strategy for enduring expressed by the mother in *River of Earth* after the mines close: "We've got to live small," she says. "We've got to tie ourselves up in such a knot nobody else can get in." Later the novel's narrator reports: "We had come through to spring, but mother [who has given birth to a child] was leanest of us all.")

In "Spring," we also find Still's tendency to see people and place as parts of one subtly interdependent whole. The condition of the people in the poem resembles that of the animals and plants that have also endured winter. "We are no thinner than a hound or mare, / Or an unleaved poplar. We have come through / To the grass, to the cows calving in the lot." In a poem entitled "Anecdote of Men by the Thousand," Wallace Stevens writes: "There are men of a province / who are that province." First in the poems, and later in novels and short stories, James Still suggests a similar identity between people and place. The physical features, characteristics, and qualities of people mirror their environment. In the poem "Troublesome Creek" men wait "as mountains long have waited." In "Epitaph for Uncle Ira Combs, Mountain Preacher" (who may be the prototype for Brother Mobberly in *River of Earth*), the preacher's faith is likened to the mountains he has looked on for so long. People are like the hills, and hills resemble people. The ridges in "Journey Beyond the Hills" are "heavy-hipped." In the poem "Court Day," the hills are so near they seem like people crowding close at the open courthouse window. A similar personification of hills occurs in *River of Earth*. On his seventh birthday, acutely aware of how much he has grown, the narrator thinks that "the hills to the east of Little Carr Creek had also grown and stretched their ridge shoulders, and that the beechwood crowding their slopes grew down to a living heart."

Like the dress of Stevens' woman of Lhassa, James Still's poems are "an invisible element" of a place "made visible." Making himself almost invisible as a speaker in the poems, concentrating not on sensibility or on social and economic views, Still allows an invisible element of a place and a people to come into sharp focus. This invisible element, the themes of endurance, perseverance, and self-preservation under harsh and unrelenting conditions, is rendered visible not only in the content of the poems but also through style and structure. The economy and concreteness of expression and the spareness of style reflect not only the laconic quality of folk speech but also conditions of life from which the language springs. Structure and content, style and theme are blended in a genuine expression of a people and a place.

The freshness of expression and point of view in Still's poems results from his having avoided the superficiality and sensationalism of local colorists and propagandists. Local colorists give the impression of having looked at mountain people and noted the quainter aspects of their traditional life. Reformers emphasize the deplorable circumstances resulting from inadequacies of that traditional life or from its destruction through the incursion of mercantile interests. Still gives the impression not merely of having looked at a place and a people but of having lived with them as he has for over fifty years. While both the local colorists and proponents of social and economic viewpoints say "they," Still says "we," by placing the speakers of his poems and the narrators of his stories and novels at the center of the action and speaking from the inside out.

James Still's work belongs to a general literary quickening which first manifested itself in the South during the late 1920s and early 1930s. In the upland South, this quickening was anticipated. In 1905, Emma Bell Miles spoke of the people of Appalachia as "a people asleep, a race without knowledge of its existence," but a literary awakening would come to Appalachia, Miles believed, once mountain people were awakened to "consciousness of themselves as a people." Echoing Miles several years later, Horace Kephart, author of *Our Southern Highlanders,* saw mountain folk as a "people without annals" who awaited their artist. Kephart wrote on the eve of a period beginning with the entry of the United States into World War I and continuing into the years of the Great Depression. During this time, events broke down the isolation of both lowland and upland South, bringing increased self-awareness, conflicts of values and the need to examine, defend, or perhaps re-define traditional life. This cultural shock released creative energy and imagination throughout the South and resulted in a Southern literary renaissance. In the upland South, the period brought forth not one artist, but several, including Thomas Wolfe, and Kentuckians Elizabeth Madox Roberts, Jesse Stuart, Caroline Gordon, Allen Tate, Robert Penn Warren, Harriette Simpson Arnow and others. James Still belongs with this group as one of the first generation of native voices from the Appalachian South.

At its best, the literature of the Appalachian region, according to the novelist Wilma Dykeman, is "as unique as churning butter, as universal as getting born." Such a combination of uniqueness and universality, found in the best literature of any time and place, is present in these poems, which are an integral part of Still's overall achievement. They are poems in which abstractions consist of what particulars ultimately mean. Like all genuine poems, they are, as William Carlos Williams puts it, "a vision of the facts."

# The Poetry: "The Journey of a Worldly Wonder"

## Jeff Daniel Marion

It's a familiar scene: late afternoon at a small southern town bus stop, already the bus filled with various sojourners, mostly rural folk returning home, a few others going longer distances, but all travelers settling back for miles of rolling hills, lush valleys, landscapes familiar to most, new to some. The engine whirrs and whines; the journey begins. But before the bus can make its turn away from the station, a lone straggler runs to the door waving his ticket and pecking on the window. He comes aboard and takes the only remaining seat beside a young man with a book balanced on his knees. Settling, the late arrival introduces himself and notes with pleasure the book perched on his traveling companion's lap. He offers the young man a magazine from his coat pocket, says there's a selection in it he'd like for him to read. So the two settle back for the journey: one to read the passing landscape, the other to journey in a world of words.

And so it is in poetry — but remember that poetry is both vehicle and destination, both journey and place of arrival. Nothing new in that idea — it's a familiar scene. When we enter the landscapes of James Still's poetry, it's a familiar scene but one that etches itself indelibly in memory, a journey that routes its way across a terrain more than mere passing scenery, a terrain of the heart and mind in the process of discovery, knowing, understanding, and enduring. As Still himself has noted,

> When I have done a thing it often seems that it preexisted and had only to be discovered. The creative act involves a person wholly. More even than he knows about himself, or could guess. The work of the great mental computer which has registered every mini-second of being from the moment of birth. Creativity involves the total experience, inherited characteristics, learning. The joys, the sorrows, the horrors.

Consider, then, some of the places of his poems, beginning with "Farm."

> In the deep moist hollows, on the burnt acres
> Suspended upon the mountainside, the crisp green corn
> Tapers blunt to the fruiting tassel;
> Long straight shafts of yellow poplar
> Strike upward like prongs of lightning at the field's edge,

*Marion, Jeff Daniel. "James Still's Poetry: 'The Journey of a Worldly Wonder.'" The Iron Mountain Review 2.1 (Summer 1984): 17–21. Reprinted with permission.*

> Dwarfing the tender blades, the jointed growth;
> Crows haggle their dark feathers, glare beady eyes
> Surveying the slanted crop from the poplar boughs,
> Opening purple beaks to cry the ripening feast,
> And flow from their perch in heavy pointless flight.
> A lizard, timid and tremulous, swallowing clots of air
> With pulsing throat, pauses at the smooth trunk
> And runs up the sky with liquid feet.

This is no cozy scene, no placid Eden, no cornucopia of eternal delights. The language itself is *alive,* energetic, moving. In an interview, Still cautioned the budding writer to be wary "of static words in composition — words registering little change. Someone has calculated that Zane Grey's work is ninety-five percent static while James Joyce's is only five percent." Note that here the acres are "burnt," the corn is "crisp," the "tapers blunt." Indeed, even the yellow poplar trees tower over the corn, dwarf it, not only in size but also in energy as suggested by their similarity to "prongs of lightning." And as every farmer/gardener knows: if the crows didn't visit the field as the corn was barely thrusting through the earth and pull it up shoot by tender shoot, pecking the germinating seed at the root, then wait until harvest time. These returning furies will then "haggle," "glare," "survey," and "cry the ripening feast." But in a poem whose energy has been generated primarily by active, sensory verbs and nouns, the central irony resides in the adjective *pointless:* the crows "flow from their perch in heavy pointless flight." Destinationless, yes, but also the crows do not fly in a distinct formation, pointless. "Pointless" vividly contrasts with "tapers," "shafts," "edge," "prongs," "blades," "beaks," and perch." But the most telling contrast is in the final three lines: the "timid and tremulous" lizard. In a poem in which we expect images such as "hollow," "acres," "corn," "crows," and "ripening feast," the lizard comes as a surprise. We react much as we might upon seeing the lizard itself. Or, as another poet has put it: "His notice sudden is." This unexpectedness quickens the pulse, sharpens our senses, focuses our perception.

But Still's attitude toward the land and its power is more than an ironic vision of the thin line between the crows' boldness and the lizard's timidity, the lightning-like yellow poplars and the dwarfed corn stalks, or the tightrope the farmer walks between hardship and harvest. In "Heritage," the persona senses other claims.

> I shall not leave these prisoning hills
> Though they topple their barren heads to level earth
> And the forests slide uprooted out of the sky.
> Though the waters of Troublesome, of Trace Fork,
> Of Sand Lick rise in a single body to glean the valleys,
> To drown lush pennyroyal, to unravel rail fences;
> Though the sun-ball breaks the ridges into dust
> And burns its strength into the blistered rock
> I cannot leave. I cannot go away.
>
> Being of these hills, being one with the fox
> Stealing into the shadows, one with the new-born foal,
> The lumbering ox drawing green beech logs to mill,
> One with the destined feet of man climbing and descending,
> And one with death rising to bloom again, I cannot go.
> Being of these hills I cannot pass beyond.

Here the land is both prison and home. The power it exerts on the speaker is such that he feels compelled to find in language an equal power to match the strength of its claim. Surely this is the claim of an artist/writer who does not see himself as separate from the land he writes of but instead is *one with* the fox, the new born foal, the lumbering ox, the destined feet of man, and ultimately one with death itself. The catalog is a revealing one: craftiness, cunning ("fox stealing into the shadows"), innocence ("new-born foal"), awkwardness of raw power ("the lumbering ox"), the arduous struggle of man ("destined feet of man climbing and descending"), and finally "death rising to bloom again." This artist refuses to reject any of the qualities of his heritage. He recognizes the universal in these local details. There is the implicit understanding that even if the hills, forests, valleys, and ridges were to be swept away, he will remain forever in place. The place is *in* him. It is thus his locus, the source he will neither deny nor abandon. This is not to say that Still's artistry depends on the source of his subject matter, however. Dean Cadle so astutely reminds us that "[Still] would be an artist in any hollow in any country. All that finally matters is the always whirling life in the ever-fresh vision in Still's mind; and once he gets it on paper there is little reason for concern over whether it ever actually existed, for hopefully neither time nor reality will erode it."

Still's poem "Wolfpen Creek" is yet another representation of his vision of the land:

> How it was in that place, how light hung in a bright pool
> Of air like water, in an eddy of cloud and sky,
> I will long remember. I will long recall.
> The maples blossoming wings, the oaks proud with rule,
> The spiders deep in silk, the squirrels fat on mast,
> The fields and draws and coves where quail and peewees call.
> Earth loved more than any earth, stand firm, hold fast;
> Trees burdened with leaf and bird, root deep, grow tall.

So the particular quality of light in a landscape enters memory, that bright pool the speaker will draw from, drink from, for a long time. And, yes, how it was in that place is reflected in this pool, this lyric of praise for "earth loved more than any earth."

How it was in that place: the journey of Still's poems is not one of landscape only. We long remember, long recall the characters and the rituals by which they live in that place, Still's world. The ritualistic processes through which we expend our energy, pass our time, find our joys, fulfill our hopes, or realize horrors are suggested by the titles of several poems: "Mountain Fox Hunt," "Horse Swapping," "Court Day," and "Dance on Pushback." Even though these poems are significant in accurately documenting cultural and social mores, folkways, their value ultimately lies in their artistry, the ways the poems themselves journey in language to substantiate reality. As Robert Frost has told us in "The Figure a Poem Makes": "It begins in delight and ends in wisdom ... it inclines to the impulse, it assumes direction with the first line laid down, it runs a course of lucky events and ends in a clarification of life ... It finds its own name as it goes and discovers the best waiting for it in some final phrase at once wise and sad." Notice how "Dance on Pushback" fulfills Frost's description.

> Rein your sorry nags boys, buckle the polished saddle
> And set black hats aslant the wind down Troublesome,
> There are doings on Pushback at Gabe Waye's homeplace
> And the door hangs wide, the thumping keg bubbles
> With gonesome plumping in the elderberry patch;
> The cider brew strains against red cob stoppers
> And the puncheon floor is mealed for the skip and shuffle,
> Ready for the stamping, waiting for the hopping,
> The Grapevine swing, the ole Virginie reeling
> In the grease lamp's fuming and unsteady gleaming.
> There are jolly fellows heading toward Pushback

In the valley's brisk breathing, the moon's white bathing,
In the whippoorwill's lonesome never-answered calling.

Gabe Waye has six fair young daughters
Who dance like foxfire in dark thickets,
Whose feet are nimble, whose bodies are willowy,
As smooth as yellow poplars in early bud,
And their cheeks are like maple leaves in early autumn,
And their breath as sweet as fresh mountain tea.
Gabe Waye has six full-blooming daughters
With dresses starched as stiff as galax leaves,
Awaiting the dancing, awaiting and hoping.

Rein-up the filly boys, hitch-up the stallion
And heigh-o yonder toward Pushback Mountain,
The katydids a-calling, the hoot-owl a-hooting,
Thick hoofs are striking fire on the crookedy trail,
For feet are yearning for the heart-leaf weaving
And a sight of Waye's daughters doing the Fare-you-well.

Gabe Waye has three tall strapping sons
Standing six feet five in wide bare feet,
And with handsome faces where laughter's never fading,
And with swift limber fingers for silver strings twanging.
The tallest picks the banjo, the thickest saws the fiddle,
The broadest plays the dulcimer with the readiest grace,
And the three together set the darkling hollow ringing
While the harmony goes tripping over moon-dappled hill.

Spur-up the nags boys, the dance won't be lasting,
Tighten up the reins and set the pebbles flying,
Heigh-o to Pushback with a quick lick-a-spittle,
Night will be fading and moonlight dying.

The cast of characters we encounter in a journey through Still's poems ranges from Uncle Ira Combs, mountain preacher, who is a mountain of faith, to Bad Jack Means, whose "sins / Killed every fish in the river," a man so intolerable that he brings the narrator to question heaven with: "Are you up There, Bad Jack? / If you are, if He took you in, / I think I'll choose the Other Place." There are also those for whom music is essential. Banjo Bill Cornett is the quintessential artist who not only has shaped his banjo by his own hands but also sings his own song: "This is his own true love / He grieves, these his winding lonesome valleys / Blowing with perished leaves and winds that starve / In the chestnut oaks, and these the deaths he dies. / His voice is a whispering water, the speech of a dove." For this artist, Banjo Bill Cornett, music is the means by which he experiences both joys and sorrows ("It [the banjo] is his tongue for joy, it is his eyes for weeping"). On the other hand, there is Clabe Mott, a man obviously not made for farming, for "The sun rakes the fields, your farm stands fallow, / The mouldboard rusts, the plowstock stands upturned, / The harness falls in heaps within your sagging barn / And your stock runs free upon the brambled hills." Nevertheless, when this man takes out his fiddle and begins to play, the world is at his command: "The waters wait, the winds break their pace, ... / The oaks go down with thunder in the singing air." Not only do we experience the presence of those who live energetically in their pursuit of some moment of joy, but there is also the lingering presence of the dead. The narrator in "Nixie Middleton" achingly tells us "I am alone and all the hills have eyed my sorrow, / And bird and fox have heard my breath along the slopes / Whistling your name." The narrator's journey is a search for his lost love, a pilgrimage that takes him "up Sand Lick, up Carr's clear waters / And the sixty-seven mile wandering of Troublesome Creek." The end of this quest is "the laurel-thicket hill / Where my love sleeps. My love waits for me still." But perhaps the epitome of Still's world is Uncle Ambrose, a man whose very being has become one with the landscape in which he lives. Like the land, he *is* strength, stability, endurance.

> Your hair is growing long, Uncle Ambrose,
> And the strands of your beard are like willow sprays
> Hanging over Troublesome Creek's breeze in August.
> Uncle Ambrose, your hands are heavy with years,
> Seamy with the ax's heft, the plow's hewn stock,
> The thorn wound and the stump-dark bruise of time.
>
> Your face is a map of Knott County
> With hard ridges of flesh, the wrinkled creek beds,
> The traces and forks carved like wagon tracks on stone;
> And there is Troublesome's valley struck violently
> By a barlow's blade, and the anti-cline of all waters
> This side of the Kentucky River.
>
> Your teeth are dark-stained apples on an ancient tree
> And your eyes the trout pools between the narrow hills;
> Your hands are glacial drifts of stone
> Cradled on a mountain top:
> One is Big Ball Mountain, rock-ribbed and firm,
> One the Appalachian range from Maine to Alabama.

Frequently details similar to ones we see woven into the life of Uncle Ambrose become occasions for poems themselves, journeys into the nature of things themselves. In the poem "Dulcimer," we see details of a world drawn into the object: not only do we see the uniqueness of the object, but by an amazing catalog of metaphors a context is also established whereby we see the greater world in which the object exists. "Dulcimer" is, then, microcosm.

> The dulcimer sings from fretted maple throat
> Of the doe's swift poise, the fox's fleeting step
> And music of hounds upon the outward slope
> Stirring the night, drumming the ridge-strewn way,
> The anvil's strength ...
>                     and the silence after
> That aches and cries unhushed into the day.
>
> From the dulcimer's breast sound hunting horns
> Strong as clenched hands upon the edge of death,
> The creak of saddle-bags, of oxen yoke and thongs,
> Wild turkey's treble, dark sudden flight of crows,
> Of unshod hoofs ...
>                  and the stillness after,
> Bitter as salt drenching the tongue of pain:
>
> And of the lambs crying, breath of the lark,
> Long drinks from piggins hard against the lips;
> And with hoarse singing, raw as hickory shagbark,
> The foal's anxiety is woven with the straining wedge
> And the wasp's anger ...
>                 and the quiet after
> For the carver of maple on a keen blade's edge.

Notice the blending of object, sound, and motion; notice the surge, the rush of everything toward "silence," "stillness," "quiet." This is the pulse of life itself, the surge poised against stillness and death, "the keen blade's edge." What William Heyen once said regarding Williams' "Red Wheelbarrow" could be said of Still's "Dulcimer":

> This is one of the reasons [it] ... is so important; as object, as thing to engage the mind, it is always there, it is matter. Perhaps the steps are sight, speech, awe, and silence. "Revision," speech again, wonder and silence again, looking up in perfect silence at the stars again, as Whitman said, "The poet's art not to chart, but to voyage." Nature itself is the Zen master who sends us back day after day for as long as we live to study perhaps one in exhaustible leaf or sound or angle of sunlight.

Again and again Still's poems do voyage, take us on journeys of the self. In "With Hands Like Leaves," we find a narrator who wanders quietly in dark thickets and discovers: "This is not a mountain I walk upon. It is a ridge / Of sleep or death, a slope hung on a night-jar's speech. / A child walks here with hands like leaves, with eyes / Like swifts that search the darkness in a perilous land. / He seeks a hill where living day shall stand." This wanderer in the fearful dark seeks light, knows the precarious balance of the self hoping to endure. We do not know whether the journey will be successful. Closely related to this wanderer is the narrator of "Eyes in the Grass" who recognizes the separation of the self from nature, particularly from the grackle and the ant whom he observes. Through this journey the narrator reaches a moment of self-awareness and says, "I think that neither the grackle's black eyes / Nor the ant's myopic sight has found me here, / Drowned in quivering stems, lost in wattled twigs / Of grass-trees. O I am lost to any wandering view. / I am a hill uncharted, my breathing is the wind. / I am horizon. I am earth's far end."

Although there are some journeys (particularly in "Hounds on the Mountain" and "Pattern for Death") that end bitterly or with the realization that there is no escape, there is the seasoned traveler in "White Highways" who arrives at a paradoxical truth: his journeying has brought him back to the starting point with the realization "Here is my pleasure most where I have lived / And called my home." The road to discovery we find turns backwards. We rediscover Emerson's truth: "Man is a knot of roots."

And now our journey leads us back to the two travelers who have journeyed by bus across Kentucky. They have reached their destinations, and as they take leave of one another, they agree to stay in touch, to write to one another, for during this journey they have found that they have common interests. The young man who sat with a book perched on his knees and who read from his fellow traveler's magazine during the trip was Cratis Williams, known to many now as Mr. Appalachia, certainly one of the region's most outstanding spokesmen and interpreters. And yes, the words he read during the trip were those written by his fellow traveler, James Still. Although this first meeting of Cratis Williams with the man James Still and his words occurred nearly half a century ago, we can certainly say of that trip and of Still's poetry: "And O the trip was a sight to the world, / The journey a worldly wonder."

# Still's Poetry and the Western Tradition

## ALEKSIS RANNIT

The story is well known. After the Victorian Age/Belle Epoque/Art Nouveau's failures and triumphs — after the flowery adjectives, poeticisms, the conversion of taste for sound and verbal rhythm into decorative patterns of high-flavored melodious verse, into a strange mixture of the sensual and the partially mystical or merely mystifying, after Tennyson, Rossetti, Swinburne, Mallarmé, and young Rilke — came revulsion. Even the Expressionists (who largely intensified and dramatized the Impressionists' colorist cleanness, rendering their play of light and syllables less fluidly and often purely graphically) rejected previous achievements and tried to return to primitive or neo-medieval form. Together with the Cubists and the Futurists, they proclaimed as holy the abstractness of hard edges and sudden sharp contrasts, now ascendant over the chromatic beauty and harmonic technique of the past. Established aesthetics collapsed, and after the First World War the way was open to the refined individualist T.S. Eliot and to Eliotism, abjuring all Romanticism and even ignoring its existence.

Two options were left: first, to follow Eliot and his associates in intellectualizing and pseudo-intellectualizing poetry to the point of becoming barren of feeling. Was, and is, the final aim of this school to perform a ritual of subtle sterilization of the word? Even if not, many American and English poets began to write predominantly for academic critics and some of them still do, cultivating a stiff dryness, an anti-musicality, a snobbery of nihilism and of the manneristically unnatural.

Or there was the other, more organic possibility: to remember Burns, Hardy, and Housman, especially Housman, in whose poetry poignantly personal feeling was embodied in "simple" verse of considerable sophistication and richness of classical association. This second line of versemakers, which later produced Robert Frost, James Still, and Robert Francis, was and is in the minority, although it looks to me that exactly these and similar poets will probably lose little in the next century, since they stand above epoch, above sensationalism and thus provisional contemporaneity. A minority, perhaps, but a remarkable one: Edward Thomas, Robert Graves, Langston Hughes (his pure lyrics, not his journalistic or political poems), Edgar Lee Masters (excluding his late pessimistic and cynical poems), William Meredith. At the end of this line may be found the skeletal excellence of the poetry

*Rannit, Aleksis. "A Commentary."* Appalachian Heritage *14.4 (Fall 1986): 21–4. Reprinted with permission.*

of James Laughlin and James L. Weil—skeletal, yes, but not stillborn. This is a company of people whose poetry does not renounce tonality, though it renounces the obtrusive musicalization, even the individualistic synthesis, of mere tunefulness. They did not cultivate an increasing self-consciousness of being original; they did not accentuate the need for every poem to be a universe unto itself. Theirs was a classical bearing of genuine modesty and willing restraint, personal and artistic. They have chosen (and James Still, the "simple" laborer of art, does it convincingly) an unforced way, a thread that allows one poetic thought to follow naturally upon another, the many virtues of moderation. Here, technical skill, at one with the naivete of a peasant-worker poet-craftsman, is patent. Sovereign ease of writing, learning lightly worn, happiness in remaining within certain conventions or at least not straying too far from them, the habit of not being afraid to please the general reader—this is what we may call Still's "classical" attitude. He possesses the art of making his poetry seem familiar, and thus, despite some contrapuntal refinements, he becomes popular and pleasing to many readers. As an authentic biological talent, James Still has achieved a germinating unity in his poems, and his best pieces calmly summarize his life as work, while mirroring his inborn feelings for the Appalachian landscape—for him, the landscape of inwardness. Born poor, he remains a harmonious, forgiving, and grateful man. He does not accuse anybody or complain and cry even when he suggests the tragic life of his Appalachian folk. The sense of style and the craftsman's skill by which he often surpasses his models are most plainly revealed in writing born of contact with life rather than with books. In so many of his poems he has spoken for the people; in "Spring" it is the people's voice that seems to speak, in the uncomplicated language of the heart:

> Not all of us were warm, not all of us.
> We are winter-lean, our faces are sharp with cold
> And there is a smell of wood smoke in our clothes;
> Not all of us were warm, though we hugged the fire
> Through the long chilled nights.
>
>                               We have come out
> Into the sun again, we have untied our knot
> Of flesh: We are no thinner than a hound or mare,
> Or an unleaved poplar. We have come through
> To the grass, to the cows calving in the lot.

Many modern poets have shouted and cried outrageously, most of them without even a sonorous voice, though some, like Maiakovskii and Neruda, have often succeeded. Yet after too many "ninth symphonies," it is good to listen to James Still's shepherd's reed. To be sure, a poem by Still is not a *begerette*, that tender French *air* of the 18th century in which shepherds and shepherdesses sing. What distinguishes Still's poetry from these idyllic, pastoral forms is the element of genuine human cognizance, a natural capacity to see the depth of things. Perhaps there are better direct or indirect comparisons, other similarities between Still's works of rural life and scenes, and the form-view of the practitioners of *Kunstmusik*. Haydn's domestic pieces, like the baryton trios or his early F major *Missa brevis,* come to mind because of their deceptive simplicity and homophonic quality. Perhaps the ideals of clarity and directness of Satie, Poulenc, and Benjamin Britten. On the American scene, perhaps Virgil Thomson's works, some of his Baptist hymns and straightforward settings of popular songs of the 19th century, and the music of Frederick Delius, the unaccompanied chorus of his *Appalachia,* for example; or, better, his *Brigg Fair* may be not too far from Still's mode of expression. But the musical chiaroscuro of Delius, however fine, is that of an English

sentimentalist, while Still remains an American poetic realist. We may also enter the territory of 19th century Romanticism, a quality present in Still's work but not demonstrative.
Perhaps Still's sensitive blending of major and minor modes and thoughts comes close to certain of Schubert's and even Wolf's songs, specifically Wolf's settings for Eduard Mörike's
lyrics, but Still actually expresses a starker and severer attitude to life, and thus has a strong
affinity With Theodor Storm, who was also deeply rooted in his own North German homeland. One may also remember other poets born out of a homeland's soil: Johann Peter Hebel,
Matthias Claudius, and Giovanni Pascoli; as well as those true geniuses of simplicity: the
Galician Rosalia de Castro and the Ukranian Taras Shevchenko. Then the famous poems of
*Doctor Zhivago* (not the melodramatic prose) have a lack of cunning and duplicity that renders them akin to Still's own verse, and are similarly rooted in the very energy of word. What
Pasternak, who as a poet changed dramatically from an ornamentalist to a classicalist,
expressed has validity in contemplating Still's poetry: poetry must become "the grain of pure
prose." Still's own prose has rhythmically the grain of pure poetry and thus is in the neighborhood of Solzhenitsyn's *Matriona's House* and Tolstoy's *Death of Ivan Ilyich* as well as the
latter's short stories, because Still, too, is able to transcend the narrow limits of experience
and produce work of universal interest.

Prestige never satisfying his art or peace of mind, Still is fundamentally a man's artist,
not an artist's artist, an artisan of plainness, of artlessness. His quest is for freedom from complexity, intricacy, elaborateness, for freedom from artificiality, pretentiousness, and luxury.
His poetry is, in a way, the by-product of sincere dedication to his own evolving aesthetic
standards. Still is ulteriorly occupied with the minimum means to an expressive end. Thus,
having reflected upon all feasible comparisons, I see in him a brother of Chardin, who concentrated on his still lifes, composed of modest wooden, copper, glass, and earthenware uten-
sils, ripening fruits, and the ingredients of meals. Not all the poems of our poet are exclusively
still lifes, but all of them are "James-Still-lifes." They have passed into the air we breathe; they
are so real that they seem things rather than words, or nearer still, living beings.

Although I come from a different land and a dissimilar culture, James Still inspires me
with his integrity as a virile, natural-born poetic writer, his fundamental simplicity, his intrin-
sic charm, and his latent hopefulness—all characteristics entirely consistent with what we
know of him (is he both a Southern and Nordic writer?). Having read his poem, "Leap, Min-
nows, Leap," which expresses his constant trust, deep expectation, faith, and the unpro-
nounced truth that man does not fight only to win, I responded in my own idiom with these
lines in humble tribute:

> I hear your tiny
> cyprinoid fish
> struggling
> in the gravelly
> dying stream,
> singing praise
> to the river of word.
> The streaming mountain
> of the Word is
> high,
> and there I see you,
> Jim,
> swimming uphill
> towards the low-voiced
> ground waters—
> beyond the mountain.

# "The Stillness After":
# Reflections on the Poetry

## ROBERT M. WEST

Perhaps the first thing to say about James Still's poetry is that it is virtually unknown by the "poetry establishment" today. The Library of America recently issued the first two volumes of its four-volume anthology of twentieth century American poetry; given his date of birth, Still should be in volume 2, but he is not. He is also omitted from the popular *Norton Anthology of Modern Poetry*, as well as from such well-known anthologies of southern literature as Louisiana State University Press's *The Literary South* and W.W. Norton's *Literature of the American South*. Although many of his poems first appeared in several prestigious publications—*The Atlantic, Poetry, The New Republic, The Nation,* and the *New York Times*—and although they have won the admiration of poets ranging from James Dickey to May Swenson, Still's poetry has yet to win widespread recognition.

Like Dickey, Still began as a poet and later turned to fiction; as was also the case with Dickey, Still's success as a fiction-writer diminished his enthusiasm for writing poetry. The first third of Still's poems were written from 1931 to 1936, the year of his first real success at publishing short stories; the poems came at a much slower pace over the next sixty years as Still diverted his energies elsewhere. He became a regular prose contributor to *The Saturday Evening Post,* which paid enough to support him as he composed his novel *River of Earth;* the enduring success of that book cemented his identity as a writer of prose fiction. Still's posthumous collected poems, *From the Mountain, From the Valley,* edited by Ted Olson and recently published by the University Press of Kentucky, offers us an opportunity to give this aspect of Still's work the attention it has long been due.

Still's poems almost always deal with the culture and landscape of his adopted Kentucky home of Knott County. He writes of the people's love of music, their politics, and their religious faith; of their farming, hunting, and work in the coal mines; of their suffering, their joys, and their dreams. He writes of their environment: the wildlife, the creeks, the mountains themselves; the change of seasons, the daily weather, the dawns. Occasionally he addresses his own identity as a poet, musing on his own life in this place. Yet, despite his Alabama origins, he never adopts the perspective of the outsider. His poetry bears witness to a people and

*West, Robert M. "'The Stillness After': Reflections on the Poetry of James Still."* Journal of Kentucky Studies *19 (2002): 126–31. Reprinted with permission.*

the world they live in, but he also always identifies himself as a part of that world. His work is not about "them"; it is about "us."

These are poems of witness, but they are first of all poems—"made things" certainly as remarkable in their craft as anything concocted by most American poets of the 1930s and '40s. As Jeff Daniel Marion writes, "Even though [Still's] poems are significant in accurately documenting cultural and social mores, folkways, their value ultimately lies in their artistry, the way the poems themselves journey in language to substantiate reality" (18). We can celebrate Still's poems for their evocation (and therefore preservation) of a society we know to be disappearing or even disappeared, but we should also be prepared to approach them as the remarkable verbal performances they are. He is capable of spinning out metrical, rhyming poems as poised and incantatory as anything Frost ever devised; he can also wield meters as supple as Pound's or Eliot's. His best poems offer dense patterns of sound: webs of alliteration, assonance, and rhyme, typically stretched over stress-heavy lines. The language is always concrete and precise; if, as Wallace Stevens says, the greatest poverty is not to live in a physical world, then Still was a wealthy man indeed. Furthermore, his language is often so economical that grasping a poem's meaning on a first reading (or listening) can be quite difficult. Sometimes his poems seem more akin to music than to speech—a fact that makes him out of place in a century when the mainstream of American poetry was obsessed with sounding like talk.

That musicality is especially apparent in Still's poems about traditional musical instruments and those who play them. Consider one of his best-known poems, "Dulcimer":

> The dulcimer sings from fretted maple throat
> Of the doe's swift poise, the fox's fleeting step
> And music of hounds upon the outward slope
> Stirring the night, drumming the ridge-strewn way,
> The anvil's strength ...
>         and the silence after
> That aches and cries unhushed into the day.
>
> From the dulcimer's breast sound hunting horns
> Strong as clenched hands upon the edge of death,
> The creak of saddle-bags, of oxen yoke and thongs,
> Wild turkey's treble, dark sudden flight of crows,
> Of unshod hoofs ...
>         and the stillness after,
> Bitter as salt drenching the tongue of pain:
>
> And of the lambs crying, breath of the lark,
> Long drinks from piggins hard against the lips;
> And with hoarse singing, raw as hickory shagbark,
> The foal's anxiety is woven with the straining wedge
> And the wasp's anger ...
>         and the quiet after
> For the carver of maple on a keen blade's edge [*FMFV* 37].

How easy it is to get caught up both in the sound of the lines and in the individual images, so that we lose the overall sense of the poem. In his preface to *River of Earth*, Dean Cadle writes that "Still's 'secret' lies in his ability to use language so that it performs the functions of both music and painters' pigments" (vi), and that is at least as true of his poetry as it is of his prose.

"Dulcimer" also exemplifies an important aspect of Still's poetry that, as far as I know, has yet to be commented on. The dulcimer evokes a variety of images and sounds—the sounds of hunting dogs, the ring of an anvil, creaking leather, the squawking of turkeys—but each stanza ends by trailing off into "silence," "stillness," and "quiet." A similar movement appears in most of Still's other poems about music. As the title indicates, his poem "When the Dulcimers Are Gone" imagines a time when the dulcimers "are mingled with the dust" (41). At the conclusion of "Clabe Mott," as loggers listen to that fiddler's playing, their "calloused hands go slack" (47), and the oaks they've been cutting fall to the earth. By the end of "Fiddlers' Convention on Troublesome Creek," "the banjos sleep, the guitars lie unstrung, / The dulcimers rest in ash dust on the mantel's breast, / And their songs are perishing from the shaggy hills" (62). "Dance on Pushback" ends with the admonition to end the dance, since day is approaching (66). "A Man Singing to Himself" speaks of a ballad in the past tense, saying of it, "This was a man's song," and "This was a man's singing"; the poem treats the ballad as the ghostly trace of the man's voice after he himself has fallen silent. In "I Shall Go Singing," the poet announces his determination to sing until extreme old age or death prevents him from doing so, yet even this bit of bravado vividly anticipates that future failing; the poem begins,

> Until the leaf of my face withers,
> Until my veins are blue as flying geese,
> And the mossed shingles of my voice clatter
> In winter wind, I shall be young and have my say [91].

The poem maintains throughout an awareness that at some point the flesh will weaken too much to be able to voice the willing spirit. Of Still's nine poems that focus on music or musicians, seven call attention to the quiet that follows the singing and playing.

His interest in stillness and quiet goes far beyond his poems about music; reading *From the Mountain, From the Valley*, it is easy to decide that a poet never boasted a more appropriate surname. Indeed, it can be instructive to trace the word "still" through his poetry. The first time it appears is in the sestet of his early sonnet "Fallow Years":

> But Mother Earth is far more faithful still
> Than man who in old age has fallow years
> To rest his hands, to ruminate on fears
> Of ending death; Earth cannot hope to fill
> The span of her eternity, nor spill
> Her life blood: Earth has only gentle tears [29].

The word itself appears here as an adverb (meaning "yet") rather than as an adjective, but it does so in the context of a meditation on the inevitable human drift into stillness. It can also he read as a playful bit of self-address ("Earth is far more faithful, Still"), as the poet makes this argument to himself. Another very early poem, "Let This Hill Rest," takes a far different attitude toward stillness: the poet yearns for a good night's rest — or perhaps for a sleep deeper than that, though he does take care to distinguish between death and the kind of sleep he desires. In the second of the two stanzas, as in "Fallow Years," we find a suggestive play on the poet's name:

> Let my heart rest this purple hour
> With slow wandering in dull passages of breath,
> In unwoven air, in sleep withdrawn from death,
> And voiceless spur the mountain's crumbling tower,
> Let me lie here unstirred, unwaked and still,
> Let my heart lean against this fallow hill [33].

Try hearing a capital "S" in "still"; if you do, you can construe the line as a suggestion that he is his truest self when "unstirred" and "unwaked." That would be in keeping with the rest of the poem's identification of the hill with the poet. If "Fallow Years" juxtaposes humankind's finitude and anxiety with Earth's immortality and unconsciousness, the voice in "Let This Hill Rest" seeks to close that gap, to replenish itself by resting within the Earth's protective embrace.

Another place where we find the word "still" applied to the poet is the mysterious "Eyes in the Grass." It begins by describing in Dickinsonian fashion a grackle hopping through the limbs of an apple tree, apparently looking for a meal on the ground. In the second strophe, the poet begins to expose his vantage point (to us, not the grackle):

> There are eyes in the grass,
> Eyes lying still beneath stalk and pod where doodles
> Drill their earthen cones, and ants march in a forest
> Of living swords.

The eyes are his, but he doesn't claim them yet; they are simply eyes, not "my eyes." Only in the third and final strophe, with its introduction of an "I," can we tell with certainty that he is the one lurking below the tree:

> I think that neither the grackle's black eyes
> Nor the ant's myopic sight has found me here,
> Drowned in quivering stems, lost in wattled twigs
> Of grass-trees. O I am lost to any wandering view,
> I am a hill uncharted, my breathing is the wind.
> I am horizon. I am earth's far end [84].

The poet takes delight in having successfully hidden himself, and he casts his hiding as a merging with the Earth: as long as he remains motionless — "still" — he appears to the grackle and the ants as just another aspect of the landscape. The union sought in "Let This Hill Rest" has been achieved, with the important difference that the poet is awake. He retains human consciousness, yet dispenses with human ego. This is a state of awareness that can take a point outside itself as the center of reference; it offers an escape from the feelings of isolation and anxiety identified in "Fallow Years." This kind of stillness, in other words, is a means of transcendence, though a brand of transcendence closer to that aimed at by Issa than by Ralph Waldo Emerson.

Some poems revolve around or move toward the stillness and silence of death in the natural world. "Wilderness" ends with the couplet "All beauty here that trudges hills and skies / Is clothed in silence and in silence dies" (36). At the end of "Mountain Fox Hunt," the poet writes that "the mellow banjos of the hounds' throats are still" — because they have caught their quarry (39). In "Passenger Pigeons" the pigeons are "a symphony of wings" now hushed (51). Another poem on the same topic, "Year of the Pigeons," ends with "the flocking millions slain": "now the boughs are still," Still writes, "Flesh, wing, and eye devoured, a countless horde brought low, / And not a slate-blue feather blows on any hill" (87).

Other poems invoke that movement to stillness as they commemorate particular human deaths. In "Death on the Mountain," the dying hillsman has no one around him to speak "the hopeful word," and, with the fiddle next to his bed silent, he has only the consolation of "remembered song" (44). "Shield of Hills," a poem for a dead child, imagines the landscape gathering up the grave in a manner reminiscent of the embrace the poet sought for himself in "Let This Hill Rest": "The earth shall rise up where he [the child] lies," Still writes, "With steady reach, and permanent" (45). The poem titled "Nixie Middleton" laments the death, apparently some time ago, of a woman the poet loved; it closes with "I have gone up to the graveyard on a laurel-thicket hill / Where my love sleeps. My love waits for me still" (82).

Poets have always found inspiration in death and other endings; what distinguishes Still in this respect is his focus on, to quote from "Dulcimer" again, "the stillness after." In his poem "Graveyard," for instance, he contemplates the silence of the necropolis:

> Nothing has moved in this town.
> Nothing at all. Only the soundless dark
> And the wonder of night that came like wind
> Unseen have wandered down these final streets.
> Only the silent have come upon this mark.
>
> There is no town so quiet on any earth,
> Nor any house so dark upon the mind.
> Only the night is here, and the dead
> Under the hard blind eyes of hill and tree.
> Here lives sleep. Here the dead are free [59].

"Graveyard" is easily paired with a poem published nearly twenty years later, "Abandoned House," which concludes by announcing "This house is filled with yesteryears and sleep" (107).

Jeff Daniel Marion and Jim Wayne Miller have both identified journey motifs in Still's writing; a journey, of course, would be the antithesis of stillness. However, the journeys in Still's poems are almost always unsuccessful; the would-be traveler stays where he is. The traveling these poems imagine is an escape from the mountains, but such an escape turns out to be impossible, as Marion and Miller have themselves noted: Marion writes that in Still's poems "the land is both prison and home" (18), and Miller comments that "[t]he mountains, a home and haven, can also be a prison" (xv). The first line of Still's sonnet "Heritage" is "I shall not leave these *prisoning* hills," and the last is "Being of these hills I *cannot* pass beyond" [italics mine] (43). "Journey Beyond the Hills" observes that the hillsmen stay within "their prisoning hills," though "Swift are their hearts upon this journey never made" (63). The poem "River of Earth" offers an image of human stillness within the mountains' slow geological flux, declaring that "Men are held here / Within a mighty tide swept onward toward a final sea" (76). "Mountain Men Are Free" argues against the dream of leaving: it asks the rhetorical question, "Mountain man, what do you need of life beyond your hills?" (97). Even in "Child in the Hills," the one poem in which someone seems to have escaped, Still argues that the journey's success is only partial: the child the escaped man used to be is left behind, now "waiting under the shadow of these hills ... / [h]is voice ... drowned in the waters of Carr" (50).

The impression left by most of these poems of silence and stillness is that of a drift of human identity into geography. Miller remarks that Still has a "tendency to see people and place as parts of one subtly interdependent whole" (xx); while that is true, *From the Mountain, From the Valley* shows us that Still inflects that constant vision of unity with several different meanings. It may be a condition of imprisonment for a whole people, but it may also be a source of strength for them. It may be a kind of transcendence sought after and achieved by the poet, but it may also be the inevitable return to the land through death. Yet it is never wholly ominous and threatening. The child in his grave is forever protected; the dead in the graveyard are free. Even when Still invokes in one poem the quiet after an apocalypse, he titles that poem "Interval," as if to suggest that the silence will not go on forever (58), that the "interdependent whole" Miller identifies will somehow survive. Still's poetry continually calls our attention to stillness, but that stillness gives way over and over to new music.

## Works Cited

Cadle, Dean. Foreword. *River of Earth.* By James Still, Lexington: University Press of Kentucky, 1978. v–x.

Marion, Jeff Daniel. "James Still's Poetry: 'The Journey of a Worldly Wonder.'" *Iron Mountain Review* 2.1 (1984): 17–21.

Miller, Jim Wayne. Introduction. *The Wolfpen Poems.* By James Still. Berea, Kentucky: Berea College Press, 1986. xi–xxiii.

Still, James. *From the Mountain, From the Valley: New and Collected Poems.* Ed. by Ted Olson. Lexington: University Press of Kentucky, 2001.

# "The Long Way Around": Space, Place, and Syntax in "White Highways"

## DIANE FISHER

Critical interest focuses more and more on issues of place — on how to "write the region," on what role place plays in individual and cultural identity, on the ethics of our relationships to places. Those who come from regions which are, as Jim Wayne Miller once called them, "more 'regional' than others" (180) might begin to hope for a reevaluation of what has long been pejoratively referred to as "the regional." Place has mattered deeply and long in the tradition of Appalachian letters and such concern, as the humanist geographer E. Relph has said, is vital to our survival:

> If places are indeed a fundamental aspect of man's existence in the world, if they are sources of security and identity for individuals and for groups of people, then it is important that the means of experiencing, creating, and maintaining significant places are not lost. Moreover there are many signs that these very means are disappearing.... [It is of] no small importance to know what are the distinctive and essential features of place and of our experience of places, for without such knowledge it will not be possible to create and preserve the places that are the significant contexts of our lives [6].

Those who want to think about the significance of place would do well to look to the hills (as well as to other of those "more regional" regions), to writers like James Still (1906–2001) — Kentucky poet, novelist, short story writer, essayist — for insight into the complicated relationships that people have to space and place.

People need both space and place. "The ideas of 'space' and 'place' require each other for definition," says the geographer Yi-Fu Tuan. "From the security and stability of place we are aware of the openness, freedom, and threat of space, and vice versa. Furthermore, if we think of space as that which allows movement, then place is a pause; each pause in movement makes it possible for location to be transformed into place" (6). Space makes it possible for us to move, grow, choose. Place is the medium in which we pause, to rest and to consider what the movement has meant, and what it may yet mean. Space and place are therefore bound up with the idea of time, which is "implied everywhere in the ideas of movement, effort, freedom, goal, and responsibility" (Tuan 118). In Still's poem "White Highways," space is associated with outward movement and the linear, forward track of time, while place implies pause — the disruption of that linear movement, that road to the horizon — and allows the mind's and the heart's eye to see the present moment and the past that lives in it:

> I have gone out to the roads that go up and down
> In smooth white lines, stoneless and hard;
> I have seen distances shortened between two points,
> The hills pushed back and bridges thrust across
> The shallow river's span.
>
> To the broad highways, and back again I have come
> To the creek-bed roads and narrow winding trails
> Worn into ruts by hoofs and steady feet;
> I have come back to the long way around,
> The far between, the slow arrival.
> Here is my pleasure most where I have lived
> And called my home.
>
>         O do not wander far
> From the rooftree and the hill-gathered earth;
> Go not upon these wayfares measured with a line
> Drawn hard and white from birth to death.
> O quiet and slow is peace, and curved with space
> Brought back again to this warm homing place.

The speaker of Still's poem seems to be rejecting his experience of space in favor of place, urging the reader not to wander, as he did, "these wayfares measured with a line / Drawn hard and white from birth to death." His repetitious "I have gone," "I have seen," "I have come back" echo an Appalachian revision of Caesar's *Vini, vidi, vici: I came, I saw, I'm going home.* But, of course, it is not so simple as that. People need their space and their future, as much as they need their home, their present, and their past. The poem knows this, and the speaker's ultimate solution is to bring the two experiences together.

Still's speaker figures the contrary experiences of space and place in terms of the contrast between the "white highways" and the "creek-bed roads and narrow winding trails" back off those main thoroughfares. His descriptions leave little doubt as to the dangers of the highway and to the surefootedness possible on the back roads. The first cluster of adjectives referring to the highways— smooth, white, stoneless, hard — reveals their particular brand of treachery. The first three adjectives have an allure; they represent a potentially attractive ease of movement. But the addition of "hard" turns the smoothness of the road into something that would hurt one if one looked up from the road for a moment and stumbled. The rest of the first stanza depicts the highways' presence in the hills in fairly violent terms: distances are shortened, as though an amputation of space had occurred; the highways push the hills back out of reach; bridges thrust across rivers like quick jabs of a fist. While such roads may seem to be "avenues of freedom," a way to fulfill "the dream of defeating time and space" (Leach 33), they come at exactly that price — the defeat of time and space. Such roads cheat us of our experience of the time we have to be walking this earth. They are, Still's speaker warns near the end of the poem, "measured with a line / Drawn hard and white from birth to death."

The speaker's return to the back roads, he claims, restores that full experience of time. Whereas his description of the highways depicts a shortening and a quick traversing of distance (which is also to say, of time), the speaker's description of the "creek-bed roads and narrow winding trails" holds out the possibility that our way through the world may be "the long way around, / The far between, the slow arrival." These roads aren't made by the pushing and thrusting of big machines, but, over the years, "by hoofs and steady feet." They don't quicken time; they are themselves accretions of time that we can access when we put our own steady feet on them. They offer the security and stability Tuan associates with place, whereas those white highways threaten to whisk us through distances and through our lives so quickly that the world and our place in it will be lost to us.

On the one hand, space, movement, the white highways. On the other, place, pause, the back roads. The contrasts are clear, but they don't tell the whole story. Although the description of the highways in the first stanza focuses on those "smooth white lines" that hurry us from birth to death, those lines may not be drawn so straight and tight as the speaker seems to want us to believe. Prepositions are telling in this regard. The highways, we should notice, go both ways: "I have gone out to the roads that go up and down." Such roads, it is true, can carry us off, but the sense of danger is mitigated if they can also carry us back, if we can go up the road, then come back down. "Up and down" may also refer to the highways' following the contours of the hills, which makes them seem less an alien presence and less readily able to carry us directly off into the distance. In spite of their distortions of the landscape — shortening, pushing, thrusting — the path the highways take is also shaped by it: they go not only "up and down" but also "between," "back," and "across" the landscape. By the time we get to the end of the stanza, we too have been "up and down," "between," "back," and "across" — we have experienced the slowing-down and backing-up associated with place within the description of hurried movement through space.

In the second stanza, the relatively static quality of place is qualified by references to motion. The roads and trails are created by the constant movement of people and animals across the landscape. And the speaker focuses on the roads, on his journey back rather than on his home itself, which appears only at the end of the stanza. The speaker's preference for place, for the long, slow way of the back roads, is clear. But that preference does not negate — it even requires — the possibility of movement associated more explicitly with the open space of the highways.

Roads are the figures through which the speaker of "White Highways" contemplates space and place. Syntax is the road by which his meditation travels to the reader, and it must enact the same tension between space and place, between forward movement and pause, that descriptions of the roads revealed. Syntactical strategies throughout "White Highways" embody both the forward motion associated with space and the pause associated with place.

The sequencing of types of sentences in Still's poem enacts the tension between forward motion and stillness, between the need for space in which to move outward and grow and the need for a place in which to make and experience meaning. The first two sentences of the poem are declarative sentences. They are essentially narrative, forward-moving, linear: the speaker's story of having gone out to the white highways, understood their dangers and their cost, and having decided to return to the stability and life-enhancing way of the back roads. Consequently, the first two sentences are built around verbs of action or motion: the speaker goes, he sees, he comes back.

The third, middle sentence of the poem, while still in the declarative mode, is no longer truly narrative (I reproduce the poem's sentences here without the line breaks, to make the syntax more visible): "Here is my pleasure most where I have lived and called my home." Rather than a verb of action or motion, this sentence is formed around a copula. It is a naming rather than a narrative, an arrival rather than a journey. Like the first two, this sentence is composed of two clauses, but here one is subordinate: the main clause, "Here is my pleasure most," and a subordinate noun clause, "where I have lived and called my home." The subordinate clause does not carry us forward to a next meaning but serves as complement to the subject of the sentence, deepening the meaning of the speaker's return to "Here." Thus, everything to the right of the copula refers back to the sentence's subject, "Here," in the initial position of the sentence. To read the sentence is not so much to move forward in a straight line, as it is to circle back around — just as the speaker makes his way back home. The sentence formed around a copula stops the forward narrative flow and gives us instead an experience of place and pause.

As we near the end of the poem, the use of sentence types enters into a more complicated relationship with the material presented in the sentences. The fourth sentence begins the speaker's direct address to his readers, his warning with regard to the white highways: "O do not wander far from the rooftree and the hill-gathered earth; go not upon these wayfares measured with a line drawn hard and white from birth to death." The exclamatory "O" at the beginning of the sentence is a sudden intake of breath that stops us in our tracks. It introduces the speaker's shift to the imperative mode, which is perhaps one of the most effective and subtle braking strategies in the poem. The speaker's venturing out onto the broad highways, the return journey, his arrival — this forward-moving narrative is further eclipsed by the speaker's mandate to the reader. We are now in the realm of the subjunctive: this sentence represents virtual actions — wandering, going — which may or may not happen. Nothing, in effect, is actually happening, aside from the speaker's appeal to the reader. The imperative mode in this sentence, by drawing the reader out of the narrative flow, enacts the staying effect that the sentence explicitly advocates. Yet we cannot ignore the appellative nature of the imperative mode. It signals a discourse overtly and emphatically turned outward to the world: these words *do* "wander far from the rooftree and the hill-gathered earth" — in order to find us. The speaker's words carry him outward as surely as do the white highways. Thus the imperative mode serves at the same time the outward motion and the slowing force of the poem, giving us the simultaneous experience of space and place which is the ultimate counsel of the poem.

With the final sentence of the poem, the speaker returns to the declarative mode and to a sentence built around a copula: "O quiet and slow is peace, and curved with space brought back again to this warm homing place." Whereas the earlier copulative sentence brought us to a nearly complete stop by referring everything to the right of the copula back to the initial single-word subject "Here," the syntax of this last sentence creates a more complicated movement for the reader and a more complex representation of the space and place dichotomy. The sentence is composed of a main clause, "O quiet and slow is peace," followed by an adjective phrase which continues the characterization of peace begun in the main clause. This syntax enacts a folding-in type of motion that mimics the substance of the speaker's appeal for a blending of space and place in this final moment of the poem. The inward point which divides the sentence, which each part of the sentence folds inward toward, is the word "peace," the subject of the sentence. The slowing impulse is strong in the main clause of the sentence. The exclamatory "O" holds us for a moment in the speaker's initial intense moment of emotion, rather than urging us immediately on to discover what follows. The use of a copula enhances the static quality of the clause. It also enacts the folding-in motion within the main clause itself, sending our attention from "quiet and slow" to "peace" and back again, to connect the subject and complements so as to complete the meaning of the clause. Nevertheless, the inversion of the subject and its complements also enhances our movement rightwise through the clause, toward the noun that will complete the meaning of the adjectives "quiet and slow." Thus, within the main clause there is pause and forward movement, and our attention is drawn, as we read, both to the left and to the right. A similar movement occurs in the adjective phrase which follows: "and curved with space brought back again to this warm homing place." Here the pivotal word that the initial adjective "curved" and the remainder of phrase both fold inward toward is "space." Their similar, embedded positioning — "peace" within the syntax of the whole sentence, and "space" within the syntax of the adjective phrase — unites syntactically these two words which the speaker is also engaged in uniting semantically. The melding of the space/place and movement/stasis dichotomy is also accomplished by the type of adjectives associated with "space" and with "place" in the adjective phrase. "Space" is most directly modified by the adjective phrase "brought back again" — the use of a past participle as adjective implies a static condition. The adjective that most directly modifies "place" is "homing," a present participle which endows place not only with agency, but with an agency specifically associated with movement. The adjective clause is long, relative to the main clause. This means that the sentence speeds up somewhat as we read along. However, since the adjective clause also refers back to the subject of the main clause, "peace," that accelerated movement, while it goes rightwise, is also directed leftwise — that is, it folds back and its movement enacts that "space brought back again to this warm homing place." Whereas the earlier copulative sentence enacts a kind of circling back to its subject, "Here," this sentence loops as in the sign for infinity: the nexus is the word "peace" and the looping motion the syntax creates on either side of that word allows for space and place, for movement and stillness, action and contemplation *all* to combine and make that peace possible. The syntax of the final moment brings the movement and freedom of space into the shelter and contemplative possibility of place.

Along with the sequencing of sentence type, sentence structure contributes to the poem's depiction of the complex relationship between space and place. Of the five sentences that comprise the poem, three (which begin each stanza and account for all but four lines of the eighteen-line poem) are composed of two independent clauses separated by a semi-colon. This structure serves the forward motion of the sentences, since in each instance the second clause doesn't need to refer back to the first in order to complete its meaning (as would be the case if the second clause were dependent) but rather carries us on to the next unit of meaning. The use of a semi-colon to link the two clauses, rather than making whole sentences out of each clause, also helps the forward flow of the sentence by avoiding the more pronounced pause of a sentence break. Nevertheless, the speed with which these sentences move forward is variable, expressive of the need for both motion and pause.

The relative length of clauses contributes to the varying pace within each of these sentences. The first sentence tells of the speaker's foray onto the white highways: "I have gone out to the roads that go up and down in smooth white lines, stoneless and hard; I have seen distances shortened between two points, the hills pushed back and bridges thrust across the shallow river's span."

The first clause is considerably shorter than the second. Paradoxically, this makes the first clause read more slowly than the second: the longer a sentence or clause, the greater the rush of the reader to get to the end, to the completion of its meaning. It also reads more slowly because, with only one exception, it is composed of one-syllable words, whereas the second clause contains seven polysyllabic words. There is a greater pause between syllables when syllable boundary coincides with word boundary, so this also contributes to the slowness of the first clause relative to the second clause. Viewed in its larger components, then, this sentence moves straight ahead, building up speed as it goes. With the second sentence of "White Highways," the speaker's attention shifts to the back roads: "To the broad highways, and back again I have come to the creek-bed roads and narrow winding trails worn into ruts by hoofs and steady feet; I have come back to the long way around, the far between, the slow arrival."

Whereas in the first sentence the initial clause was shorter and the second longer so that the sentence gathered speed, here the opposite occurs. The greater length of the first clause, followed by the shorter second clause (again with a greater density of one-syllable words) favors our slowing down as we follow further along the speaker's trek into the "creek-bed roads and narrow winding trails." The fourth sentence begins the speaker's direct address to his readers, his warning with regard to the white highways: "O do not wander far from the rooftree and the hill-gathered earth; go not upon these wayfares measured with a line drawn hard and white from birth to death."

Here the pacing within the sentence represents a more complicated experience of space and place, motion and stillness. In the first and second sentences of the poem, the variable speed of the sentences keep pace, so to speak, with the experiences represented: the relative length of clauses causes the sentence focused on the broad highways to pick up speed as it goes along and causes the sentence focused on the little back-roads to slow. As we near the ultimate synthesis of motion and stillness in the poem, the relative length of the clauses causes us to pick up speed as we read through the sentence, even though the speaker's counsel at this moment is for stillness. Syntax thus adds a simultaneous experience of forward motion and space to the experience of stillness and place represented by the "rooftree and hill-gathered earth." (As we've already seen, the syntax of the last sentence follows the same dynamic, although it is composed of a main clause and an adjective phrase, rather than of two clauses.) In each of these sentences, the larger sentence structure advocates the forward motion associated with space and the poem's "white highways," while the relationship between each sentence's largest components (the relative lengths of the two independent clauses) varies pacing of forward motion, creating also the experience of slowing and pause associated with place and with the poem's "creek-bed roads and narrow winding trails."

Within these large sentence structures, more localized syntactical strategies such as compound syntactical units, series, repetition and inversion work to further nuance the poem's enactment of the complex relationship between space and place. Compound syntactical units — couplings of like syntactical units by a conjunction — appear frequently throughout "White Highways": "up and down," "stoneless and hard," "To the broad highways, and back again," "creek-bed roads and narrow winding trails," "hoofs and steady feet," "where I have lived and called my home," "the rooftree and the hill-gathered earth," "hard and white," "quiet and slow." In each case, the conjoining *and* carries our attention forward. At the same time, however, it creates a closed syntactical unit, a kind of circular unity with a centripetal force contrary to the forward motion of the sentence. Two slightly more extensive series in the poem have a similar, though perhaps more subtle, effect. The first occurs in the first stanza: "I have seen distances shortened between two points, / The hills pushed back and bridges thrust across / The shallow river's span." The three phrases beginning with "distances," "the hills," and "bridges" are a series of noun phrases functioning as direct objects. The other series occurs in the second stanza: "I have come back to the long way around, / The far between, the slow arrival." Here the three prepositional phrases function as noun phrases which function, in turn, as objects of the prepositional phrase "back to." Although there is not exact equivalence between the elements in either of these series and their connections to each other are not as tight as in the case of the compound units, nevertheless the elements of each series echo each other semantically enough to cause a slight backward pull on our attention even as we move forward through the series. This effect is somewhat stronger in the second series, which is structured in a slightly different way than the earlier basic series: the conjunction between the final two elements of the series is omitted, replaced by a comma. This kind of arrangement, Virginia Tufte suggests, heightens "the implicit parallelism in the series" (104) and so enhances the series' backward tug on our attention at the same time that the speaker is turning back toward home.

Repetition may be one of the most effective strategies for merging a sense of motion with a sense of stillness, since we must move forward in order to encounter a repeated element, and then immediately move our attention backward, to previous occurrence(s) of that element, in order to recognize that a repetition has occurred. Repetition, in other words, draws us forward while keeping us in the same place; it makes us look both ways at once. Lexical repetitions throughout Still's poem create a sense of both forward movement and of backward-looking pause. "Roads" first appears in the first line of the poem, where it seems to refer simply to the "white highways" of the title. When it recurs in the second line of the second stanza to differentiate the "creek-bed roads and narrow winding trails" from the highways, the repetition causes us to reconsider the meaning of the word. We have to stop — just as we think the right road has been set before us — and look back again at the vista of white highways that confronted the speaker in the initial moment of the poem, before we follow him down the back roads. The "smooth white lines, stoneless and hard" at the beginning of the first stanza reappear near the end of the poem as "a line / Drawn hard and white from birth to death." Here, near the conclusion, where we think we are about to sit down and stay put, we are sent back to the beginning of the road that goes from birth to death, made to recall and re-experience our journey from that first step. The repetition fuses motion and stillness, the journey and the arrival.

One of the most noticeable repetitions in Still's poem involves the recurrence of first-person present perfect verb forms throughout the first three sentences. The first sentence begins with "I have gone." "I have seen," which begins the second clause of that same sentence, sends the mind's ear back to that same verb form at the beginning of the sentence. Even though the composition of the sentence by two independent clauses tends to serve a forward-moving impulse, the repetition of the verb form adds a contrary effect, causing the first motion that the second clause sets into play to be a backward one. Where we thought to be moving forward, we are brought up short and caused to look back. This effect is intensified by the directness of the repetition that occurs in the second sentence. "I have come" occurs in both of the sentence's clauses and is compounded by the preposition "back" in both cases (though the position of the preposition varies). The occurrence of a verb of motion in each clause should enhance our sense of movement, but the repetition arrests that feeling of forward motion by sending our attention back to the first clause when we encounter the repeated verb in the second. In the third sentence the first-person present perfect verbs occur in a more condensed form, both in the second, dependent clause: "where I have lived and called my home." The elision of "have" with the second verb draws less attention to the repetition of the verb tense, as does its appearance only in the second clause. Indeed, more than calling attention to the repetition within this sentence, the verbs here seem to call attention to the recurrence of the present perfect verbs throughout the poem. This tense is itself a sign of repetition. The present perfect tense draws us through the past incidences of a verb — here, the long history of the speaker's living and calling this place his home — and bundles all the past actions into the act of the present moment. The effect is similar to that of the description of the back roads "worn into ruts by hoofs and steady feet": the past has a staying power; it accumulates into the present moment, which doesn't leave things behind but rather stores them up. The present perfect tense itself and its repetition throughout the first three sentences of the poem thus create a sense of motion and of linear time, associated with space, because they express a series of actions. At the same time, they create a sense of stillness and containment associated with place because they gather those past actions together with the present one within a single shell.

Inversion produces a dual direction of attention in much the same way that repetition does. Most of the inversions in this poem are fairly subtle, as in the placement of adjectival elements after the noun that they refer to. This occurs in the first two lines of the poem, where the speaker describes the highways as "roads that go up and down / In smooth white lines, stoneless and hard." Our attention must circle back over the intervening adjective clause to "roads"—which appears back near the beginning of the sentence—in order to connect the adjectives "stoneless and hard" with their antecedent. The delaying of those adjectives enacts syntactically the experience that's being represented: we step into the smooth path of the sentence only to find the real information at the end that will send us back to the beginning, just as the speaker is lured by the smoothness of the road before he discovers its hardness. While those smooth white lines are carrying us forward, they lead us on to adjectives that will carry our attention backward, that subtly complicate our own journey through the poem. Inversion serves as a strategy to postpone key elements in the third sentence of the poem: "Here is my pleasure most where I have lived / and called my home." "Here is" functions in this sentence much like a *there*-transformation, allowing the new information of the sentence— the announcement of "home"—to come in the most emphatic position, the delaying syntax of the sentence matching the speaker's story of journey and return. Near the end of the poem, inversion is occasioned by the imperative mode when the speaker cautions us: "Go not upon these wayfares measured with a line / Drawn hard and white from birth to death." On the one hand, the inversion seems to support the speaker's mandate by braking the forward movement of the sentence in the same way that the speaker recommends to the readers that we stay put. The absence of the auxiliary verb "do," which necessitates the inversion of the verb and the negative, makes the negative command all the more emphatic. Also, the inversion causes a backward movement in the reader's attention, since the meaning of the negative is completed by a verb that precedes it. On the other hand, the inversion has a curious, opposite effect. Since we read the sentence from left to right, there is an instant in the initial reading in which the "go" appears as a positive command. This is not the case in the first clause of the sentence. In "do not wander" the possibility of wandering is rejected before the word "wander" even appears; but the possibility of "going" hangs, alive, in the air for a moment at the beginning of the second clause before the speaker rejects it. Even at this first moment after homecoming, the syntactical strategies that enact the staying of the speaker's journey are complicated by strategies that keep our sense of movement alive.

    In all of these cases, the inversions are relatively subtle, either because the connections between the inverted elements remain easy to see or because the inversions correspond to familiar variations of the normal sentence pattern. This is not the case, however, in the first clause of the second sentence of the poem, which begins the second stanza: "To the broad highways, and back again I have come / To the creek-bed roads and narrow winding trails / Worn into ruts by hoofs and steady feet." It begins, not with the normal subject-verb order so strongly present in the two clauses of the first sentence, but with two prepositional phrases, "To the broad highways, and back again," functioning as adverbs to modify "I have come." One effect of this syntax is the dual direction of attention that we have seen in the other instances of inversion. On the one hand, the introductory syntax speeds forward motion of the clause, since we have to hurry on to the verb before the meaning of the adverbial phrases becomes clear. On the other hand, once we get to the verb, our attention turns back, to the left instead of the right, to get at the complete meaning. This looking-both-ways-at-once is reinforced by the semantics of the two phrases. "To the broad highways" links semantically with the preceding sentence, sending our attention all the way back to the first stanza. "And back again" sends it forward, to whatever will follow the verb (though this segment of the inversion still contains its own embedded inversion, "and back again I have come," which is very striking). The remainder of the clause is a long prepositional phrase with a compound object, "to the creek-bed roads and narrow winding trails," followed by an adjective phrase, "worn into ruts by hoofs and steady feet." The placement of the adjectival element after the nouns it modifies casts the reader's attention backwards, as does the use of the passive construction, which places the subjects (hoofs and feet) after the verb (worn). These aspects of the syntax are not so noticeable as the convolutions in the initial moments of the sentence; still, they slightly tug the reader's attention backward. The whole inversion dynamic in the clause, then, enacts a kind of syntactic tug-of-war, drawing the reader's attention forward and backward such that we're held momentarily in the middle, at a crossroads, just as the speaker at the beginning of this second sentence stands looking at the white highways on one side, and the back roads on the other. Inversion has an additional effect here, not so much present in the other, more subtle instances. Tufte explains: "Some inversions simply beg for attention. They are self-conscious, artificial. People do not speak that way, so when a writer writes that way, his inversions have a decidedly literary turn.... [T]he ultimate effect of the more striking inversions is to call attention, not to any sense unit within the sentence, but to the self-conscious style itself" (137–39). Just as the speaker declares that he is turning back to the creek-bed roads and to home, that he is turning away from the white highways that would carry him outward and away, his language takes a decidedly outward turn. In the moment of leaving the outside world, the speaker reaches out to it — the self-conscious, inverted syntax as an appeal for the reader's attention. On this level too, the inverted syntax enacts for us the dichotomy of motion and stillness, of the need both to reach outward through distance and to claim a home base in which to rest and consider what to send out into the world.

What "White Highways" sends us is no simple answer for the competing claims of space and place in our lives. Undefined space is as necessary to the making of meaning as is a known place — a home — from which to ponder on what waits be defined. Still's speaker braids together, through the poem's road imagery and its syntactical resources, the experiences of space and place in such a way that both are open to us. "The possibilities for maintaining and reviving man's sense of place do not lie in the preservation of old places," Relph says, " ... nor can they lie in a selfconscious return to the traditional ways of placemaking — that would require the regaining of a lost state of innocence. Instead, placelessness must be transcended" (145). The speaker of "White Highways" overcomes the threat of the highways not by simply turning his back on them and embracing the already meaningful home place, but by folding the open space of the highway back into "this warm homing place." He takes us up the road, and back down: the long way around.

# Works Cited

Leach, William. *Country of Exiles: The Destruction of Place in American Life.* New York: Vintage Books, 1999.

Miller, Jim Wayne. "Regions, Folk Life, and Literary Criticism." *Appalachian Journal.* 7 (1980): 180–87.

Relph, E. *Place and Placelessness.* London: Pion Limited, 1976.

Still, James. "White Highways." In *From the Mountain,* *From the Valley: New and Selected Poems.* Ed. by Ted Olson. Lexington: University Press of Kentucky, 2001. 77.

Tuan, Yi-Fu. *Space and Place: The Perspective of Experience.* Minneapolis: University of Minnesota Press, 1977.

Tufte, Virginia. *Grammar as Style.* New York: Holt, Rinehart and Winston, 1971.

# V

# THE WRITINGS ABOUT AND FOR CHILDREN, AND THE FOLKLORIC WRITINGS

James Still beside Jethro Amburgey (on left), master dulcimer builder, in the Hindman Settlement School woodworking shop, 1935. Amburgey allowed Still to live in the Amburgey family's log house beside Wolfpen Creek, Kentucky; there, Still wrote many of his finest works, including much of *River of Earth* (courtesy of the Hindman Settlement School).

# "We'll have to do something about that child": Representations of Childhood in the Short Stories

## KATHY H. OLSON

James Still was one of the few writers of Appalachian literature for adult readers who excelled in the characterization of children as well as of their behavior and their perspective on the world from which they emerge. An examination of Still's fiction provides a plethora of characters who internalize values of Appalachian culture far beyond their years. These children reflect an interesting mixture of adult values and childish innocence. They stand in awe of the world around them while encompassing an adult vision of reality that transcends the often austere limitations of the place in which they live. This results in the paradoxical, unique nature of their personalities. Still exhibits in his fiction firsthand knowledge of the nature of an Appalachian child.

Still's writing reflects a time and place that, for most of us, exists today only in stories and songs. The culture of Still's Appalachian region arises from a group of people tied to land and family. The mountains that surround them and the valleys that house them represent the world as they know it, and within these natural walls Still's characters find their voice. Presenting a clear and distinct portrayal of people, places, and events, Still's writings reflect the Appalachian culture's valuation of simplicity and durability.

The changing outside world reverberates quietly in the remote setting of the Kentucky mountains where Still's stories take place. The land envelopes its inhabitants, protecting them from change and isolating them from some of the more ephemeral shifts in American culture. The mountains are a physical obstruction to change, and the people from the Appalachian region possess a natural constitution that obstructs change from within as well. The constancy of these characters and the durability of the physical environment complete the setting for Still's portraits of people who value the land for its beauty and also for its familiarity.

Still's short stories and novels sometimes explore the nature of this constancy through the consciousness of a child narrator. The child, often male, ranges in age from seven years old to twelve years old. According to critic Cleanth Brooks, the young narrator in

Still's writings "has a boy's curiosity and freshness of vision. He is alert and properly inquisitive about the world in which he finds himself" (Brooks 1978, x). Still's choice to speak through the voice of a child is often criticized or questioned by scholars who do not believe that such a narrational representation could possibly be accurate. Can children speak with such vision?

In an interview by Laura Lee in the book *The Wolfpen Notebooks,* Still says of his Alabama childhood, "We children worked alongside our parents, hoeing and chopping and picking and pulling.... By the age of twelve I could pick a hundred pounds of cotton a day" (11). This quote gives us an idea of the world in which the author came of age. Still's childhood was much different than the world experienced by many children today, more closely approximating the world of the characters found in his stories. In Still's world, children worked with their parents. Members of families lived in close proximity to one another, and children mingled with adults in a watchful existence that permeated their child-world, exposing them to aspects of life not found in the lives of contemporary American youths. Parents did not shelter their children from the often harsh realities of life. These children experienced plenty and famine, birth and death, sickness and healing alongside their fathers and mothers.

The realities of life become the childhood experiences of the youthful characters and Still's narrators. Children learn from these very real experiences. According to child development theorist Jean Piaget, the individual child plays a huge role in his or her own development. While environmental and genetic forces influence cognition, a child's interaction with the world around him or her influences how and what knowledge he or she will acquire. Knowledge is the result of the interaction between the environment and the individual child.

This knowledge base, or structure, allows children to know their world. Structures represent the child's reality. According to Piaget, with age and subsequent experience, children's structures change (Piaget 1969, 114–59). Still's narrators experience life in a world that is unpredictable since it is inseparably tied to nature and the physical world. Fate and determinism play a part in this life. Things happen — life is not fair or unfair. Still's characters live in close association with the land and with nature, and there is a sense of acceptance, respect, and fear. We see an attempt to balance man's individual insignificance with a general need to survive. This balance often depends on forces outside of one's control.

Where children are concerned, life is outside their control. By looking at four short stories, we can get a sense of the changes taking place in Appalachia and the reaction of eastern Kentucky people to those changes. The voices that relay those changes are children. In "I Love My Rooster," Still's eight-year-old narrator's thoughts and visions tell us of the coal boom in the mines and his own, as well as his family's, subsequent reaction. "The Proud Walkers" presents an example of the young narrator, again age eight, who is longing for adventure and for the courage of an adult, but who is frightened by the implications of adulthood. "On Quicksand Creek" shows the nine-year-old narrator's experience with the broader world of human nature and his subsequent disappointment. With "Journey to the Forks," Still brings his twelve-year-old narrator to the brink of decision-making, choosing between a past that is known but volatile and a future of possibilities and new ideas. Looking at these short stories, we see the inherent wisdom in Still's choice of speaking through a young boy; we see the difficulty this choice dictates; and we see the environment, both the inner environment of the people and the outer environment of a changing landscape and marketplace economy that is stretching into this once somewhat remote and self-sufficient culture.

The lack of control is manifest in the nature of the land, jobs, and seasonal variations. In "I Love My Rooster," the narrator is eight years old. Randolph Runyon calls this story a "tale of Appalachian innocence" (Runyon 1991, 57). The realistic vision we experience in the words of the narrator mimics the world he comes from. The characters experience life at home in the midst of the entire family. In this particular story, a coal boom has hit the mine camps, and the narrator's family will profit from his father's increased wages. Gathered in one room, the children hear the plans and decisions that go into the distribution of this bounty. The narrator merely reports the events as they happen. He does not comment on them or pass judgment. We do not get authorial intrusion or subjective interpretation. The children are very literal in their respective understanding of the facts and the musings of their parents. At one point the father, excited about the increase in coal prices, remarks, "I say it's ontelling what a ton o' coal will sell for. They's a lack afar north at the big lakes, and in countries across the waters. I figure the price will double or treble.... Yon blue sky might be the limit" (1). The children are puzzled by this expression, and the narrator says, "Our heads turned toward the window. We saw only the night sky, dark as gob smoke" (2). They did not understand the implication of their father's sentiment. The father looks toward the blue sky with hope and imagination. His vision is trusting and with it comes a desire for freedom from the everyday struggle to survive. The narrator does not try to clarify these details for the reader. Quite the contrary, he leaves the reader to his own speculations and conclusions. The father laughs quite often, while the mother is quietly reserved and cautious. She exhibits a desire for self-sufficiency and security when she suggests saving the extra income to build a house. On the other hand, the father wants new expensive boots. This desire for clothing is imitated by the children. They want store-bought shirts and a dress. The narrator wants a shirt and a rooster. The father's jubilation and childlike attitude is shown, not by a comment from the narrator, but in the reportage of the father's actions and desires in his time of plenty. The father is interested in the here and now, in better food, in finer clothes, and in the excitement of a feast: "Why, we're going to start living like folks. Fitten clothes on our backs, food a body can enjoy" (3). He appears excited at the prospect of freedom from struggle, if only for a short time.

The narrator also possesses a child's curiosity about the unknown. He expresses a strong desire to see behind the eye-patch worn by his nine-year-old friend Fedder Mott. Written from the viewpoint of a child, we read: "I studied the eye patch. It was the size of a silver dollar, hanging by a string looped around his head. What lay behind it? Was there a hole square into his skull? I was almost ashamed to ask, almost afraid" (7). Not only are we aware from this passage of the child's desire to experience the unknown, we are also aware of the inherent fear that accompanies this desire. While the father desires the unknown, the mother desires security. This fear is echoed throughout Still's stories. The child's fear of the unknown mirrors the adult's fear of the unknown and their subsequent struggle with change. Differences, often manifested in Still's stories by child characters who were physically deformed or mangled, suggests that outer deformities reflect inner psychic wounds caused by nature or the world in which the characters participate. The children are not protected from accidents. There is an underlying acceptance of these occurrences, viewed simply as part of life. But fear is there as well.

Once again, the children mirror their parents' acceptance of their fate. The mother in this story fears the future. She knows, from past experiences, that the boom will not last forever. She warns, "I say this boom can't last eternal" (5). Planning for the future, for a roof over her family's heads, is her main concern. And she is right. The story ends when the boom ends. However, by this time, she has saved enough money to build a house, as well as enough to spend on luxuries for the family.

In using a child narrator, the author manages to emphasize the qualities of the adults with a clarity of vision that would not be possible from another adult. By merely reporting the events and the conversation, the young boy gives the reader information without commentary. We have an objective viewpoint, unsullied by subjective admonitions about the actions of the adult characters involved in the story. The eight-year-old narrator does not have experience to qualify his statements or to defend or condemn the characters. Adults have experienced life, and writing objectively about other adults experiencing life can be difficult. The child's point of view allows Still to emphasize the adult problems and constraints by mingling the actions of the parents closely with the actions and observations of children.

In Still's story "I Love My Rooster," the narrator wants a rooster. Here we see the narrator take an icon of the adult world, the fighting cock, and see him as a pet rather than a way to make money or gain esteem with his peers or a portion of the larger adult world. By trading the rooster, the narrator can have the store-bought shirt he longs for and see underneath the patch on Fedder Mott's eye, part of the bargain of the sale. As with the adults, compromises are made, and the children compromise just like the adults they imitate.

This conflict mirrors the conflict with their limited resource — money. The boy saves his nickels but ultimately trades them for a rooster. He then trades the rooster for a store-bought shirt with long tails that can be tucked inside his pants. The mother dreams of the permanence and security that a house would provide. She says, "Fair times and bad, we'd have a rooftree" (3). The father lives more for the day-to-day enjoyment of fulfillment, wanting to appear as others appear, wearing shiny boots that reek of affluence and prosperity. The mother does not like the constant movement of the family as they follow the coal camps and the jobs with money. The father does not seem to mind the movement. A certain freedom is intimated by this way of life, a way that he has grown used to and is comfortable with. The narrator is torn by his desire for a pet, which would give a sense of permanence (a living thing), and a shirt, a commodity that is disposable and, by its very nature, will eventually be rendered useless as the boy's body outgrows his purchase. Finally, he will see what is underneath the eye patch of Fedder Moss. The curiosity mixed with fear imitates the uncertainty of the lives of these characters.

A child's life is filled with fear and uncertainty. Children are used to these sensations, however, and they approach these feelings as they appear — as part of the reality of life. There is little attempt to understand the fears. The inevitability of the outcome is tantamount to their reaction to, and acceptance of, their lives. What better way to emulate these feelings than to use children as narrators? The innocence of the children focuses our attention toward a central idea of the innocence of these people, being both sheltered and isolated from the larger world. The characters in Still's stories inhabit a world that encompasses poverty and hunger. At the same time, individuals have dreams and do not live unmarked by the outer world. As they move from place to place, both figuratively and literally, we sense the hopelessness of the journey and the constant struggle against a changing environment.

Change is inevitable in the lives of these characters. They rarely move far, but they are mercilessly dependent on an economy that has little to do with the lives led within the surrounding mountains and has everything to do with the price and "ondoings" in the outer world. The people in Still's stories, though touched by the outer world, may not recognize the sensation. In "I Love My Rooster," the differing views of Mother and Father — a permanent dwelling obtained by sacrifice and hard work versus an easier, shinier day-to-day existence that is ultimately fleeting — illustrates the changes taking place in the region. The narrator's struggle between his desire for a shirt, a rooster, and courage mimics the parents struggle, encompassed within one individual.

In the story "The Proud Walkers," we clearly see the narrator's conflict between his curiosity and desire to be an adult, and the fear of facing the unknown. After overhearing his father tell of seeing strange people with square heads walking along the ridge, the narrator goes outside to feed the mare and look for tracks of these mysterious people. We read: "I went before eating, being more curious than hungry.... I found a nest of brogan tracks set in the mud; I saw where they printed the ridge. 'If I was growed up,' I spoke aloud, 'I'd follow them steps, be they go to the world's end.' Then I ran to the house; I ran so fast a bluesnake racer couldn't have caught me" (21–22). Conflict, in this instance, is a curiosity about the unknown, mixed with a fear that almost paralyzes one. But not quite. The narrator goes outside and investigates his father's story. He wants to be brave and follow the strange tracks, confronting the unknown on his own just as he did when he looked behind Fedder Moss's patch. Yet he realizes he is not "growed up" and he retreats to the safety of the cabin.

We see the narrator constantly moving through his experiences toward adulthood — often much faster than can be imagined from the point of view of a reader in the twenty-first century. These experiences take one beyond a location or an economic environment. They take us to a central family role, an early inclusion and participation in the most rudimentary of family struggles. These experiences were an integral part of the adult world, and the children moved fluidly back and forth between that world and the world the children concocted for themselves. Adults do not create a separate environment or world for children. The children must take their chances as members of the culture.

The curiosity of childhood and the desire for money and adventure begin to overcome the inherent fear of the unknown. In the story "On Quicksand Creek," readers see Still's narrator moving from innocence to experience. A successful neighbor who sells cattle comes to visit. Aaron Splicer's clothes are described by the narrator. His expensive dress puts him in an economic category above the boy and his family. The narrator admires Splicer's dress and its trimmings. He thinks to himself, "I'm liable to be a cattleman when I'm grown up, and go traveling far. Yet it'd take a spell to get used to thorny boots. I'd be ashamed to wear 'em" (49). These boots far surpass the expensive boots worn by the narrator's father, which had been bought with the money saved after the coal boom. Youthful and innocent, the young boy is drawn by the allure of the cattleman. Splicer hires the narrator to drive his calves to Mayho town. He promises to pay a silver dollar for the thirteen miles round trip that the boy will travel. Excited at the prospect of the adventure, the boy agrees to go. When he reaches his destination, he finds that the promise has not been kept. Waiting for him is another boy with a message that they are to drive the cattle a day longer to a place called Quicksand, with the promise of two dollars pay at the end. We read: "'My poppy'd be scared, me not coming straight home,' I complained. 'I hain't never been on Quicksand. I oughtn't to go.' I felt a grain hurt. 'Aaron said he'd send me a dollar. A silver dollar'" (51). The narrator begins to see that the adult world is not always to be trusted. He is scared and his feelings have been hurt. The innocence of youth begins to crumble. The process continues when Aaron refuses to pay at the end of three days' work. Splicer says, "'I'm broke tee-total'" (54). He wants to give the boys a heifer to split between them. The boys refuse the offer, but the promised pay is still not forthcoming.

This life-lesson in the treatment of children by an adult is a difficult one for the narrator. His own innocence is exploited by a smooth-talking, well-dressed, prosperous-looking man. Splicer's dishonesty in his dealings with others becomes apparent as the story progresses. Splicer takes advantage of the starry-eyed youth, and, other than the trick played on him by the boys at the end of the story, there are no recriminations. He is not forced to settle his debts or adhere to his promises. The narrator's father is also fooled. His trusting nature was emulated by his son, who did not know better because of his inexperience. The father's innocence and gullibility is on display in this story as well. We see the ease with which exploitation occurs when people encounter a culture of which they are not familiar. Yet their very survival depends on their ability to adapt to this culture, seeing through the coverings and deceptions, and thereby developing an understanding of a new reality. New rules will be made, and new lessons learned.

But these images, as Still uses them, are subdued and easily missed. They are common, and Still makes them not only credible but expected. Fred Chappell discusses the "understatement" in both James Still and Rudyard Kipling. Chappell comments that understatement is achieved "by the strategy of narration, a voice reporting almost objectively from inside a context only dimly comprehended by the larger world outside" (Chappell 1981, 196). The reader easily identifies with a child's perspective. Through youth, we see innocent encounters with many of the difficulties of a harsh world. In "Journey to the Forks," Still writes about the narrator, now twelve years old, and his younger brother going to school. They are frightened of the unknown. The younger child, Lark, is missing two fingers. The physical deformity is found on the child who exhibits the greatest fear of this endeavor. But fear of the unexpected is apparent throughout the story. The boys meet an adult, Cain Griggs, who warns them of the problems of school and education in general, thus reflecting an undercurrent of distrust toward education within this Appalachian culture. Cain says, "I never put much store by all them fotched-on teachings, a-larning quare onnatural things, not a grain o' good on the Lord's creation" (46). The narrator, older and wiser than in the first story, replies, "Hain't nothing wrong with larning to cipher and read writing" (46). The dispute continues, but the narrator finally tells his little brother, who has been much worried by the ominous warnings of Cain: "Cain Griggs don't know square to the end o' everything" (46). As the two brothers descend the last few yards to the schoolhouse, the reader realizes they are descending to the unknown. It is not only the school and its ways that are unknown, but the changes symbolized by knowledge.

By using a child as narrator, we get the sense of the curiosity and bravery of a twelve-year-old boy, even when encountering the fears and limited viewpoint of the adults that surround him. The eight year old's fear is much like that of the adult, Cain, in the story. Lark is still young enough to be heavily influenced by the adults he encounters, with their superstitions supreme in their mind. But the narrator, a young boy of twelve, is ready for new adventure and longs for freedom. He rides away from the family toward a new society with different values, ready to experience the journey of growth. He rejects Cain's idea that his father sent them to the school, taking responsibility for the decision: "'Poppy never sent us,' I said. 'We made our own minds'"(45). The narrator is willing to brave the stories and the superstitions in order to change and face his fears and his fate. With the narrator being a youth, the approach to the forks takes on a symbolic meaning: "We came upon the forks in early evening and looked down upon the school from the ridge. Lights were bright in the windows, though shapes of houses were lost against the hills. We rested, listening. No sound came out of all the strange place where the lights were, unblinking and cold" (47). The author gives his reader a sense of the foreboding landscape as well as a glimpse into the minds of the boys. A combination of fear is mixed with a calm acceptance of the reality of the future as the reader stands with the brothers on that ridge. The boys are ready to face the problems the future may bring as they move to connect the past to the future. The future, from the narrator's eyes, is full of new ideas, providing one with a new vision. Tied to nature, he has followed his people in an acceptance of the world around him. But the world he views is changing, and the outside world and its influences will continue to invade the culture of Appalachia.

The rugged environment and austere landscape of Appalachia present a child with surroundings that are unlike other places in America. These four stories give a realistic portrayal of children in Appalachia by mirroring the culture that shapes them. Still's young narrators possess disparate views of childhood from those considered normal for many children. Youth takes on special meaning as values arise from a juxtaposition of reality and innocence that comprises the world of the child. The values inherited from the family in general and the environment in particular have their roots in a childhood singularly linked to place. A careful study of these works reveals a writer with firsthand knowledge of the nature of an Appalachian child. Still's children are exposed to a life of hard work as well as the realities of life and death. The landscape, both interior and exterior, invariably takes the form of a structured pattern of life normally reserved for a much older personality. Through the eyes of a child, the reader becomes aware of the strangely intertwined qualities that combine to give one a realistic view of a changing Appalachian culture.

## Works Cited

Brooks, Cleanth. Foreword. *The Run for the Elbertas*. By James Still. Lexington: University Press of Kentucky, 1980. x.

Chappell, Fred. "The Seamless Vision of James Still." *Appalachian Journal* 8 (Spring 1981): 196–202.

Piaget, Jean, and Barbel Inhelder. *The Psychology of the Child*. New York: Basic Books, 1969. 114–59.

Runyon, Randolph Paul. "Looking the Story in the Eye: James Still's 'Rooster.'" *The Southern Literary Journal* 23 (Spring 1991): 55–65.

Still, James. "I Love My Rooster." *The Run for the Elbertas*. Lexington: University Press of Kentucky, 1980. 1–15.

_____. "The Proud Walkers." *The Run for the Elbertas*. Lexington: University Press of Kentucky, 1980. 16–29.

_____. "Journey to the Forks." *The Run for the Elbertas*. Lexington: University Press of Kentucky, 1980. 43–47.

_____. "On Quicksand Creek." *The Run for the Elbertas*. Lexington: University Press of Kentucky, 1980. 48–58.

_____. *The Run for the Elbertas*. Lexington: University Press of Kentucky, 1980.

_____. Interview with Laura Lee. *The Wolfpen Notebooks: A Record of Appalachian Life*. Lexington: University Press of Kentucky, 1991.

# Journeys of Childhood
## in the Fiction

CAROL BOGGESS

"Some fellers don't never get growed up. They git killed down," begins the story of a young boy in a 1942 newspaper article by James Still. The humorous narrative following this dramatic declaration was told to Still by a real child from Leslie County, Kentucky. The boy elaborates all the narrow escapes he has had in his life of eight years by describing each adventure in the context of an excursion. Again and again his trips verge on disaster, but his entertaining narrative carries the reader along to a final stopping place — the same place he started — wondering about "how fellers git growed." If we look at Still's fiction for the answer to the young boy's question, we can conclude that children grow up by going on journeys of discovery.

Readers have long appreciated Still's authentic rendering of his Appalachian world. Critics and journalists have repeatedly noted the man's attachment to place. Living in and around Hindman, Kentucky, for seventy years, Still exemplified a person who stayed put and loved thoroughly the place where he had put himself. The familiar closing line of his best known poem, "Heritage," expresses a permanent connection to his place: "I cannot leave. I cannot go away." While he never left his mountains for good, he was an avid traveler all his life.

His first trip, one of his few one-way voyages, represents a major point of self-discovery. He left his family's home in Alabama in 1924 to attend Lincoln Memorial University in Tennessee. Eight years later he settled in Hindman, Kentucky, where he found his permanent home, but his traveling had only just begun. He was drawn from his quiet life in the hills to numerous writers' conferences in New England, to World War II experiences in Africa and the Middle East, to family reunions in Alabama, to the Mayan temples of Central America, and the historical houses and cemeteries of England and France. In his later years, he continued to travel to colleges in the Appalachian region to teach classes and read his works. Throughout his 94 years, Still made long and short journeys away from home but always returned to his roots in Knott County. For him, traveling was a way of expanding his world and sharpening his vision, a means of learning and growing.

If being a traveler who valued permanence was one paradox of Still's life, another was his thorough knowledge of children. Although the sixth born in a family of ten children, after he left his home to enter college he had very little contact with children except those who attended the Hindman Settlement School where he worked as librarian. Still never married nor had children of his own, yet he possessed a remarkable insight into family life and understood well the minds and hearts of young people. Frequently his protagonists or narrators were boys. At least four of his works are intended for young and young-at-heart readers: *Sporty Creek* (1977); *Jack and the Wonder Beans* (1977); *Rusties and Riddles and Gee-Haw Whimmy-Diddles* (1989); and *An Appalachian Mother Goose* (1998). Toward the end of his life, Still openly displayed his affection for children by assuming the informal role of godparent to babies and toddlers belonging to his friends and neighbors; finally, at the age of 90, he legally adopted a grandson.[1]

When Still's understanding of children merges with his passion for travel, the result is a recurring metaphor of young characters on the move. All children are destined to grow in spurts, and that growth involves expanded horizons, new experiences, and the alternation of security and comfort with

Portrait of James Still, in uniform while serving in U.S. Army Air Force, 1945. Courtesy of the Hindman Settlement School.

strangeness and challenge. In Still's writing, this growth is best expressed through journeys out from home and back again, experiences that involve discovery and learning. As has been noted by scholars and critics, the journey metaphor is not unique to James Still.[2] One source of power for the metaphor is that it echoes a common theme in life and literature. Another source is that Still repeatedly plays with this childhood journey motif, threading it through his entire canon.[3]

Yet it is in the stories that Still never seems to tire of the excursions children make. "Run for the Elbertas" tells the tale of adolescents Godey Spurlock and Mal Dowe traveling with Riar Thomas to Georgia; these same two boys take "A Ride on the Short Dog." In "The Stir-Off," a young boy goes alone to a neighbor's sorghum making and has his first experience with a girl. "On Quicksand Creek" is another story of a nine-year-old boy who is "old enough to go traipsing, to look abroad upon the world," and that is exactly what he does when he drives yearling calves on a thirteen-mile round trip. One of the most memorable trips in all of Still's fiction is the story of a twelve-year-old and his younger brother making their "Journey to the Forks," a physical trek to the boarding school that initiates their journey of the mind.

To explore this childhood journey motif in some detail, this study will focus on four of Still's best known prose pieces that span his writing career: first and most recent is his well-loved 1977 rendering of the classic folk tale, *Jack and the Wonder Beans*; another is the powerful story, "The Nest," which he first published in 1948; third is "Mrs. Razor," submitted to *The Atlantic* during World War II and published in July 1945; and, finally, his 1940 novel, *River of Earth*. These works illustrate his understanding of children, his appreciation of their special voice and unique perception, and his metaphoric use of the journey to reflect the human

story of growth and discovery. All these narratives employ the basic motif of a child's journey out from home and back again, yet the circumstances and characters differ widely, and
the motif is skillfully altered to serve the theme of each story.

Although they share the central journey metaphor and the presence of youthful characters, the four pieces represent a variety of style and tone that illustrates Still's versatility and
his commitment to real children who had touched his life. Jack, of course, is not real unless
such a familiar folk figure can be said to generate his own reality. When Still recreated Jack,
he liked what he saw and was not shy about saying so, boasting to Jerry Williamson the year
after the book was published, "All my powers and my gifts, such as they are, came together
in those few pages. The news that some children are sleeping with this book and that their
elders are reading it with some delight tickles me" (53–54). Readers do delight in Jack's personality and achievement when he sets off on his journey with direction and purpose and meets
with success. "The Nest," which brings readers the opposite of delight, is the profoundly disturbing story of a six-year-old girl, Nezzie, who literally roams about in the forest on her
figurative journey of the heart, searching for a secure nest of love. Nezzie's search ends tragically. When asked why he wrote such a disturbing story, Still reported that he wanted to
release himself from the haunting experience a young local girl must have had when she
became lost in the woods. The only way he knew to get it out of his mind was to put it in a
story (talk at Hindman). Another of his characters who comes alive on the page was also
inspired by a real little girl belonging to a neighboring family. Elvy, alias Mrs. Razor, tours
the imagination, seeking an unknown, fantasy destination. Like Jack, Elvy delights readers,
yet her story is not a predictable folk tale but a complex psychological study that invites exploration and analysis. The foundation of Still's childhood journey motif began with his 1940
novel, *River of Earth*. Though the unnamed narrator is a universal "every boy," Still claimed
that the character was initially inspired by a young student at the settlement school, William
Lee Parks, the same child who reported his experiences of getting "killed down" instead of
"growed up." The boy of the novel engages in many small expeditions that fit together like
concentric circles and propel him along his large journey of growth, life, and learning on the
river of earth.

* * *

Still's version of the classic Jack and the beanstalk story tells of a young mountain boy
facing an adult problem — he and his mother need money. His task is to provide that money
but also to prove that he is not a simpleton. Jack's story unfolds through two kinds of journeys. The first is the literal trip to town to sell the cow. Apparently he fails this test, for he
foolishly trades their one asset for only three beans. The mother's adult reaction is under-
standable; in her fury she hurls picturesque insults at the boy: "Upon my word and deed and
honor, you couldn't be trusted to pack slops to a sick bear! You don't know beans!" Of course,
being the determined lad that he is, Jack, with a little help from the beans, sets out to prove
his mother wrong.

His success, however, must come through a trial involving a second kind of journey; he
must climb the beanstalk and confront the giant. Jack — being "Independent as a hog on ice.
Ready for anything"— never hesitates: "He stepped onto the path and went where it went."
Still's mountain Jack is cocky, fearless, and resourceful. Instead of being cowed by the giant,
Jack is challenged. He easily outwits the overgrown fool, and his reward is the sack of gold.
Thus, Jack gains his first objective — money.

Practical adults would advise Jack to quit while he is ahead, but as Still puts it, "He
hadn't got his barrel full. And curiosity was stinging him." So Jack makes a second journey up

the beanstalk, this one for pure adventure. He repeats the visit to prove himself. Jack finds things much the same with the giant and his wife. Once again, Jack narrowly escapes, this time with the magic hen, and he runs down the beanstalk shouting orders to his mother to get the ax. The reversal of roles could not be clearer — now Jack is doing the shouting. After this second trip, he does have his barrel full. The story ends on a positive note; Jack has solved the problem of no money and has proven himself in the process. The last words echo: "And nobody could rightly say Jack didn't know beans." His round-trip journey of discovery ends happily as do most folk tales and fairy tales.

*    *    *

Still's inspiration for the Jack story was the traditional folk tale, but the germ for "The Nest" was based on a real life event that took place in Knott County. Still wrote the story to forget it. Ironically, the result is a story that involves the reader in a painful, unforgettable experience. The structure and tone of Nezzie's story differs dramatically from Jack's. While "The Nest" contains elements of the fairy tale, its ending is not happy, and its tone is not in any way triumphant.

Nezzie Hargis is a young girl engaged in a simple task involving a short journey. The story opens with her in the woods on the way to her aunt's; gradually we learn, through her thoughts and flashbacks, that she has been sent there for the night while her father, step-mother, and their baby son visit her ailing grandfather. Her father's instructions are to "fol-low the path to the cattle gap," the way they had gone before. He has set the task for her in what sounds like reasonable terms to an adult, even describing it as a test of maturity. "You're over six years old ... Now, be a little woman" (43). Possibly he realizes that he is pushing her out of the nest prematurely, because his efforts to bribe her with a "pretty" reveal his con-cern for her ability to make the trip. "If you'll go willingly to your Aunt Clissa's, I'll bring you a pretty. Just name a thing you want, something your heart is set on" (44). Throughout the story, Nezzie never names the thing she wants.

Unlike Jack, Nezzie does not know what she wants, and we see her confusion manifested in her physical lostness. "Cow paths wound the slope, a puzzle of trails going nowhere" (43). She is in a different world than Jack who "stepped onto the path and went where it went." Nezzie is not seeking adventure, nor is she making a simple journey up and down the beanstalk; she is looking for a safe haven, surroundings of warmth and love, a sense of secu-rity. The fairy tale elements of the story suggest not the triumphant Jack but the perilous jour-ney of Red Riding Hood or the dilemma of Hansel and Gretel, abandoned in the woods by a weak father and an unfeeling stepmother. Their ingenuity (with a bit of fairy tale luck) saves them in the end, but Nezzie lives in a real world, full of conflicting emotions and shifting contingencies. Nezzie's journey is neither simple nor successful. It aborts in the woods where she finds her nest, a cold, abandoned rabbit bed.

Readers watch Jack make his journey and smile, but with Nezzie they go along and suffer. The structure of the story, like her journey, is a maze of trails. Her confusion and aloneness are evident from the beginning, because when the story opens she is already lost. Through flashes of imagery and bits of remembered conversation, the story pieces itself together like a puzzle, and the reader sees the paths that have wound her to this spot. A trail of memory emerges: her baby brother in his cocoon of quilts; her stepmother forever crying to her "Go tend the chickens"; her father's words of advice, "Be a little woman." All this time she is walk-ing and searching for the route to safety. Yet, physical limitations and tough conditions wear her down. What little sense of purpose and linear movement the journey possesses at the beginning of the story is completely lost by the middle. Her physical struggle mirrors her emotional state. Like her thoughts, the images and memories become more jumbled as her relationship to the physical environment becomes less certain. Time also blurs as night falls and dream mixes with reality. Her mind recalls bits of conversation about the future of the baby and fuses them with thoughts of the present. She follows a circular mental pathway connecting the three generations of males in the family: "And seeing her grandfather she thought of his years, and she thought suddenly of the baby growing old, time perishing its cheeks, hands withering and palsying" (50). Finally just before sleeping, she sees her mother's face and imagines the warm safe nest of her arms.

When the last section of the story begins with the words "She waked to morning..." (51), readers feel that with daylight the girl will complete her journey or be miraculously saved. But a sentence or two later, the world takes on a dreamlike quality. Her sense of darkness and confusion is replaced by dim sight and meaningless sounds; her pain of the night before has become merely languor. She loses a shoe and hops through the snowy pasture, laughing at the bush that steals her bonnet. As the cows walk by in a fog, drowsiness overcomes her. The reader feels uncertainty and sadness upon finally realizing that her incomplete journey is over. Hers will not be a round trip (unless the rabbit's nest and the closing vision of her mother are thought of as her only real home). Nezzie's journey is less successful in material terms than Jack's, but her human story is more engaging because it is more real. This story is no fairy tale.

*   *   *

A third narrative involving a different kind of childhood journey is "Mrs. Razor," a delightful story with an ending that is no less ambiguous or profound but certainly is less tragic than Nezzie's. Like "The Nest," this story's protagonist is a young girl and was based on a real child. Elvy's childhood journey is not obviously emotional or psychological or even physical — hers is imaginative. This six-year-old lives in an imaginary world involving a Nowhere Place called Biggety Creek; she has three children and is married to "a lazy shuck of a husband," known as Razor. Elvy has created an identity for herself not as a dependent child but as a responsible mother and shrewish wife.[4] Like Jack and Nezzie, she cannot live in a vacuum but must relate to her family, a necessity which creates conflict in the story. Like Jack's mom and Nezzie's dad, Elvy's parents want her to grow up. They are waiting for her to put aside the childish habit of living in her imaginary world. The family has two other children, one of whom, Elvy's older brother, tells the story. The narrator and her younger brother, Morg, are involved in the conflict as both witnesses and participants. Each child has a different capacity for make-believe: Elvy actually lives a story; Morg, in contrast, can "never make-like"; it is the narrator, the storyteller, who has the power to move from imaginary to real and to pull the two together into a fiction of his own.[5]

The story he tells belongs primarily to Elvy and her father and climaxes when the father decides to take real action that will jolt his daughter out of her fabricated suffering. Earlier that afternoon Elvy had met her father at the barn gate with news of Razor's tragic death; she insists that they hurry to Biggety Creek and rescue her children. The father himself had made up the place of Biggety Creek "where heads are the size of water buckets, where noses are turned up like old shoes, women wear skillets for hats, and men screw their breeches on" (2–3); his daughter has inherited his talent and embellishes it with total belief. He tries to force Elvy back to reality with a literal journey to Biggety Creek. The whole family climbs into the wagon as night falls. Elvy points them in the right direction, then nods fitfully as she struggles to keep awake.

The reader becomes absorbed in this family situation, and once again Still closes with an intriguing ambiguity. The story's concluding sentence, "We traveled six miles before Father turned back" (6), lets us know that Mrs. Razor's journey is round trip, but we cannot be sure if this literal journey has buried Elvy's no-good husband once and for all, thereby symbolizing her passage into an adult world which insists on separating real from make-believe. The uncertainty puts power in the narrative because this story exists somewhere between the father's mind and the girl's imagination. It lives in the words of the young narrator, the storyteller or artist who can weld fact and fiction and who will carry the reader along for the ride.

*       *       *

A similar young nameless narrator is the protagonist in Still's novel *River of Earth*. The motif of the childhood journey threads throughout the work and informs both plot and theme. The story asks the basic question of how young fellers grow and answers it by looking at the narrator's life from age seven to nine. How this particular boy grows and learns is part of the larger, more universal question voiced by Preacher Sim Mobberley in his sermon: "Oh, my children, where air we going on this mighty river of earth, a-borning, begetting, and a-dying — the living and the dead riding the waters?" (76). The whole story, then, questions the cyclical human journey along the river of life, a journey which contains all and controls all. Within that large journey, the story raises specific questions. The boy's immediate family dramatizes an Appalachian social conflict of the 1930s: the father's urge to move from one coal camp to another in search of work pitted against the mother's inclination to root her family to one spot of earth. The story ends with the Baldridges preparing for another move to yet another camp, adding significance to the questions of where they are going and why. Within the large metaphysical expedition and through these family wanderings indicative of social migration, the narrator repeats small journeys, out from home and back — each time, like the mythic hero, discovering more about his identity and destiny.

Of the many small journeys that fill the novel, three are especially noteworthy. The first takes place on the child's seventh birthday. When a neighbor comes to seek help for his mare in labor, the father unexpectedly carries the boy along. At the beginning of this initiation experience, the boy observes that they are soon beyond any place he knows. The trees and hills are different; he has left home and his familiar surroundings. His anticipation grows when his father hints that he might get the colt. At their destination, the boy experiences the trauma of the foal's birth and what he calls "the pain of flesh coming into life" (27). He also fights with the neighbor's son, Oates, for the right to own the foal. After shamefully turning his eyes from the birth and losing the fight to the larger boy, his bitter comfort is the knowledge that the colt dies and so is spared the cruelty of his adversary. The father and son return home without triumph. "Being seven on that day, and bruised and sore from fighting, the years rested like an enormous burden on my swollen eyes. We went on, not stopping or speaking until we saw our hill standing apart from all the others" (32).

This first journey establishes a pattern for subsequent ones: he leaves home and familiar surroundings, experiences difficulties, learns lessons from people of the present or past, and finally returns with greater knowledge to his own hill, house, and family.

The entire second part of the novel is a sojourn for the boy; he is sent from Little Carr to help Grandma at Lean Neck. More importantly, she helps him by telling stories of the heritage they share. The Oates boy of the earlier trip had taunted him with the words that he was a Middleton; now, in this visit with Grandma Middleton, he learns what it means to be who he is. While on this long visit, he makes short expeditions away from his grandmother's house; one is in the chapter beginning: "She's a traipsing fool" (138). Jolly is speaking here of

Grandma, but the chapter also tells of the legendary wanderer, Walking John Gay, a source of fascination to the boy. The end of the chapter finds young Baldridge walking to the site where his grandfather was murdered, to explore the legend surrounding Boone Middleton. The boy's experience on this trip is more positive than that of the first venture. As he leaves the site, he meets a strange man walking in the woods, his own version of Walking John Gay. The boy rehearses the story of discovery he will tell his grandmother: "I spoke the words aloud to know their sound." His return home this time is triumphant, for he is discovering his creative voice as well as his identity. He compares the experience to a resurrection when he says, "I turned down the creek, going back the way I had come, going from this death place as from a new grave" (147).

A third important journey takes place near the end of the novel, after the boy has returned to his immediate family now living in the coal camp of Blackjack. Almost nine, he explores on his own and keeps his wandering a secret from his family: "I went barefooted through the camp, going where I was of a mind" (224). On one particular trek, the boy sets out to find and ride the blind mules that were kept at the foreman's place. As he leaves, his mother asks him to check on his Uncle Samp, who had not slept in his bed for two nights. The search for Samp leads the boy into the local store. As on the first trip, he is accosted by adversaries, men who are disgruntled at losing their jobs in the mines. This time the fight is not physical but verbal and psychological. The men plague the boy and question his father's connections to the mine operators because, unlike them, he is still employed. They scoff at the boy when he blurts out that he will never be a miner. Full of anger and frustration, he bursts out of the store, running to escape the taunting of the men and the frightening reality of their declaration that no matter what he wants to be, he'll "end snagging jackrock" (227). No matter how hard he runs, the boy cannot escape that truth. Finally, he seeks peace as he stands by the fence where the mules should be, but they are not there. His earlier journey to see the birth of the colt is mirrored at this point when he discovers that he is too late, that the mules are dead. His brief conversation with the foreman's wife concludes the chapter:

> "I come to ride the little mules," I said.
> The woman peered out of the bonnet. "They've been tuck away."
> "Gone?"
> "Old, and blind, and puny. A sight o' feed it tuck, and times are getting hard. They'd a need to be put out o' misery."
> "Gone?"
> "Gone to dirt" [229].

This scene foreshadows the very end of the book and the profound question the boy asks while facing his grandmother's coffin: "Grandma, where have you gone?" (245).

The boy's question echoes and makes specific the preacher's question "Where air we going on this mighty river of earth?"(76). At the conclusion of the novel, the boy's journey is not over; his question is not yet answered. He is only just beginning to ask it. Nor is the journey over for his family. The story ends with the new baby crying in the far room and the father's promise that they will move on to another coal camp. Clear-cut endings are hard to find in Still's stories because they are rare in real life.

Perhaps Jack lived happily ever after, but the children of Still's fiction do not inhabit a fairy tale world. The journey of life is not always simple or beautiful or even successful. It can be filled with confusion, hunger, and death, just as it can contain exploration, humor, and compassion. The circumstances that the characters face are real, and like real children, they have vivid imaginations as well as the ability to reformulate their experiences through words. That is what Still himself did so well in his stories. The Leslie County boy, William Lee

Parks, who told Still his tale so many years ago, makes us wonder how children ever grow up — except, of course, in fairy tales. Yet, most of them do, and they continue to make journeys, repeated journeys that explore their individual identities and their place in the continuum of human experience. The boy's question — How do fellers git growed? — and the preacher's — Where air we going? — weave together to provide the central theme of James Still's fiction. Never attempting a simplistic answer to the big questions, Still takes readers on a journey of discovery, a childhood journey that begins and ends in his own permanent spot in Appalachia but that merges with the universal quest for meaning.

## Notes

1. In 1998, when Still officially adopted Teresa Reynolds, he became the grandfather to her two children: Kayla, age 15, and Jacob, age 4.

2. See Rebecca Briley's study, "River of Earth: Mythic Consciousness in the Works of James Still," for an exploration and analysis of Still's use of the quest myth as an archetype that reflects universal experiences.

3. Jim Wayne Miller introduces *The Wolfpen Poems* with an essay probing Still's use of journeying in the poems as well as the prose.

4. While most of Still's young protagonists are boys, these two stories illustrate his empathy and understanding for young females, their place in the family and role in society. Danny L. Miller includes a discussion of both stories in his chapter on James Still's Mountain Women.

5. For an interesting discussion of the roles of the members within the family, see Joyce Hancock's article "Creative Energy in James Still's 'Mrs. Razor.'"

## Works Cited

Briley, Rebecca L. "River of Earth: Mythic Consciousness in the Works of James Still." *Appalachian Heritage* 9 (1981) and 10 (1982).

Hancock, Joyce. "Creative Energy in James Still's 'Mrs. Razor.'" *Appalachian Heritage* 8 (1980): 38–46.

Miller, Danny L. *Wingless Flights: Appalachian Women in Fiction.* Bowling Green, OH: Bowling Green State University Press, 1996. 102–123.

Miller, Jim Wayne. Introduction to *The Wolfpen Poems* by James Still. Berea, Kentucky: Berea College Press, 1986. xi–xxiii.

Still, James. "Hit Like to 'a' Killed Me." *Courier-Journal Roto-Magazine* [Louisville, KY] 19 April 1942: 22.

_____. Interview with J.W. Williamson. *Interviewing Appalachia: The Appalachian Journal Interviews, 1978–1992.* Knoxville: University of Tennessee Press, 1994. 49–66.

_____. *Jack and the Wonder Beans.* New York: Putnam's, 1977. Illustrated by Margot Tomes.

_____. "Mrs. Razor." *Pattern of a Man and Other Stories.* Lexington, KY: Gnomon Press, 1976. 1–6.

_____. "The Nest." *Pattern of a Man.* 43–52.

_____. "On his Life and Work." Interview with Judith Jennings. *Heritage* recording. Appalshop. 1992.

_____. *River of Earth.* Lexington: University Press of Kentucky, 1978.

_____. Talk with visitors at Hindman Settlement School. Hindman, Kentucky, 10 July 1997.

# "Read my tales, spin my rhymes": The Books for Children

## TINA L. HANLON

"I'll say this from my heart, I'd rather light up a child's eyes than earn a grunt of approval from a dozen of their elders" ("Interview" 124). This statement from a 1979 interview reveals an essential characteristic of James Still that lies at the heart of his long career as a librarian, writer, and teacher. Although he did not publish books marketed for children until the 1970s, Still's interest in children was central to the events that first took him to eastern Kentucky after he finished graduate school in 1931, and kept him there for seventy years. He went "to Knott County, Kentucky, to help Don West and his wife, Connie, with a vacation Bible school and a recreational program." There, Still organized boy scout troops and baseball teams, camping and playing with the children all summer (*The Wolfpen Notebooks* 15–16). Then he accepted a job as librarian at Hindman Settlement School, where he worked for the first three years with no salary. His devotion to the library and to the children of the county, recorded modestly in autobiographical essays, became legendary: "Aware that the many one-room schools in the county were without access to a library, I began spending one day a week—my own undertaking—walking from school to school with a carton of children's books on my shoulder; I would change the collections in these schools every two weeks.... Often as I approached a school I would hear the cry, 'Here comes the book boy'" (*From the Mountain* 17). While his jobs varied over the next seven decades, Still never stopped serving the region through his positions as volunteer, employee, and neighbor at Hindman, motivated by strong convictions about the value of a well-stocked library. He believed that children needed to read well and to experience good literature, not just school textbooks.

Like May Justus, who lived near the Highlander Folk School in eastern Tennessee through most of her long career and wrote more than sixty books for children, Still spent most of the twentieth century enjoying and assisting the rural communities of Knott County, Kentucky, devoting much of his time to children. Justus and Still concentrated their energies on participating in the life of the community, teaching, and writing creative literature that grew out of their own lives and observations, rather than joining social or political groups or writing didactic literature. Unlike Justus, Still also spent much of his time traveling widely and wrote just a handful of children's books, publishing more stories and poems for adults than

**James Still working as librarian, the Hindman Settlement School, Hindman, Kentucky (courtesy of the Hindman Settlement School).**

for children. But he was also the kind of author who wrote from the heart without separating his work for children and for adults. He said in 1979, along with the comment about his preference for lighting up a child's eyes, "I don't write for children—children alone. My so-called 'children's' books are for all ages, and I have knowledge adults are reading them. If children find books of mine they can and will read, I could not be more pleased. I'm not writing for any particular age group" ("Interview" 124). He wrote *about* children throughout his career, in stories and poems based on his own childhood in Alabama, a summer job as a social worker, and a lifetime of experiences with children and families. His novel *River of Earth* is narrated by a boy who is less than ten years old through most of the story, and some of his most highly regarded short stories for adults are about childhood, such as "The Nest" and "Mrs. Razor."

While Still told stories to children and read classic books to them throughout his life, he produced his own books for children in the later years of his career, and his four children's books from the 1970s were all reprinted at the end of the century. In 1974 and 1975, his two slim volumes of riddles and other folklore and poems were published: *Way Down Yonder on Troublesome Creek* and *The Wolfpen Rusties*. He blended some of his realistic short stories into the novel *Sporty Creek*, which is closely related to *River of Earth*. His picture book *Jack and the Wonder Beans* appeared in the same year as *Sporty Creek*, 1977. In 1998, when he was over ninety years old, he was persuaded to publish a collection of nursery rhymes, *An Appalachian Mother Goose*. It may seem unusual that the author best known for the intense, earthy realism of *River of Earth* and his short stories—who would produce one book of similarly realistic stories for young readers about mountain life during the Great Depression, in *Sporty Creek*—would produce other children's books containing fantasy and nonsense in the form of folktales, nursery rhymes, and riddles. However, both the realistic fiction and the folklore are rooted in Still's long immersion in the folklife of eastern Kentucky. References to traditional stories, rhymes, songs, and superstitions appear throughout the realistic stories as part of the every-day lives of the characters. Folktales and nursery rhymes blend practical, psychological, and social realities of life with nonsense and fantasy in ways that modern adults often overlook.

Moreover, Still's children's books in these different genres are consistent with several different trends in American culture and education that were influencing literature for children by the 1970s. A revival of storytelling led to publication of many new books based on oral traditions—not only retellings of classic fairy tales and collections of nursery rhymes, but also, due to growing interest in providing multicultural literature for children, books based on folklore from previously marginalized cultural traditions. May Justus's book *The Complete Peddler's Pack: Games, Songs, Rhymes, and Riddles from Mountain Folklore* appeared in 1969, a few years before Still's folklore collections. On the other hand, *Sporty Creek*'s use of the spare modernist style and unsentimental, realistic perspective on the hardships of mountain life that Still had developed since the 1930s was not out of place in a children's book of the 1970s because of the rise of New Realism in fiction for children and young adults. *Where the Lilies Bloom* by Bill and Vera Cleaver, a popular novel about a family of orphans living off the land in western North Carolina, appeared in 1969. *Bridge to Terabithia*, Katherine Paterson's realistic story of a more contemporary Virginia farm boy struggling with problems of class and gender and the sudden death of his best friend, was published in the same year as *Sporty Creek* and won the 1978 Newbery Medal for children's fiction published in the U.S.A. Like these other writers, Still wanted to give children well-told stories about the real joys and sorrows of life without condescension, without hiding painful realities or simplifying the language. It was through his distinctive command of language that Still combined humor, folklore, and realism in subtle ways in his children's books. Kentucky author George Ella Lyon commented on the day after Still died in 2001, "He had a perfect ear. He could convey so much of character and place without using the sort of dialect that's graphically depicted. He did it in the rhythm, the word choice and the metaphors; not by using apostrophes and strange spellings.... The beauty of his language and the fact that he wrote in so many genres was really a model for me" (qtd. in Egerton).

## *Sporty Creek*

*Sporty Creek* is James Still's second and last novel, his only work of realistic fiction classified as a book for children. Published in 1977 with the subtitle *A Novel about an Appalachian Boyhood* (and without the subtitle in the revised edition of 1999), the book has an unusual literary genealogy that reflects Still's lack of interest in segregating his readers by age, as well as his continuing interest in writing about childhood and family in rural Kentucky during the Great Depression. Seven of *Sporty Creek*'s ten chapters appeared earlier as short stories in magazines and books for adults, beginning with "The Ploughing" in 1939, which became *Sporty Creek*'s first episode, "Simon Brawl." Some of the same stories have been reprinted since 1977 as well. *Sporty Creek* is a sequel to *River of Earth*, Still's highly acclaimed novel of 1940, and yet not exactly a sequel, although the two books and their characters are closely related. Their narrators are cousins, young boys in growing families that move from place to place through the episodic chapters of each novel as their fathers struggle to support them. Their stories overlap in theme and style more than in specific incidents or characters, except that genial, comical Uncle Jolly plays a significant role in both books. In fact, the same plowing episode with Uncle Jolly that opens *Sporty* Creek is a middle chapter in *River of Earth*. New babies weave their way through both books, bringing as much joy and laughter as work and worry; in *Sporty Creek* a long wait for the baby to be named ends in the last family scene when the father calls him Little Jolly.

Migrations between the homeplace, where these families live off the land, and mining camps or towns, where jobs are offered and then terminated as the coal business changes, show the effects of industrialization and economic depression on families with conflicting loyalties, thwarted ambitions, and a need to feed and clothe their children. The mothers who long for the security, natural beauty, and garden plots of the homeplace follow their husbands to bleak camps where neighbors die of lung diseases, mine owners and thieves dismantle everything when the mines close down, and neighbors throw rocks at the windows as soon as someone moves out. The mine and the chapter about these events in *Sporty Creek* are appropriately named "Low Glory." The father in this novel is especially ineffectual in his decisions about waiting for mining jobs to reopen, and another time he moved the family too far into the woods, overestimating the abundance of ginseng and game in Tight Hollow, but in Low Glory his wife insists on pinching pennies and saving for their return to Sporty Creek.

These characters have much in common with the inhabitants of Wessex in the fiction of Thomas Hardy, one of many authors who influenced Still. Their characters occupy landscapes of rural beauty, based on places that these authors loved throughout their long careers, but some characters are destined to wander around their region and suffer, victimized by effects of modernization on rural communities as well as their own inner weaknesses, flawed relationships, and inflexible traditional values. The parents in *Sporty Creek*, for example, are similar to Tess's parents in Hardy's *Tess of the d'Urbervilles*, although not as dysfunctional or class conscious. Tess's drunken father indirectly causes the horrible death of the horse they need for their livelihood, putting too much of the burden of work on his children, while the father in *Sporty Creek*, with the help of his family, brings a bloody episode called "The Force Put" to a successful close by saving a neighbor's choking calf, which his son is then allowed to keep. The narrator is ashamed of his own fear and inability to help as his brother does, but he is not destroyed by family troubles like Tess. His mother's belief that berries are poisonous during a "locust summer" could have have had disastrous consequences for a hungry family, if the herb doctor had not come along to declare them edible. His angry sister's lie about giving away the baby to the childless doctor's wife horrifies the boy, and it might be true in a Hardy novel such as *The Mayor of Casterbridge*, but this American baby stays home playing with his parents and "growing bigger than the government" (74). Hardy and Still also include much humor and human sympathy in their affectionate depictions of the varied personalities, daily lives, folk customs, and regional dialect of the communities in their novels. They write about struggles and joys that are both universal and rooted in particular times and places.

Still's choice of youthful narrators in both of his novels helps keep the focus away from the tragic fates that ruin lives in Hardy's later novels, where characters suffer through wanderings and deprivation without the level of hope in family love and education that flows through Still's writing. His boys are confined by the destinies of their parents and wander with them — they can't take off suddenly to climb a magic beanstalk or slay a passel of giants like their favorite folk hero Jack, but they have their own adventures and initiation experiences, large and small, along the way. When the baby takes his first steps alone and the narrator calls him "independent as a hog on ice" (*Sporty Creek* 106), Still is using he same phrase that describes Jack as he starts up the beanstalk in *Jack and the Wonder Beans*. At the level of the children's perspective, thwarted ambitions take the form of universal boyhood experiences in attempts to gain independence by going away from home for errands or pranks, learning new skills, longing for possessions that adults may or may not provide, trying to earn their own money, and figuring out how to manage a complex array of emotions associated with home, school, and the wider world.

When the boy in *Sporty Creek* insists on learning to plow in the first chapter, Uncle Jolly says, "A tadwhacker never caught on too young" (2). The boy longs for his own colt but its arrival and temporary loss (when the family moves) are mentioned briefly in Still's understated style, overshadowed by dramatic exploits with cows and bulls, so the boy imagines himself a cattleman. When family finances improve in the mine camp, he becomes fascinated with game roosters, but he trades his rooster for a striped shirt with a collar that he has coveted, even though he has grown to love the rooster; then the shirt appears "too loud for the times," fades after poverty returns, and reappears as a baby garment (43, 106).[1] The boy does not complain that his fate is tied to the hard journey of his parents' lives even though he is developing his own dreams and skills. The children explore the world around them at their own pace and amuse themselves in spite of hard times. The attention paid to their reading and schooling, and their ability to learn all kinds of things at all ages, suggests that they may find their way out of the ruts in their parents' lives. The smart sister Holly makes dolls with tiny clothing out of the gingseng that keeps eluding their poor father's attempts to sell it for profit.

There is much common ground in *River of Earth* and *Sporty Creek*, and Still did not condescend to young readers in children's books or avoid references to the harsh realities of life and death, whether he was writing realistic fiction or nursery rhymes. Nevertheless, from the title to the end, *Sporty Creek* is like other children's books in the way it takes a lighter and more optimistic approach to the subject than *River of Earth*. Both families are poor, but their situation is more desperate at the beginning of *River of Earth,* where the mother comments on the first page that they don't have enough to feed the four children, and the cousins who wear out their welcome staying with the family cause so much distress that she moves into the smokehouse and burns down the old house. *Sporty Creek* opens with more emphasis on humorous childhood experiences. The boy's plowing lesson ends comically when the mule licks Uncle Jolly on the mouth, paying him back for laughing so hard at the frightened boy flying wildly across the field in all directions behind the wayward mule. Rebecca Briley notes that this scene, which juxtaposes working the land and education, establishes the central conflict in the book (75). The second chapter about school sets the boy's success as a student against his frustration with the torn and missing pages in the textbooks. While the teacher's stinginess and inadequate community support for schools cause the problems that the children perceive as a disgrace for their school, Uncle Jolly provides comic relief again, pulling pranks at the school that amuse the children and destroy the old books so they will have to be replaced.

*Sporty Creek* also ends with a stronger emphasis on the children's independence and hopes for their future. *River of Earth* closes with Uncle Jolly's trip to bury the grandmother and talk of his plans for marrying and farming. His visit enables the young narrator to grapple with death while the coffin is in his house overnight, but in *Sporty Creek* Uncle Jolly precipitates the boys' own journey at the end. He has suggested that a settlement house education would be best for the narrator's brother Dan after he loses some fingers in an accident. Uncle Jolly has the foresight to envision misfortune as an advantage; since the mines and military won't claim Dan, "it opens up the world" (94). Uncle Jolly (who was inspired by Still's own great-grandpa and a cousin) also recognizes that the narrator has brains and ought to go to a better school as well. Thus, the last chapter, "Journey to the Forks," focuses on the two boys alone, on their long walk to Hindman Settlement School.

The boys' homesickness affirms their attachment to home; as in other stories by Still, "journeying out into the world serves only to heighten the sense of belonging to one familiar spot of earth" (Miller 21). Dan also has doubts about being a scholar, especially when a neighbor denigrates the "tomfoolery" of too much learning and "fool notions" that contradict the Bible (115–18). But the narrator chatters about the wonders he has been told he will find at the school, especially the novels by Twain, Stevenson, and Defoe that another boy has described. As in many other twentieth-century children's books, the boy perceives that adults can be foolish and ignorant; the narrow-minded neighbor knows little and must be ignored, while the boy has a chance to be the first "pure scholar" in the family who might go "clear through the books and come out on yon side" (116). Adults make the journey necessary by not providing better country schools and, in their father's case, not thinking to move the family closer to any school, but the narrator insists that they made up their own minds to go to the Forks. He said earlier that he wanted to "live everywhere" and do everything in the world (93). He recalls the baby's first steps away from his tearful parents, and the calf they adopted after saving its life, now grown into a cow. Many details in the novel show how children make their own decisions that parents can't control — when to walk and talk, when to give up dolls, when to sneak off to cockfights and purchase a forbidden rooster. Then, game roosters and fancy shirts are left behind as the boy seeks more serious work with farm animals and saves his money for boots that he will wear in the world away from home.

It takes a great writer to weave humorous details and imaginative references to folklore and fantasy through a novel of intense realism that deals with life's harshest realities — as Katherine Paterson does in her novels about the struggles of a foster child, the death of a child's best friend, and other stories for children, some of which are set in Appalachia. Still's realistic novels and short stories about childhood seem to contrast dramatically with his books of folklore, full of magic and fun, but close comparison of his children's books shows that the folklore is rooted in realism as well as imagination. Images that link characters in *Sporty Creek* with Jack in *Jack and the Wonder Beans* — the baby walking like a "hog on ice," the boy called a "tadwhacker" who makes deals involving cows and seeds (his one-eyed friend has plans to sell seeds to buy a glass eye) — raise the question of whether the realistic characters are being compared to folktale heroes, or the folktales are based on everyday realities of rural life, or these links result from the author's consistent and authentic use of dialect in eastern Kentucky. The answer is probably all of the above. The boy and his family are depicted in the context of very particular places and experiences, but, as Briley observes, the absence of the narrator's name in the text helps to give his story mythic significance as his character develops toward manhood (67). Most names in the book, on the other hand, are both realistic and deeply ironic or amusing. Sporty Creek is not so sporting for the family without enough income to stay put on the land they love, and Sporty Creek school does not provide all that the children deserve, but children and adults do have fun together. The family is often described playing with the baby, and the father's talk is full of colorful, humorous expressions. At home and in school, the characters tell riddles and retell exciting stories from legend and history, just as Still describes Kentuckians of the past doing in the introductions to his *Rusties and Riddles* books.

Uncle Jolly is described from the beginning as a trickster, a scamp, and a "witty." He sings bits of humorous folk songs about fools and stubborn mules, and recites traditional rhymes such as the one counting out the baby's fingers (94). People link him jokingly with the devil through a variety of folk expressions, because of his pranks. He is kissed by a mule for napping and laughing at the plowing, but we see no evidence that he is succeeding in his hunt for a wife. He mocks the schoolteacher, distracting the class as if he is still an adolescent prankster by chanting the taboo phrase "school butter." He is not the only trickster, however, as tricks are used throughout the book, just as they are in Jack tales, for getting the best of a more powerful opponent. The mother in *Sporty Creek* doesn't resort to real violence, like Alpha in *River of Earth* burning her own house, but she tricks the father into moving away from Tight Hollow. She makes him laugh when he realizes she has fabricated hints and images of intruders or attackers. The sly sister Holly, like a wild child or witch woman with her ginseng dolls and secret friendship with skunks, gets revenge on her brother for invading her privacy when she tricks him into thinking the baby was given away. The boys, who take some risks in the night to play a trick with a noisy "dumb-bull" on a neighbor who won't keep his promises about paying them for work, acquire a calf in the end. These incidents, narrated in an unsentimental and sometimes understated manner as folktales often are, could be contests with witches, giants, or beasts if some of the realistic details were replaced with the exaggerated images of folklore.

Uncle Jolly's tricks provide more than jolly comic relief as well. The school children expect to be amused by him, and while he pretends to snore, they get to live out one of their fantasies by re-enacting the story of Gulliver and the Lilliputians at length. On the surface, Jolly seems like a stereotypical bachelor hillbilly—napping, joking, laughing, thriving without hard work, and wandering casually through different scenes. He's the subject of local legends about standing up to the Law with shocking audacity. But he's also a teacher, comforter, advisor, and provider of food. He's Jack and the folk hero's magic helper or godfather, or at least an imaginative helper, at the same time. Beneath the surface, we realize that the best ideas in the novel come from Uncle Jolly. He behaves outrageously at school to trick the authorities into getting new textbooks, his rhymes about being a fool comfort an injured nephew, and he provides better advice than the parents about the value of education. He jokes about having little schooling himself, but, without taking all the credit, he inspires the boys to go and seek knowledge, giving them apples for the journey. At the very end, they must control their own fears and climb by themselves down the stony ridge in the dark toward the lights of the new school. Uncle Jolly couldn't give them seeds for a magic beanstalk or enchanted shoes that would climb a magic mountain, and we don't know whether they will live happily ever after, but the narrator, carrying the boots purchased with his "first dollars earned," is ready for the new teachers who, as Jolly foretold, will help make him "fit ... for living in a hard world" (95).

## Jack and the Wonder Beans

In wonder tales from the oral tradition, the hero can have the kinds of adventures that the boys in *River of Earth* and *Sporty Creek* long for. Still's autobiographical essays describe his childhood epiphany about the magic of oral storytelling:

> One day, when I was hoeing cotton, my sister Inez began to tell a story from the next row— a true story, I thought. It continued for hours as our hoes chopped and pushed and rang against stones. Then I learned that her story was a fabrication. She had created it while she was working. From that moment my horizon expanded into the imaginary. I could make my own tales and did. Oral ones [*From the Mountain* 7].

Elsewhere Still explained his methods of telling oral tales, such as "The Three Little Pigs," to the younger children while he was librarian at Hindman, and his enjoyment of the natural storytelling talents of his neighbors (*Wolfpen Notebooks* 36). He called store owner Mal Gibson a trickster who told him he'd have to learn to tell lies and chew tobacco in order to hang out at the store. Gibson played jokes on everyone and ended up appearing in more of Still's notebook entries than anyone else (*From the Mountain* 20). One of his concerns about publishing the sayings and short tales he recorded in his notebooks over the years was that the printed page would not do justice to the oral flavor of the material. Nevertheless, he did select material from his notebooks in the late 1980s for publication in *Foxfire* and then *The Wolfpen Notebooks.* And earlier he published one traditional folktale as a picture book—*Jack and the Wonder Beans*, with engaging illustrations in earth tones by a prominent New York illustrator, Margot Tomes. It was republished in 1996 and also adapted by Larry E. Snipes as a musical play in the 1990s, with lyrics by Mark Noderer and Vivian Robin Snipes.

In fiction and nonfiction Still refers to folks telling legends and Jack tales in rural Kentucky homes. And the narrator's complaint in *Sporty Creek* about having to "splice ... together" two defective school books to read "Jack the Giant Killer" provides a glimpse of their long history in print, in chapbooks and school readers accessible to people who didn't have libraries or bookstores. Although the boy begins his assignment of studying the dictionary that day with enthusiasm about learning new words, it is not hard to imagine why he is soon tempted to "slack off" and read about Jack's exciting adventures (*Sporty Creek* 9). "Jack and the Beanstalk," the most popular Jack tale in the world, is usually called "Jack and the Bean Tree" by Appalachian storytellers. Still's emphasis in his Jack tale book on "wonder beans" enhances the magic in this tale about an ordinary country boy who acquires something that looks like ordinary country bean seeds, but soon finds himself climbing an extraordinary beanstalk to a magic kingdom in the sky.

Although Jack's seemingly foolhardy trade of their only cow for three beans angers Jack's hungry mother, Still never characterizes Jack as the lazy or foolish boy who appears in some versions of this story and other Jack tales.[2] Still's book makes a point of noting that although "hit looked like Jack was being tooken, ... Jack was no simpleton." He knows he needs food, and he carefully avoids getting taken in by other worthless offers, such as swapping for a gee-haw whimmy-diddle or a poke to catch snipes, but he trusts in the gypsy's promise that the wonder beans will feed him for life. Later, Jack's independence, curiosity, and fearlessness are stressed more than his desire for riches, when he climbs the beanstalk without hesitation and then returns a second time to "[give] it another crack." The young boy in *Sporty Creek* is realistically apprehensive when he leaves home to learn and experience new things, but, as a folk hero, Jack embodies the idealistic fantasy that a self-confident and resourceful boy, one who is "cocky as they come" when he needs to stand up to a dangerous opponent to pursue his quest, can make his wishes come true no matter how gigantic the obstacles.

While Still's story line does not depart dramatically from other English and American variants of "Jack and the Beanstalk," his text is most distinctive in his use of dialect and his artful blend of realistic and fantastic details. He described the book as "my re-telling of Jack and the Beanstalk as it could only have been told back in Knott County" ("Interview" 124). The text includes some real place names and evokes the tradition of local storytelling by claiming that "some tell" that Jack's "homeseat was here on Wolfpen Creek." Yet, since the narrator isn't certain of the details of time or place, Jack's story also entices us into the mysterious world of once upon a time — or "way back yonder," in the opening words of this book. Still, who often expressed his desire to use authentic and exact language in both narrative and dialogue, wove an abundant array of colloquial phrases and colorful expressions through this tale. For example, the narrator declares "Right! Right as a rabbit foot. They were bean vines. The beans had come up. They were twisted together into a stalk thick as a black-smith's arm" and "You know Jack. Independent as a hog on ice." While discussing the difficulties of preserving oral tales in writing, Briley affirms that Still's "printed page has captured that oral spell," describing him as "a troubadour with such a fine ear for the music of the tradition and the language of the people and their tales" (Summer 75). The similes that use striking visual images to unite the realistic and the fantastic, or the abstract and the concrete — such as anger that "sizzled like a red-hot horseshoe in the cooking tub" — employ the same powers of imagination as Still's collections of riddles and nonsense rhymes in his other children's books.

Jim Wayne Miller has observed that Still's folktale and short stories describe journeys to "otherworldly places ... in familiar worldly terms" (22). Thus, as both Miller and Briley note, the giant in another world, seventeen feet tall and fond of eating boys like Jack, becomes familiar through description of his "feet like cornsleds, hands like hams, fingernails to match bucketlids, and the meanest eye ever beheld in this earthly world." The ominous "Fee fie fo fum" lines are so well known in world folklore that it is fun to compare variations on the giant's rhyme in different retellings of this tale. Still's giant tromps in twice, "a-saying": "Fee fie chew tobacco" and "Fee fie, pickle and cracker / I smell the toes of a tadwhacker." His wife's attempts to dismiss his suspicions and hide Jack, so she can eat him without her husband devouring all the meat, add more folksy details to a bizarre, suspenseful situation — a humorous kind of domestic rivalry as the backdrop for Jack's escape from the dozing husband and the wife preoccupied with polishing her kettle. This blend of ordinary words and images with wondrous motifs from older fairy tales is a common source of interest and humor in Appalachian retellings of European folktales. At the top of the incredible beanstalk, Jack finds "a castle house," where a "high tall giant woman" feeds him crumble-in to fatten him up — the same humble dish "made of plain bread and milk" that he and his mother have been surviving on at home.

Jack takes a bag of gold and then a hen that lays golden eggs from the giant, but the hen produces only regular brown eggs on Earth — "an odd thing!" Even though Jack is like his counterparts in other variants of the tale because he acts on his adventurous compulsion to climb the beanstalk more than once, in Still's story Jack is destined to obtain just enough riches to make himself and his mother comfortable before he does the giant in by chopping down the beanstalk. For readers accustomed to endings in which Jack acquires more wealth, and sometimes even a princess bride, it may seem laughable that a pretty "second cow with ribbons to her horns" and a return to a mountain cabin mark the conclusion of Jack's quest. Perhaps the more modest endings published by Still and by North Carolina storyteller Ray Hicks, in his book of Jack tales, reflect their own preference for a humble way of life in the mountains, where they tended gardens and farms as well as spinning yarns. In "Appalachian Literature at Home in the World," Miller emphasizes that Still's characters are "rooted in a particular environment," while they are also "forever journeying through the world" (21). Still observes sensibly that "Jack had his barrel full enough" once he and his mother have plenty to eat with their garden, hen, and cow.

Jack's success as a smart and plucky individual seems more important to Still than material gain. A final joke at the end of the tale, echoing an insult from his mother when she was angry about the beans, asserts that "nobody could rightly say Jack didn't know beans." Briley's analysis of mythic consciousness in Still's books concludes that "Jack is content, for the journey for adventure is over and the penetration into the supernatural has been profitable" (Summer 75). The magical union of Jack's mythic heroism and loyalty to home is symbolized in Tomes's first and final illustrations within the main body of the story, by a soft black sky full of huge stars above the same humble brown house. Only the proportions within these illustrations are different, as the sky and stars are much bigger than the house at the end, spilling over the gutter into a final blank page beyond Jack's front porch.

Thus Still's retelling of a wonder tale is not so different from his realistic fiction in this final emphasis on the hero's attachment to home as well as his desire for adventures that develop his inner self in relation to the world and the supernatural. Richard Chase's introduction to Appalachian Jack tales notes that Jack's "fantastic adventures arise often enough among the commonplaces of existence, and he always returns to the everyday life of these farm people of whom he is one" (xii). Like Chase, who published two picture book retellings of Jack tales in the 1950s, Still recognized the enduring value of this storytelling tradition and set a high standard for authors of Appalachian picture books who came after him at the end of the century, such as Gail E. Haley, William H. Hooks, Paul Brett Johnson, and Tom Birdseye. Critics often comment on the achievement of timelessness in Still's writing, and Still recognized the timeless appeal of well-told folktales like his when he said, "It may be that this book has a chance of greater longevity than any of my other works. All my powers and my gifts, such as they are, came together in those few pages. The news that some children are sleeping with this book and that their elders are reading it with some delight tickles me in a spot that is hard to get to" ("Interview" 124).

## Rusties and Riddles and Gee-Haw Whimmy-Diddles

While *Sporty Creek* and *Jack and the Wonder Beans* are prose stories interspersed with verses and traditional witticisms, Still's other children's books focus on folk rhymes and riddles, accompanied by some longer prose passages of wordplay and commentary. Two collections of riddles, *Way Down Yonder on Troublesome Creek: Appalachian Riddles and Rusties* (1974) and *The Wolfpen Rusties: Appalachian Riddles and Gee-Haw Whimmy-Diddles* (1975) were reprinted as one volume in 1989. Titled *Rusties and Riddles and Gee-Haw Whimmy-Diddles*, the combined volume includes Janet McCaffery's black and white woodcuts from the original editions on every double-page spread. These titles reflect Still's special interest in specific places and playful folk traditions, especially wordplay. The first book explains that rusties were "turns of wit, tricks of words, or common pranks." In the second book, *gee-haw whimmy-diddle* is defined as a "toy whittled from the prong of a tree limb" or "anything of small worth."

The titles and the contents thus suggest that these are collections of nonsense and silly amusements, but Still framed the riddles and rusties with ample evidence that they are not all trivialities of small worth. While *Jack and the Wonder Beans* has no preface or source notes, Still introduced each of these volumes with a short overview of the landscape, place names, language, daily lives, and cultural traditions of the place for which it is named: "Troublesome Creek country" and the valley of Wolfpen Creek. Writing more than thirty years after he began living among the people in these places, he describes their customs in past tense as a culture that is passing away although it is "within living memory." As they amused each other with tales about "the legendary Jack," about ghosts and witches and historical explorers and pioneers such as Daniel Boone, Still adds, "They sprung riddles and pulled rusties." Although Still himself quotes a statement by John James Audubon about the simplicity of past times on the Kentucky frontier, the common conception that rural life was simple in the past must be weighed against the wealth of details about work, play, school, history, crafts, and nature that Still packed into a few pages in these introductions. The riddles and rusties he records are part of a rich cultural heritage with ancient roots.

Still also combined nonsense with realism in these books by including epigraphs and poems among the riddles and rusties. The first book opens with a lyrical quotation from Sarah Orne Jewett, an earlier writer of realistic stories about New England rural life: "Bring your gifts and graces and tell your secrets to this lonely country child." This line reflects Still's respect for the cultural traditions he recorded and his lifelong devotion to enriching the lives of children. The four titled poems in *The Wolfpen Rusties* originally appeared in such national publications as *Saturday Evening Post, Esquire,* and the *New York Times* (some as early as the 1930s), and in Still's later poetry collections. "On Wolfpen Creek" (originally titled "Beloved Place" and ultimately retitled "Wolpen Creek"), a short poem reprinted before the riddles, is about remembering the beauties of nature, about "Earth loved more than any earth." While the realistic images all represent a specific place, they are also deepened through metaphors that compare light with a pool of water, and describe "maples blossoming wings, the oak proud with rule, / The spiders deep in silk." Many of the riddles, of course, are also based on metaphor and more playful ambiguities in language.

One of the other poems reprinted in *The Wolfpen Rusties* among the riddles, "Apple Trip," celebrates the "worldly wonder" of the rich variety of apples for sale and barter at Hurricane Gap, with just a hint of dialect in compound phrases such as "tooth-ticklers" and "grin-busters." At the very end of *Sporty Creek,* Still included specific names like the ones listed in this poem, revealing the young boy's precise knowledge of apple varieties and their different pleasures, as he shares apples with his brother. The poems "Granny Race" and "Dance on Pushback" contain many more examples of regional dialect and humor. Old Granny's hasty trip on horseback to deliver a young couple's first baby is described with details of folk traditions associated with childbirth, as well as jokes about the new father's need for "a nip" of spirits as he anxiously waits to find out he has a son. "Dance on Pushback" is also full of energy and even more fun, urging boys to hurry to "Gabe Waye's homeplace" in the moonlight to dance with his "six fair young daughters" while his three sons play banjo, fiddle, and dulcimer.

Each book also contains a selection of untitled verses that contrast nonsense and practical matters, as collections of nursery rhymes often do. *Way Down Yonder* begins with a short rhymed account of "the last earthly things I expect to see," a list that mocks the devil by progressing from the silly impossibilities of "a mouse picking a cat's teeth" and a mule plowing by itself to an image of "Old Horned Scratch praising the Lord." Another verse that turns ancient supernatural beliefs into absurdities depicts a witch on Wolfpen who gets cooked herself when she steals the "moon-ball" and "sun-ball" to make food with them. In two later short rhymes, speakers claim to engage in implausible actions, such as riding on a horse's tail and jumping both ways off a train track, losing one's trousers to avoid an oncoming train. The stubborn mule Simon Brawl appears in another humorous verse, similar to the song sung by Uncle Jolly in *Sporty Creek*'s first chapter about learning to plow.

More practical traditions of children's folklore and education are represented in some lines providing a mnemonic sentence for learning to spell "geography" in "Sporty Creek fashion," and in the verses about books on the final pages of each book. "Book protection" is the label used by English folklorists Iona and Peter Opie for inscriptions that express the owner's fear of loss or theft of the book. Still's last rhyme warns any "young whippersnap" against stealing the book, "For nickels and dimes / It cost-éd my pap." Both this verse and the two lines in *Way Down Yonder* asking for its return if the book gets lost are very similar to rhymes the Opies collected from English schoolchildren in the mid-twentieth century (*I Saw Esau* 91). Like *Jack and the Wonder Beans*, many of Still's rhymes show the continuation of European folk traditions with regional variations in the oral traditions of Appalachia.

Over 130 riddles comprise the central contents of the two books. The answers printed upside down under each riddle and the lively variations in the design and placement of Janet McCaffery's folksy woodcuts add to the novelty and fun of these books. One riddle is shaped in a spiral of words like its answer — a snail, illustrating the literary tradition of concrete poetry. The Opies observed that adults lost most of their interest in riddles three hundred years ago, relegating them to the realm of childhood amusements (*Oxford Dictionary* 14). But folklorists and literary historians remind us that riddles have an ancient history in oral traditions, in teaching, and in literature, as riddle contests have serious consequences in *Oedipus Rex*, the Bible, and fairy tales. Still observes that the riddles of his Kentucky folk "had been handed down from their ancestors," with so many obscure variations and frequent changes "that the answers were lost" in some cases (*Way Down Yonder*). The variations selected by Still for these volumes include some easy riddles about everyday objects that any contemporary child could guess. The verse starting "Riddle, riddle, randy crow / I can't move but here I go / Two black hands to cover my face" is obviously about a clock, but the rhythms and occasional nonsense lines in some of the rhymes provide as much fun as guessing the answers. The majority of the riddles are based on descriptions of everyday objects—from sawdust ("a pile of timber ... so limber" that you can't "whack it" or "stack it") to a duck with yellow shoes or a wagon (sticking its tongue out under the bed at night). Most are images from nature or household objects, and some require knowledge of rural life or past customs that are not so well known today (wagons have tongues). Occasional footnotes explain regional vocabulary and superstitions that appear in some of the rhymes and riddles. A long riddle about the Trojan horse shows, like some of the details about school discussions and boyhood reading in *Sporty Creek*, that Still's mountain folk knew about world history and literature just like more sophisticated people in the world.

Some of the riddles can be solved by figuring out poetic descriptions of objects such as a pumpkin ("a yellow homeseat lacking a thatch") or the wind. Others involve personification, such as a tree saying "In summer I'm dressed fit to marry the Queen of Sheba," and sometimes inanimate objects even have names, such as "One-eyed Priscilla" and "Jonathan No-arms" for a needle and thimble. Many of the riddles depend on puns and other types of wordplay, drawing attention to the abundance of semantic ambiguity in the English language. Riddles that bring together dissimilar things with similar names sometimes trick the listener with apparent paradoxes: corn has ears that can't hear, a potato has "eyes staring yet cannot peep," you can't wear a lawsuit, and a criminal who "broke out" couldn't leave the jail if he broke out with measles. The *Larousse Dictionary of World Folklore* explains that "rather than the practical wisdom or the creation stories of a culture, riddles contain its thought associations, which can often be startling or beautiful and are usually witty." Solving riddles "develops the capacity for sustained, imaginative application in the individual intellect of both children and adults" (Jones 368–69). The solutions might depend on ignoring distracting details in the riddle, such as the exact dimensions of a hole, which have no bearing on realizing that the amount of dirt in a hole will always be "none." A poem in which the speaker is traveling to Noe is similar to the classic "As I Was Going to St. Ives," encouraging the listener to add up the many creatures going in the opposite direction when the only answer needed is that one is going to Noe.

Other tricks and paradoxes require focusing more than we do in ordinary discourse on properties of language such as spelling and pronoun reference. The word "short" can be made "shorter" by adding letters. Removing two letters from a five-letter word ("often") will leave "ten." "Butter" can be spelled with four letters ("goat"). Questions asking for comparison or contrast might be referring to spelling rather than other attributes of the items named. The ambiguity of pronoun reference can be used to trick the listener into spelling a long phrase rather than answering "i-t" to spell it. Some of these seem like rather crude tricks or silly rusties, especially to listeners who feel foolish if they don't catch on, yet many of the riddles give us profound new insights into everyday realities. How often do we think about yesterday as something that "every living, breathing creature on the ball of the world has seen," but "to their dying day" will "never see ... again"? Briley discusses Still's riddles as reflections of the "mythic element" in everyday language and the "quest for knowledge of life and self" (77). She observes that "the most vivid of all the riddles are those dealing with the concepts of the cycles of nature and of the inevitability of old age and death" (78). In addition to the riddles she cites that describe aging in natural objects and humans, it is worth noting that the last riddle in the second book is about a coffin, the source of some of life's final paradoxes, since "you couldn't give it to the man who made it" and "the man who used it never set eyes on it."

Most of these riddles refer to common nouns, but names are also important throughout both books of riddles and rusties. A number of selections take the form of miniature stories with named characters, such as Lucas Magoffin, the criminal who breaks out with measles after being jailed for vandalism at school. Some of the riddles mention eastern Kentucky place names, and several items in these books focus primarily on the use of interesting names. Briley notes that colorful names are a way of unconsciously "creating metaphorical myths in order to make observable realities in nature accessible to human understanding" (77). *Way Down Yonder* ends with the longest piece in either book, a three-page tale of Riar Tackett, the Dirk postmaster whose "anticky" family likes to play games with the "quare place names" he strains his eyes to read. His son tells a long story full of italicized words, each of which is a Kentucky place name. For example, "Watch out for a *Viper* at *Hot Spot*, and behave *Lovely*." Still notes at the end that many of these post offices have been closed since they appeared in the 1923 Kentucky postal guide, "but the *places*— towns or hamlets— remain." As we see these names transformed through history from ordinary words to place names and back to common nouns in a traditional family game, Still shows that language is both ambiguous and precise. His collections of rusties, riddles, and nursery rhymes preserve the dual nature of oral folklore, recording culturally specific details from the history of real places and people that Still wanted us to remember, while also showing how their language and culture belonged to a much broader history of European-American traditions that were constantly changing as humorous and serious folklore passed from one speaker to another for generations.

## An Appalachian Mother Goose

*An Appalachian Mother Goose* seems like Still's most fanciful book of all, but, as in his earlier collections of folklore, traditional rhymes recited for fun also provide insights into regional culture and universal human experiences. The short Preface describes children in one-room schools reciting their lessons in unison. They learned "'by heart' the Mother Goose rhymes and often changed them to match their time and place and understanding. And sometimes they created their own." Still obviously participated in that process himself and never tired of it, since he was over ninety years old in 1997 when he told novelist Lee Smith, while she visited him during an illness, that he probably wouldn't publish any more books. She coaxed him into showing her the "little verses" he said he had written. Still later noted, "One day, I thought about Jack jumping over the candlestick ... and it just occurred to me that he scorched his britches, and I put it down.... I didn't know I was working on a book" (Breed). After Smith encouraged him to work on the book, he expressed surprise that the University Press published the collection of more than eighty nursery rhymes the following year, and that it sold so well: "I did that book just for fun. I was just playin'" (qtd. in Parales). Smith also recognized the deeper significance of the rhymes: "I think that this is very serious writing.... These little poems are about very important things. I mean, Mother Goose poems always are. They address all sorts of things that children fear or hope for, and they're very magical. What he adds is the real element of poetry" (qtd. in Breed).

Like some of the folklore in the *Rusties and Riddles* books, many of Still's nursery rhymes resemble familiar rhymes recited by children throughout the English-speaking world for centuries. They show how oral traditions evolve, as new silly rhymes build on and parody the old nonsense rhymes that European immigrants brought to Appalachia; there, like the Jack tales, the rhymes developed interesting blends of Old World and New World language and images. In some cases, a familiar line introduces an entirely different subject, as in the rhyme beginning, "Diddle, diddle dumpling, my son John / Caught a catfish forty feet long." The old rhyme about John going to bed in his shoe and socks turned into a miniature tall tale about fishing. "Jack and Jill" became a satire on marital relations, as Jill "died of laughter" when Jack fell down, but after she revives and marries him, she and her daughter have to fetch all the water, while the illustration shows lazy Jack dozing at the bottom of the hill. A rhyme similar to "Pussy cat, pussy cat, where have you been?" seems to have been updated for the modern democratic world, since the cat does not go to look at the queen, but says instead, "I petitioned the judge to give cats the vote" (49). Typical nursery rhyme nonsense and impossibilities are also found in the rhymes about Charlie Mann, who "Skipped the custard, /Ate the pan," and "Rowdy, dowdy, Jitney Jones," who "Bought a dog with no bones," so Jim Oak "carried the dog in a poke" (11, 24).

Some of the fantasy disappeared from other rhymes, replaced by down-to-earth humor about Jack Be Nimble scorching his pants and the dog laughing at the musical cow and cat in "Hey Diddle, Diddle," where "the cow sang ballads to the moon" instead of jumping over it (32). One "baked bird" in "Sing a Song of Sixpence" wonders pragmatically, "Why didn't we up and fly?" (5). Little Bopeep's sheep get burrs in their tails, while the sheep in "Baa, Baa, Black Sheep" gets sunburn and feels cold in the shade after being sheared so close (10). No-nonsense morality seems to dominate one of the rhymes about school: the boy addressed is a "bad creature" who got smacked for taking a snail to his teacher, but there is still fun in repeating the lines that start "Tadwhacker, tadwhacker" (35).

The King's men are gone from "Humpty Dumpty," which is no longer a riddle as the speaker explicitly longs for the lost egg for breakfast. And "Little Nancy Etticoat" isn't the traditional riddle about a candle with a white petticoat and red nose. Still's Nancy got "a pretty petticoat" at the Isom Fair and it made her vain. There are riddles in the book, though, such as "Why did Ole Jerb Bowen take a bale of hay to bed with him? *To feed his nightmares*" (42). Another riddle, more melancholy than most of the nursery rhymes, is about grave-digging. The old woman in a shoe is more resourceful and humane than her European ancestor (who beats her children), since she *does* know "what to do" with young'uns: wash them, give them a treat, and put them to bed (36). "Old Miss Buxom Hubbard," however, is cruel compared to Old Mother Hubbard, since her cupboard is full of delicacies but "Her flea-bitten dog got none" (1).

As in his other books, Still uses real Kentucky place names in some of the rhymes, such as Isom and Bulan Town. A question about the number of rocks in Carr Creek's bed illustrates the tradition of insults in children's folklore, since the answer is, "As many rocks as are in your head." Hazard replaces Norwich, England, in "The Man in the Moon Came Down Too Soon," which is now a funny rhyme about a blizzard. The English man in the moon's "cold pease-porridge" has disappeared, but other rhymes feature regional "victuals" such as stack cakes, turnip greens, and fried pies ("eat too many and you're apt to split"). Jack Sprat and his wife get to eat something specific together in their Appalachian rhyme: "If baked opossum was on the table / They both ate as long as able" (31). "Grabbling [digging] taters" and "hunting ginseng" are mentioned in a poem that spins off the saying about raining cats and dogs, expressing chagrin that the speaker was always occupied elsewhere when miracles happened, such as "the day it drizzled silver dollars" (48). A rhyme about Isom Fair mentions other regional objects: "A new gourd fiddle, / An old whimmy-diddle" (34).

Paul Brett Johnson, a native of the Kentucky mountains who writes and illustrates children's books, studied with Still when Johnson was a high school student at Hindman. His black and white drawings in this book enhance the rhymes' blend of homey charm and silly humor. Johnson's cow posed daintily on two back legs singing ballads is more amusing than most of her predecessors as they have been depicted jumping over moons by generations of nursery rhyme illustrators. Most striking is the double-page spread of Old Boney Face, who "loved his ease" and on hot nights "slept entirely raw" (16–17). Still's short rhyme becomes more hilarious with Johnson's image of two prim ladies, one shocked and one bemused, peering in the window at the long horizontal figure of the nude man.

Still's gifts for understatement and the economic poetic forms of the nursery rhyme are evident in his version of a traditional rhyme about a crow on a clod:

> There was an old crow
> Sat dozing on a clod,
> That's the whole story,
> Crow, nod, clod [37].

A very unusual review of *An Appalachian Mother Goose* in *Virginia Quarterly Review*, only a few lines long, begins, "Ancient rhymer, grand old timer, seeks his inner child. Plays fast and loose with Mother Goose, drives this reader wild." The rest of this brief book note does not seem complimentary, with phrases such as "fondest rhymes defiled," but this reviewer should have understood that playing fast and loose with everything is the essence of the nursery rhyme tradition. The "old crow" rhyme mocks the process of storytelling by introducing a story that goes nowhere, except to a clever three-syllable summation of the protagonist, the plot, and the setting. Smith, like other writers and critics, appreciated Still's achievement in short comic rhymes as well as longer and more serious works of literature. She observed that "there's a freshness and originality of language that I think is childlike.... He has access to that part of himself that I don't think most of us do" (qtd. in Breed). In his poem "I Shall Go Singing," Still wrote, in 1938, "And the child in me shall speak his turn, / And the old, old man rattle his bones" (*From the Mountain* 91). As the nursery rhyme tradition combines the songs of childhood with the insights of adults who reshape and repeat the rhymes, occasional glimpses of wisdom and human wishes appear among the absurdities. One of Still's rhymes full of nonsense about money falling like rain ends with an intriguing, energetic line that seems to express undying enthusiasm for the endeavors of this world and the next: "The minute this world comes to an end / I believe I'll start all over again" (48).

When Noah Adams interviewed James Still and Lee Smith on National Public Radio in 1995, they were in a class with dyslexic children at Hindman. Adams observed that Still had noticed how adults sometimes ignored younger people, but he enjoyed the company of children when he stayed at Hindman during the winter. It seems, then, that the children of the region and the world deserved to be the primary recipients of one of Still's last gifts, his book of Appalachian nursery rhymes. Adults also appreciate his children's books, but we know that Still would be especially gratified to see children continuing to enjoy them, taking him up on his invitation to "Read my tales, spin my rhymes" ("My Days," in *From the Mountain* 151).

# Notes

1. The rooster episode in "Low Glory" is from the short story "I Love My Rooster," which has been reprinted and discussed by critics a number of times.

2. Gail Haley's later picture book, *Jack and the Bean Tree*, also emphasizes that Jack feels the magic when a mysterious man offers him the beans. A version by Ray Hicks, on the other hand, reveals that Jack lazily wants to be rid of the stubborn cow, then he is skeptical about trading for one bean, and then he feels silly about the trade by the time he gets home. Some variants, such as Richard's Chase's "Jack and the Bean Tree," have no trading of the cow for beans, but simply open with Jack's mother asking him to plant a bean she finds in the house.

# Works Cited

Adams, Noah. "Still's Love of Life Reflected in Novels and Poetry." *All Things Considered*. National Public Radio. 10 Nov. 1995. NPR.org. Transcript. rpt. *James Still Homepage*. Ed. Sandy Hudock. Colorado State University–Pueblo. 10 Mar. 2006 <http://faculty.-colostate-pueblo.edu/sandy.hudock/jsnpr.html>.

Breed, Allen G. "Celebrated Author Gives New Sauce to Mother Goose." *The Shawnee News-Star* [Shawnee, OK] Web posted 2 Oct. 1998. 30 Jan. 2006 <http://www.newsstar.com/stories/100298/art_mgoose.shtml>.

Briley, Rebecca Luttrell. "The River of Earth: Mystic Consciousness in the Works of James Still." *Appalachian Heritage* 9 (Spring-Summer-Fall 1981): 51–55; 64–80; 70–80.

Chase, Richard. *The Jack Tales*. Illus. Berkeley Williams Jr. Boston: Houghton Mifflin, 1943.

Egerton, Judith. "Author James Still, Known for Love of Appalachia, Dies at 94." *The Courier-Journal* [Louisville, KY] 29 Apr. 2001. Metro. Rpt. *The Black-listed Journal*. Ed. Al Aronowitz. 1 May 2001. 10 Mar. 2006 <http://www.bigmagic.com/pages/blackj/column59b.html>.

Haley, Gail E. *Jack and the Bean Tree*. New York: Crown, 1986.

Hardy, Thomas. *Tess of the d'Urbervilles*. 1891. New York: W.W. Norton, 1991.

Hicks, Ray. *The Jack Tales*. As told to Lynn Salsi. Illus. Owen Smith. New York: Callaway, 2001.

Jones, Alison. *Larousse Dictionary of World Folklore*. New York: Larousse, 1995.

Mayhall, Jane. "James Still: Quality of Life, Quality of Art." *Shenandoah* 48 (Summer 1998): 56–73.

Miller, Jim Wayne. "Appalachian Literature at Home in this World." *Iron Mountain Review* 2 (Summer 1984): 23–28. Rpt. *An American Vein: Critical Readers in Appalachian Literature*. Eds. Danny L. Miller, Sharon Hatfield, Gurney Norman. Athens: Ohio University Press, 2005. 13–24.

Opie, Peter, and Iona Opie, eds. *I Saw Esau: The Schoolchild's Pocket Book*. Illus. Maurice Sendak. Cambridge, MA: Candlewick Press, 1992.

_____. *The Oxford Dictionary of Nursery Rhymes*. 2nd ed. Oxford: Oxford University Press, 1997.

Parales, Heidi Bright. "First James Still Fellow: Christina Parker." *Odyssey* Spring 1999. University of Kentucky. 29 Jan. 2006 <http://www.rgs.uky.edu/odyssey/spring99/still.html>.

Review of *An Appalachian Mother Goose* by James Still. "Notes on Books." *Virginia Quarterly Review* Spring 1999. <http://www.vqronline.org/viewmedia.php/prmMID/7958>.

Runyon, Randolph Paul. "Looking the Story in the Eye: James Still's 'Rooster.'" *The Southern Literary Journal* 23 (Spring 1991): 55–64.

Still, James. *An Appalachian Mother Goose*. Illus. Paul Bret Johnson. Lexington: University Press of Kentucky, 1998.

_____. *From the Mountain, From the Valley: New and Collected Poems*. Ed. Ted Olson. Lexington, University Press of Kentucky, 2001.

_____. "An Interview with James Still." *Appalachian Journal* 6 (Winter 1979): 121–41.

_____. *Jack and the Wonder Beans*. Illus. Margot Tomes. 1977. Lexington: University Press of Kentucky, 1996. N. pag.

_____. *River of Earth*. 1940. Lexington: University Press of Kentucky, 1996.

_____. *Rusties and Riddles & Gee-Haw Whimmy-Diddles*. Illus. Janet McCaffery. Lexington, KY: University Press of Kentucky, 1989. N. pag.

_____. *Sporty Creek*. 1977. Lexington: University Press of Kentucky, 1999.

_____. *Way Down Yonder on Troublesome Creek: Appalachian Riddles and Rusties*. New York: G.P. Putnam's Sons, 1974.

_____. *The Wolfpen Notebooks: A Record of Appalachian Life*. Lexington: UP of Kentucky, 1991.

_____. *The Wolfpen Rusties: Appalachian Riddles and Gee-Haw Whimmy-Diddles*. New York: G.P. Putnam's Sons, 1975.

# The Wolfpen Notebooks:
# A Record of Appalachian Life

## JIM WAYNE MILLER

"There are twenty-three of them, six by four inches, wire-hinged," James Still has written of the notebooks he began keeping more than half a century ago, soon after moving to a two-story log house between Dead Mare Branch and Wolfpen, on Little Carr Creek in Knott County, Kentucky.[1] The original notebooks are preserved in Special Collections at the University of Kentucky. Their contents are now available in *The Wolfpen Notebooks: A Record of Appalachian Life* (Lexington: University Press of Kentucky, 1991).

An extraordinarily multifaceted record, *The Wolfpen Notebooks* reveal much about the life of the scattered community Still became a part of. The entries often suggest sources for Still's poems, short stories, and novels. They are especially revealing for what they tell us about the folk speech of Still's chosen place, where he has lived and listened attentively for more than half a century. Asked to account for the way people in her community spoke, a Knott County woman observed: "The people here not having been told what to do or say 'the right way,' do things their way." Her explanation not only accounts for the speech of her eastern Kentucky neighbors, it is also a fair explanation of folk speech in any place, at any time. For folk speech is unconcerned with the criterion of correctness. Consequently, folk speech frequently manages to be eloquent without being grammatical or correct. Folk speech is too busy improvising, making do with what it has to work with. While folk speech often deals with general propositions and universal experiences, its materials are the particulars of local life. So it is little wonder a Hindi proverb maintains that language changes every eighteen or twenty miles!

The improvisational spirit of folk speech accounts for its color and vividness. Folk speech employs verbs in striking ways: "You'd better *throw* a little air into them tires. They're about to go flat and *hunker* up."—"I used to be the worst drunkard ever was and I *throwed* it down. If I could, anybody can." Verbs become nouns, nouns verbs. A man speaks of being able to *belly* up to a table. Someone tells about a man with a head so big he can hardly *pack* it around. Someone is accused of telling a *pack* of lies.

Folk speech is often close to poetry because, like poetry, it deals with abstractions

*Miller, Jim Wayne. "The Wolfpen Notebooks: James Still's Record of Appalachian Life." Appalachian Heritage 19 (Summer 1991): 20–24. Reprinted with permission.*

by discoursing in concrete circumstances and particular instances. Folk speech is verbal *bricolage,* discourse made from the materials immediately at hand. Thus, not having recourse to the *Kama Sutra* or to one of the several treatises on love from the Middle Ages, an eastern Kentucky sage whose words James Still recorded distinguishes and names his own categories: "There's two kinds of love: the 'ground-hog case' and the 'cholera case.' The ground-hog case you can get over. With the cholera case it's marry or die."

*The Wolfpen Notebooks* reveal that the folk speech of eastern Kentucky, like folk speech everywhere, contains numerous instances of naming — of plants, animals, seasons, places. Such naming is a fundamentally poetic activity, for it relies on the drawing of analogies and the expression of implicit and explicit metaphors. Thus the castor bean is known locally as dog tick (because it resembles a tick on a dog). The brown thrush is known as the corn-planter bird (because it is seen and heard at the time when corn is planted). The cold spells of spring are redbud winter, dogwood winter, blackberry winter (because they occur in conjunction with the blooming of these plants). An ear of corn with variously colored grains is skewbald, the same word used to describe a horse of brown and white coloring. (In a folksong about a famous racehorse, the word has become corrupted to Stewball.) An herb believed to cure incontinence is known as pee-in-the-bed.

In the naming of people, places, and things, folk speech is rough and ready. A prized rifle is called "Death o' Many." A man named Ulysses, notorious for his laziness, is known as "Useless." A sot known to drink rubbing alcohol when nothing better is available is referred to as "John Rub." When two Joneses in the same neighborhood are named Reecy, one is known as "Reecy-right-here," the other as "Reecy-up-there." A place difficult to get in to, and just as difficult to get out of, is known as "Helechawa" (Hell Each Way).[2] Rain that makes the corn grow is a "nubbin-stretcher." Depending on how much falls, a rain might be judged a "middle-splitter," a "sod-soaker,' or a "Devil's foot washer." A necessary thing is a "force-put," as in: "I ain't going to use a walking stick until it's a force-put."

In the folk speech of eastern Kentucky, carrion (decomposed flesh unpleasant to smell) is pronounced "cjarn" — and use metaphorically in statements such as: "If he treated me that carriony, I'd kick his rump until his nose bled." As in "carriony," folk speech improvises suffixes: "He never worked a day in his life to anybody's know*ance.*" Or: "I made a big mistake, but I've right-*ified* it with the man I done it to."

The concreteness of folk speech is illustrated by these examples from *The Wolfpen Notebooks:*

— Best corn crop a crow ever flew over.
— Step back about two ax handles, so I can take a swing at you.
— He can load twenty-one shuttle buggies of coal a day, and every one with a graveyard hump.
— Your garden is getting away from you. If you don't hoe it soon you'll have to buy a snake rake.
— We had a pretty good chunk of rain yesterday.
— The water coming down Yellow Creek out of the mine will eat the fenders off your truck. It'll rot horses' hooves, too. What do you figure it will do to your belly?
— I'm off to see the prettiest girl that ever wore shoe leather, and if I don't come back write me at Blue Eyes, Kentucky.
— They feed you good at their table. You'll never see the bottom of their dishes.

The concreteness of folk speech is often incidental to vivid and apt similes and metaphors. An eastern Kentuckian describes a politician "working" a funeral "like a bee a rosy-brier." A drunk is said to be as "loud as a jackass in a tin barn." A small bus running between two towns is known as "the Short Dog." (See Still's short story, "A Ride on the Short Dog.") Occasionally a general observation, expressed in particular terms, resembles a proverb, as in: "If you don't pick the goose, you won't have any feathers."

The immediate world of the speaker is reflected in such observations as these: "You'd better shave before somebody steps on you for a woolly worm." "You boys are like hogs under an apple tree. You eat and sleep and never look up to see where it's coming from." "They had me on the witness stand and I didn't like the pick-lock questions the lawyers asked me." "He sets on the courthouse steps and whittles as regular as geese go barefooted." "When you buy a pint of likker you're just buying a club to beat your brains out." "Bread dough turns sad [i.e., it will not rise] if it's left to set too long." "They're as poor as whippoorwills and live nasty as buzzards." "What a girl! What a looker! Why, I could pick her up in my mouth like a kitten and carry her off."

Occasionally folk speakers will revive a dead metaphor: "He sowed his wild oats — as long as they would sprout." And through the use of metaphor, this speaker comments wryly yet with some delicacy on a local woman: "So, she actually found her a man and got married! Well, she won't have to lean against a tree to grind her corn from now on. She can get her younguns in bed."

Employing metaphor, folk speech achieves an economy of expression that rivals, and often bests, the self-conscious literary craftsman. "On Groundhog Day the sun came out warm as wool." A wife is a "doughbeater." "The Cross Bar Hotel" is a whimsical euphemism for a jail. A "sunball" is a watch. ("I always carry a sunball in my pocket. Else how am I going to know in the bowels of the coal mine when it's quitting time?")

Other poetic devices found in the folk speech collected in James Still's *Wolfpen Notebooks* are personification employed in the naming of a baby's fingers (Little Man, Ring Man, Long Man, Lick Pot, Thumbo), and hyperbole: A man is "so drunk he couldn't hit the ground with his hat." A baby is "spoiled so sweet, salt wouldn't save it." A person is warned: "Somebody's going to knock ten kinds of green apples out of you someday." A certain individual is "the crookedest man that ever screwed britches on." Another is "as slow as a schoolhouse clock."

As many writers have acknowledged — Eliot, Yeats, and Frost among them — the beginnings of literary expression are found in folk speech. James Joyce kept a notebook of his wife Nora's expressions, noting such things as "He looked at the time." "A knock came to the door." "Will I do as I am?" "Can't believe a word out of his mouth."[3] Such expressions would be perfectly at home in *The Wolfpen Notebooks,* where Still has recorded examples of his neighbors' folk speech, such as: "The truth never walked his lips." "That dog has teeth in his eyes."

Still overheard and recorded this observation on the willfulness of women: "I know positive yore woman rules you. Mine will have her way even if she has to burn the waters of the creek. The woman is the boss in this country." The remark is the germ of Still's short story "The Burning of the Waters." Still recorded in *The Wolfpen Notebooks:* "I wrote a meal sack full of letters and he never answered a scratch." Compare this with Still's short story, "The Sharp Tack," about a mountain preacher who carries on a one-sided correspondence with a returned World War II veteran, who never answers the preacher's letters.

Some of the more striking features of folk speech are nothing more than obsolete or archaic forms and usages, together with metaphorical extensions of meaning. In *The Wolfpen Notebooks* we find: "Reach me some more of that likker. Hit's got a *whang* I like." What is a *whang?* Here it seems at first to mean a distinctive taste or flavor. *The Random House Dictionary* gives these meanings: "Whang. 1. a resounding blow. 2. the sound produced by such a blow. 3. Dial. a thong, especially of leather, cf. whang leather. Alter. of thwang, early form of thong." Thus, liquor that has a *whang* delivers a blow. There are similar meanings in current drug culture. Certain drugs are said to deliver a kick (there's drug-culture talk in Cole Porter's song "I Get a Kick Out of You"). One speaks of a "hit" of cocaine.

The folk speech of eastern Kentucky preserves the other meaning of *whang* (a leather thong) in a "call" used by horse traders in Knott County. A mare due to foal in the spring is described in a rhymed couplet as: "Round and sound, tough as a whang / Two good eyes and four in the spring."

Other words and expressions recorded in *The Wolfpen Notebooks* that might be considered archaic or obsolete usage are: *jasper, ramp, rue back.* "I wouldn't associate with that jasper." Here the once common name Jasper, a form of Casper, is generalized to apply to any male. "He wants to ramp and rave and cuss." Here "ramp" is a verb, little used as such in contemporary standard speech, meaning to rise or stand on the hind legs. But a form of the word is preserved in the word "rampant," which, in heraldry, describes, for example, a lion on a coat of arms, standing on its hind legs, in a menacing posture. The expression "rue back" might seem strange at first, but it adheres to the root meaning of "rue" as used in Housman's line, "With rue my heart is laden." If a person trades a horse, car, or gun with no "rue back," this means the deal is final.

Folk speech preserves the history of the language in such items as these recorded by Still in *The Wolfpen Notebooks*: "hit [it]"; "sass patch [garden]"; "budget [valise or bag]"; "poke [sack or bag]"; "blinky (also blinked) milk [soured or spoiled milk]"; "rigmaroar (also rigamaroar) [confused, convoluted situation]." Each of these usages is a window into the past. "Hit" is an old neuter pronoun. (And it should be noted that speakers who use this form also use "it." "Hit" tends to be employed in emphatic, "it" in unemphatic positions.) "Sass" is a version of sauce, and may come from the English of the Scots-Irish. "Budget" is an obsolete word for a bag or pouch, still listed in *The Random House Dictionary*. "Poke" as a noun, meaning a sack or bag, is probably related to the word "pocket." "Blinky" or "blinked" milk, i.e., milk that has soured, probably refers to a folk superstition according to which some supernatural creature has given the milk the "evil eye," that is, "blinked" at it, causing it to turn sour. "Rigmaroar" / "rigamaroar" is a version of "rigmarole" / "rigamarole," which is thought to be a corruption of the *rageman,* a roll of names from the fourteenth century.[4]

The slippage from "rageman roll" to "rigmarole" / "rigmaroar" and their variants is similar to the misunderstanding that results in a malapropism, examples of which from Still's *The Wolfpen Notebooks* are: "Three Door Roosevelt" (for Theodore Roosevelt); Silver War (Civil War); nit-name (nickname, itself a corruption of "ekename," i.e., an "also" or "extra" name)[5]; bam gilly (Balm of Gilead). *The Wolfpen Notebooks* also provide the example of "cave" as a corruption of "cavil," as in: people "caving and huffing in the courthouse hall." Still's examples also illustrate the difficulty folk speakers have in grasping medical terms. A woman who suspects she is a hypochondriac says she has been "hypoed."

In an "afterword" to *The Run for the Elbertas,* James Still wrote that the stories in that collection might "amount to a social diagram of a folk society such as hardly exists today [and might] even include some of the uncharted aspects of the Appalachian experience."[6] A similar claim might be made for *The Wolfpen Notebooks,* which are sure to be of interest to anyone concerned with the history, heritage, language, and literature of Appalachia, and especially to students of the region's folk speech and of folk speech generally.

## Notes

1. *Foxfire*, Vol. 22, No. 3, Fall 1988, "The Wolfpen Notebooks," p. 150.

2. Robert M. Rennick. *Kentucky Place Names* (Lexington: University Press of Kentucky, 1984), p. 137, characterizes this derivation of the name as "a popular account." According to Rennick, Helechawa, in Wolfe County, was named by W. Delancy Walbridge, president of a now-defunct railroad, who combined parts of his daughter's name *Helen Chase Walbridge*.

3. McCrum, Robert, William Cran, and Robert McNeil. *The Story of English* (New York: Viking, 1986), p. 251.

4. Hendrickson, Robert. *The Facts on File Encyclopedia of Word and Phrase Origins* (New York: Facts on File Publications, 1987), p. 450.

5. Hendrickson, p. 375.

6. James Still. *The Run for the Elbertas* (Lexington: University Press of Kentucky, 1980), p. 144.

# VI

# THE MAN AND HIS ART:
## REASSESSMENTS

James Still in the doorway of the log house, located beside Wolfpen Creek, Knott County, Kentucky (courtesy of the Hindman Settlement School).

# Man on Troublesome

## DEAN CADLE

"'When you write him, please give him my love,'" Marjorie Kinnan Rawlings wrote from her home in Florida to James Still in 1942, in passing on to him the regards of her house guest, Norwegian Nobel Prize novelist Sigrid Undset. "She was immensely happy to hear that I knew you, and asked me many questions about you and your life.... She picked up your *Hounds on the Mountain* with keen interest, and said that she read your two other books. She said that she was very certain that in time you would be one of our major American writers."

It is doubtful that Mrs. Rawlings was able to answer Miss Undset's many questions, since she likely knew no more about Still than do most of his other friends. For those who know him as a writer and teacher are almost wholly unfamiliar with his routines at home among his friends along Troublesome Creek in Knott County, Kentucky; and among his neighbors, most of whom are farmers and coal miners, his prestige rests mainly on his being a sound man, a capable farmer, and keeper of the library at Hindman Settlement School. And even in the county seat of Hindman, eight miles from Still's home, one of its leading citizens, who is owner of a hotel and consequently one of the county's sources of information, can talk passably about other Kentucky writers but paused for a moment when asked recently about Still, then said, "Oh, the librarian. Yes, I've heard he writes some, but I've never read anything by him."

Still welcomes his obscurity, and contrary to the popular opinion held that most authors want and promote self-publicity, and in flagrant disregard of the encouragement that publicity can give a writing career, he has worked diligently to protect his privacy and to insure separation between his personal life and any critical acclaim that might adhere to the name James Still as writer. Three patterns of living, perhaps more the result of inclination than of design, have contributed to his obscurity. He has chosen to live and write in isolation, he has refrained from inviting attention to himself and has run from it when he could, and he has published relatively little. "I have remained intact" is the way he evaluates his choice of living, implying all the conditions of health, geography, and attitude that are necessary if a person is to continue writing unhampered and owe nothing as a writer to anyone but himself.

In the early 1930s, when it was still fashionable and perhaps somewhat necessary for beginning writers to congregate in Paris or Greenwich Village or in any artistic community that offered sustenance, Still moved into an ancient log house in Knott County, accessible only by eight miles of dirt road and two miles of creek bed. He arrived there from his home

*Cadle, Dean. "Man on Troublesome." The Yale Review LVII.2 (December 1967): 236–55. Reprinted with permission.*

in Alabama by way of universities in Tennessee and Illinois, with bachelor's degrees in both arts and sciences and a master's degree in English. Throughout his life there he has supplemented his meager earnings as a writer and farmer by whatever means would assure him time to write: two Guggenheim fellowships, occasional grants in the form of room and board from foundations and writers' colonies, intermittent work as a librarian, and for the last few years as a teacher at Morehead State College.

During the years Still has been writing, he has shied away from the public relations activities that most writers seem to thrive on. Although he has published poetry and fiction in numerous magazines, he has never met an editor. He declines to talk to civic clubs or, about writing, to any group outside the college classroom, and he does not respond favorably to invitations that promise to point in any way to James Still the writer. He has cooperated in giving only two interviews, each with a reporter he realized had respect for his sense of integrity.

Such implied reluctance, plus his inability at the time to accept an appointment from Columbia University as Phi Beta Kappa Poet or to accept in person an award of the American Academy of Arts and Letters in 1947 or to record his poetry for the Library of Congress, has created the impression that his avoidance of publicity is merely a pretense. On the only trip he has taken to acknowledge an honor for his writing, when he went to New York City to share in the Southern Author's Award for *River of Earth,* a reporter for a major New York daily, finding he was getting nowhere with the questions that normally produced a flood of answers, asked, "Is it Southern shyness or a false front?" Still replied, "It's self-protection."

And his remark concerning another occasion when he declined to be courted by an

James Still receiving honorary Doctorate of Humanities, Berea College, Berea, Kentucky (courtesy of the Hindman Settlement School).

influential person says much about his sense of independence, and perhaps about his concept of his life as a writer: "I prefer to view the throne from a distance, for those standing closest are the first to lose their heads."

However, Still is not the "romantic" or the "literary hermit" he has been called occasionally by readers who allow their uninformed opinion of him as a person to infect their interpretation of his writing. Rather, he is quite cosmopolitan, and his orientation toward life and writing is more that of the scientist than of the idealist, as anyone knows who has talked with him for long or has observed the objectivity and the exactness of detail present in his written accounts of seasonal changes and of the relationships between man, animal, and nature. On weekends and at other free times, in the proper season, Still can be found in any one of a number of places: in the mountains "sapping" or hunting for mushrooms, at a sorghum stir-off, at the livestock sale a few miles from Hindman, at home tending his bees or working his garden, or on a fishing expedition to Norris Lake.

But his local interests mirror only a part of the man. In addition to teaching and writing, he reads several books each week, perhaps his only exacting rule on subject matter being that they not be fiction with an Appalachian setting, for he wants his view of his region to be his own, undistorted by anyone else's vision. Periodically he visits Louisville to see a play or movie and to listen at the public library to the latest taped and phonograph recordings of plays and poetry. As an invited guest in 1959 he attended the dedication ceremonies of the Robert Frost Room at Amherst College. And occasionally he visits in Florida or New York City, where in 1965 he spent a play-going week as the guest of a Knott County woman and her husband, who is a leading Broadway stage producer.

Eugene Burdick, Taylor Caldwell, Harold Robbins, Irving Wallace, Herman Wouk, to list only a few of the more conspicuous names, are writers who have come into wide public notice during the years in which Still seems to have plodded along, publishing only occasionally, seemingly unmoved by, even unaware of, the furious production around him of words and fortunes. He has published only three books, all by Viking Press: *Hounds on the Mountain* (poems), *River of Earth* (novel), and *On Troublesome Creek* (stories), and thirty-nine uncollected poems and seventeen short stories.

His stories have been reprinted in several anthologies and textbooks, including three in *Best American Short Stories* and four in *O. Henry Memorial Award Prize Stories*, but perhaps not nearly so widely as they deserve. Certainly the author's refusal to act as "salesman" for his writing has played some unmeasurable role, but the real reason likely rests in his deceptively simple narrative technique.

The difficulties of writing about Still's prose are akin to those presented by the best stories of Chekhov, of Katherine Anne Porter, and of Bernard Malamud in that the reader is placed in the position of a listener enjoying classical music. The listener does not have to be able to relate an accompanying narrative or recognize the techniques employed in order to appreciate the music. It is true that if his listening apparatus is supplemented by a knowledge of such concrete and mechanical facts he might be able to discuss his appreciation more factually and more intelligently. But what is more important is that he and the music are conducting an exhilarating conversation in which any form of kibitzing would be deadening. Like music, Still's better stories (such as "A Ride on the Short Dog," "Mrs. Razor," "The Run for the Elbertas") and *River of Earth* are more meaningful if they are "experienced" rather than read critically and analytically, if they are approached as incidents happening rather than as stories that are being read. Their effect is closer to that gained from hearing an oral tale or from watching a staged play.

The reader who approaches Still's writings equipped with the kit of critical tools now issued with most college diplomas is apt to dismiss them as exercises in regional naïveté or terminate his tinkering in bafflement because his custom-made tools do not fit the model. For there is little conscious use of symbols, no allusions to classical or other literatures, and no reference to anything outside the immediate situation in which the characters are involved.

However, the machinery is there, just as it is in all writing, or in any other artistic creation — the only difference being that the nuts and bolts and pistons are fewer and are more finely tooled than in most writing.

Qualities that a careful reader may find in Still's writing are his convincing characterizations, the exactness and colorfulness of his language, his emphasis on sense of place, his reliance on poetic interludes, his use of humor, and his themes. Perhaps less obvious, but equally as important, are his point of view and his use of foreshortening.

Because his methods of characterization are unobtrusive and because the characters do and say what seems appropriate, the reader's impression likely is that character delineation must be the easiest part of writing for Still. We do not learn the traits of the characters from either the author or his narrators. Rather, Still unfolds characterization by implication in much the same way a skillful dramatist presents it on stage: through dialogue, through gestures, and through remarks that characters make about each other. And it is to Still's credit that he succeeds without the dramatist's crutch of stage directions preceding the acts, in which we too often are told point-blank the nature of the individuals we are about to meet, or what changes have transpired in their attitudes since last we saw them.

A character is revealed gradually in response to the friction of the other characters and to the incidents he must contend with. Presentation in this manner can be a series of surprises as the reader watches the character react as he thinks he should but is not always certain he will. It can also be a disastrous method in the hands of a writer not thoroughly familiar with his characters.

In "The Run for the Elbertas" we first see Riar Thomas as he glances at his watch, then stops his truck to pick up two teen-age boys who are to make the trip with him to South Carolina. He pulls the cardboard out of the broken window and opens the door from the inside, because "it's cranky." "Let's go," he commands the boys; "a body can't fiddle in the peach business."

However, there is considerable "fiddling" as the boys prod, prick, cheat, and prank, and draw out the character of Riar. His character is implied in the short opening paragraph: He is punctual, thrifty, honest, determined, irritable, business-like, suspicious, and a bit impatient. But it is only after many miles of defensive argumentation and after numerous delays initiated by the boys that we realize that the entire story is a development of the implications of the opening paragraph.

What is perhaps most delightful in Still's writing is the colorfulness and exactness of his language. Whether the individual words are strange or familiar, it is the manner of expression that gives them conviction and demonstrates that the author is a creator, as well as a listener and lover, of language, and that he sees and hears with the senses of a poet.

The language can create a picture: "Morning was bright and rainfresh. The sharp sunlight fell slantwise upon the worn limestone earth of the hills, and our house squatted weathered and dark on the bald slope. Yellow-bellied sapsuckers drilled their oblong holes in the black birch by the house, now leafing from tight-curled buds." And a sound: "January was a bell in Lean Neck Valley. The ring of the ax was a mile wide, and all passage over the spewed-up earth was lifted on frosty air and sounded against fields of ice."

It can be filled with factual knowledge, as in the account of removing a cob from a calf's throat in *River of Earth*:

Father dug fingers into the calf's throat, feeling the proper spot, seeking a place free of large veins. The blade flashed in the lamplight; it slid under the hide, making a three-inch mark. Mother looked away when the blood gushed. It splattered on her hands, reddening them to the wrists.... Father opened a space between the muscles of the calf's neck, steering clear of bone and heavy vein. The calf made no sound; only its hind legs jerked a bit.... At last Father put the knife aside. He eased thumb and forefinger into the opening, and jerked. The cob came out, red and drenched.

As dialogue the language can be idiomatic:

"I've seen women's flesh fall away like a snow-melt." "Hey-o, you wife-beaters, how are you standing the times?"

And Brother Mobberly's sermon in *River of Earth:*

He snapped the book to. He leaned over the pulpit. "I was borned in a ridgepocket.... I never seed the sun-ball withouten heisting my chin. My eyes were sot upon the hills from the beginning. Till I come on the word in this good Book, I used to think that a mountain was the standingest object in the sight o' God. Hit says here they go skipping and hopping like sheep, a-rising and a-falling. These hills are jist dirt waves, washing through eternity. My brethren, they hain't a valley so low but what hit'll rise again. They hain't a hill standing so proud but hit'll sink to the low ground o' sorrow. Oh, my children, where air we going on this mighty river of earth, a-borning, begetting, and a-dying — the living and the dead riding the waters? Where air it sweeping us?"

Still's language is so filled with the creations of a real people, with his own experiments, and with folklore and Elizabethan expressions and influences, that perhaps a linguist could not easily separate the borrowings from the creations. However, even a waving familiarity with Elizabethan literature can help us spot numerous words and expressions in Still's work that have passed out of common use in English but have remained lodged in the mountain language, some unchanged and others twisted to fit the tongue, as apt reminders of what the Elizabethan spoken language sounded like. Especially noticeable is that the people have retained one of the more marked and lively peculiarities of the Elizabethan language, that of using any word as almost any part of speech.

The following words and phrases picked at random from the dialogue of *River of Earth, On Troublesome Creek,* "A Ride on the Short Dog," and "The Run for the Elbertas" are no longer standard English but can be found frequently in the works of Chaucer, Spenser, Shakespeare, Evelyn, Philip Sidney, Thomas Nashe, Robert Greene, Thomas Deloney, and in the King James Bible (1611):

FAIR: almost, plainly, completely ("I figure they're fair ready for biling.")

NIGH: almost, nearly ("I'd be nigh ashamed.")

BONNIE: pleasant, fair, pretty ("As bonnie a chap as ever I saw.")

WHAP: to strike, hit ("Whap him and even up.")

PLEASURE: as a verb ("I made it to pleasure him in his last sickness.")

FITTEN: as an adjective meaning suitable, proper, likely developed from the Middle English adjective *fitting* ("I hain't had a fitten meal since I left Lean Neck"; "I've not got on a dress fitten.")

It may seem far-fetched but is entirely likely that the sententious, elegant deflection of the language that came to be known as Euphuism, primarily written rather than spoken, may be partially responsible for the brief, balanced, often witty, proverbial statements of the mountain people which Still enjoys hearing his characters speak. Predecessors of the following proverbial statements from Still's work can be found in the writings of many Elizabethans, especially those of John Lyly, who popularized the form, and in thirty-seven of Shakespeare's plays:

"You point me to a plumb honest feller, and I'll show you a patch of hair growing in the palm of his hand."

"Nowadays you can hear everything but the truth and the meat a-frying."

"Hello, Coot, what'll you give to boot?"

"You're as useless as tits on a boar."

"I'll see you later, when I can talk to you straighter."

"It's better to keep your eyeballs on things nigh, and let the rest come according to law and prophecy."

"A man's backbone don't print through his clothes."

Quoting disjointed passages of vernacular dialogue can be unfair to Still, for it implies that he does not differentiate between the freshness of literate expression and the burdensome quaintness that characterizes the work of Mary Noailles Murfree (Charles Egbert Craddock) and of earlier and later journalists and tourists.

A more distinctive use of language can be found in Still's emphasis on sense of place and seasons and in his use of poetic interludes. He once said that any writer who concentrates on description of place and climate simply out of fascination for them should be working for "the U.S. Bureau of Climate and Terrain."

A people who have lived in a place for a long time and who depend for their livelihood on seasonal changes of the land and the weather become very much aware of the appearance and behavior of both. Specific valleys, ridges, and trees and how they look in different seasons—whether the tree is "That big old blood-red maple on the nigh side of the footbridge" or "That big old branchy sycamore yonder side of the pond"—become ever-changing signal lights for them.

The attention to place may be either a cataloging of names of well-known markers, or a picture of movement along a familiar route, or a scene-setting passage. Here is a bus ride: "We passed Hilton and Chuck Jones's sawmill and Gayheart and Thorne. Beyond Thorne the highway began to rise. We climbed past the bloom of coal veins and tipples of mines hanging the slope; we mounted until we'd gained the saddle of the gap and could see Roscoe four miles distant." The setting for a family's sojourn in a mining camp: "The slag pile towering over the camp burned with an acre of oily flames. A sooty mist hung over the creek bottom. Our house sat close against a bare hill. It was cold and gloomy, smelling sourly of paint, but there were glass windows.... We went on the porch and looked up the rutted road. Men walked the mud with carbide lamps burning on their caps." And sometimes the love for place can be only a vision: "Forever moving yon and back, setting down nowhere for good and all, searching for God knows what.... Where air we expecting to draw up to? ... Forever I've wanted to set us down in a lone spot, a place certain and enduring, with room to swing arm and elbow, a garden-piece for fresh victuals."

Some of Still's best writing appears in rhythmic passages that may be called poetic interludes which he uses as transitional devices to bridge space between scenes or to indicate the lapse of time or change of locale. Usually they deal with the look of a place or the change of seasons, and they are always brief, sometimes no more than a sentence.

The mountains fell back, the earth leveled and reddened, the first peach orchards came to view.

The days shortened. The air grew frosty. Nights were loud with honking geese, and suddenly the leaves were down before gusts of wind. The days were noisy with blowing, and the house filled with the sound of crickets' thighs. There were no birds in the bare orchard, not even the small note of a chewink through the days.

Fall came in the almanac, and the sourwood bushes were like fire on the mountains. Leaves hung bright and jaundiced on the maples. Red foxes came down the hills, prowling outside our chicken house, and hens squalled in the night.... Hounds hunted the ridges, their bellies thin as saw blades. Their voices came bellowing in the dark hours. Once, waking suddenly, I heard a fox bark defeat somewhere in the cove beyond Flaxpatch.

A discussion of humor can be as unreliable as the writing of it. Nothing can spoil so soon or stay fresh so long. There are few guides, no assurances. What seemed humorous yesterday may be embarrassing today. The printed page often becomes a paper coffin for what in real life is hilarious. And exactly because of its mercurial nature, from what was entombed in Egypt and Greece centuries ago there may yet sprout full-blown laughter in outer space.

Still knows this, and so what may be humorous in his stories is not often specifically intended as such. His use of humor is inescapably a part of characterization and of theme. For instance, when Han and Tibb Logan, the wild, undisciplined brothers in *River of Earth*, cut off the thirty-year-old, carefully-tended mustache of Uncle Samp, the incident may be humorous. But the real function of the act is to characterize them, to show the reader that their lives are sustained by such practical jokes. And Godey and Mal in "A Ride on the Short Dog" and in "The Run for the Elbertas" turn to practical jokes and speak only in clever, cliché remarks not because they necessarily enjoy them or because they possess a sense of humor but as a means of relieving the tension, of reducing the monotony, of their static lives.

Such acts and such language are presented as inherent human reflexes that act as alternatives against loss of will, against defeat. They serve as pacifiers and preoccupiers, in somewhat the same way that counting the bricks of his cell guards the prisoner against insanity. And while they may be humorous today and even several generations from now, Still is too wise a writer to bet on humor. On Uncle Jolly, a humorous character he has written knowingly about, he has more than one relative pass judgment: "There goes a born fool."

Just as one mentions point of view in discussing Laurence Sterne or William Faulkner because they made an art out of misusing and overusing it, so it is mentioned here because Still has rendered it as nonexistent as possible. The reader is so little aware of point of view in his stories that it is difficult to recall whether they are told through the third person or the first. Actually, most of them are related by a first-person narrator. But Still has skirted most of its traps and has evaded the violations which some writers read into their license to use the first person. He has veritably erased the author.

In *River of Earth* and *On Troublesome Creek* Still chooses the even more risky path of taking the reader into the immediate world of a seven-year-old boy. He uses the unnamed narrator as an eye or window to keep the reader's attention riveted at all times inside the story, and to keep the narrative "tight," never accepting the privilege granted the author to wander or to use the narrator as a chorus. And what remains to delight the reader even years after reading the stories is the seen, heard, and felt child-view of a small mountain world, with hardly a false note to betray its passage through the mind of the author.

When Still's themes are enumerated outside his writings they seem as blatant as trumpet blasts, but when their almost unobtrusive weavings are traced through his stories they are no louder than the simple, traditional affirmations that have always plagued and honored mankind: concern with love, loyalty, hunger, death, and with the reactions of the individual when he is cornered, when he reaches the breaking point, either by force or choice. Reworded, they mean the will to endure, self-preservation.

More than twenty years before the Appalachian region was labeled a poverty pocket and before the somewhat artificial reactions of experts and government officials to the problems of poverty, as though they had encountered some recent wonder, Still had presented in *River of Earth* the heartbreaking account of what it means for a human being to live out his life hungry and cold. His is not a socioeconomist's collection of figures, causes, and possible cures, but the dramatized plight of human beings accepting poverty without accusations or judgments and without rantings against ephemeral institutions.

Acceptance of life as it is and refusal to admit defeat aptly describes the philosophy of most of Still's characters. They are always on the move in search of better living conditions. Like migrating birds, they move with the seasons back and forth from coal camps to hillside farms, always confident that this is the last move, that a life of plenty is ahead.

The father in "The Burning of the Waters" sees Tight Hollow as a paradise in which "We can sit on our hands and rear back on our thumbs." And with the coming of each fall Brack Baldridge in *River of Earth* announces: "A long dry spell it's been, but they'll be working at Blackjack," or "We'll feed right good down at Blackjack this winter. I hear tell the mines are to open the middle of October — this time for good."

And when the mines close and the crops fail, there is little complaining. They simply pack up and move again, accepting, hoping, laughing to make their misfortunes bearable. After the father has pitted himself against common sense, the advice of friends and family, a merciless winter, crop failure, and even the animals of Tight Hollow, which betray him by taking food from his traps and then escaping, he bends to his family's pleas. But he is undaunted, and even as they prepare to move, "A gale of laughter broke in father's throat."

When Riar Thomas is pushed to the edge of lunacy in "The Run for the Elbertas" by his teen-aged tormentors, he fends them off until they near the Kentucky line, putting up every reason at his command against their case for the joy to be found in revenge, then he strikes back in the only way he knows will be effective, in their own manner. For him it is a difficult choice, but he realizes it is necessary.

Family loyalty, independence and self-reliance, and a sense of honor are themes that are prevalent throughout Still's writing. Season after season Brack Baldridge boards his relatives when there isn't even enough food for his children. "I can't turn my kin out," he argues with his wife. "As long as we've got a crust, it'll never be said I turned my folks from my door."

When Grandma Middleton's husband is murdered, she calls her sons together and has them swear against their will to an oath: "There's been blood shed a-plenty. Let Aus Coggins bide his time out on this earth. Fear will hant his nights. Hit'll be a thorn in his flesh. Let him live in fear. He'll never prosper nor do well. Let him live in sufferance." And he does. We never see or hear Aus Coggins nor even know what he looks like. But we do know that here is a man who has lived in sufferance.

If social injustice is one of Still's themes, then it is present only by implication, for his people never begrudge the better fortune of others nor express a desire to move farther than the few miles that separate mining camps from hillside farms. "Being of these hills," Still seems to say in prose as well as in poetry, they not only "cannot" pass beyond them but have no desire to. They complain, of course, the men less out of a sense of social maltreatment than because they must work a garden patch instead of dig coal, the work they do best; and the women's complaints are softened into good-natured resignation: "It takes a man-person to be a puore fool," or "Oh, man-judgment's like the weather. Hit's onknowing."

Still's interest in endurance, self-preservation, and the reactions of people under stress are themes he likely finds akin to the motives that drive men to climb mountains. Not the Appalachians, but the big ones which are spoken of as being "scaled" and "conquered," the ones of which records are kept, those which men continue to challenge in the face of promised death: Everest, K2, Kangchenjunga, Nanga-Parbat. And from his interest in and knowledge of mountain climbing Still has derived the word "foreshortening," which he applies to his practice of giving early in a story a synopsis, or telescoped view, of the entire narrative, characterization, and theme. It is a geometrical term applied primarily to the effect of visual perspective, meaning "to cause an object to be apparently shortened in the direction not lying in a plane perpendicular to the line of sight." In painting a mountain or other large object, for instance, a painter must shorten some lines and make some parts disproportionate in order to create an illusion of true perspective. Since he must crowd a tremendous bulk of earth, stone, foliage, snow, and shadow onto a small canvas, it is the illusion, not the true picture of the mountain, that the painter wishes to present. For when a viewer looks at a mountain from a distance, he sees it all at once. But he does not realize its distance, size, details, or complexity until he gets close to it.

Likewise, in the first paragraph or early in a story, Still attempts to give a preliminary view of the entire narrative, a silhouette. And just as foreshortening in painting is a misrepresentation in order that the complete figure will have visual proportion, so Still's practice is a negative form of foreshadowing, for what transpires in the story is often the opposite of, and at the same time much larger than, what is implied.

When Wick Jarrett in "A Master Time" invites the narrator in the first paragraph to attend a hog killing, he says, "Hit's to be a quiet affair, a picked crowd, mostly young married folks. No old heads like me — none except Aunt Besh Lipscomb, but she won't hinder." But she does hinder. In fact, she and her hindering become the point of the story. As a midwife she has delivered all of the twelve couples present, and when at the end of the story she tells the narrator, "I'll endure," we realize that she has come to represent more than just a granny woman interfering with their "master time."

"If ever I could see smoke or hear an ax ring, I'd know the way," the lost six-year-old Nezzie thinks in "The Nest." Ironically, next morning belied cows blowing smoke puffs of breath pass and a fox horn sounds in the distance as Nezzie lies frozen into drowsiness in a clump of broomsage.

When the father in "Mrs. Razor" says, "We'll have to do something about that child.... I figure a small thrashing would make her leave off this foolish notion," he indicates the destructive path the story seems likely to take. In fifteen hundred words Still has accomplished the moving and amazing feat of capturing the wonderful country of fantasy to which most children for a time swear allegiance. In six-year-old Elvy's make-believe world she is married to a no-good Mr. Razor who has abandoned her and her three children. Most children grow out of this real un-real life, but a few remain there, as Elvy might if the story were to follow the action implied by the father's words. And an ironic parallel is that the father has helped create this alien country with his tales of "Biggety Creek where heads are the size of water buckets, where noses are turned up like old shoes, women wear skillets for hats, and men screw their breeches on." It is through the mother's understanding and her gentle persuasion that the story turns away from its foreshadowed course, and the entire family heads toward Biggety Creek in a wagon to rescue Elvy's abandoned "chaps ere the gypsies come." They travel six miles in the darkness before Elvy falls asleep.

It is in "The Run for the Elbertas," Still's most humorous and in some ways his best story, that we are given the clearest example of his foreshortening. The story opens with this paragraph:

> As Riar Thomas approached the Snag Fork bridge, the truck lights picked up the two boys sitting on the head wall. Glancing at his watch, he saw it was nearly one o'clock. He halted, pulled the cardboard out of the broken window, and called, "I'll open the door from the inside, it's cranky." The boys sat unmoving. "Let's go," he said, "if you're traveling with me. A body can't fiddle in the peach business."

Telescoped into a few words and foreshadowing the entire action of the story, we are given an exact location, an initial characterization of Riar which is expanded as the story develops, two boys who have a will of their own, the dilapidated truck whose cranky window might be considered an extension of Riar's own personality, and the implication that this peach trip may be unlike any other Riar has taken. Which, in fact, it is. For there is likely more "fiddling" here than in any other modern American story. But the "fiddling" is only the surface action.

Unlike most writers, Still does not want to put into writing or have printed what he has learned about the theories or techniques of the craft of writing, perhaps feeling that putting it into print would be equivalent to establishing a system of rules, which, like a law that has been put on the books, would be most of all binding on the maker, as though he fears that any opinion in black and white might assume the authority of a dictum that would somehow permeate to the source of his creativity and do irreparable damage.

And even when he talks about writing it is often in a puzzled, questioning tone, as though he is not certain how it is done and would not object to finding an inclusive code that would not be dangerous, one that he would not have to claim if the time came when he found that it instead of his characters was dictating to him. "A writer has to stay wild," he once said. "He shouldn't be trained. He's got to stay in the woods. He must be like a cat. No matter how domesticated you make a cat, it's all on the surface. You can never tame one." And at another time he said, "The writer is like a surgeon probing for a nerve. Unless I touch a nerve the story has no life."

He believes that the flaw in most writing is that the writers have constructed barriers between the reader and the story. "The reader has enough trouble without the author muddying the water. Even the simplest, most artistic arrangement of words is still a screen between the story and the reader. The perfect story would be like a copper wire stretched from a generator to a light bulb.

"My intention is to tell a story. The form of the story is something that just comes, and everything that hinders the story sort of eliminates itself. Writing is about people. The big temptation in fiction seems to be to write philosophy and geography. They don't make good stories. Fiction is drama. I include only actions I can visualize, and I have to hear the characters talking. When they quit talking to me I know something is wrong. In one story I left a character tilted back in a chair for two years because he quit talking to me."

Although Still won't — or simply is unable to — discuss his own stories critically, he relaxes and talks freely about the historical development of any story up to the point where he began the actual writing.

"Pattern of a Man," for example. He had known for several weeks exactly what the story should contain, but in this case the usual narrative form, requiring long transitional passages that would deaden the interest, was out of the question. A letter from a candidate soliciting his vote solved the problem.

The "trigger" for "A Ride on the Short Dog" was simply the remark he overheard from a neighbor woman describing her husband's health: "He's doing no good," which is the closing sentence of the story.

"The Run for the Elbertas" had its beginning shortly after the Second World War when Still went on a peach-hauling trip to South Carolina. But it was not until 1958 when he saw a pile of rotting peaches dumped by the roadside that he knew the story was ready to be written.

"Mrs. Razor" came to him complete, "like a bright light being turned on," one evening at dusk as he stood under a tree on Wolfpen Creek.

Whatever the immediate motivation for any story may have been, it is certain that Still's "notebook" has played an important role in his writing. A mixture of fact and imagination, the "notebook" exists as a steel cabinet filled with hundreds of manila folders arranged alphabetically by subject. In addition to being a thirty-year history of the people in and around

Knott County — their culture, their relationships with each other and with the land in all seasons — it contains dialogue sequences and sketches which can almost stand alone as short stories.

Still is an exacting writer. "I've got to live with a story until it's ready to be written." And although he publishes infrequently, he is a fast writer. He writes a first draft at one sitting, sometimes so fast that some words blur off into wriggling lines. Then he "plays around" with the story until he is satisfied that every word is right.

In one story, however, he admitted defeat on one word he wanted to describe the peculiar quality of light on a windy spring-clear December morning with the sun shining brightly through thin clouds. He used the most descriptive word he knew and published the story, and ten years later the word he had wanted came to him.

He thinks most writers are too wordy. They try to describe a scene or a person or an emotion completely in words instead of suggesting it, instead of working for the one word or one phrase that would capture and transmit it clearly. "A major flaw of even the best writers is that they write around the subject. Hemingway was right."

If there were a redundancy machine through which a writer's work could be run to measure excesses of language, Still would doubtless rank as one of the cleanest, most restrained of American writers. Certainly no one has written more effective prose about the Appalachian South. But, like the four-lettered detector of which Hemingway occasionally spoke, the only known redundancy detectors come built in.

More than once he has emphasized his belief that exactness pays off. "A writer doesn't have any choice between being exact or sloppy, with either facts or emotions. Many readers and most writers demand exactness of facts yet are not bothered by emotional sloppiness.

"I feel that much of the writing being done comes more from need than from talent. It may be a need to make money or to become 'known' or to 'prove' oneself. But you get good writing only when there is genuine talent combined with an *artistic* urge to create. It would be enough if I were to write one book of enduring merit in my lifetime, or even one short story. That's more than most writers do. Just consider how much is being published, and how little is really good."

Still is practically free of the self-loving "artistic hypochondriasis" that drives so many artists to expend their psychic energy enhancing the fiction of their superiority. And he views with humorous disdain their need to exhibit themselves rather than their art. Of one writer he says, "We can't know how good a writer he is unless we can forget how great he keeps telling us he is.

"I don't think a writer should allow himself to be used to promote his writing. That sort of deceptivity is more appropriate for politicians and automobile dealers. My writing speaks for itself. What I wear or have for breakfast or even my opinions have nothing to do with my writing once it is finished. Such things don't get writing done, and they don't make writing any better."

Yes. But one can't listen for long to Still talking about writing without realizing he is attempting to give body to the artistry that shapes his fiction. At one time or another, nearly every writer does it, most of them in written words. And it is fascinating, at times a bit startling, that Still's concept of the artistic temperament echoes the diary-like commentary that Flaubert wrote in his letters to Louise Colet and Maxime Du Camp during the four years he was isolated in the country writing *Madame Bovary*:

> To "become known" is not my chief concern — that can afford complete satisfaction only to very mediocre vanities.... Even to one's self, illustriousness is no proof that one has accomplished great things, and obscurity no proof that one has not. I am aiming at

something better — to please myself. Success seems to me a result, not an end in itself. I have conceived a certain manner of writing and a certain beauty of language which I wish to achieve. When I think that I have gathered the fruit of my efforts I shall not refuse to sell it, and I shall not forbid applause if it is good. If on the other hand when it is gathered no one wants it, that can't be helped.... If a work of art is good, if it is authentic, it will be recognized some time — and if one has to wait for recognition six months or six years or until after one's death, what is the difference?

# Jim Dandy:
# James Still at Eighty

## JIM WAYNE MILLER

When his first published poem appeared in the *Virginia Quarterly,* James Still sent a copy to the benefactor who had made his graduate education possible by the award of a scholarship. Not at all certain that a boy who wrote poems had benefited from his expenditure, Still's patron, heir to a sash-and-blind fortune, wrote for advice to Edgar A. Guest, then probably the best-known poet in the country. Edgar A. ("It takes a heap o' livin' in a home t' make it home") Guest's terse reply came promptly: "Leave this young man alone. He may draw up at a place you know nothing of."

Still drew up at the Hindman Settlement School in the summer of 1931, in the depths of the Great Depression. The next three years he worked there for no salary at all, and for another three for an amount which averaged out for the whole time, he once figured, to six cents a day. In 1939 he moved from the Settlement School to a two-story log house on Dead Mare Branch. A neighbor said of him: "He's quit a good job and come over in here and just sot down."

He sat down to finish the novel *River of Earth* but soon realized that this was the place he had been looking for all his life. The log house, built before 1840 and now on the Kentucky Register of Historical Sites, was left to him as a lifetime inheritance following the death of dulcimer maker Jethro Amburgey. Except for time spent in military service, traveling, and teaching, Still has called the log house home ever since.

Over the years Still has kept his private life and his life as a writer separate — in order to remain "intact." Those who knew him as a teacher and writer knew little about his day-to-day life among neighbors (for the most part, farmers and miners); and his neighbors knew next to nothing about him as a writer. To them he was a farmer, gardener, and the librarian at the Hindman Settlement School. His success at keeping separate his private life and his life as a writer has led to misunderstandings about both his life and his writing. A woman in his neighborhood asked him: "Do you do your own writing?" Still replied: "No, I have seven dwarves."

Moreover, Still has made little effort to advertise himself, or to promote his writing (except to cooperate with publishers). So he has been perceived as a recluse, a hermit-writer.

*Miller, Jim Wayne. "Jim Dandy: James Still at Eighty." Appalachian Heritage 14 (Fall 1986): 8–20. Reprinted with permission.*

This romantic notion is a misperception and has resulted in more things being known about James Still that are not true than about any other writer in the country.

These things are true: He was born in Appalachian Alabama (Lafayette) on July 16, 1906, and grew up among "barrels of relatives, dozens of cousins" (Jacksons, Lindseys, Stills) who visited back and forth. His mother, a Lindsey, was born in the North Georgia *Foxfire* country. He was born in the same county as the champion prizefighter Joe Louis (who was Joe Barrow in Alabama), and is related on the Jackson and Lindsey sides of the family to George Lindsey of *Hee Haw*.

On his first day of school, the teacher, a Miss Porterfield, wrote his name in chalk on his desk, handed him an ear of corn and showed him how to spell his name by placing grains of corn on the chalk. "By the end of the day, I knew its shape," Still says. (His full name is James Alexander Still Jr. His father always signed his name J. Alex Still. James Jr. didn't like the diminutive "Jimmy" and chose the simple and direct James Still, which is, as someone observed, balanced, like John Keats.)

During grade school he gave what was to be the first of many public readings, reciting "Birdie with a yellow bill / Hopped up on the window sill"—with his fly open. And brought the house down.

Years later, while a student at Vanderbilt University, he ran into his first grade teacher, Miss Porterfield, who was taking classes at Peabody College. She remembered him —could recite the names of all the students in his class— and volunteered that she never thought he "would be the one" to attend college and graduate school. The confession pleased Still, who likes to surprise, and who considers his whole life —certainly his career as a writer— a long shot.

Still is a paradox. "You talk smart but you've got country wrote all over you," a stranger remarked to him. Rather well-known for being a recluse, he is actually quite gregarious, merely selective in his associations. "The soul selects her own society," he says, quoting Emily Dickinson. He is urbane and well-traveled. While he appeared to be living an isolated life in Knott County, Kentucky, Still was a constant reader of the *Nation*, the *New Republic*, and the *New York Times*. He was publishing in the *Atlantic Monthly*, the *Yale Review, Poetry*, and many other magazines and journals. His stories have been included in the *Best American Short Stories* and the *O. Henry Memorial Prize Stories*. He has been the recipient of two Guggenheim Fellowships and the Southern Authors Award. He was twice honored by the American Academy and Institute of Arts and Letters, and has received the Milner Award, conferred by the Kentucky Arts Council, the highest honor awarded in the arts by the state of Kentucky. He has been invited to McDowell and Yaddo, the writers' and artists' colonies, and numbers among his acquaintances Marjorie Kinnan Rawlings, Katherine Anne Porter, Elizabeth Madox Roberts, and Robert Frost. The "Man on Troublesome," as a scholarly article in the *Yale Review* dubbed him, is remembered by a classmate at LMU as "a friendly man" but one who "would not tolerate any ridicule of a minority group or any person with a disability."

The man on Troublesome is also the man in Central America, caught up in a revolution. (In February 1977, he was on the main street of San Salvador when the street was blocked off by tanks, and soldiers fired into the crowd. Before the day ended, over two hundred people had been killed.) He is also the man at Yaddo, the writers' colony at Saratoga Springs, New York, playing ping pong with Katherine Anne Porter, Eleanor Clark, and Elizabeth Bishop. He is the man who was once one-third owner of a monkey (against military regulations while stationed in Africa during World War II); who roller-skated in Florida with Robert Frost.

Still is the private man on National Public Radio (he reported on the "snow of the century" from eastern Kentucky for NPR in the winter of 1985 and has contributed commentaries to NPR's "All Things Considered" for the last five years). He is the "recluse" featured in

James Still riding a camel (center of photograph), in Egypt during his World War II military service (courtesy of the Hindman Settlement School).

"KentuckyShow!" and who has served on the Kentucky Humanities and Arts Councils. ("I'm a classical humanist. I don't know exactly what that means, but it sounds good.")

Far from being a recluse, Still has a penchant for making news or for turning up by chance where news is being made. "If you want something to happen, stay around James Still," a man in Hindman, Kentucky, observed. "If it ain't happening, it shortly will be." On the day *River of Earth* was published, in February 1940, Still witnessed a murder in Jackson, Kentucky. In a letter of thanks to *Time* magazine, where a very favorable review of his novel had just appeared, he reported on the murder, coincidentally, and his report appeared in the letters to the editor column.

At mealtime at the Hindman Settlement School, where he continues to serve as consultant to the Settlement School staff and its executive director, Mike Mullins, Still says: "Even if I'm not going to have soup, I like to reach around in front of Mike Mullins and stir the pot." Still likes to keep the pot stirred. Once, while traveling with him, I returned to the car and apologized for making him wait. He finished a note he was making. "I don't wait. I do something."

Still is endlessly surprising. The man who declined to accept the Award of the American Academy of Arts and Letters because he lacked bus fare to attend the occasion is nevertheless cosmopolitan in his tastes and habits, having read several hours a day for more than fifty years. His favorite writers are the Scandanavians and the Russians, especially Anton Chekhov, Nikolai Gogol, and Ivan Turgenev.

The man who did not accept an invitation to be Phi Beta Kappa poet at Columbia University in 1940 because he lacked suitable clothes for the occasion (as well as bus fare) has spent eleven winters in Mexico, Guatemala, Honduras, and El Salvador studying Mayan culture and civilization. Alluding to Thoreau, who said he'd traveled a lot in Concord, Massachusetts, Still once told me: "I've been in most of the states of the union, and I've traveled a lot in Knott County and environs. But I don't *know* this place without reference to other places. The local language is not fully appreciated without reference to Chaucer."

The man who raised his own food on Dead Mare Branch ("I dried apples, hilled potatoes") has for about forty years kept daybooks on what he has seen and heard, recording "every facet of the Appalachian experience," with particular attention to speech. "I have attempted to record some of the non-reflective energy of people about me." His journals, as yet unpublished, have been copied and are among his papers at the University of Kentucky. They constitute a unique record because, as Still observes, "they could never be done again, as that era has passed." These journals, along with his stories, poems, and novels, deal with some of what he calls the "uncharted aspects" of the Appalachian experience.

He considers himself "something of a botanist" and has experimented with the development by natural selection of the wild strawberry and wild violet. He is a man who knows that there are two thousand varieties of leaf miners (tiny insects); who calls plants "hardworking citizens of the world." The ground around his house on Dead Mare he has described as "a cross between a botanical garden and an experiment station."

If you went there looking for him, you might be greeted by the sound of Mozart coming from the log house. "Beethoven composed his music," Still says. "Mozart discovered his." Still has also been known to attend Kenny Rogers and Willie Nelson concerts.

With degrees in both arts and sciences, Still has brought the temperament, habits, and, to some extent, the methods of the scientist to his writing. A neighbor on Dead Mare Branch said to him: "You bring up big subjects." Still says he only brings *out* the big subjects implicit in small talk. His novels, poems, and short stories do just that — bring out the big subjects in familiar, everyday affairs by combining the near and the far, the unique and the universal.

But for all his familiarity with other times, places, and cultures, Still has not felt isolated in Knott County, and considers himself fortunate to have lived there, lucky to have been assigned Box 13 at the post office when he first came to Hindman. In the early days, "Hindman was surely the only place you could cash a check at four a.m. and call for your mail at midnight. The cashier was an early riser, the postmaster an insomniac."

In August 1985, James Still and I left Hindman after the Settlement School Writers Workshop had ended to drive through the mountains of eastern Kentucky, southwestern Virginia, eastern Tennessee and western North Carolina. At the outskirts of Hindman, he said, "Now we're on vacation!" And he began a loosely associated mix of literary allusion, arcane scholarship, random recollection, and observation. Quoting Thoreau, he said: "We leave the desperate city and enter — the desperate countryside! Drive slow along here — so many children. A boy got killed right here not long ago." He remembered a boy who couldn't keep his grades up at the Settlement School because he couldn't stay away from his dogs. "Loved them so much he couldn't take time away from them to study." When Still was a boy he'd wanted to be a cowboy or a railroad engineer, "the only two professions open to little boys."

We were going the old road he had known for half a century. Hardly a foot of ground failed to yield a story, a recollection, or to elicit a memorable phrase. He pointed to a place up a holler that was "a perfect bowl"; a place where a man had been burned to death; where a woman used to stand naked in the window. A road sign reminded him of a man who, seeing a new sign by the road that said "Litter Barrel," remarked: "Dadburn, this place has been named Kellytown ever since I can remember." He recalled a man's explanation for his early marriage: "Me and her was running across the pasture one Sunday and she fell down and I fell down too. We didn't get up soon enough."

We passed through a divide where a raindrop "could split," half of it going into the Kentucky River, the other half taking a very different route. It was August 10. On the first of August, Still said he'd heard a cricket singing at midmorning, and it was as if he'd crossed a divide. "I knew then it was the far side of summer."

I repeated the phrase. "'The far side of summer.' Sounds like a title." He wrote it down, then told about how he got the title for a short story. "Troublesome Creek has a fork called Betty Troublesome, probably named for the oily scum on the water. In colonial times—I looked it up—there was such a thing as a betty lamp, just a cup of oil with a wick. 'Betty' goes back to an Anglo-Saxon word that means oil. A man said there was so much oil on Betty Troublesome 'you could strike a match to it, it'd burn.' I thought: 'The Burning of the Waters.' I had a title, but no story. Two or three years later I heard a man say his wife would have her way 'or burn the waters of the creek.' Then I had a conflict."

Although "nobody in twenty years, hereabouts" told him they'd ever read a book of his, Still recollects that his neighbors on Dead Mare Branch and Wolfpen Creek tolerated his efforts at writing—as a pastime of no consequence. "Few probably knew of it." What they judged him by were his corn patch and vegetable garden, and his willingness to help others at harvest. But once he was leaving the house when the branch was in flood, and had to cross a footlog with both suitcase and his typewriter, also in its case. A neighbor, seeing the crossing would be precarious, took the typewriter and said: "You go on, I'll bring your wife."

Still's personal library, which contains fine works of history, literature, discovery, and exploration, always stood open to his neighbors. Once a neighbor came by and asked if he might borrow a book. After being told to pick one, and after examining several hundred volumes, he said, "Well, I don't believe I'll borrow one today." The would-be borrower reported to a neighbor: "Jim Still has got a lot of books but they hain't nary a one of 'em any good."

When he first went over to Dead Mare to live, his neighbors cast him in the role of greenhorn. Once he passed some neighbors who were chopping down trees. They asked him to chop one down. Never much of a hand with an ax, Still nevertheless tried. His neighbors laughed at his efforts. They seemed to enjoy themselves so much, Still clowned for them, never striking anywhere near the same place twice. His neighbors roared with laughter.

Often they played pranks on him. Once he came home to find a pile of wood all chopped and neatly stacked. No one ever acknowledged doing it. Knowing of his interest in terrapins and box turtles, neighbors would pick them up and toss them over into his garden. "Some loafers" mailed him one, and made sure they were present at the post office when Still opened the package to find the box turtle with "ha ha" written on its back.

Sometimes Still retaliated. Once he found "one galosh" by the road, an outsized one. He put it on and walked on up the road, stepping carefully so he would leave no track but that of the "one huge galosh"—and started a "Bigfoot" story among neighbors who came along the road; they gathered, looking at the strange track, wondering who or what it could have been.

His neighbors also liked to represent Still as a know-nothing gardener. "They told that I would work in the garden, and run in the house and read a book to see how to do the next thing. It wasn't true. It was true that I took a field guide to plants into the woods and fields with my neighbors. And I'd ask them what they called various plants. I wanted to know what *they* called them, and why. For example, they called a certain plant 'pee-in-the-bed' because you could make a tea out of it if you were incontinent."

The many pranks, deceptions, and rusties in Still's novels *River of Earth* and *Sporty Creek,* and in the short stories collected in *On Troublesome Creek, Pattern of a Man,* and *The Run for the Elbertas,* are based on Still's familiarity with his Knott County neighbors. The novels, poems, and stories reflect a grasp of community values which is both subtle and profound. "People will acknowledge your weaknesses, faults, and shortcomings, but redeem you by pointing out: 'He'll work!' The second most important thing is: 'He pays his debts.' You can be a drunkard, thief, poor provider to your family, but if you'll work and pay your debts..."

Martha Foley, editor of the annual *Best American Short Stories,* and who often reprinted Still's work, praised his language for being "as unspoiled as when Chaucer and the Elizabethans first made it into glorious literature." Foley envied Still his home on Dead Mare Branch, calling it "a Kentucky Walden." But Still does not think the comparison with Thoreau altogether valid. He says he had not read Thoreau when he moved to Dead Mare. And although he lived there much as Thoreau lived at Walden, he did so for very different reasons. Still's tastes and views regarding material possessions are unlike those of the austere Thoreau. Still likes the best in books, music, food. "I have gone mad with possessions," he recently remarked. "I'm a book junkie!" In making the point that he is not necessarily a plain liver, he reminds one that in his *Jack and the Wonder Beans,* his delightful retelling of "Jack and the Beanstalk," Jack buys a second cow with ribbons on her horns— symbolic of Still's love of light and color. "Prize animals at stock fairs are beribboned."

He will recall, however, a passage from *Walden* about two women who visited Thoreau at his cabin. Thoreau reports overhearing one of them remark as they left: "He even swept under the bed." Still says he received a similar visit from two women at his house on Dead Mare and overheard one of them make the same remark as they were leaving.

But visitors were not frequent. "I used to go for days and not talk to anybody," Still says. "I didn't want to talk. I didn't have anything I wanted to say. I'd be around other people. I'd listen to what they had to say. I was interested. But I didn't want to say anything. For weeks. Months, sometimes. Monroe Amburgey [a neighbor and long-time friend] used to say to me, 'Say something, dammit!'"

Though alone much of the time, Still was not lonely on Dead Mare. For a long time he had the company of a "banty hen that laid an egg just about every day." He remembers putting cracked corn in the cuff of his trousers whenever he stepped out the back door; the hen would come, sit on his shoe, and eat. If he forgot and came out without the corn, the hen would "fuss at me and quarrel."

He also had the company of characters in the novels and short stories he was writing. Typically, they appeared to him in vivid scenes in his imagination. He observed their behavior and listened to them talk. They continue to appear to him. One morning at Yaddo, Still told me: "Long before daylight Godey Spurlock [a character in some of his short stories] waked me and started talking. I got up and started taking down what he said."

Writing is not just work for Still. "All waking and sleeping hours are in a sense devoted to it. I never looked upon writing as a calling, a profession, a vocation or avocation. I have looked upon it ... as a *life,* a way of life. A whole life. A cradle-to-grave affair." The actual writing comes, for him, almost as an afterthought. "A story is just my playpen," he says. "Starts that way. But I get excited. One sentence, a phrase, so condensed that it suggests more than it says— that's my reward. But I play hard. I'm competing with everybody in the world — and with nobody." (A table that used to be in Still's house on Dead Mare Branch, now in the

James Still Room at Morehead State University, has notches cut in it. "I cut a notch in it every time I finished a story," Still said.)

Since writing is for him a way of life, Still is always writing. He was in bed one morning when I came by with coffee. "When you came in," he said, "I was making up a sentence." We talked about the various shapes a sentence can take. "I write telegrams," he said. "I write tight. Then I have to loosen it [the writing] up." He referred to punctuation as "mental breathing" and added that, trying to read some writers, "In some sentences I run out of mental breath."

Still justifies making hundreds of notes by reference to a passage in Lewis Carroll's *Through the Looking Glass:* "'The horror of that moment,' the king went on, 'I shall never, *never* forget!'—'You will, though,' the Queen said, 'if you don't make a memorandum of it.'"

The rich detail of Still's narratives and poems, his uncannily accurate ear for folk speech, are the result not only of his note-taking, but of an extraordinarily retentive memory and unusual powers of observation. He says his memory isn't what it used to be; if not, it is still remarkable. He remembers what a man said whose wife was making the ten-year-old Still a set of underwear that proved too tight: "Hit's pinchin' his little fixin." He recalls a neighbor's term for an illegitimate child ("fencerow child") and for the child's mother ("fencerow gal"); immigrants on a train in Alabama in the 1940s, one of whom looked out the window and remarked, "Yust like Roosia!" He remembers that when he was a student at Vanderbilt University in 1930–31, living in a boardinghouse, he blew "speckles of soot from the railroad yards" off his pillow at night. He recollects an automobile accident, years ago, and the Kentucky state trooper's description of it as a "dogfall"— his term for an unavoidable accident in which both drivers were equally blameless and equally at fault; a little boy buying an ice cream cone in a Hindman drugstore, leaving, and returning later with the empty cone to say: "Here's yore horn back"; a child commenting on his father's blasphemy: "Daddy doesn't know enough adjectives."

Explaining his approach to writing, Still quotes Whitman: "There was a child went forth each day." He says he tries to go at writing every day as if he were a child, with "all the innocence I can muster." But innocence is compatible with experience. He once explained why he advised anyone aspiring to write to learn to type. "A confirmed writer gets ready to enter the profession, just as a truck driver learns to operate a truck. I'm fairly certain Chopin didn't compose his works on the piano with one finger, or even two. The preparation is the point. I know 'poets' who don't own a dictionary or have access to an encyclopedia. I've encountered aspiring short story writers who never read a story by Chekhov, never heard of Katherine Anne Porter, or Flannery O'Connor. Most of the would-be writers I know don't subscribe to any of the magazines they purport to contribute to."

Still brings a prepared innocence to his writing. He watches, listens, remembers, connects. "Nothing happens in my life, I guess, that ... if you give me time, I'll use it. Nothing is wasted. Unless you want to call the whole thing a waste."

And every day brings a gift, sometimes only a single word, but one he has been looking for. Somewhere in southern New York state, while I pumped gas, he watched a truck driver walking to his rig. I saw Still make a note. He has a character, he explained, who walks like the truck driver. Watching the trucker, Still suddenly knew the exact word he needed for his character, a word that, instead of *telling* you how he walks, *shows* you. "You see it."

As the poet Robert Francis once said of him, Still works at prose as carefully as he works at poetry. Other perceptive readers have made similar observations. After she had read both *Hounds on the Mountain,* Still's first book of poems (1937), and *River of Earth,* his first novel

(1940), Katherine Anne Porter wrote to him that the novel was "an extension of the poems, as the poems are the further comment on the experience which made the novel.... In the South ... the poets write the best prose, too."

Still may draft a poem very quickly, but the quickly-accomplished draft may have grown out of a long period of silent watching, listening, reflecting. Just after we had started out in the car one morning, Still shifted in the seat and took out pad and pen. "My pentameters are bothering me this morning," he said. Quickly he wrote down the beginning of a poem. "One of my throwaway poems," he characterized it.

Sometimes the experience that gives rise to a poem and the first draft of the poem come close on one another. In December 1982, in a letter, Still mentioned an incident: "Last night, driving at moderate speed, I ran a fox over. Suddenly there was a brilliant flash of golden fur directly in my car's beam, and then the fatal thump." A few days later came a poem, "Death of a Fox." A year after that he revised the poem, changing one word.

When Still talks about how he writes stories, he often resorts to metaphor. "I try not to put all the furniture in one corner of the room," he says, explaining how he drops in necessary information at various points throughout the story, so naturally the material is not perceived to be necessary exposition. Or he will say, matter-of-factly: "You have a problem in every paragraph. You solve them."

Still demands that a story's parts fit together in a way that suggests more than is said, as in a poem. There should be no extraneous thing. If anything is left over, it should be something unexplained, mysterious. "Never tell all." And a story should be like a boulder, hard enough to stand the weathers of all time.

After years of familiarity with his work, and careful study of it, I have often been astonished by yet another facet of Still's artistry. Once when he said he avoided using the "perpendicular pronoun," I reminded him that *River of Earth* is a novel narrated by a young boy, and written in the first person. Still pointed out that, nevertheless, the pronoun "I" seldom occurs. I realized, looking back through the novel, that he was right. I had not, until then, appreciated what an extraordinary accomplishment the novel is in this respect: a first-person narrative in which the first-person pronoun rarely occurs. Such sleight of hand is an important clue to Still's narrative art. "Fiction," he once said, "falls into two distinct categories. In the first, the story is being *told* as by the fireside, the reader being aware, if only vaguely, that there is a narrator at his elbow weaving the tale, throwing the shuttle to vary the pattern, pressing the pedals to spur the action. In the second, the author is nowhere to be discovered. The story is *itself*, breathing and alive in its every action, in its language, and driving toward a resolution no hand could have changed or influenced."

Still intends to create this second kind of fiction. If he is present as author anywhere in his stories and novels, it is only in "some little distinction between the speech [of the characters] and the narrative." Otherwise, he is invisible. He wants the story to flow, like a stream, but does not want the author's shadow reflected in the stream. "And of course, the big thing is immediacy. As the story opens, I want to have the motor running, and be able to say to the reader, 'Let's go.'"

I reminded him that's pretty much the situation in "The Run for the Elbertas," where at the outset Riar Thomas stops to pick up Godey Spurlock and his sidekick:

> As Riar Thomas approached the Snag Fork Bridge, the truck lights picked up the two boys sitting on the headwall. Glancing at his watch, he saw it was nearly one o'clock. He halted, pulled the cardboard out of the broken window, and called, "I'll open the door from the inside, it's cranky." The boys sat unmoving. "Let's go," he said, "if you're traveling with me. A body can't fiddle in the peach business."

Still pointed out, too, how many things were planted in the opening of this story — a seat spring sticking out, a pocket knife — things that "paid off" later. He cited Chekhov's requirement that if a shotgun over the fireplace is mentioned in a story's opening, it must be discharged at some point; otherwise, it should not be mentioned. "You can't spring things on the reader. You have to prepare him. Life's not logical, but fiction has to be. And if it's going to stay around, it has to be psychologically sound."

In an essay entitled "Slick as a Dogwood Hoe Handle" (*Appalachian Heritage,* Volume 11, No. 3, Summer 1983), Joe Glaser analyzes Still's short story "I Love My Rooster," showing how all the seemingly irrelevant details finally pay off. Glaser finds the story to be "as elegantly plotted as a scene from Restoration drama ... and almost any other Still story or episode would show the same narrative deftness." He speaks of the "clockwork construction" of Still's stories.

Glaser puts Still in a category of "scofflaws and scamps—fellows whose profession and amusement it is to confound the unwary." He describes Still as "a supremely artful man who mixes indirection in everything he does. In his public statements about his work, there is a large element of recreational flimflam. In his fiction, the same duplicity is put to more complicated uses. It shapes his plots, controls the unfolding of events ... enriches his characterizations with unexpected turns, and even determines the basic tone of his fiction. With Still, guile is a prime ingredient of his art. His trickery is essential to his work's fundamental nature and appeal."

In conversation Still typically proceeds by indirection. He sidles up to his real purpose. He seems without purpose when most purposeful, unintentional when most intent. He knows that whispering, when everyone else is shouting, is apt to get attention; that appearing to conceal something is a way to reveal it; and that appearing to reveal something is also a way of concealing something else. Once when I was helping him sort letters, we came across one from the 1930s—which had never been opened. I said I thought that was remarkable — his never having opened the letter — and asked if he wanted to open it now. "No, I know what's in it," he said, and didn't elaborate. Once, telling a story, he referred to "a man, whose name I don't think I'll mention"— and went on. In conversation he will frequently find himself too close to something painful or troubling. He will pause, and after a long while, say, "no matter," or "however," and go around that point in the telling.

Over lunch at Yaddo in August 1983, Still began telling me about the early days at Hindman. (I would not realize until later that Hindman was not his subject at all.) His life at Hindman in the thirties was far from idyllic. He had no days off; he was always on duty, seeing after children, supervising them. A nephew in school in Florida wrote asking if Still could send him ten dollars a month. Still was making, by that time, fifteen dollars a month. "Missionary barrels" that came to the school contained clothes, and although Still desperately needed clothes, the Settlement School policy was that these things were not sent for staff members. Yet, when he hardly had shoes himself, he bought shoes for a little boy who walked by his house in ice and snow. He bought the boy shoes, admittedly, to put his own mind at ease, for he couldn't endure knowing the boy walked with wet or frozen feet.

After taking the M.A. degree at Vanderbilt he had accepted the only scholarship available to him, one from the University of Illinois leading to a degree in library science. He came to the Hindman Settlement School as librarian. But he was never a "desk librarian." He voluntarily included in his activities the job of carrying boxes of books to outlying one-room schools, which involved considerable travel on foot. He believed then, as now, that the primary job of the school is to teach children to read well. (Later, he taught ten years in the Department of English at Morehead State University, accepted short-term teaching positions at Ohio

University and Berea College, and held seminars at the University of Kentucky.) Now he says, "I'm apparently left with one honest job in life: librarian," a role he defines as "reader's advisor."

When he carried books to remote schools in Knott County, he would ride a bus across the county, get off with his box of books, carry them on foot in to a school, and pick up books he had left on a previous visit. He was able to reach about four schools a day in this manner. He was a bookmobile on foot.

But it would be a mistake to assume that this voluntary work of bringing books to children in isolated areas, from homes where there were no books, was necessarily met with gratitude. One school superintendent banned Still from going into schools because the books Still circulated were taking children's minds off their studies! The superintendent referred to the books, thoughtfully chosen by Still for their appropriateness, as "them old books."

When word got around that Still was carrying books, a woman administering welfare programs in adjoining Perry County informed Still he might qualify under one of her programs (this was during the Depression years). He might earn $22.00 a month for his work. Still recollects receiving one check before the school superintendent prohibited him from going into the schools.

At this time there was a school in the remotest area of Knott County, so out of the way that one had to leave Knott, go through parts of Perry and Breathitt Counties and then back into Knott in order to reach it. It was a school, Still remembers, with eight students "taught by an ignorant boy." Still wanted to live there and teach the school. But although he had two bachelors degrees and an M.A., he was considered unqualified to teach the school.

Nor did he find favor with the one public health officer in the county during the early years. Still had a child with a rheumatic heart condition and epilepsy admitted to Children's Hospital in Louisville, where the child underwent treatment for about two years. (He is credited with saving the lives of two children through his referrals.) The county health officer resented Still's not making a referral through her. He reminded her that she had known about the child's condition and had done nothing. Again, when he referred cases of trachoma out of the county, he met with resentment from the county health officer and from teachers— because it reflected on them for not having identified the problems.

While Still talked, we lunched leisurely and went through our mail. Still showed me, as a current example of how he is perceived in the place where he has lived and worked for over half a century, a letter from someone who urged him to "get forgiveness of his sins." The letter was unsigned. "But I know who wrote it," he said. And he laughed. "All my sins are sins of omission," he said.

In the midst of talking about writing, Still brings up cooking. He prepares several stir-fried dishes, in some of which he uses almonds ordered a gallon at a time from California, while in others he uses pecans and walnuts from farther south. Has Still wandered from his subject? Hardly. This is more indirection that pays off. When Joe Creason, the *Courier-Journal* columnist, once asked him how he learned to cook, Still replied: "I got hungry." One learns to write for much the same reason, Still maintains. "You get hungry for what writing does for you. It feeds you, nourishes you, sustains you."

The connection between cooking and writing was established, after a fashion, quite early in one of the first things he remembers having written. His mother had gone to visit relatives for a week, and Still missed her. Not wanting to admit that, he wrote her a note: "Mama, come home. Lois [his sister] is baking the biscuits too big."

Still does not give advice. But sometimes, he says, "I lend my experience." He has lent me his experience with respect to being a writer:

- A writer has to get used to being widely unknown.
- Never use a word of two syllables until you have exhausted the possibilities for a word of one syllable.
- Generosity in life, parsimony in language. Marshall Best, my editor at Viking, once accused me of trying to eliminate "all the words."
- Students are forever asking me my advice. I'm nowadays quoting a rear bumper sticker I lately saw: "Don't follow me. I'm lost."
- He once gave me an excellent tip for getting ink stains out of shirt pockets.
- There is always erotic interest in writing. It's like salt, though: if you taste it, it's too much.

And surely the most important tip:

- Be someone who's hard to round up.

Whether he intended to or not — and he probably did — he has lent me experience on:

- Motives: All our motives are unknown.
- The army: It seemed there never had been anything else, never would be anything else.
- Progress: When I learned, years ago, that a machine had been invented to pick strawberries, I knew we would eventually go to the moon.
- Colonel Sanders: Fried chicken was the least of him. He could cuss the angels out of heaven.... Glad I didn't know him. Glad to know about him.
- Eloquence: Of a man who boasted to Still of a daughter's accomplishments, Still said: "He wanted to be eloquent — and what else could he do but shout?"
- The artist's life: Don't ever think anybody's going to understand — not your mother or father, your wife — anybody. Unless they have the disease themselves, they can't understand the rewards an artist derives from the work.
- God: Still admires the Quakers, and believes no one should tell anyone else what their relationship to God should be. To people concerned about his soul, Still says: "Did you ever look closely at a Serotica [moth]?" The question implies that the other person's god may be narrower than his, who, as one of his smallest accomplishments, can create the miracle of this moth.
- What's important: After you have clothing, food and shelter, then what? Young people ought to think about that. The "then what?" days will come.
- Himself: People have told me I'm an enigma. Woodrow Amburgey, who has known me for over thirty years, told me once he didn't understand me. I'm as simple as the sun. The only secrets I have are those of other people ... my own vanity. I'm proud of my Phi Beta Kappa key. When I feel especially ignorant, I wear it (out of sight). I ride off in all directions at once, on wild horses, without rein or saddle — looking for someone in the wilderness of the world who understands my visions, my joys, my losses.
- Appalachia: ... that somewhat mythical region with no recognized boundaries.... I trust to be understood for imagining the heart of it to be in the hills of eastern Kentucky where I have lived and called my home and where I have exercised as much freedom and peace as the world allows.

James Still "drew up" at the Hindman Settlement School in 1931. Fifty-five years later, on July 16, 1986, he drew up to his 80th birthday, in good health, still working, a "reasonably happy" man. Reasonably happy because "Guilt is not one of my faults. I forgive myself easily." And because "I gift myself." He observes his own private holidays. "March 10 is my own holiday," he once told me. "Because of something that happened to me on March 10." So is June 10. He doesn't elaborate on either date. And for his own reasons he has repeatedly visited an out-of-the-way cemetery in the Powell Valley in Tennessee. (It is generally understood that these visits are to the grave of a college classmate; she died in her junior year at Lincoln Memorial University.)

A friend of Still's, Helen Muchnic, author of *A History of Russian Literature*, once remarked to him: "You are the only truly happy man I know. You know what you want to do and you are doing it." If he is reasonably content, Still says, it is because he accepts personal limitations cheerfully. "I do not write better because I don't know how," he says. "I've done what I could." That sounds as if he's broken his pencil. But not so. Recently he counted up fifty-two things he wants to write. At eighty he is as curious about the world as the boy narrator of *River of Earth*, who wants to go traipsing to "the scrag end of creation." Still wants to see it all. This desire has taken him to six countries in Africa, to Brazil, Israel, and again and again to Mexico and Central America. Pursuing an interest in Mayan civilization and primitive peoples, he returned, in February 1986, for the eleventh time to the abandoned sites of the intellectuals of the Meso-American culture ("At one time their calendar was more accurate than ours.") In August 1986, he traveled to Iceland.

Still likes to go traipsing, but he loves home, too. And he is not so driven as a writer that he can't spend a long winter evening going through seed catalogs, anticipating spring, planning a garden. In a postscript to a letter, Still wrote me once: "There is simply nothing to match an Appalachian spring. It makes me feel new, reborn, shriven of all my sins. I have a new rototiller. My cup is running over."

Still was asked to read his poem "Heritage" at the funeral of Congressman Carl Perkins in August 1984. That well-publicized event — practically the entire United States Congress was in attendance — more than anything else, Still estimates, best presented him and his work to his neighbors, and explained his life to them.

His novel *River of Earth* was published many years ago and is still in print. It is worth considering what has kept the book alive. Does the book continue to live because of the folklife it deals with? Because it was the only novel written about that part of eastern Kentucky at that time? Is it because *River of Earth*, though fiction, is a historically accurate presentation? All of these considerations may be partial explanations. But Still's achievement as a writer is best suggested by what a Knott County resident once told him: "I've lived here all my life, but until I read your novel *River of Earth*, I'd never really seen the place." This is the function of the writer — to help us see, and see into, our place, our experience, our lives in the world. Still's poems, short stories, and novels are a distinguished, unified body of work, at once unique and universal, illuminating a particular place, people, and way of life by providing a poetic vision of the facts. Still's people, swept along on the "mighty river of earth," constitute a metaphor for the essential human experience.

Many things happen in Still's writing — humorous things, and almost unbearably sad things. He has not hesitated to narrate what George Eliot called "the harsh unaccommodating actual." But whether humorous or sad, we experience his characters as living, breathing people. "Your heart begins to beat with theirs. That's what I hope to do, anyway," their creator says. But it is the seeing, and seeing into things, which occurs when we turn from the poems and stories and look back into the world and see it as if for the first time — this is what Still is best at making happen.

On July 16, 1986, his friends and colleagues, students and admirers of his work, James Still Fellows from the Appalachian Center at the University of Kentucky, people from near and far gathered at the Hindman Settlement School for "A Master Time: James Still's 80th Birthday Celebration." With support from the Kentucky Arts and Humanities Councils, Berea College published under its reactivated College Press imprint *The Wolfpen Poems,* Still's collected poems. The poems were released as part of the 80th birthday celebration.

Quite aware that "no man lives forever," James Still continues to do what he wants to do. Still making things happen, honored where he has chosen to live and call home, he is a state resource, his work a national treasure.

# The Seamless Vision

## FRED CHAPPELL

James Still's novel *River of Earth* was first published in 1940; it was reissued in 1978 by the University Press of Kentucky, with a brief but enlightening foreword by Dean Cadle. Here is a paragraph from the novel:

> The waters ran yellow, draining acid from the mines, cankering rocks in the bed. The rocks were snuffy brown, eaten and crumbly. There were no fish swimming in the eddies, nor striders looking at themselves in the waterglass. Bare willows leaned over. They threw a golden shadow on the water.

I do not know what writers may have had influence over Still's style and conception. From internal evidence in some of his short stories, one might guess at an eighteenth-century author like Swift. But if his prose reminds me of anyone else at all, it would have to be of Kipling. Still's severe and telling economy, his selection of pointed detail, the use of color, the cool and almost innocent dispassion — these qualities we find in the best of Kipling's fiction, and almost nowhere else in English literature. And a comparison might be drawn between Still's unobtrusive use of the Appalachian expression "waterglass" and some instance of Kipling's sprinkling-about of East Indian words and expressions.

Above all, one is struck by the force of understatement in both authors; and by the strategy of narration, a voice reporting almost objectively from inside a context only dimly comprehended by the larger world outside. These latter two qualities lend to Still and Kipling their manner of quickly established authority. They both have suffered the times and places they write about; and while they hold to deeply caring attitudes, they are equally unsurprised at any vicissitude or inequity they find.

In his much too short "Afterword" to his book of stories, *The Run for the Elbertas* (University Press of Kentucky, 1980), Still says, "My writings drew on everyday experiences and observations. I only wrote when an idea overwhelmed me." A reader who has gone through Still's stories with even minimal attention will surely believe his latter sentence here. The stories are set down too clearly, too forcefully and economically, to have been written by someone writing for money, or writing for the sake of writing; each of them seems as necessary in its place in the universe as every piece of metal or glass, every scrap of cloth, to be found in a mountain cabin.

*Chappell, Fred. "The Seamless Vision of James Still."* Appalachian Journal *8.3 (Spring 1981): 196–202. Copyright* Appalachian Journal *and Appalachian State University. Reprinted with permission.*

But a reader might wonder about what Still would describe as an "idea" for a story. His stories seem not to have ideas in the usual fictional way; they are not stories about what would happen *if* (as in, say, Hemingway's "The Short Happy Life of Francis Macomber" or James's "The Aspern Papers"), but about what *did* happen *when.* "The Fun Fox," for example, and "The Stir-Off" and "A Master Time" (the latter in *Pattern of a Man and Other Stories,* Gnomon Press, 1976) are not stories in the usual sense; they are accounts, so severe in the restriction of authorial intrusion that to the unaccustomed eye they might look like reportage. There are no surprises, no unexpected twists. Once the basic situation is set up — the conflict between a schoolmaster and a local mischief-maker, or merely a celebration party — it plays itself out to the end. And when the situation comes to its natural ending, the story concludes. As simple as that. And as difficult.

Still's story lines are as clean and strong as the lines of Shaker furniture. In one of his best stories, "The Nest," a little girl is sent by her parents to spend a night with her Aunt Clissa. She loses her way and dies of exposure. That's all there is. The narrative line is simpler than that of "Little Red Riding Hood," simpler even than Bill Monroe's ballad, "Footprints in the Snow."

Yet it is an effective story, and deeply moving. Here is the final paragraph:

> Nezzie came down the slope. She lost a shoe and walked hippity-hop, one shoe on, one shoe off. The pasture was feathery as a pillow. A bush plucked her bonnet, snatching it away; the bush wore the bonnet on a limb. Nezzie laughed. She was laughing when the cows climbed by, heads wreathed in a fog of breath, and when a fox horn blew afar. Her drowsiness increased. It grew until it could no longer be borne. She parted a clump of broomsage and crept inside. She clasped her knees, rounding the grass with her body. It was like a rabbit's bed. It was a nest.

Ironic pathos gives this paragraph much of its strength. Nezzie has survived a freezing night alone on the mountain, only to succumb when very close to shelter and the comfort of kinfolk. (It is her Uncle Barlow sounding the fox horn in order to direct her steps.) The choice of detail reinforces that ironic strength; she is close enough to her destination to meet the cows coming from milking, those cows whose warmth ought to be solace and comfort, their "heads wreathed in a fog of breath." Still allows himself few allusions in his prose, and when he does they are to the basic and primeval texts, to the Bible or to folk myths or fairy tales. Here he enjambs two allusions to nursery rhymes, "hippity-hop, one shoe on, one shoe off," emphasizing not only Nezzie's extreme youth — she is six years old — but also to the lost protection of her family. Earlier she had remembered how her father sang to her baby brother, "Up, little horse, let's hie to mill." The bush snatches off her bonnet to wear; it is anthropomorphized as in an Arthur Rackham illustration for a children's book. The last two sentences underscore both Nezzie's close feeling for the world of nonhuman nature and her terrible true distance from it: "It was like a rabbit's bed. It was a nest."

Still's poem "Spring on Troublesome Creek" (first collected in *Hounds on the Mountain,* Viking Press, 1939, and retitled "Spring" for later collections) begins, "Not all of us were warm, not all of us." That kind of bitter, half-mocking statement exemplifies the litotic attitude toward natural hardship throughout all his work. His idea seems to be that we can know nothing of nature until we have endured it in its calamitous aspects. Knowledge of nature must be earned; love of nature must be earned, and can be. The same poem ends, "We have come through / To the grass, to the cows calving in the lot."

Human nature is no less a trial than nonhuman. Many of Still's characters have hard protective shells and thorny borders, and other characters must undergo certain ritual tests in order to make and to preserve friendships. Characters rarely meet one another; they are ritually initiated into each other's confidence. There are even bad characters — villains, if you will — in Still's work. I would name Aus Coggins and Han and Tibb from *River of Earth,* and maybe Crafton Rowan from "Pattern of a Man," though he is treated humorously. Should we include Hodge Muldraugh from *River of Earth?* He has probably murdered — Still does not absolutely say so — the schoolmaster. Should we include Godey Spurlock from "A Ride on the Short Dog"? Godey is no more than uncontrollably obtuse and mischievous, but see what destruction results. Yet if we mark down Godey Spurlock as a "bad" person, why not Mace Crownover or even that marvelously alive character, Uncle Jolly?

One factor that complicates our moral categorizations is the ancient mountain tradition of the "rusty." To play a mischievous prank on someone, especially a prank that causes him to lose face, is "to pull a rusty." (To do something merely foolish, to make a fool of oneself, is "to cut a dido.") But the rusty is susceptible of ambiguous social judgments. To clip a man's overalls' galluses while he stands talking is a good rusty; to cut the cinch strap of his saddle is unacceptable behavior. Every rusty demands revenge; the victim is expected to return prank for prank, but when it gets out of hand — as in the case of a cut cinch strap — then revenge amounting to bloodshed may be called for.

"The Run for the Elbertas" is a story that is a string of rusties. On a 500-mile round trip to pick up ripe South Carolina peaches to sell, Godey Spurlock and Mal Dowd torment the entrepreneur Riar Thomas unmercifully, and are satisfied only when the whole truckload of peaches is spoiled and finally dumped. The personal fault attributed to Riar is avarice, though no hard evidence is adduced to support the accusation. The reader is at a loss how to place his sympathies until the end of the story, when Riar dumps sacks-full of stinging peach fuzz down the shirts of the two adolescent boys. Then there is a refreshing sense of relief. Even as outsiders we realize that the boys' tricks have been just too mean and costly. But it is a funny story all the way through, if we can accept the rough-and-ready tradition of the Old Southwest humorists. A similar episode occurs in *The Adventures of Huckleberry Finn,* where Huck pulls such a rusty as to make his friend Jim believe him dead. Again, a reader's sympathies are confused until Huck apologizes, humbles himself "before a nigger." Then there is the same feeling of relief, of justice restored, that we feel at the end of "The Run for the Elbertas."

Still has rung a very effective change on this pattern. In "A Ride on the Short Dog," we meet Mal Dowd and Godey Spurlock again, this time in company with an unnamed narrator, a boy of their own age. One favorite primitive rusty among boys is to "frog" someone's arm, to give him a blow that raises a charley horse. Godey is expert at frogging, and this is a recurrent motif in a story full of other sorts of rusties. His frogging of the narrator's arm finally reduces the speaker to tears, whereupon Godey, feeling an unaccustomed remorse, invites the narrator to return him a "rabbit lick," a powerful chop at the base of the neck. Godey fears nothing. But the enraged narrator strikes with all his might and does Godey grave if not mortal injury. They have been riding a bus, and one of the other passengers inquires what is wrong with Godey Spurlock. "Mal opened his mouth numbly. 'He's doing no good,' he said."

How are we to feel about this story? Godey means no one any serious harm; he merely likes to irritate people and mock their pretensions, and to see if he can find in them any hidden vein of cowardice. He does not deserve his accidentally terrible punishment. Or does he? Our sympathies are never quite with Godey; we share with the other passengers — as we did with Riar Thomas — their indignation and consternation. Godey intends no evil, but he has been taking unconscionable liberties with the tradition of the rusty; he is just barely this side of being purposely cruel. But who is to say when he oversteps the line? The rusty permits a wide latitude of freedom, even to the point of cruelty. One hint we may take is that Godey is rude to Liz Hidey, an old lady; rudeness to one's elders is one of the worst breaches of Appalachian manners.

Finally, though, Still imputes no blame. Even his characters rarely judge one another on moral grounds. They do often fling about the epithet "witty," meaning fool, but this is mostly in judgment of a man's capacities as breadwinner. The law too makes no moral judgments, and seems to have little connection with justice.

There is a point in reading Still at which we take his restraint, his careful understatement, as impassiveness. The reader must supply all the feeling about the events of the fiction. Still's objectivity and reticence are so unrelenting that we have few hints about what kind of feeling to supply. Some of the stories are almost as difficult to interpret as a poker player's face. Still's intention is not hard to descry; he soaks his fiction in the same attitudes his characters share: a stoic indifference to physical discomfort and pain, a straight (but not always entirely clear) code of behavior, a fierce and even harsh independence of spirit, and a certain cold insularity of understanding.

It may be that this latter quality is in some respects a drawback. Still's characters are never highly educated; the wisdom they possess they have acquired by dint of harsh personal experience. Much of their information is mere superstition or misinformation. Yet they hold stubbornly to their notions, right or wrong, and are skeptical about the knowledge and intuitions of others. There is something a little suffocating about their narrowness, and the reader is so thoroughly immersed in their milieu that he can form no accurate judgment about how the characters are to be perceived outside it. Yet his curiosity is aroused. How would a doctor or qualified veterinarian — if only there were some around! — receive all these smug home remedies and folk homilies?

In "The Sharp Tack," we have a clash between an enlightened world-view and an extremely narrow fundamentalist mountain world-view. It is an epistolary story; the ignorant backwoods preacher, Jerb Powell, begins to write a series of fire-and-brimstone letters to Talt Evarts, a veteran of the Second World War, newly returned to Baldridge County, Kentucky. The Reverend Mr. Powell is riled because Mr. Evarts claims to have visited the Holy Land while in service, crossed the River Jordan, toured the town of Bethlehem, and returned home with a sprig from a cedar of Lebanon. The preacher regards these tall tales as mortal sin, damaging to the beliefs and even to the salvation of local gullibles. Powell does not believe the Holy Land exists on earth; it is the geography of the afterlife. "The Holy Land is yonder in the sky and there's no road to it save by death and salvation." Talt Evarts, then, with his accounts, is an instrument of Satan, if not the Antichrist himself. "Hell's bangers! Are you in cahoots with Beelzebub? Aye, your tongue is a viper which continues to wriggle even after its head has been cut off."

"The Sharp Tack" is a funny and also a clever story. All the letters are from Preacher Powell; his adversary never answers. But the ranting minister gets his come-uppance little by little, as he becomes more informed about the character and war record of his antagonist, and about the geography of the world. "I learnt a speck. I'll admit it," he says. But even at the end, he has accommodated the facts of the case to his narrow fundamentalist notions. "I'm willing to allow you visited a town called Jerusalem. I hold it was labeled after the city On High — like Bethlehem, Nebo and Gethsemane here in Kentucky. The Holy Land on earth is the namesake of the Country Above." This silly notion satisfies him; it reduces the unknown to his own small purview and familiarizes the unimaginable truth. The veteran Evarts is content to let him rest with this idea, and the schoolmaster and postmaster, who have been scorning the old fundamentalist, follow Evarts' tolerant lead.

A clever and funny story, as I say. It is good to see Jerb Powell distressed and good to see the humane tolerance of Evarts; the story regards the old preacher as an antediluvian throw-back, out of touch with reality, a loud but harmless nut. But might that be too simple a view? Jerb Powell's mentality is the kind that is liable to break out in social violence and to incite others to violence. He is funny partly because he is isolated and powerless, but suppose that he had a television station at his command. Would he not then be capable of major harm? This stiff-necked militant ignorance has possibility for real danger; it is not just a Pickwick-ian foible.

I am not criticizing Still for not writing a story he had no intention of writing. And surely he is correct in taking satire as his mode; laughter is the best weapon against the kind of atti-tude Jerb Powell represents. But maybe the satire is too gentle and the story too hopeful. "The Sharp Tack" was first published many years ago; but the world-view it attacks has not lost force with the passage of time and the spread of education — as Still evidently surmised would happen. This world-view is still very much with us, and at this hour comes nigh to being the most socially acceptable one in American society.

Well, we do not hold even science fiction writers to blame for not accurately predicting the future. "The Sharp Tack" is instructive about Still's mild and cheerful liberalism because this is one of his few stories that deal with change and with the relationship of Appalachia to the outside world. Most of his stories depict his Appalachia as sealed away in time and space, resistant to and mostly unknowing about the forces of larger history. The changes his fiction depicts are the most ancient ones, the changes of seasons, the changes of human life, from youth to maturity to old age to death.

In that masterful novel *River of Earth* change is restricted indeed. It consists mainly in change of season and change of landscape. The Baldridges move from a coal mining settle-ment to an almost idyllically drawn farm and then back again to the bleak mines. The life depicted is impecunious, even precarious, and dangerous, but not miserable. The joys the Baldridge family experiences are as deep and genuine as their sorrows, and it is this knowl-edge about life and poverty that sets *River of Earth* far apart from so many facile protest nov-els.

The center of the novel portrays the happiest time for this family. They have moved to a farm, found a healthy and provident environment, sent the boys to a pretty good school, and gathered a plentiful harvest. The farm represents a kind of Paradise Gained, but it is soon Paradise Lost, as the family moves back to the Blackjack coalfields.

They move back because the father, Brack Baldridge, is a coal miner by calling as well as by profession. He gives hay fever as an excuse, but the truth is that he is called to mining the way another man might be called to baseball or religion. "I'm longing to get me a pick and stick it in a coal vein," he says. The notion of such dangerous sad drudgery as a vocation is startling but true nonetheless. Clancy Sigal's fine documentary novel, *Weekend in Dinlock,* is a corroborative and more thorough examination of this feeling.

And so the Baldridges move to Blackjack, back to the hunger, uncertainty, apathy, and tragedy. The younger son, Fletch, loses most of his hand in an accident with dynamite, and the grandmother, who is not present in Blackjack, dies. These events are not consequences of the move back — though it may seem so to the young narrator — but they do contribute to the darkening of the book. The vision of the free sunny farm life has flickered and dimmed like a dream unraveling from memory. Here is the beautiful final paragraph of the book:

> I waked, trembling with cold, and it was morning. The coffin box had been taken away. The chairs sat empty upon the hearth. I ran outside, and there were only wagon tracks to mark where death had come into the house and gone again. They were shriveled and dim under

melting frost. I turned suddenly toward the house, listening. A baby was crying in the far room.

A reader will discern from this quotation that it is James Still's prose style, as much as his observation and characterization, which lifts his work, ennobles his themes and gives them latitude and broad application. In a letter written to Still, dated October 5, 1940, Katherine Anne Porter remarked on the style of the book:

> I love the evenness and unity — do you know what it is like to me? A man telling an old beautiful tale who almost imperceptibly drops into poetry at the right point, saying again what he has just said but in different rhythms and deeper words, and then taking up his narrative again.

Still's style is indeed consistent, maintaining a certain level of intensity and lyricism which becomes, in a certain manner, unobtrusive, and thus able to handle the more mundane concerns of a novel, those entrances, exits, introductions, and transitions which are necessary if a story is to get told. A reader after awhile accustoms himself to style on the writer's special level, and is able to detect a lowering into dullness for requisite mechanical passages or a straining for effect in lyric set pieces. But there is none of that in Still; his style is very nearly seamless.

Here is a quick sketch of mountain folks going to attend a funeral:

> Beyond, at the mouth of Defeated Creek, we came on folk walking toward Seldom Churchhouse. The men wore white shirts, with collars buttoned. One had a latch-pin at his throat, for the button was gone, and another fellow's neck was wrapped around with a tie, roostercomb red. The women walked stiffly, dresses rustling like wind among corn blades, their hair balled on their necks. They carried yard flowers and wild blooms in their arms; honeysuckle and Easter flowers, and seasash.

This paragraph marks no special dramatic point in the novel. In fact, it is a preparatory section, leading us to the sermon by Sim Mobberly from which the book takes its title. But the lyric use of specific detail is admirable. There are the irresistible and characteristically bleak place-names, "Seldom," "Defeated." There is the buttonless shirt collar with its telling — and colloquial — "latch-pin." There is Still's customary touch of primary color, the "rooster-comb red" necktie. Here are the women, modest and sapless, as much a part of their environment as plants, but given an underecho from the biblical story of Ruth. And the paragraph ends appropriately — since a preaching is a real celebration for these people — with a mass of flowers, named by their local names.

But what engages one most is Still's restraint. In his careful distinguishing between similar, but never identical, tones, in his tipping-in of the single bright color, in his intently faithful localism, he is reminiscent of the Dutch landscape painters of the seventeenth century. I think particularly of Albert Cuyp or Meyndert Hobbema, who produced subtle and searching canvases of scenes that an Italian or French artist would have found unpainterly, flat and monotonous and indistinguishable. He shares also with the Dutch painters their love of generic anecdote and of characteristic personal detail — the disposal of a sleeve or collar, the positioning of a hand that tells us so much about a character we believe it is all we need to know.

None of this works if it is obtrusive. It is the consistency of Still's style which allows these effects to achieve themselves. And I think that this consistency has been accomplished by the writer's imbuing himself thoroughly with the values of the region and the inhabitants he treats with. Not an easy preparation, perhaps especially not easy for an Appalachian writer, whose background accommodates literary training with some difficulty. Writing requires a fair amount of sophistication, and an Appalachian writer has been brought up to distrust sophistication, to distrust bookishness. So that composition is for him often a matter of re-achieving a kind of nonliterary (and even nonliterate) innocence, of going back into a world of values he no longer fully shares. And this he must do without guilt or condescension.

Still is able to bring it off. His mastery of values that he must have in some sense passed beyond, his very reticence and restraint, argue for a steadfast self-confidence on his part. He knows what person he is; he understands and fully (though I would wager, not easily) accepts his relationship to his heritage. In fact, in his sonnet "Heritage," he has spoken of this relationship in positively determined language. Here is the sestet:

> Being of these hills, being one with the fox
> Stealing into the shadows, one with the new-born foal,
> The lumbering ox drawing green beech logs to mill,
> One with the destined feet of man climbing and descending,
> And one with death rising to bloom again, I cannot go.
> Being of these hills I cannot pass beyond.

# A Master Language

## WENDELL BERRY

If one believes, as I do, that James Still is a master of the short story — one who in execution is virtually flawless, in touch and ear so nearly perfect that the difference does not matter — then one must ask why this is not more generally recognized. This may seem easily explained by prejudice against country people and country things, whatever is perceived as regional or local; and yet in Mr. Still's lifetime other rural writers have risen to favor with both critics and the reading public.

The problem, more likely, is his reliance on the native dialect of the Kentucky mountains (perhaps he would prefer to *say* the native dialect of Knott County) that always informs the language of his stories. And so any assessment of his work must begin with an examination of his language.

Mr. Still has given his whole attention to a people who not only are regional, rural, and "backward," but who until fairly recently spoke a regional dialect that was intact and vigorous; it had the accuracy and expressiveness of a common language rising out of common experience. To present-day Americans, whose speech always contains a deference to the invented dialects of specialists and experts, the language of Mr. Still's characters must seem to come from another world — which it does.

But the critical question is not whether or not a writer uses a dialect, or whether or not the dialect is old or obsolete, but whether or not that dialect has benefits to confer on the writer who uses it, and whether or not the writer has benefited. Mr. Still's short stories give proof that the dialect of his people had plenty of benefits to confer, and that he benefited plentifully.

It is evidently tempting, when speaking of this body of work, to carry it into the neighborhood of words such as "folk," "primitive," "archaic," and "Americana." Thus an incoherent culture condescends to a coherent one, and in the process overlooks the artistry of James Still, whose work claims our interest, not as a display of folk speech or folk knowledge, but because of his superb storytelling, the richness and subtlety of his understanding of character, and his extraordinary clarity of feeling.

Mr. Still's language is not that of "local color" or "regionalism." It is neither "realistic" nor "picturesque" nor "quaint." It involves no condescension to the local. By it, simply, he gives his prose the economy, liveliness, and density of poetry. The speech of his characters is elegant — and eloquent. It is certainly not an obstacle to get over in order to learn the story,

Berry, Wendell. "A Master Language." The Sewanee Review 105.3 (Summer 1997): 418–21. Copyright 1997 by Wendell Berry. Reprinted with the permission of the editor and the author.

any more than is the language of Chaucer or Shakespeare. The story is in the language in which it is told, and nowhere else.

Searching for a way to take this work as seriously as I believe it deserves to be taken, I came upon this: "He had got emotion, the driving force he needed, from his life among the people, and it was the working in dialect that had set free his style." That is from Lady Gregory's essay on John Millington Synge in *Our Irish Theatre*. And, turning to Synge himself, I found the following passage in his preface to *The Playboy of the Western World*: "In countries where the imagination of the people, and the language they use, is rich and living, it is possible for a writer to be rich and copious in his words, and at the same time to give the reality, which is the root of all poetry, in a comprehensive and natural form.... On the stage one must have reality, and one must have joy."

Laying aside the difference that Synge's "life among the people" was tragically shorter than Mr. Still's, it is useful to think of the several likenesses between these two lives and bodies of work. Both men went to live among the people they wrote about. In the work of both you feel, behind the presence of the writer, the presence of a solitary, endlessly patient listener and observer. And in both you apprehend an intense, uncompromising artistry. Neither of them offered as dialogue the raw chatter that writers use when they want to show off their provincial characters to urban readers. The language of each is in no sense merely "found," but is a splendid artifice. The dialect is not used for any form of display, but for what it lends of energy, particularity, metaphorical richness, wit, economy, and swiftness. Every speech reveals character and moves the story forward.

The energy and richness of Mr. Still's language permit him to enter right into the story with no more scene-setting and character description than if he were Shakespeare. By this language, in which the community speaks along with the individual, even a small girl or boy, speaking, is surrounded with a distinctive landscape and culture.

Mr. Still's stories give us the reality that Synge called for, and the joy as well, but they do not accomplish this, I think, by what is called realism. There is, of course, a difference between realism and what Synge called reality. Realism is the most fraudulent of literary illusions because it promotes in its theory the illusion that it is not an illusion. Reality in art is life made immediate to the imagination. Like Synge's plays, Mr. Still's stories feed on observation and hearsay, but they give us, not what has been seen and heard, but what has been imagined. The story set before us moves us because it is imaginable as lived life; its language is imaginable as spoken speech. We do not read as observers of putatively "real" events that have been observed, but rather as participants in events that have been so fully imagined that we too cannot help but imagine them.

Nothing that I have said takes away from the fact that these stories can be read as "a social diagram of a folk society such as hardly exists today," as Mr. Still himself once said. They are that — though I am more and more inclined to distrust the word *folk*. That we can learn from them about a society that no longer exists is a part of their value, as it is part of the value of Homer or Jane Austen. But it is also true that, as the writer of these stories, Mr. Still is never a collector or a researcher — not a sociologist or a folklorist or an anthropologist. We will continue to read them, and to want to read them, because they were written by a surpassing artist.

Of course, there is no way to separate the issue of language from the issue of subject. That Mr. Still's characters, who speak a dialect now hardly heard, are members of a society that now hardly exists may be one more reason why some readers would like to classify them as exhibits of "Americana" or "folklore." Mr. Still began to know these people in 1932 when their traditional ways were already under extreme pressure from the industrial economy imposed on their region by the coal companies. One of the themes of his work is the tension felt in families between the opposite pulls of their old agrarian life and their employment, however undependable, in the mines. The old life had not yet died; it was still present, still observable, its outline clarified perhaps by its passing away, and in some of his stories Mr. Still seems to be reaching toward it, attempting to see it whole in his imagination.

But, as with dialect, the critical question about "folk society" as a subject is not whether or not it is used but whether or not it is useful. What does it have to offer? To Mr. Still his experience of the doomed traditional society of the Kentucky mountains offered, I believe, not archaism but coherence, not Americana but a vision of life lived elementally. The coherence of culture provided for a coherence of character, perception, and event such as the world will not soon know again. A writer, writing about such a culture, is invited to see it whole, as it sees itself. He will see its tragedy and its comedy, its pathos, meanness, and cruelty, its kindness and its beauty; and he will see each of these without looking away from the others, compassionately and humorously.

It is tempting at this point to begin a description of the various stories, speaking of the delicacy of "Mrs. Razor," the pity and terror of "The Nest," the outright horror of "The Scrape," or the hilarity of "School Butter." But readers can read the stories, which is better than reading descriptions of them. I would like to speak instead of the instructiveness that arises from a certain difference between our own present society and that earlier "folk society such as hardly exists today." The difference is that certain matters that were merely private or communal in the old society have now become ferociously political.

Kentucky's one-room rural schools of the old days have always been held up as symbols of backwardness and deprivation. Yet I could not help but notice, in reading again Mr. Still's stories of mountain schools, how permeable was the boundary, for better and for worse, between community and school. The state educational bureaucracy was remote, and the school was the community's concern — two facts that are undoubtedly related. This is nowhere the point of Mr. Still's stories, but is observable in them.

And I could not help wondering what modern feminists and anti-feminists would make of "A Master Time," in which there is sexuality and sexual contention but no sexual politics. (When there is no thought of a "public" the private cannot become political.) An unnamed storyteller, evidently a bachelor and something of an outsider, is invited to a hog-killing that is also an all-day and overnight social event. The company is made up of six young married couples, the storyteller, and an ancient midwife, Aunt Besh Lipscomb. The work of the hog-killing is accomplished; there is a great deal of cooking and eating; the women laughing in the kitchen while the men eat; and there is — for the men — a churn of good whiskey in the smokehouse. Perhaps because of the whiskey, a little estrangement begins and grows between the husbands and the wives. It is carried on in jokes and laughter, but it is there, it is finally strong, and it is resolved deliciously, and convincingly too, in a snowball fight! This is very much a story of individual people, but it is also a ritual drama in which the community first expresses and then dissipates an old discord that it knows will go on interminably. There is a residual bitterness in Aunt Besh, whose trade, after all, has been childbirth and suffering, and who is partial both to the young wives and to the whiskey. "Kill 'em," she cries to the women during the snowball fight. And, at the end, finding that the churn is empty, she says, "I'll endure." So must the young couples, and bitterness will not help them much. That is why their reconciliation has an emotional charge that carries us far beyond the hilarity of its means.

This story seems to me almost a miracle. It is absolutely lovely, quick and alight with shifting tones. It is a little globe, a world called into existence, reality and joy, by a master workman.

# Quality of Life, Quality of Art

## Jane Mayhall

From a certain point of view, James Still, Alabama born, Kentucky endowed, is a very lucky man. For some fifty years, his life as a novelist and poet has been almost or entirely separate from the literary rat race. Apologists for the belief that art must ply the mercenary would be amazed at the Still position. For a bucket of reasons, he has been able to elude the machinations of the popularity market (and with neither a covert eye on trends, nor virtuous renunciation of them).

Though the credentials are innumerable, and the dazzlement of a lifetime in endless supply, his prominence to date is modest: appearance on PBS, sharing platforms with distinguished names, local awards, celebrations among state leaders and university presidents, and a sprinkling of bluegrass singers.

His national reputation is not extensive. Certain documentary films noting his achievements have touched university towns and New York City educational TV circuits. Parenthetically, Still was appointed Poet Laureate of Kentucky in 1995 (the term ran out in 1997)—an honor, he might say, more civic than glamorous.

Actually, James Still never aspired to go unnoticed. His aims are broad, and he knows whereof he speaks. At age 91, he has the same neat candor as always. Writing of the late 1940s and into the 1980s, he commented: "Although my stories and poems were appearing in *The Atlantic, The Yale Review, The Virginia Quarterly,* I had three published books, I do not recall encountering anybody who'd read them." And, "Whether this is good or bad, I cannot say."

Still resists the codification. He's a maverick, but not an outsider; original, but not eccentric. It would take an inkblot test of one's own literary accounting to say where he does, or doesn't fit. To extract a chronology from his life would be like trying to disentangle a precious metal from its source—to be sure, to be used for a different purpose. Still never tries to force the accuracy of his material into a specified time frame.

This is particularly true of *The Wolfpen Notebooks* (the University Press of Kentucky, 1991), a volume of sayings from his backwoods neighbors that Still collected over the years. The personal interview that goes with it has a bearing, Still talking off the cuff. Incidentally, the reminiscences are offered to a group of high school students from Rabun County,

*Mayhall, Jane. "James Still: Quality of Life, Quality of Art." Shenandoah: The Washington and Lee University Review. 48.2 (Summer 1998): 56–73. Reprinted with permission.*

Georgia, and they display great enthusiasm for the man and his attitudes. At the core is the educational experience. Still's memories flow in a clear progression: early forebears, childhood, places, travel; and all interconnected, future, past, present, all are (as it were) the roots of some ever-enlarging universe.

Still says in this interview: "When I was a child, we were told that if we looked into the water well we might see ourselves in our coffins. Thus I dare not peer too closely into the well of creativity. The true how and why. It might desert me. The best I can offer is a personal observation. I write best when I've achieved a state of free association."

The ramifications are private, free choice. In Still there are few calendar dates; and no in-beat historic obligations for the author to lean on. The essence of his art is that of total immersion, into the actual physicality of human experience. In character and dialogue there are seeming irrationalities and gaps, depths of hidden meanings. As Tolstoy said, few people talk in straight educated sentences. But Still (like Tolstoy) gives the effect of everyday, recognizable speech. The examples I'll come to shortly.

I first met James Still at Yaddo in the early 1950s, when we were both writers-in-residence. It was only at his leave-taking that it clicked who he was. I had offered to drive him to the Saratoga train station, a story by itself. Yaddo is a retreat for artists (in upper New York state) and at the time, grateful for a workplace oasis, one scarcely kept track of fellow occupants. I hadn't identified James Still until in the car. Coincidentally, some years before, Delmore Schwartz had recommended Still's work to me. Schwartz (still in the flowering of his own talent) had said: "This man has something special."

Still's novel *River of Earth* made an impact. Though not until years after did I catch its brilliance. I was pleased to talk with Still. Gingerly, I mentioned that I was from Kentucky also, and we fell into an animated exchange. It wasn't patriotism but (on my part) a genuine relief to be talking to someone who *knew*. And Still had known personally Elizabeth Madox Roberts and Marjorie Kinnan Rawlings, writers who had opened doors for me, as well as the legendary Allen Tate and Caroline Gordon. Conversation moved on to Chekhov, Flaubert; nobody looked at a watch. Still almost missed the train.

I didn't hear from him for years. Then he wrote a letter to say that he was recommending me for a summer teaching job in Appalachia, where he lived. This was after I had published a novel, and had been teaching in New York City. I don't know if I had made the grade (I felt that Still was far above me), but it seemed at our first meeting I had the right trappings. Not inverse snobbery, but that day in Saratoga Springs, the car I had been driving (it belonged to my husband) had been among the last of the four-cylinder 1939 Fords. Second-hand, reliable, unpretentious. Or maybe he wasn't impressed; it was hard to tell what was his yardstick.

Much of Still's fiction takes place during the American Depression: remote lives, dirt farming, coal mine struggles. Bare Appalachia, at the period of economic breakdown, in the hills of eastern Kentucky, represents the dramatic substratum. What is inherently sophisticated is that James Still doesn't apply any social theory. The human perspective evokes the larger questions.

His first novel, *River of Earth,* came out at nearly the same time as John Steinbeck's *The Grapes of Wrath*: 1940. Both were published by Viking. The subjects appear to be similar, a working class family victimized by economic powers beyond them. The Steinbeck characters are Okie immigrants, going west to California. Still's people are confined to Kentucky.

Some critics contend that *The Grapes of Wrath,* though highly successful, is not and was never up to the standards of *River of Earth*. At the time, Alexander Woollcott called *The Grapes of Wrath* "the great American novel," and it was featured throughout the country in every bookstore. Prior to publication, Steinbeck's editor, Pascal Covici, spent $10,000 on pre-publicity and Viking did an initial run of 50,000 copies. With the bolstering of numerous translations and widespread publicity, including the Henry Fonda movie, it was an acclaimed moneymaker. In 1962, Steinbeck won the Nobel Prize for Literature. *The Grapes of Wrath* is still in print.

Still's book was on another rung. It was championed and supported by Katherine Anne Porter, Carson McCullers, Eudora Welty, and Robert Frost — writers whose voices were not yet in the mainstream. In a recent issue of the *Journal of Appalachian Studies*, Ted Olson puts forth a fiery but reasoned analysis that says the Still novel is far superior to *The Grapes of Wrath*. He accuses Steinbeck's novel of being laced with stereotypes and journalistic commentary.

The book's topicality would make an essay by itself. But it has little to do with the Still vernacular, or his concerns. One can imagine in 1997 a New York TV "literary" panel, where money and ratings would hold the stage.

The above details are from an introduction by Robert DeMott to the current paperback reissue of *The Grapes of Wrath*. No moral issue to be drawn. But in DeMott's sympathetic appraisal of Steinbeck, who was a skilled and prolific writer, in alluding to other Steinbeck works, there are detected uneasy qualms of guilt.

Steinbeck worried about his own method, and he spoke of another of his own books as a "vulgar tract" and said, "It's bad because it isn't honest." This reveals an underside. Steinbeck's method involved having to flesh out his main characters, to a large extent, by field trips and research. The unsaid part is that he had not lived their lives.

Still comes directly from what he writes about. One is tempted to pull in contemporary definition, to illustrate the differences between the two writers. The analogy would be: James Still as "hermeneut" — in Greek mythology, from Hermes, messenger of the gods (truth) and bearing witness to that authority. And Steinbeck in the stance of "exegete," searching for his reality in the truth of others. Nobody has to take sides. Steinbeck's expository style, less personally implicated than Still's, nevertheless had its effect. Due to *The Grapes of Wrath*, the labor laws were changed in California. Propaganda worked, and for a high cause.

In James Still's work, there's a psychological layering and care in language akin to James Joyce's *Dubliners*. The failure of Still's book can't be laid at the door of good writing, if this may have been a factor, but critics have discerned that the fault came from the general public, and its wrong expectations. The Still novel was lumped into mistaken categories, including the world of Jesse Stuart and Erskine Caldwell, both decent but basically orthodox writers.

James Still deflects anticipation, and the way he does it is not always immediately apparent. In regard to him, we can evoke the typical American image. But Still's background isn't simple, and divergent elements don't add up. In *The Wolfpen Notebooks*, he tells us that he was born a short distance from Lafayette, Alabama, on Double Branch Farm in 1906. The household was almost devoid of cultural objects. His curiosity was omnivorous, boredom was no problem. His father was a self-taught veterinarian, dirt farmer, Jack of all trades.

The three books in the Still house were (after The Holy Bible) *The Anatomy of the Horse*, *Palaces of Sin*, and *The Cyclopedia of Universal Knowledge*, a short catechism of science and literature. A tongue-in-cheek truth hangs about the Still report. When quite young, he latched onto, and memorized, Keats and Byron. Why did he do that?

His upbringing was stoic, rooted in English and Scots-Irish tradition. In another mini-autobiography (*Biography of Contemporary Authors*, 1993), there's a large backdrop of ancient relatives, neighbors, and at times an almost aphoristic reconstruction of place and event. His life is remarkable in its utter lack of privilege. Difficulty was regarded as run-of-the-day. Still records with zest the experience of cotton picking at the age of twelve — he packed a "hundred pounds a day." As deftly, he catches the quality of his mother, a diminutive pioneer who, when the reader thinks of it, weighed less than the cotton he picked, ninety-three pounds. But she was a "hardy worker," cook, canner, bottler, who also "joined the men" to work in the fields.

The family was constantly moving. Poverty mixed with antebellum (Grandma's flower beds, "the buckets of water thrown on the cape jasmine on summer nights to enliven the fragrance") garnered with memories, recounted in a manner both obsessive and intelligent. At a certain period, the Stills are living in a neighborhood where the grandfather of Woodrow Wilson taught weekdays at the Presbyterian Church. Still is as well aware that the grandfather of Joe Louis, the boxer, lived in the same area not far away.

A stringent note of evaluation touches whatever he means to say. When James Still was in the ninth grade, his first poem, published in *Boy's Life*, was entitled "A Burned Tree Speaks."

In the life, as in the art, one can make a zillion inferences. Still was one of ten children, eight of whom survived. He is the only writer among them. The odyssey of intellectual development holds the same lone-rider paradox. It appears that Still was always on good terms with family; he didn't fight them or succumb. Likewise, in his formative years, he was deeply affected by friends and associates. But he was never psychologically swept away by them.

All evidences (in the Still telling) run together, and he literally shies away from giving moral credence to any one event. For instance, his receiving a scholarship from Vanderbilt University must have been a cultural turning point. The emotional currents were strong, and the surroundings likely were ultra-dynamic. For a poor boy, education was a battle. As a student (preceding Vanderbilt) at Lincoln Memorial University, he had literally starved. During the Depression, Still remembers himself and other students being glad to have "free walnuts and apples" from the trees.

In conversation, though he's more coolly objective when he writes, Still doesn't hold back on names and simple gratitude. Loyalties for Vanderbilt faculty and fellow students are clear fact. And the participatory warmth of being in the company of John Crowe Ransom, Andrew Lytle, Allen Tate — there is an educational emphasis amounting to renaissance. These were (to refresh the reader's backlog) among the originators and members of the Southern agrarian movement of the late 1920s and 30s — and oversoul of the earlier Fugitives. Ransom, particularly dominant, imbued students with interest in contemporary poetry, including T.S. Eliot, and inaugurated a "method of close reading of poetic texts."

All water under the bridge. For Still, at the time, the interplay of literary influences was compost for his talent. Though his response was more solitary than of the classroom. He was no doubt affected by the critical ideas on literature, and the agrarian sway, but he never officially joined the movement. In terms of agrarian influence, worth noting is a study made by H.R. Stonebeck (*Kentucky Review*, 1990) in which he points out that "Still's version of agrarianism, clearly, is not a call to political action, not a symbolic stance from which to go forth into the world of letters and peripatetic academic career, as it was for so many other agrarians. It is a design for living. It need not be insisted that this is a deliberate position, a conscious stand-taking for Still."

Put delicately, James Still is more a doer than a joiner. The conscious "stand-taking" runs through a lifetime. As part of the student movement, for instance, at Lincoln Memorial University, Still delivered food and supplies to the coal fields and miners' families, putting his life at risk. But he never officially became a member of any union.

The same goes for his odd, academic biographical zig-zag. Still was a fine teacher, and to be sure was prepared (had earned several diplomas from institutions), but this was not his preference or calling. Incidentally, due to the Depression, Still went into a series of poorly paid and definitely non-teaching jobs. Needless to say, a renegade richness abounds. He tried the C.C.C. and didn't get in, rode the rails and hitched rides, attempted selling Bibles, picked cotton in Texas. In a way, it was a writer's freedom. Eventually he landed in a significant niche, or a place that could satisfy a first-rate mind, and the independent sensibility of his lifework. Still took on the librarianship at Hindman Settlement School, in Knott County, Kentucky, and he admitted to the sense of home. He had been employed in the capacity of librarian, off and on, since 1931. But this was a decision. The first three years, no salary. But as the Depression let up, he was paid a few dollars: "I had worked six years for six cents a day."

He liked the library, and savored the kind of school that Hindman was. "The students eager," he said, "the staff motivated." To leap over the multifarious, one may (in the case of Still) observe the positive underlay. First, a quick picture of Hindman that scarcely does it justice. The Hindman Settlement School is one of those seminal places in Kentucky that grew out of selflessness and work. An eastern Kentucky mountain school founded in 1902 by two Kentucky women who were graduates of Wellesley, it was an institution "begun in a tent" and gradually turned into eight buildings. It came out of a village of "two hundred souls."

No fairy tale lore involved. Among those aware of the educational possibilities was a man named Don West, a classmate of Still's at Vanderbilt. It was West who introduced Still to Hindman and helped him get a job there. Interestingly, West himself went off later to found the Highlander Folk School, "where they trained blacks and whites in social awareness and union organizing." Never to press a moral point, James Still notes, as if fleetingly, that two of the Highlander students were Martin Luther King, Jr., and Rosa Parks.

At Hindman, the literary output cohered with daily rounds. Still was finishing his novel, and in 1937 Viking published a collection of his poems, *Hounds on the Mountain*. Still's poetry, then and now, is lyrical and unmired by cliché. In the early poem "Pattern for Death," his word choices, "The crane-fly / quivers its body," and the unadorned lines at the end, "Who reads the language of direction?" suggest what Robert Frost saw in his novel: a modernity, enhanced by the sensitive feel of tradition.

Still's new home was a two-story log house, built in 1837. It was on the outskirts of town, and hadn't been lived in for years: "Once a farm, now long fallow"; the road was a creek-bed. Long after Still fixed it up — electricity, improvements on the outhouse (though it remained quite rustic, with vines over the door), flowering gardens, and a path — I was invited in the 1950s for a visit during my summer Kentucky teaching job at Morehead State (that Still had arranged). Incidentally, the Morehead staff was by no means "countrified," and students were not simply passive vessels. This was true of the other summer writing classes at Kentucky schools that Still was connected with, including Alice Lloyd College and, of course, Hindman. At one of them, I gave an assignment of the William Carlos Williams short story "The Use of Force," and the response was electrifying. Literature moved on the same track as daily life. From Morehead, I spent a couple of nights at Still's house, not far away. In the mornings, I awakened to a lovely phenomenon. The wide chinks between the ancient logs allowed hits of blue sky and young tree branches to straggle through.

Still had a feeling for the Knott County people, but initially he must have seemed to them an oddball. During the first years, after he had moved to his log house, he slept on an army cot and cooked on a two-burner stove. His work-table was two stacked steamer trunks, supporting a portable typewriter. When a neighbor asked who James Still was, the reply came from another neighbor, "We don't know yet. A man person. We call him the Man-in-the-bushes."

He formed friendships with Hindman townsfolk, farmers, dulcimer makers, coal miners, blacksmiths and, after Still began to teach regularly at the Settlement School, with the faculty members there. He raised his own produce: beans, potatoes, turnips, squash, tomatoes. In the range of experience, there is apparently no cleavage between Still's semi-illiterate childhood and the educated adult.

The same double-perspective can be found in the Still development. He made use of what was offered. For instance, while a student at Lincoln Memorial, he had the job of night janitor at the University library, and, after cleaning up, he would fall asleep on a pile of newspapers and awaken in the middle of the night to read Thomas Hardy, Joseph Conrad, Jane Austen, Balzac. Nobody told him to. The regrouping of his intellectual habits seemed undetermined.

Still had no objection to being called "hillbilly." He said, "I count it as an honor, except when used as a slur." At the same time, Vanderbilt appears to have never vanished as a part of his life. The highly polished curriculum studies of T.S. Eliot and I.A. Richards have the same instantaneous currency in his thinking as the planting of vegetables and clearing the land. Still places himself directly in the experience. In conversation, his brief references to serving in the military are vivid and alive. He was with the U.S. Army Air Force in Africa and the Middle East, from 1941 to 1945. Equally vital in speaking of his numerous travels to the Yucatan, Guatemala, South America, as well as Europe, he displays a levity and absorption as if it were happening today. Any chronological design is, if not avoided, of small significance. The date is less important than the human contact.

Still's fiction evokes this sense of timelessness. The grandmother in *River of Earth* imprints on the "present" a layered reality. Speaking of the murder of her husband in the prime of his life, she is equally at one with the white cotton shirt he was wearing, as with the incident and the meaningless psychology of the killers. We are there. And as quickly we are moved into her recollections of her own father, and an applewood button box he whittled and then to the "latch-pins in it. This pure silver thimble, it was fotched across the waters by my gran. Fotched o'er from England in the ol' times." The effect is almost impressionistic. The many ribbons of thought are never didactically articulated, but run seamlessly from one chapter to the next.

Somewhere, James Still writes that he never thought of *River of Earth* as necessarily being a novel. He could think of it as a series of short stories or scenes. Parts did appear in magazines—*The Atlantic, Harper's*—and each seems sufficiently rounded. And yet, the secret flow of the whole book is uppermost. Like Dostoyevsky's *The Brothers Karamazov*, there is a certain haunting connectiveness, an attitude, that draws chapters into focus.

In his 1978 introduction to *River of Earth* (republished by the University Press of Kentucky), Dean Cadle clicks into what he calls the Still manner: "unposed, and with the perception and restraint that denotes an imagination as honest and controlled as the needle of a compass." The feat of the paradox is the "honesty" with "control." This conjunction is no more neatly performed than on the first page, first chapter, of *River of Earth*. The protagonist is a seven-year-old boy, beginning the tale simply. But the first paragraph is already rich with language color, naturalness of speech, and (in terms of plot) fact and direction.

> The mines on Little Carr closed in March. Winter had been mild, the snows scant and frost-thin upon the ground. Robins stayed the season through, and sapsuckers came early to drill the black birch beside our house. Though father had worked in the mines, we did not live in the camps. He owned the scrap of land our house stood upon, a garden patch, and the black birch that was the only tree on all the barren slope above Blackjack. There were three of us children running barefoot over the puncheon floors, and since the beginning Mother carried a fourth balanced on one hip as she worked over the rusty stove in the shed-room.

In the complex drama the heroic and complex Mother character burns down the house to rid the family of two parasitic relatives—in the short space of the next ten pages! But it must be said that anything of a shock in the Still theatrics is very much distilled in truth, and not for random entertainment. The larger conflict in the novel is between the poor family and the mine owners. This creates a fugal contrast with the sparring that goes on inside the family itself. These are alternately surrounded by the forces of ignorance, education, defeat, cynicism, and the contrapuntal dramas and the consciousness of generation. And not to be overlooked, also, is the enormous cloud of coming industrialism that hangs over the rural Appalachian hills.

In a way, the Still chapters are stories unto themselves. One of the most telling occurs in the middle of the book. This would appear to be a simple descriptive section about a boy learning to plow. Actually, though he is only seven, it's a life-changing event. The narrator (the boy), the soul of insight and reservation, is, in conquering the plow, learning to be a man.

This chapter must be cited because of its inherent style, an interweaving of physical experience, nearly too deep for words. But how Still brings it through, to the accompaniment of folk idiom, almost raucous humor, plowing technique and poetic sensuality of being among furrows, is a gratifying outlay. Uncle Jolly, who is teaching the boy, is an exaggerated rhapsodic mountain type but interestingly so, and he sounds forth with the cryptic in-betweens like "what's folks going to live on when these hills wear down to a nub?" And the mule, pulling the plow, is traditionally stubborn, but has a personality of his own: "The mule didn't budge. He lifted his ears and looked back at me, sly and stubborn." But the crest of sensibility is in the boy's relatedness:

> The earth parted; it fell back from the shovel plow; it boiled over the share. I walked the fresh furrow and balls of dirt welled between my toes. There was a smell of old mosses, of bruised sassafras roots, of ground new-turned. We broke three furrows. Then Uncle Jolly stood aside and let me hold the handles. I felt the earth flowing, steady as time.

But the confirmation doesn't close with poetics. Following in the rest of the chapter are high jinks and colorful interchange. Doubt and frustration are the rule, delicate comedy. The boy falls down after the fifth row and Uncle Jolly goes into a fit of laughter, all wittily dramatized. But a *pièce de résistance* at the chapter's very end is what puts Still's work at its conscious effectiveness; that can't just be a lucky strike. As happens in Still's fiction, one can read in a superficial remark a double-entendre. Here is the same vitality, with Uncle Jolly's sniggering, and the narrator watching. And seeing what is happening: "... and I saw a fresh throe boiling inside of him, ready to burst. The mule raised his head suddenly. He licked his yellow tongue square across Uncle Jolly's mouth."

The act of the mule could be either affectionate, or an attempt to shut Uncle Jolly up. But more than that is the somehow corrosive delight of the "yellow tongue" itself and the sensuous "licking." And the final coup is the boy's comment; down to earth or mysterious, but definitely worldly: "'I bet there's a wild enough taste,' I said scornfully."

Here Still may be providing a whammy of a three-fold meaning. And only the discerning reader might get it. Clearly, there is lodged throughout his prose unexpected turns of ideas. The wild taste could be associated with nature, or nature's affront, and the boy's sense of new-found confidence, at learning to plow, that can give him both the "scorn" and enormous humor; it is Uncle Jolly (and not himself) who got licked by the mule.

As artist, James Still has been called a master storyteller, wit, Appalachian classicist, an American Chekhov, as well as the warmly evocative hermit craftsman — while, I will add, the babble of commerce tumbles in cities afar. The latter has been my feeling about Still's work over the years. In everything he writes, there is unique tone and voice. The speech is generally Kentucky dialect. But in little asides, there is an unusual flavor that doesn't belong to the stereotype.

Cleanth Brooks thought the magic resided in the language. In his introduction to Still's story collection *The Run for the Elbertas* (1980), Brooks held that the culture, though primitive, is not "brutish." And that the patterns of so-called common speech, in prose and dialogue, were moving from a culture and history that stemmed from the English poets, Anglo-Saxon form (with a whiff of Scottish), and might be traced to antiquity.

Not that Still paused, while writing, to pick up so many forerunner ancillaries. But it can be suggested that he caught in characters, and in his Kentucky experience, a thread of language that connected with earlier times. From them, he was able to gather a broader nuance than just "folk." William Faulkner, Eudora Welty, and Flannery O'Connor are brilliant wielders of the colloquial, though (with even all the riches of portrayal) the use they make of it is mainly to advance the plot.

In the James Still anthology pieces such as "Locust Summer," "I Love My Rooster," or "The Stir Off," the very words that he employs serve not only as instruments, but also take on the same importance as the human actors and their plight. It's a sort of balancing. Experimental poets write this way, and in the current scene (and in some current novels) the hodge-podge of sound and rhythm becomes the abstracted message. In Still it's not abstract. And there's a secure hold on realism.

Nevertheless, one may say that in many of the stories there is a light peppering of the lyric, flickers of old speech, turns of phrase that seem to offer a recognition concerning the *nature* of communication. In the case of James Still, it's a sense of what Wallace Stevens meant when he said, "Every word was once a poem."

This is often demonstrated by what Brooks refers to as the James Still use of "compound terms." These are mixes like "gamble-cards," "lie-tales," or "sun-ball." Interestingly, current black language has that kind of vigor, street talk, the spontaneous compression. Anyway, in Still's work there is a kind of "Shakespearian" excess. Artistically speaking, it's an overcharge that points to not just the telling of the tale, but to some empathic exuberance (like the love of music) for speech itself.

A good example of the verbal enthusiasm appears in the story "On Quicksand Creek," though, to be sure, Still keeps it to a discreet sort of running, spikey music. The plot involves a young boy in cold weather, on his first day of cattle driving. All, the animals, nature, the environment, have separate identities. The language is taciturn, but appealing to the auditory senses:

> I set off behind the yearlings with daylight breaking, and before the sun-ball rose I had reached the mouth of Shoal Creek and turned down Troublesome. The yearlings pitted the mud banks with their hooves, and I sank to the tongues of my brogans. My coffee-sack leggings were splattered; my feet got stone cold. A wintry draft blew, smelling of sap.
>
> The sun-ball rolled up a hill, warming the air, loosening the mud. The yearlings nearly ran my leg bones off. I cut switches keen to whistling; I herded the day long, knew then how it was to be a cattleman.

The mood is accurate, a country life. But one can't help being aware of the isolate beauty of the language.

Still's fiction is filled with moments of high drama, cruelty, and death. Evil appears in its embryonic stage. A most chilling example of violence is the story "A Ride on Short Dog." An ordinary bus-ride journeys into fear and claustrophobic nightmare. It ends in the inadvertent murder of a sadistic bully, who has been torturing, by psychological abuse and physical assault, several of the bus occupants. The voice of the author maintains the poise of acceptance. Still never steps out of objectivity. Events are horrific. Of the dying monster: "he slumped and his gullet rattled," funny, but not funny. Head-on ugly. The crisp, everyday telling stirs the reader more than exaggeration could do.

Minimalist technique has cropped up all over the place in the last twenty years. Sherwood Anderson cleared the way for Raymond Carver. Gertrude Stein and Hemingway were shaped into Ann Beattie: imitators have increased along with university workshops. But in 1945, Still was already practicing his undercut abbreviations. When a passenger asks about the dead man, "What's wrong with him?" the man across the aisle says numbly, "He's doing no good." Economic, fatalistic.

When such understatement is applied to an intimate circumstance, as to the death of the much-loved grandmother (at the near end *of River of Earth*), the emotions are immense. Cold facts make the poignance:

> Uncle Jolly ran fingers along the coffin lid. The rio lamp shone fully upon it from the mantel, and the lamp fry and clock tick pitted the air. On the walnut sides of the box there was not a single grain bur. A good sawyer had built it. The box lid was raised an inch. I dreaded to look, though Fletch stood close and unafraid, and I believed he did not know Grandma was inside. Uncle Jolly balanced the lid on the joints of his fingers. "Want these chaps to see now?"

The reductive is one of Still's best tools. Nowhere does he give a formula for writing. The closest he comes is in the issue of *Foxfire* (1988) when he meditates on poetry. "We do know that in writing there are a host of things to do at once. All that you can know and are and can be come together and is concentrated on a single point, like a glass drawing fire from the sun." If this sounds like enigma, there is science to it also.

Wendell Berry, the Kentucky poet and novelist, has given a fine secularity to the Still mode of composition. In an address at Chattanooga, Tennessee, in 1997, when James Still received the Special Achievement Award from the Fellowship of Southern Writers, Berry brought to the occasion a decided relevance, emphasizing the degree of hard work, and the mystery of the talent. Incidentally, Still received the award in absentia (due to a temporary illness), but he had some photocopies made of the speech, and I'm lucky enough to have one. A model of observation, Berry goes to the heart of the discipline, and having met Still when he (Berry) was young, and since then always had in mind, "and particularly as I have read and re-read James Still, that quick-caught imaginary glimpse of a man quietly serious rising early and sitting down to work in the dark of the morning." And going on to the essences: "I know that he was imagining something and putting it down so skillfully in words that whoever read them could not help but imagine the same thing; I know that to do this, he was employing talent, perception, and art, and was probably ignoring or forgetting the issue of publication." And Berry recounts two elements in Still's writing, the first, the mystery: "I really don't know how he has done what he has done, and finally I must understand his work just by admiring it." And secondly, the sensitive relation of the author to his subject (and one can go off on a slew of importances, having to do with specific historical "writer attitudes" in fashion, both yesterday and today). To quote Berry: "Because, perhaps, of its artistic integrity this body of work [he's speaking of the short stories here] never exploits or condescends to its subject, a region that has been condescended to and exploited almost by convention."

Whether we agree or not, there is something to the school of opinion that Still, in his way of life and work, has set off. In the case of Wendell Berry, himself a modest and powerful writer, one has the example of a career that has been kept out of the best-seller deliriums, though his novels and poems are well-published and enjoy a serious following. As a full-time farmer, like Still, and with the same anonymity and dedicated hours of writing as touchstone, Berry's life itself is special. The same can he said of other younger Southern authors in their prime, like Fred Chappell and Chris Offutt, to name a couple.

It has been said that the characters James Still wrote about and the readers who might want to read them no longer exist. The question is moot. Or rather, it's a lining up of beliefs on what constitutes "American" life. We can look back to book reviews, say, in the Sunday *New York Times* of eighty or ninety years ago, and few of the literary adulations would suggest a quality winnowing. This, of course, doesn't exclude the bad press received by some of the best of the then-modernist and experimental ground-breakers. But selectivity in reading, as well as moral personal behavior, have never been really predictable. Nobody has to read pulp fiction, even if it is in vogue.

The lean toward vulgarity and emptiness (and, appreciably, cult "newness") is a matter of choice, like everything else. In a marvelous little story, "Journey to the Forks," Still presents the best ironic defense of ignorance I've ever come across. It's delivered by a teen-age illiterate, trying to persuade two younger boys that education is against God and nature. The older advocate against learning (appropriately named Cain) says he'd "let nothing but truth git through my skull." He figures "the Lord put our brains in a bone box to sort o' keep the devilment out." These ideas hit home, and could be turned into a present day fanatic's discourse on the preservation of stupidity and blind instinct. We are not as safe from simple-minded self-justification as supposed.

Equally, let TV rant and non-books count their winnings. Latent in James Still's work is a kind of stimuli that has nothing to do with selling. Whatever the underpinnings, his writings are shamelessly devoid of hype. I think that James Joyce (when he could bear to read anybody else) and the odd-ball early Knut Hamsun (ultimately no angel, but of initial humanistic impulse) and the early Tolstoy and that esthete-moralist Baudelaire would all have given hearty reception to any of the James Still stories.

Not that anybody has any proof. But certain facts, and almost non-definable depths of affinities, have a place of working value. On the other hand, no deterministic big deal — but a sort of camaraderie of excellence. But as James Still would say, one of his favorite comments: "No matter." A moving on to other items, or no explanation need be.

# A Man of the World

## HAL CROWTHER

James Still was the last — and least known — of America's "Greatest Generation" of writers.

> The earth shall rise up where he lies
> With steady reach, and permanent.
> A shroud of cedars be his mound
> This shield of hills his monument.
> —"Shield of Hills," James Still [1906–2001]

In a country tribute to James Still's longevity, one of his neighbors told him, "You're the last possum up the tree." The last of his generation in Knott County, Kentucky, the neighbor meant to say. But Still, who died in April [2001], a few weeks short of his ninety-fifth birthday, was also the last of the undisputed "Greatest Generation" of American writers. William Faulkner, Ernest Hemingway, Robert Penn Warren, Thomas Wolfe, F. Scott Fitzgerald, Thornton Wilder, John Dos Passos, Allen Tate, and John Steinbeck were all born within a single decade at the turn of the last century, and it was their fiction and poetry that introduced most of the world's readers to the riches of American literature.

Still, born in 1906, was the youngest of these giants and the least celebrated. There are respectable readers, even English teachers, who fail to recognize his name. In contrast with ceremonies for the great Eudora Welty, mourned like an empress this past summer by Mississippi and the literate world, Still's wake was an Appalachian family affair. His limited renown, his admirers argue, was due entirely to regional prejudice and Still's reluctance to practice our culture-defining art of self-promotion.

"I think that up there in Knott County, well off the main track of the literary world, Still became a nearly perfect writer," wrote Wendell Berry. "His stories consist of one flawless sentence after another." Such reckless praise invites a closer reading of the venerable Sage of Hindman. Take the time. Though Still outlived all the rest, he was not prolific; his pursuit was perfection, not saturation. If you read the classic Appalachian novel *River of Earth* (1940), the new collected poems *From the Mountain, From the Valley* (2001), and the story collection *Pattern of a Man* (1977), you haven't covered James Still by a long shot, but you've measured him fairly. If you're not impressed — if you're new to Still and you're not astonished — then possibly literature isn't your strong suit after all.

Acclaim has not been stingy. The poet Delmore Schwartz, hardly an Appalachian partisan,

*Crowther, Hal. "A Man of the World." The Oxford American (Fall 2001): 11–13. Reprinted with permission.*

once called *River of Earth* "a symphony" and wrote of Still, "This man has something special." For his humanity and the psychological subtlety of his fiction, Still was described as an Appalachian Chekhov; for his populist humor with its marbling of black irony, he was compared with Mark Twain; in his fierce hermit's independence and minute observation of the natural world, he reminded readers of Henry David Thoreau. Stories like "Mrs. Razor," "Maybird Upshaw," and "A Master Time" are tone-perfect, simultaneously heart-vexing and hysterical, and so finely crafted that Berry rightly describes one as "almost a miracle." They'd have dazzled Twain or even the author of *Dubliners*.

Still's loyalty to the native dialect of eastern Kentucky made him a hero in Appalachia but may have cost him the international reputation he deserved. His characters speak as their models spoke, in the vernacular of his neighbors on Troublesome Creek before the Second World War. To jaded urban ears a story in any regional dialect sounds like folklore, and critics and publishers are among the most jaded of urban animals. ("Thus an incoherent culture condescends to a coherent one," as Berry laments.)

Still himself once conceded that his stories are "a social diagram of folk society such as hardly exists today." But *Moby-Dick* is no less powerful because summer celebrities have replaced Nantucket whalers. *War and Peace* loses nothing human because Pierre's lost society of aristocrats lies buried under centuries of social upheaval and disaster. No "true" story crafted by a writer of genius ever becomes archaic.

James Still, a subsistence homesteader in a time before paved roads, a man who favored overalls and straw hats, denied that the label *hillbilly* ever bothered him: "I count it as an honor, except when used as a slur." But before he settled in Knott County, the Alabama native earned three university degrees, including a master's in English from Vanderbilt, where he was a contemporary of the famous Fugitive poets. Among his countless prizes and distinctions were two Guggenheim Fellowships; as a young man he summered at the Yaddo and MacDowell writers' colonies with most of the literary lions of his day. By standards far more cosmopolitan than Knott County's, he was a man of the world — a traveler who had visited twenty-six countries and made fourteen trips to Central America to study Mayan culture.

Yet for most of seventy years you could find him in Hindman. When an artist of Still's stature lives so long in a place so remote, he begins to draw pilgrims and generate myths, some of a quasi-saintly nature, like the story of the suit coat he left hanging on a bush for months because he refused to disturb a bird who built a nest in its sleeve.

Still loved the birds and beasts. But he was no St. Francis, no beaming, haloed presence. He was proud, private, sometimes a little prickly. He could be flattered, but he wasn't one to roll over and wag his tail every time someone gushed, "I *love* your work." He could be distant, even impatient, with academics, poetasters, and literary day-trippers. He preferred the company of children, animals, and poets—creatures without agendas, without *careers*.

"I've often remarked that he would be happy if there were only children in the world," said his friend Mike Mullins, director of the Hindman Settlement School, where Still had served as genius loci since 1932.

"He's very innocent in a certain way," wrote my wife, Lee Smith, with whom Still loved to flirt. "I don't mean to say he's childish. But there's a freshness and originality of language that I think is childlike. He has access to that part of himself that most of us have lost."

Not surprisingly, the narrator of *River of Earth* is a seven-year-old boy. At Still's funeral one speaker revealed that "my dog Jack," immortalized in the poem "Those I Want in Heaven with Me Should There Be Such a Place," was a dog the poet's father had given away when Still was seven years old — a wound he nursed for most of a century.

In his seventies, Still began to write for children, retelling — inimitably — Mother Goose rhymes and the "Jack" tales of Appalachian storytellers. When someone asked him why "the Dean of Appalachian Literature" was fooling with nursery rhymes, Still replied, "I've been foolish the whole time." At the same time, he was consuming literary magazines and journals; if you doubted that he kept abreast of the latest trends in fiction and poetry, he was always poised to set you straight.

Hillbilly intellectual, log cabin hermit with a thousand luggage stickers, the oldest possum with the youngest heart — James Still sounds like a walking circus of contradictions. But contradictions trouble people who live and think inside the box; if Still ever knew the box existed, he never let on.

Conventional souls, often envious, call a man like James Still "a character." He wasn't an eccentric so much as a natural man who found a sanctuary where his idiosyncrasies were indulged. In Kentucky, his world was subdivided by creeks and ridges, and among them he found all that he ever needed to write about. Despite his travels, there seems to be only one published piece — a poem set in Belize on one of Still's Mayan expeditions — that didn't find its inspiration in Knott County.

At his memorial service in Hindman, one speaker after another tried to express how entertaining it was to know Mr. Still. (You called him "Mr." Still unless you were a writer he admired, a woman he fancied, or his rare equal in years — a "Brother to Methuselum" like ancient Uncle Mize in one of his best stories.) They labored to capture his grand sense of mis-

In 2003, the section of Kentucky Route 160 stretching from the Hindman Settlement School to the intersection of Route 160 with Kentucky Route 15 at Carr Fork Lake was officially named James Still Highway, in commemoration of the author's life and work. James Still traveled this same stretch of road regularly (photograph by Ted Olson).

chief—his dark, deep-set eyes fairly glittered with it, right up to the end. They remembered him stretched out snoring on the reading table in the library, and his delight in smuggling six-packs and Kentucky Fried Chicken to the Trappist monks at Gethsemane Abbey, which housed that other garrulous hermit Thomas Merton.

This started me thinking about longevity. It's obvious that there are no special extensions for the pious or the virtuous, or the rich or wise either. Yet here was the oldest man for miles around, and by far the most interesting. Maybe Fate or the Reaper or whoever cuts our strings is actually a connoisseur like Scheherezade's Sultan, and couldn't bear to interrupt Mr. Still in the middle of a wonderful story.

The most eloquent eulogist was Appalachian scholar Loyal Jones. To honor Still, Jones said, is to honor "art and integrity, and the need for some people to be different from the rest of us."

For me it was an august honor to do a couple of readings with him; I saved the programs. I excused his attentions to my wife because he was almost forty years older than we were, though no doubt I underestimated him.

He was a strange and unforgettable man, and most people who knew him must have moments when he seems present, yet. One morning I was reading Still's collected poems on a mountainside in North Carolina—a deliberate exercise, with one eye on the blue ridges and one hand on my dog. I was deep in "Year of the Pigeons" when an emerald hummingbird descended on a flame-red phlox plant just six feet away. The poem and the bird struggled for my attention, until I imagined a voice I knew as well as the ageless face that I often studied on the sly. "Set that poem aside," it said, "and mind the hummingbird."

# Index

252